Art Center College of Design
Library
1700 Lida Street
Pasadena, Calif. 91103

# The Ecology of Architecture

Art Center College of Design
Library
1700 Lida Street
Pasadena, Calif. 91103

720.47
Z46
1996

# The Ecology of Architecture

*A Complete Guide to Creating the Environmentally Conscious Building*

*Laura C. Zeiher*

Art Center College of Design
Library
1700 Lida Street
Pasadena, Calif. 91103

Whitney Library of Design
*an imprint of Watson-Guptill Publications/New York*

The information and sources included in the text are provided in good faith as reference material for the purpose of creating the environmentally responsive built environment. The author does not endorse any specific products or businesses, including those provided in this book. Please contact the author in care of the publisher with comments or further information regarding both ecologically and socially responsive building design.

Cover design: Jay Anning
Interior design: Abigail Sturges
Production Manager: Ellen Greene

Copyright © 1996 by Laura C. Zeiher

First published in 1996 by Whitney Library of Design, an imprint of Watson-Guptill Publications, a division of BPI Communications, Inc., 1515 Broadway, New York, NY 10036.

Library of Congress Cataloging-in-Publication Data

Zeiher, Laura C., 1955-
The ecology of architecture: a complete guide to creating the environmentally conscious building / Laura C. Zeiher.
p. cm.
Includes bibliographical references and index.
ISBN 0-8230-1596-3
1. Architecture—Environmental aspects. I. Title.
NA2542.35.Z45 1996
720'.47—dc20 95-44416
CIP

All rights reserved. No part of this publication may be reproduced or used in any form or by any means—graphic, electronic, or mechanical, including photocopying, recording, taping, or information storage and retrieval systems—without written permission of the publisher.

Manufactured in the United States.

First printing, 1996

1 2 3 4 5 6 7 8 9 /02 01 00 99 98 97 96

Acknowledgements

*The Ecology of Architecture* could not have been written without the continued support of many important people. I am grateful to the architects, engineers, consultants, and owners who provided much of the material for the book, as well as a great deal of inspiration for it. I would like to thank the many professionals at Architects/ Designers/ and Planners for Social Responsibility for their spirited endorsement, and the American Institute of Architects for significant research information. I am most grateful to Whitney Library of Design, specifically to my editor, Micaela Porta, for her hard work and particular enthusiasm, and to Senior Editor Roberto de Alba for his interest. This book is dedicated to my family, dear friends, and professionals and leaders who believe that the purpose of their work is to serve and to restore.

# *Contents*

# *Preface*

The Ecology of Architecture is dedicated to the notion that an inherent ecology exists in all architecture. Whether or not ecological sensitivity has been respected, the design and construction of architecture has a powerful and lasting effect on the balance of ecology and on the human condition. The information in this book recognizes and underscores a deep respect for natural and human resources and ecological consciousness as fundamentals in the practice of architecture. There is no doubt that the future of all architecture must integrate this attitude of stewardship. The quality of our lives depends on it, and conversely, creates the quality of our environment. Whether we are in tune with this force or not, all of us as professionals and citizens are an integral part of our natural and built environment, and are empowered to influence it.

This book was written for professionals in all practices of environmental design and construction, as well as for the layperson. Many, many others outside the building professions have an important impact on the built environment, whether it is through real estate development, scientific research, education, or product manufacturing. Every government, business, and household will need to make decisions about physical resources. *The Ecology of Architecture* is therefore written for everyone, because your knowledge of resources affects your quality of life.

*Laura Zeiher*
*New York City*

# *The Elements of Ecology and Architecture*

## AIR

The air we breathe consists of under 21% oxygen, over 78% nitrogen, small amounts of carbon dioxide, argon, and other trace elements, with water vapor present to some degree. Everything else is considered a contaminant. For millions of years this composition has remained stable. If the amount of oxygen or nitrogen were to drastically increase, all life would be at risk.

### *Chlorofluorocarbons*

In 1896 the Swedish scientist Svante Arrhenius first established that the use of fossil fuels could double the carbon dioxide in the atmosphere and cause a rise in the average global temperature of about 41˚F (5˚ C). In 1930, Thomas Midgley, a research scientist working for the Frigidaire Division of General Motors, was asked by his employers to produce an alternative for the unsafe ammonia thas was then used as a refrigerant. In only two days he developed a group of inexpensive, stable chemicals called chlorofluorocarbons (CFC) that would do the job.

The greenhouse effect, or global warming, results when heat is retained near the Earth instead of radiating out into space. Created by chemical changes in the atmosphere that alter the amount of absorption and heat retention, global warming was estimated in 1973 to increase the surface temperature of the Earth at 34˚F (1˚C) per year. Main contributors to the greenhouse effect are carbon dioxide, carbon monoxide, methane, volatile organic compounds (VOCs), nitrogen oxides, chlorofluorocarbons, and surface ozone, otherwise known as the greenhouse gases. Activities such as the burning of fossil fuels, deforestation, the regular use of primary refrigerants, CFC, HCFC, Halon, and agricultural sources continue to increase greenhouse gases.

CFCs remain a primary source of refrigeration in buildings but are scheduled, according to an international agreement in London in 1990, to be reduced by 50% by 1995, by 85% by 1997, and phased out of use by the year 2000. Approximately half of the CFCs produced around the world are used in buildings, refrigeration and air conditiong systems, fire extinguishing systems, and in certain insulation materials. In addition, half of the world's fossil fuel consumption is attributed to the servicing of buildings. Architects and others can significantly reduce global warming by carefully reviewing these systems and specifying alternatives.

### *Air Pollution*

Almost any substance is capable of polluting the air if it is light enough or, in the case of solids, small enough, to be airborne. Gases, liquid droplets, solid particles, or a combination of these can contaminate the air. Primary sources of air pollution are placed in two major categories: point sources and nonpoint sources. Point sources are identifiable and nonmovable sources such as industrial or municipal plants and mines. Nonpoint sources include automobile emissions, aerosol cans, smoke from wood fires, or dust from eroding fields. Criteria air pollutants are among the most problematic. These include ozone, particulate matter, carbon monoxide, sulfur dioxide, lead, and nitrogen dioxide. Hazardous air pollutants include asbestos, berylium, mercury, vinyl chloride, arsenic, radionuclides, benzene, and coke oven emissions.

Other air pollutants are formed when gases are combined. A photochemical reaction takes place when nitrogen oxide, primarily from automobile exhaust, hydrocarbons, and other organic compounds mix in the air in the presence of sunlight, which triggers the creation of toxic nitrogen dioxide and ozone. This is the reaction that forms smog, a visually murky, physically irritating, and dangerous form of air pollution.

### *Indoor Air Quality*

The Environmental Protection Agency estimates that over $60 billion dollars per year in medical costs in the United States can be attributed to the poor quality of interior environments. As the public becomes more aware of the issue of indoor air quality, greater steps are being taken by building professionals and managers to ensure safe, non-toxic homes and workplaces.

## WATER

In its natural state, water contains mostly hydrogen and oxygen. Minerals, salts, trace metals, nutrients, bacteria, and organic matter are present in smaller amounts. At normal low levels of concentration, these substances are harmless, and some are even beneficial. Scientists cannot agree on the exact composition of "pure" water or on what levels of various substances pose a health threat. Governments generally have the responsibility of determining maximum contaminant levels. In the United States, maximum contaminant levels (MCLs) are set under the Safe Drinking Water Act (SDWA). The MCLs related to health are called Primary Drinking Water Standards. Secondary Drinking Water Standards indicate aesthetic alterations in color, taste, odor, hardness, salinity, pH levels, and turbidity. The Environmental Protection Agency has identified over 700 regular pollutants in drinking water. Of these, twenty are known carcinogens. There now are hundreds more pollutants found in drinking water, but as of 1991 only sixty of them were regulated by the SDWA. For many of them, tests are never done or do not even exist due to a lack of scientific knowledge.

### *Acid Rain*

As in air pollution, the hydrologic cycle is being gradually changed by industrial chemical processes. Industrial, agricultural, household, and municipal use of water is rapidly increasing the threat of contanimation. Agricultural pesticides and fertilizers, industrial waste dumping and landfilling, effluents and radioactive wastes, leaks from underground tanks and pipes, household toxic wastes and septic tanks each flow into rivers, lakes, and groundwater supplies. The combustion of fossil fuels, in particular coal and oil, produces sulphur dioxide, nitrogen oxides, and hydrocarbons. As global energy consumption rises, these substances are put into the air in increasing quantities. In the atmosphere they combine with water to form sulphuric and nitric acids, while hydrocarbons and nitrogen oxides also interact with sunlight to form the tropospheric ozone that causes air pollution. The additional airborne supply of contaminants mixes with these pollutants during the hydrologic cycle to form smog and acid rain.

Acid rain dissolves certain natural building materials. The ancient monuments of Athens have been more damaged in the last twenty-five years from acid rain than in the last twenty-four centuries. Serious damage is taking place around the world—in London, Rome, Venice, Cologne, Washington, DC, and many other major historic cities. Scientists believe that the stained glass in cathedral windows will fade within decades.

Infrastructural systems are also affected. Rapid corrosion of railroad tracks is attributed to acid rain, resulting in slowed schedules and serious accidents. In 1974, the Environmental Protection Agency estimated that sulphur dioxide emissions caused two billion dollars in damages annually to buildings in the United States.

Acid rain's effect on the natural world is catastrophic. Throughout Europe and North America, fish from freshwater lakes are being killed by the increasing acidity of the water. Twenty percent of Sweden's lakes are acidified. In many Swedish lakes the pH of the water is at five, a level that is lethal to salmon eggs.

Every ton of fossil fuel burned—most of which is used for heating and cooling buildings—adds polluting substances to the atmosphere that will be returned to the Earth in rain. Zoning and other community issues recognize that buildings such as out-of-town developments lacking access to mass transit depend on long distance travel in cars, which increase the quantity of pollutants.

### *Manufacturer Impact*

One of the primary causes of river pollution is industrial waste, of which mining and manufacturing are among the largest sources. Architects and others who specify and order materials are increasingly making a difference by requiring the manufacturers of the products they use to incorporate environmentally and socially responsible practices.

### *Ocean Dumping*

Oceans have traditionally been regarded as too large to be damaged by human activities. The sewage from 12% of Britain's population is discharged untreated into the sea, and 30% of the UK's sludge is dumped there as well.

### *Water Use and Conservation*

Most of the water provided for human use comes from rivers. About 3% of the Earth's water is freshwater, two-thirds of which is frozen in the polar ice caps. The quantity of available water isn't really the problem; it's the amount of available drinking water. The same rivers that provide drinking water receive toxic wastes from industry, run-off from pesticides and fertilizers, and effluents from sewage.

Our level of consumption also affects water supply. Average domestic consumption is 160 litres per person per day in the United Kingdom, while in the United States it is at 220 litres per person per day. In the UK, domestic consumption of water accounts for 1/3 of the total water use. It takes 3,600 litres of water to make one ton of cement. A ton of steel requires 300 tons of water. Concrete manufacturing not only requires water for the mixing process, but also for the washing of aggregates. The manufacture of one ton of steel uses 300 tons of water.

After a building has been completed, the amount of water it consumes depends on its function. In residential and commercial buildings, the toilet is the single largest consumer of water, using one-third of the domestic water supply. Domestic use of water can be identified as follows:

| *Activity* | % |
|---|---|
| Toilet flushing | 32 |
| Personal hygiene | 28 |
| Laundry | 9 |
| Washing up | 9 |
| Drinking and cooking | 3 |
| Garden watering and car washing | 6 |
| Losses | 13 |

Under half of domestic uses require water of drinking quality, but drinking water is typically supplied to satisfy all of these functions. Ecologically conscious buildings are changing the structure of building water systems. Graywater systems, for instance, recycle water for uses such as gardening, car washing, and heating. Other systems include on-site water purification.

## EARTH

Iron, glass, concrete, steel, aluminum, and even plastic are all produced by first being taken from the Earth. The most economically important ores typically exist in low concentrations and the refining process involves concentrating a small part of the excavated material. The spoil that is left around the mine creates a chemical hazard. Land frequently cannot be reclaimed after mineral extraction. In open pit mines, the spoil banks typically exceed the area of the mine by three to five times. Every phase of mining and manufacturing produces land use changes and environmental contamination. The processes of extraction, refinement, fabrication, and delivery are all energy-consuming, and this use of energy adds vast amounts of pollution to the earth, air, and water. The total energy consumed during these processes is known as embodied energy. The embodied energy of a material should be considered since it offers a general guide to the amount of pollution involved in its manufacture. Typically, low-energy materials are the least polluting.

The distance traveled to the site is an additional consideration. Choosing materials that are local or regional makes good sense. Local materials are usually more economically viable and climatically appropriate, thereby contributing to natural energy conservation. Supporting a local or regional economy is equally important as a cultural contribution.

The choice of material is further complicated when one considers the manner in which it is used within the building or combined with other materials after reaching the site. The manufacture of Portland cement contributes about 8% of the carbon dioxide to atmospheric global warming. According to Robert Berkebile, American Institute of Architects Council on the Environment Founder and President, aluminum is the most energy consumptive material used in the building trade. "Not only is tropical rainforest stripped to unearth the bauxite, but vast amounts of power are used to process it into aluminum. In many ways, however, the aluminum industry is doing a better job of recycling than almost anyone else. We need only to use aluminum more intelligently to increase our current amount of recycled aluminum from 17%. If an architect specifies recycled instead of virgin aluminum, 95% of the energy consumption and 96% of the pollution in the bauxite conversion process is avoided."

## FIRE

Burning finite fuels to meet the growing demand for energy and increasing population creates the single largest cause of destruction to the Earth's environment. This process is the greatest direct cause of air pollution, water pollution, and loss of the Earth's resources. The damages to the American economy from continued global warming alone could total $350 billion annually—a third of the federal budget or over $1,000 a person, according to a study by the Institute for International Economics.

Nearly all of our activities require some kind of energy consumption. Types of available fuels used can be separated into two groups: finite and renewable. Finite, or fossil fuels include coal, oil, natural gas, and uranium. Renewable fuels are derived from natural resources and include solar energy, wind power, wave power, biomass, and timber.

Fossil fuels form the basis of modern life in industrialized countries, providing 88% of all energy purchased. They have become dominant because they have been accessible, efficient, portable, and have worked in controlled combustion devices such as automobile engines, furnaces, and turbines that produce electricity. Fossil fuels are responsible for accellerating the greenhouse effect and global warming through the release of carbon dioxide and methane. The combustion of fossil fuels, in particular coal and oil, produces sulphur dioxide, nitrogen oxides, and hydrocarbons, the primary causes of air pollution. Over half the sulfur dioxide and 30% of the nitrogen oxides are produced in the burning of coal alone. Every ton of fossil fuel burned, most of which is required for heating and cooling buildings, adds polluting substances to the atmosphere that will be returned to the Earth in the form of acid rain.

Fossil fuels are declining resources. At their current rate of use, reserves of 60 years for oil, 120 years for natural gas, and 1,500 years for coal have been estimated.

The design and construction of new buildings accounts for the single largest amount of energy consumption in the United States. Some 54% of all energy used in America is related to construction, and over 30% of our nation's landfills consist of construction debris. Architects who carefully choose low-energy materials, energy conservation systems, and renewable energy systems make a significant impact in reducing over half of all energy consumption.

## FENG SHUI

The art and science of feng shui reflects cultural convictions expressed throughout the traditions of the Far East that nature commands man and must be respected. The ancient Chinese found that a house sited halfway up a hill on the north side of the river facing south received optimal sun, was protected from harsh winds, avoided floods, and had access to water for crops. In such surroundings it was easiest to survive: crops grew easily in the sun, animals grazed comfortably on lush grass, and a house stayed relatively warm in winter. The comfortable and harmonious environment helped its inhabitants to survive and grow successful and prosperous. The Chinese frequently contribute success or failure to the mysterious forces of the Earth, known as feng shui—literally "wind" and "water."

Besides arranging spaces for optimal comfort of mind and body, feng shui includes numerous psychic aspects. The proper channeling of water and harnessing of wind, the forces of c'i, the term for the life force or energy that ripples water, creates mountains, breathes life into all living things and propels man along a life course, are crucial. "He who controls water, governs the empire," goes an old Chinese saying. For all the mystery that surrounds it, feng shui evolved from the simple observation that people are affected, for good or ill, by their surroundings. The Chinese concluded that if you change your surroundings, you change your life.

Feng shui, a key to understanding the dialogue between man and nature, fulfills a need to intuit and interpret the natural environment. The traditions of Asian culture show great respect for the power of nature, a belief which is quite opposite to the cultural beliefs of Western societies. Born of ancient Greek philosophy, religious and cultural expressions throughout the Western hemisphere illustrate the underlying belief that man is at the center of the universe. Perhaps an understanding of these two very different outlooks can help create an equilibrium and harmony between the natural environment and humankind. Technological possibilities for global communication offer increasing opportunities for cultures to understand one another.

## THE THIRD WAVE

The period from the discovery of global warming to the initiatiation of a response to the problem took over 130 years. It is frightening that the industrial and chemical processes that have been shown to deplete our ozone layer, increase global warming, and cause irreversable damage to our natural resources have continued to be those on which our society depends. Most alarming is the fact that even after 100 years our industries, professionals, and technical specialists have shown little ability in making necessary changes in design and construction methodologies. How many life-threatening statistics must be revealed? Why aren't we responding to the direct relationship between the increasing numbers of serious illnessnesses and premature deaths and the extent of our chemical society? As students of architecure, we experience a reverence for the spirit of natural resources and the land with which we work. Why, then, do we forget this as professionals? This book is offered as a reminder and, moreover, as a call to action. "A new civilization is emerging in our lives and blind men everywhere are trying to suppress it, "writes Alvin Toffler in *The Third Wave*. "Without really recognizing it, we are engaged in building this new civilization from the ground up." As building professionals, it is up to us to meet this challenge to literally construct a better future.

# The Ecology of Architecture

**Chapter 1**

# *A History of Ecology in Architecture*

*The precondition of any civilization, old or new, is energy. First wave societies drew their energies from human and animal muscle power, or from the sun, wind, and water. Second Wave industrial societies began to draw their energy from irreplaceable fossil fuels—oil, coal, and natural gas. This revolutionary shift meant that for the first time a civilization was eating into nature's capital rather than merely living off the interest it provided. Third Wave civilization must and will draw on an amazing variety of energy sources—hydrogen, solar, geothermal, tidal, biomass, lightning discharges, perhaps advanced fusion power, as well as other energy sources not yet imagined.*

—*The Third Wave,* Alvin Toffler, 1980

## HUNTING AND GATHERING CIVILIZATION

During the first two million years of human history, people lived almost exclusively in small mobile groups. Food was not stored because extra goods hindered the nomadic way of life, and items such as tools and utensils could be easily replaced with readily available local materials. Humankind's early societies survived by gathering food and, more rarely, by hunting animals, a difficult and hazardous practice undertaken only when necessary. Recent archeological evidence indicates that the variety of nutritious food available was so great that obtaining it occupied only a small portion of the day, leaving more time for leisure and ceremonial activities.

In order to provide adequate food and shelter for themselves, hunting and gathering groups depended on a profound knowledge of their local environment. Every aspect of their lives revolved around seasonal changes, a fact concretely illustrated in their architecture. Diverse, ingeniously constructed buildings that respond well to local climate, are built of local materials, and rest comfortably in the landscape can be found all over the world. These structures have incorporated thousands of years of trial and error, withstanding the test of time because they were constructed with regional materials and their design proved comfortable and efficient for the shelter's inhabitants.

For instance, the Anasazi Indians built Pueblo Bonito in Chaco Canyon, New Mexico, in the 10th and 11th centuries A.D. Local topography provided this early human habitat with security and shelter from cold winds and hot sun. Its tiered, semi-circular structure once housed up to twelve hundred people. Sacred, underground ceremonial chambers called kivas were built within its stone and adobe terraces. Cut deep into the wall of a natural canyon and oriented to the sun's summer and winter solstices, it maintained a balanced temperature year round, day and night. The Acoma Indians constructed a terraced "sky city" on a sheltered mesa near Albuquerque, New Mexico, whose design utilized to its greatest potential its lowest point in winter. The design of North American Indian tents, created with animal skins and slender lodge pole pines, provided a minimal structure that offered protection from the elements and accommodated a nomadic life.

This is not to say that hunting and gathering groups had no effect on the environment. Their most damaging impact was through the hunting of animals. A number of animals became extinct in Eurasia on a relatively small scale, but elsewhere in the world the destruction was massive. In Australia, 86% of large animals have become extinct over the last one hundred thousand years. A likely explanation is that hunting by Aboriginal groups over the last forty thousand years could have led to their extinction. In addition to hunting, the destruction of these animals' natural habitats and food resources contributed to their demise. The loss of 80% of large animals in South America and 73% in North America is equally remarkable for this reason.

Nevertheless, the hunting and gathering way of life was highly stable and lasted for hundreds of thousands of years. Then, about ten thousand years ago, the methods that humans used to obtain their food and create their shelter began to change. The devel-

*Pueblo Bonito, Chaco Culture National Historical Park, New Mexico. The largest known archeological ruin in North America, Pueblo Bonito covers three acres and contained at least 695 rooms, four to five stories high in places. All evidence indicates that the structure was designed by the occupants and took 150 years to complete. The first major construction period began early in the 10th century. The second surge of building occured in the 11th century. Photo: Jonathan A. Meyers/FPG .*

*The tepee, or tipi, was typical in North American Indian tribes living on the Great Plains. The structure was made by arranging poles into a conical frame and spreading animal skins tightly over it, leaving an opening at the top through which smoke from the campfire could escape. Not only were these dwellings extremely portable, but they provided strong shelter against the elements. Photo: No. 335511 by Curtis, courtesy Department of Library Services, American Museum of Natural History.*

*The Eskimo igloo, made of blocks of snow arranged in a spiral formation, is a simple dwelling still in use today. While it can provide protection for weeks in severe cold, it is usually used as a temporary shelter while traveling. Photo: No. 231921 by D.B. MacMillan, March 1915, courtesy Department of Library Services, American Museum of Natural History.*

opment of permanent settlements and agricultural cultivation brought about a radical change in human history, one which is fundamental to all subsequent social developments.

## AGRICULTURAL CIVILIZATION

Around 8000 B.C., the emergence of villages and towns and an increasing population concentrated the demand for food and resources, and efforts to increase supply inevitably imposed significant strains on smaller areas. Agricultural civilization was born and demands for new and a greater variety of goods increased, especially concerning construction materials for permanent buildings and homes. While the construction of creative indigenous architecture continued throughout following periods in history, a rise in the construction of monumental architecture typifies the period of agricultural civilization with its development of organized settlements.

From its beginnings, monumental architecture has been associated with licentious attitudes toward resources, suggesting that architecture is available only for those who have enough wealth to afford luxury.[1] From 5000 B.C. in Egypt, 2000 B.C. in Greece, and 500 B.C. in Rome date not only the divorce of architecture from the common and the ordinary, but also its relation to an economic surplus necessary for the creation of art. Architecture became associated not with the production of shelter, but with the expenditure of resources for a particular stylistic effect. Classical monumental architecture relied on slavery and the exploitation of distant resources. In order to build their temples and cities, the Egyptians, Greeks, and Romans procured armies of slaves to bring huge quantities of stone from far-away areas. "It is tempting to suggest," write Robert and Brenda Vale in *Green Architecture,* "that the development of the arch by the Romans was a way of coping with the shortage of resources for a more concentrated population."

***Step Pyramid, funeral monument of King Zoser, 3rd Dynasty, Saqqara, Egypt. The Egyption tomb began as the mastaba, an underground burial chamber marked above ground by a simple mound faced with brick or stone. The pyramids evolved from these mounds into monumental tombs for the pharoahs who were lavishly laid to rest in the cavernous chambers beneath. The huge size and scale of the pyramids required enormous amounts of labor and resources to be constructed, exhibiting the importance of the pharoahs and the belief in divinity in Egyptian society. Photo: Werner Forman/ Art Resource, NY.***

During the development of villages and cities, the requirement for wood to build houses, heat homes, and cook food steadily rose, and forests began to suffer as a consequence. Local deforestation led to soil erosion. According to Clive Ponting, author of *The Green History of the World,*

> Recent evidence indicates that as early as 6000 B.C., and within one thousand years of the emergence of settled communities, villages were being abandoned as soil erosion caused by deforestation resulted in a badly damaged landscape, declining crop yields, and the eventual inability to grow food. The increasing demand for food surplus, the creation of artificial environments for agricultural production, and the steady growth of communities meant that it was far more difficult for humans to escape the consequences of their actions. In particularly sensitive ecosystems with greater human concentration, these civilizations began to collapse.

The first signs of widespread damage emerged in Sumer, Mesopotamia, an area where the most extensive modifications to the natural environment were first made. In 1936 Leonard Woolley, one of the excavators of the early cities of Sumer, wrote a book about his work entitled *Ur of the Chaldees.* "Only to those who have seen the vast Mesopotamian desert will the evocation of the flourishing ancient world seem so incredible, so complete is the contrast between past and present," writes Woolley. "It is difficult to realize that the blank waste ever blossomed and bore fruit for the sustenance of a busy world. Why, if Ur was an empire's capital, if Sumer was once a vast granary, has the population dwindled to nothing, the very soil lost its virtue?" The answer to his question was that the Sumerians themselves destroyed the civilization that they painstakingly created out of the difficult environment of southern Mesopotamia. Around 3000 B.C., the Sumerians became the first literate society in the world. Detailed administrative records kept by the temples of the city states provide a record of the changes in the agricul-

tural systems and an insight into the development of significant problems.

The valley of the twin rivers of the Tigris and Euphrates created huge challenges, particularly in the south. In the spring following the melting of winter snows, the rivers were at their highest. During the months between August and October, when crops need the most water, the rivers were at their lowest. The seasonal cycles dictated that water storage and irrigation were critical for crops to grow, yet the irrigation and water storage systems involved both advantages and disadvantages. High summer temperatures quickened water evaporation from the land surface, thereby increasing quantities of salt in the soil. The soil itself had low permeability and a slow rate of drainage, factors which contributed to its being waterlogged. The amount of silt coming down from the rivers, probably caused by deforestation in the highlands, added five feet of silt and caused the delta of the two rivers to extend about fifteen miles every millennium. As the land became more waterlogged and the water table rose, salt settled on the surface. To restore the soil, the land needed to remain fallow and unwatered for long periods of time. Internal pressures of the society for food made this impossible. Short-term demands outweighed any consideration of the need for long-term stability and the maintenance of a sustainable agricultural system.

In the Early Dynastic period, which lasted over six hundred years until about 2370 B.C., the major city states Kish, Uruk, Ur, and Lagash were militaristic and organized the food surplus to feed their bureaucracies and armies. All were dependent on the large-scale production of both barley and wheat, of which equal amounts were being grown in 3500 B.C. But wheat can only tolerate a salt level of half a percent in the soil, whereas barley can tolerate twice this amount. By 2500 B.C., wheat had fallen to only 15% of the crop. By 2100 B.C., Ur had abandoned wheat production and it had declined to 2% of the crops grown in the entire Sumerian region. By 2000 B.C. the cities of Isin and Larsa no longer grew wheat, and by 1700 B.C., salt levels in the whole of southern Mesopotamia were so high that no wheat at all was grown.

More important than the depletion of wheat was the general decline of crop yields. Until about 2400 B.C. crop yields remained high. Between 2400 and 2100 B.C. crop yields fell by 42%, and by 1700 B.C. they were decreased by 65%. In 1936, Leonard Woolley wrote in *Ur of Chaldees* that in 2000 B.C. "the earth turned white," a direct reference to the devastation of salinization. The independent city states survived until 2370 B.C. when the first outside conqueror established a new empire. In the following six hundred years, the new empire was again conquered and by 1800 B.C., the conquest of the area by the Babylonian kingdom centered on northern Mesopotamia. Crop yields continued to fall, the agricultural base of Sumer effectively collapsed, and Sumer declined into insignificance as an underpopulated, impoverished back country.

***The granary is of great significance to the household and community, and a separate shelter is built in order to store and protect its contents. This adobe granary in the village of Niofouin, Ivory Coast, is, like most, raised on stilts to keep rodents from burrowing inside and to provide ventilation for the grain to remain dry. Photo © Carollee Pelos.***

Although the script used by the inhabitants of the Indus Valley has not yet been deciphered, much evidence exists that the same forces that prevailed in Mesopotamian civilization brought about the downfall of the Indus Valley. The Indus settlers created a complex and highly centralized society that emerged around 2300 B.C., flourished, and lasted only five hundred years. The Indus River's tendency to flood and change course created the single greatest problem for the inhabitants. Extensive systems were fabricated to contain the river, irrigate the fields, and to produce the food that supported and fed the ruling elite, priests, and army. The hot climate of the valley raised the water table and produced salinization, leading to the gradual decline of crop production.

Deforestation was the other factor that under-

***Deforestation in China resulted from agricultural cultivation that began around 3000 B.C. Though the soil was rich, it quickly eroded once the natural vegetation was removed. By the 18th century, all of the original forests had been cleared. Photo: Yuan Li.***

mined the environment of the Indus Valley. Originally, the area had been richly forested with a plentiful supply of wildlife, yet part of the land was cleared to provide agricultural fields. More important, however, were the dominating construction techniques used. To build their temples the inhabitants used mud bricks that were dried in ovens, a process that required vast amounts of wood. The surrounding trees were rapidly cut down, exposing the soil and causing erosion and the impoverishment of the soil quality. In 1900 B.C., the Indus Valley civilization came to a sudden halt. Environmental degradation through salinization and deforestation reduced the available food surplus to such a degree that it may have led to the reduction in the size of the army, thereby increasing vulnerability to external conquest.

In China, beginning around 3000 B.C., the cultivation of millet on the fertile soils of the northern regions created the base for agricultural development and the rise of early societies. While the soil was rich, it easily eroded once the natural grass cover was removed to make way for the millet. Rapidly, huge canyons developed as hillsides were simultaneously cleared of trees for fuel and construction. The deforested area increased until by about two hundred years ago, all of the original forests of China had been cleared. The general loss of trees was also one of the main causes of the flooding of the Yellow River, named for its color, created by the soil it carried from upstream erosion.

The same problems led to the downfall of the great medieval Christian kingdom of Ethiopia. In the northern area, originally the center of the state, deforestation severely degraded the environment until it could no longer support shrubs of grass. By 1883, the kingdom shifted south to a new capital in the central highlands, only to have the process repeated once again. What happened at the new capital, Addis Ababa, after becoming the capital of Ethiopia in 1883 illustrates how quickly and completely inhabitants can transform their environment. Within twenty years a zone of one hundred miles around the town was devastated–stripped of its trees by charcoal burners producing fuel for the capital.

The process of long-term environmental decline can be traced around the Near East and Mediterranean in every area. It is now estimated that no more than 10% of the original forests that once stretched from Morocco to Afghanistan even as late as 2000 B.C. still exist. The hills of Lebanon and Syria were one of the first areas to suffer. The natural forests there were rich in the tall, straight cedars for which Lebanon became famous. Prized by the states and empires of Mesopotamia as building materials, control of forests and trade was a high priority. The cedars later became the mainstay of Phoenician commerce and were widely traded. Gradually they were cut down and reduced to a remnant; there are now just four small groves of cedars left in the region, maintained as a former symbol of glory. The Mediterranean landscape of olive trees, vines, low bushes, and strongly scented herbs is the direct result of massive environmental degradation brought about by the relentless pressure of long-term settlement and a growing population. The region's original vegetation–a mixture of oaks, beech, pines, and cedars–was cleared bit by bit to provide land for agriculture, fuel for cooking and heating, and construction material for buildings and ships. Increasingly sheep, cattle, and goats grazed the land, ensuring that the vegetation could not regenerate.

Early signs of large-scale environmental degradation in Greece began around 650 B.C. The main problem there was overgrazing on the eighty percent of the land that was unsuitable for the cultivation of crops. Within a couple of generations the hills of Attica were bare. In 590 B.C., cultivation on steep slopes was banned because of soil erosion. Plato wrote in his *Critias:*

> What now remains compared with what then existed is like the skeleton of a sick man, all the fat and soft earth having wasted away, and only the bare framework of the land being left. There are some mountains which have nothing left but food for bees, but they had trees not very long ago . . . There were many lofty trees of cultivated species and . . . boundless pastures for flocks. Moreover, it was enriched by the yearly rains from Zeus, which were not lost to it, as now, by flowing from the bare land into the sea; but the soil it had was deep, and therein it received the water, storing it up in the retentive loamy soil, and . . . [it] provided all the various districts with abundant supplies of springwaters and streams, whereof the shrines still remain even now, at the spots where fountains formerly existed.

In Italy, similar events occurred a few centuries later as population rose and Rome grew from a small city into the center of an empire which stretched across Europe and the Near East. Around 300 B.C., Italy and Sicily were still well forested, but the increasing demand for wood resulted in rapid deforestation. As the soil eroded, earth was carried down the rivers, silting up the ports and estuaries. The southern port of Paestum silted up entirely and the town decayed. Ravenna completely lost its access to the sea. Ostia, the port of Rome, survived by constructing new docks. The Pontine marshes were created about 200 B.C. in an area which had supported sixteen Volscian towns four hundred years earlier. The Roman empire placed pressure on the Mediterranean region as demand for food increased. After 58 B.C. the citizens began to receive free grain for political reasons and many provinces were turned into granaries. From what were once the most productive provinces of the empire in North Africa remain a series of impressive Roman ruins, surrounded by vast desert. After the fall of Rome the process of erosion intensified as Berber tribes brought their large flocks of grazing animals which did away with the remaining vegetation. The Roman provinces of Asia Minor were completely deforested by the 1st century A.D., and a few decades later the emperor Hadrian restricted access to the remaining forests of Syria. Some regions were less affected and continued to flourish until the early Byzantine period. Both are now ruins and the limestone hills of the area have lost up to six feet of soil. While historians continue to debate the reasons for the fall of the Roman empire, most agree that it was the result of a number of factors causing internal decay and vulnerability to external pressure. After the fall of the empire, liberated from some of the demands of the imperial system, some areas were able to recover land and create secondary forests, but other areas continued to decline.

The development of civilizations in the Americas created the same sequence of events as in Eurasia. Historians believe that the collapse of the great city of Teotihuacan in the valley of Mexico and some of the early city states along the coast of Peru were linked to the collapse of their agricultural bases. The clearest case of environmental degradation leading to the fall of a society comes from the Maya who created one of the most extraordinary civilizations ever known in what is now Mexico, Guatemala, Belize, and Honduras. Some of the first explorers to find the "lost cities" in 1830 were at a loss to understand what happened to the flourishing settlements. The Mayan script has only been partially deciphered, but increasingly sophisticated techniques used in archeology have given us new insights. Until the 1960s, it was widely believed that the Mayans were generally peaceful people governed by religious castes. In the last thirty years these ideas have been replaced with a different picture of the Maya, explaining why the civilization collapsed so abruptly. A new reading of the texts found on the stone stelae typically found in elaborate ceremonial centers in all Mayan cities tells of the conquest of cities through warfare. By the 1st century A.D., a large number of ceremonial centers were developed throughout the region. After the decline of the Mexican city of Teotihuacan in 600 A.D., the Mayans entered their most spectacular period. Then within a few decades after 800, the whole society began to disintegrate. No stelae were erected, the ceremonial centers were abandoned, and the population abruptly declined. Archeological fieldwork in the 1970s determined that an elaborate agricultural system provided sustenance for the foundation of the Mayans' great achievements. The first signs of declining food production are evident before 800 A.D., when the skeletons

***Most of the landscape in Italy is cultivated, public land resources are limited, and timber is costly. The Tuscany region in north central Italy (shown here) is covered with low brush, small pine forests, grape vineyards, and olive groves. Many areas of southern Italy are rocky, arid, and have low scrub vegetation and olive trees which thrive for many years with little water and poor soil. Photo: Laura Zeiher.***

*Uxmal, Yucatan, Mexico, 6-10th century. Uxmal is one of the greatest of the peninsula's remaining Mayan ruins. In the Mayan language, Uxmal means "thrice built," because the Mayans abandoned and returned to the site several times due to drought. The city had no wells, and relied entirely on rainwater. When the rain and the crops failed, people moved on in search of fertile land. Photos: Marian Appellof.*

from burials of the period show higher infant and female mortality rates. The declining resources resulted in increasing warfare, and within decades the cities were abandoned. Only a small number of people continued to live in the area. The deserted fields and cities were not found again until the 19th century.

The most striking example of a sustainable balance between the natural environment and the demand for resources can be found in Egypt. For about seven thousand years after the emergence of settlements around 5500 B.C. in the Nile valley, the Egyptians were able to incorporate the annual flood of the Nile River as the basis of a succession of states; from the dynasties of the Pharaonic era, to the Roman Empire, under the Arabs and the Mamluks, until new technology in the 19th century began to undermine the system.[2] The agricultural system adopted by the ancient Egyptians and used by later successors stabilized the environmental effects by exploiting a natural process with a minimum of human interference. The inhabitants were also recipients of fortunate geographical and seasonal occurrences. Each year the Nile river flooded the length of the lower valley, depositing huge amounts of silt from its sources in Ethiopia and Uganda. At present it is estimated that the Nile carries a hundred million tons of silt per year. The heavy rainfall occurred in the upper regions in June, and the flood reached Egypt two thousand miles away in September, depositing rich soil and providing water in time for the sowing of autumn crops. The absence of salinisation is demonstrated by the increasing output of wheat.

In the 1840s, the first artificial irrigation systems in Egypt caused waterlogging and salinisation in newly cultivated areas. In the early part of the 20th century, the first attempts were made to control the Nile floods by building a dam on the upper Nile at Aswan so that water could be released as required, avoiding shortages downstream. The construction of the present dam in the 1950s would finally undermine the long established agricultural system. Although the dam regulated water levels, by retaining the silt, rich soil was no longer deposited. The natural fertility of the land was destroyed and replaced by artificial fertilizers."[3]

## INDUSTRIAL CIVILIZATION

Each archeological study of the course of flourishing civilizations demonstrates environmental degradation leading to their decline or extinction. Some civilizations were able to survive longer than others, yet the struggle to provide adequate resources and food supplies is one of the central features of each. Energy

sources clearly represent a driving force in the development of human history. For all except the last several hundred years, energy sources were few and the quantity of energy generated was limited. The use of renewable resources such as human and animal power, wood, and water typifies the development of early civilizations. With screaming velocity, the exploitation of the earth's non-renewable resources and a massive increase in energy consumption from fossil fuels mark the rise of industrialization.

The first significant use of water power took place in Egypt in 100 B.C., with the development of an automatic irrigation wheel and grain mill. The spread of water power was slow and for centuries was limited to grain production. Mills were constructed across Europe throughout several centuries. Built primarily on rivers, water mills provided power for tanning leather, making cloth, driving iron forges, sawing wood, operating bellows, and making mash for beer from around 1100 in Europe. The early industrialization of China produced acute wood and coal shortages in the 13th century. At this time China was the most industrialized country in the world with the development of highly sophisticated hemp spinning machines powered by water, a technology which was not produced until the 18th century in Europe.

In Europe and in China, wind was the main supplement to water power. Windmills, first developed in Tibet and China as prayer wheels, were not common in China as a source of industrial power until the 13th century. The development of windmills in Europe occurred as a completely separate phenomenon. The first windmills in Europe were built in England around 1200 and within one hundred years, they could be commonly found. By the 16th century the Netherlands had more than eight thousand windmills which were used to power saws, lift mine equipment, mill cloth, dress leather, make gunpowder, roll copper plates, and silk.

As water and wind power proved irregular and subject to climatic and seasonal changes, the world's main source of fuel during the early development of the industrial period was wood. The advantages of wood were many; it was readily available, easy to collect, it burned easily and reliably, and in many cases was free. Supplies seemed inexhaustible and little attention was paid to treating wood as a renewable resource. Forests were destroyed to provide more clear land for agriculture and for fuel and construction material. Wood was relied upon for construction of all kinds: houses, fortification, bridges, casks, furniture, vats and machinery, and shipbuilding. In the 14th century, the construction of Windsor Castle resulted in the felling of over four thousand oaks in ten years.

The first signs of a shortage of timber in western Europe can be identified in the shipbuilding industry in the 15th century. Venice, a great medieval maritime power, exhausted local timber supplies and came to rely on imported wood while imposing draconian laws in an unsuccessful attempt to protect the last of its domestic oak supplies. In 1715 in France it was reported that wood was so scarce and the price so high that the poor had to do without fires. Illustrating the need for wood to be treated as a renewable resource, Edmund Howes wrote in the early seventeenth century,

> Within man's memory, it was held impossible to have any want of wood in England. But such hath been the great expense of timber for navigation, with infinite increase of building of houses, the making of household furniture, caskes, and other vessels not to be numbered, and of carts, wagons and coaches, besides the extreme waste of wood in making iron, burning brick and tile, that at this present, through the great consuming of wood and the neglect of planting of woods, there is so great a scarcity of wood through the kingdom.

By 1775, North America was stripped of the very tall pines needed for the mainmasts of the English Royal Navy.

The growing use of coal in place of increasingly scarce and expensive wood in Europe marked the beginning of the use of non-renewable fossil fuels in

***Indigenous architectural devices for catching the wind were used in ancient Egypt and at least twelve hundred years ago in Peru. Today, in southern Pakistan, hundreds of "windcatchers" or windscoops grace the skyline of a desert community, creating unique abstract sculptures and cooling and ventilating building interiors. A moderate southwest wind blows across the Sind region's flat desert from April until June, coinciding with the hottest days of the year, when the temperature reaches 107°F. The windscoops consist of three angular planes supported by simple post-and-beams and tilt forward at about forty degrees. They face the summer winds and turn their backs on the winter winds, when it is not needed. Their origin, like most indigenous design, is unknown. Photo: © Carollee Pelos.***

*Top: Stonington House, Stonington, Connecticut. In the 18th century, residents of Stonington, Connecticut constructed simple clapboard homes from plentiful regional forests. The use of paint, limited to homeowners with ample means, was uncommon. When the clapboards became worn from the elements, only the individual damaged pieces were replaced. Later, shingles were used to cover building exteriors since they proved sturdier at withstanding the harsh New England climate. This change led to the vernacular "Shingle Style" architecture. Photo: Ezra Stoller/Esto.*

*Bottom: Round Stone Barn, Hancock Shaker Village. Built in 1826, this barn was designed to feed large numbers of cattle from a single trough located at the center. The trough was quite effortlessly refilled by only a few men. Manure is collected below the floor to fertilize the fields and gardens, and natural air and light provide necessary ventilation. The round form, materials of local stone and timber, and exquisite detail typify the innovative practicality, beauty, and craftsmanship found in Shaker architecture. Photo: UPI/ Bettman Archive.*

order to meet energy demands. While the main coalfields of Europe were in production by the 13th and 14th centuries, large-scale development of deep mines came later, after the increasing costs of wood offset extra costs and technological ability was developed.

Industrialization in America in the 19th century followed very different patterns of growth, mainly because large supplies of wood were still available. In 1850 wood accounted for 90% of the U.S. fuel supplies and half of the nation's iron was produced using charcoal. Steam power was not widely adopted before the 1880s and transport, iron production, and all stoves and boilers were designed to use wood. Steamboats and railway locomotives in the U.S. used wood and after 1890, when supplies began to increase in price, coal quickly became the primary source of fuel. By 1910, coal provided 75% of the nation's energy.

The 19th-century shipping industry provides a particularly clear illustration of the worldwide transition to fossil fuels. Technological developments led to the adoption of iron hulls around 1853, and steel hulls ten years later enabled sailing ships of greater tonnage to compete with the more costly steam-powered vessels typical of the 1840s. By the end of the century, the amount of shipping not only increased substantially, but the fundamental change to the nonrenewable resource of coal had effectively taken place. Almost every ship manufactured was powered by coal, so England subsequently built a chain of coaling stations around the globe to sustain the Royal Navy. The world's dependence on coal peaked early in the 20th century. Although world production has regularly increased throughout this century, world energy consumption has fallen from 90 to 30%. Coal is now the second most utilized energy source after oil.

As coal proved to be the means to support the expansion of industry in the 19th century, the availability of cheap oil has been the primary sustainer of continued economic growth in the 20th century. The world consumed about ten million tons in 1890, rising to ninety-five million tons by 1920, and then to 294 million tons by 1940. Since 1940, oil consumption has doubled every year to reach 2500 tons per year by the 1970s—more than a two hundred-fold increase. The United States has been one of the major producers of oil since the 1860s. Russia has been the largest producer of oil in the world since 1900, and the rise in the production of oil in the Near East since World War II continues to play a regular and central role in world political structures.

A by-product of oil production, natural gas is a naturally occurring burnable gas that includes primarily methane (50 to 99%) as well as hydrocarbons, hydrogen sulfide, carbon dioxide, nitrogen, and helium. It is generally considered to be the cleanest of the fossil fuels. Recent studies, however, suggest that leakage during transmission and distribution may contribute disproportionately to the greenhouse effect and global warming. Natural gas is traditionally carried by pipeline across country and underwater, and building and maintaining production sites creates considerable ecological damage. Nearly all of the world's gas consumption is concentrated in the industrialized world. Russia is the world's largest producer of natural gas.

One of the most significant developments over the last century has been the growth in the use of fossil fuels to provide a highly convenient form of secondary energy: electricity. The first hydroelectric power station was built in 1886 in Niagara Falls, but the vast majority of electricity was generated by fossil fuels–first coal, then oil and natural gas. Electricity replaced steam-powered machinery in industry and made possible far greater production processes. It provided energy for completely new industries like aluminum production, which has quadrupled in output since World War II. The energy required to manufacture a ton of aluminum requires six and a half times the energy required to make a ton of steel. Almost every home in the industrialized world is connected to a utility supply to provide heating, air conditioning, lighting, cooking, and general power for a vast array of household goods. Rising electrical consumption has been one of the main causes of increased energy consumption around the world. Although electricity is convenient, it is also highly inefficient. According to current estimates, power stations are only about twenty-five percent efficient. The average output of a power station in the 1920s was 30,000 kilowatts to 600,000 kilowatts in the 1970s. Current power station demands in cities such as New York and Los Angeles are the basis for energy rebate and grant programs as utility companies realize that it is more cost effective for them to provide reduced rates to their customers than to build new plants to provide more power. The continually increasing demand for oil to generate power for domestic and commercial building use as well as for manufacturing and transportation creates rising demands to meet most of the world's energy needs.

Throughout the last one thousand years there has been a remarkable continuity of attitudes in the patterns of consumption of fossil fuels. Short-term considerations have been emphasized, as though supplies of fossil fuels were inexhaustible. It is difficult to estimate the quantity of the world's fossil fuel reserves, but most agree that there is enough coal to last several hundred years, while reserves of oil and natural gas may last for less than a century. Before supplies are exhausted and they become more difficult to obtain, severe problems will be encountered, not the least of which are the economic and political repercussions related to the control of fuel resources.

**NUCLEAR GENERATION**
*Percentage of power generated by region*

|  |  |
|---|---|
| New England (CT, ME, MA, NH, RI, VT) | 51% |
| Middle Atlantic (NJ, NY,PA) | 39% |
| South Atlantic (DE, DC, FL, GA, MD, NC, SC,VA,WVA) | 29% |
| East North Central (IL, IN, MI, OH,WI) | 22% |
| West North Central (IA, KS, MN, MO, NE, ND, SD) | 18% |
| Pacific Contiguous (CA, OR,WA) | 16% |
| East South Central (AL, KY, MS,TN) | 15% |
| West South Central (AR, LA, OK,TX) | 14% |
| Mountain (AZ, CO, ID, MT, NV, NM, UT,WY) | 9% |
| Pacific Noncontiguous (AK, HI) | 0 |

The advent of nuclear power represents a clear level of desperation. The first nuclear power plants were built in the 1950s, a by-product of military programs in the United States. After thousands of deaths, billions of dollars in operational costs, damage, and repairs, the use of nuclear power is slowly being reduced. In 1979, the partial core meltdown at Three Mile Island focused world attention on nuclear energy hazards. In 1986, the Chernobyl meltdown was responsible for hundreds of immediate deaths, and tens of thousands of following deaths. Three hundred and twenty thousand people were evacuated, and the damage created by radioactive fallout remains acute as far away as Scotland. The land and animal life of thousands of square miles occupied by four million people is poisoned for centuries to come, continuing to cause premature illnesses, birth defects, and death. Eventual withdrawal from nuclear energy seems eminent but the elimination of uranium reserves from commercial as well as military resources remains an additional concern, and the problems remain unsolved. Nuclear waste reserves will continue to increase while power plants remain in operation.

About four hundred stations are still in operation worldwide. In 1991, there were 110 commercial reactors still in operation, with more than fifty aging reactors reaching their licensed age the next twenty-five years, and sixteen subsequently closing. Japan–twenty-eight percent nuclear–continued to build reactors until the monumental accident at Chernobyl altered any future plans for further development of nuclear power. In Russia, Eastern Europe, and India in 1991, forty-six new reactors under construction never reached completion. Only in France–where nuclear power represents 75% of electricity production–does support for the development of nuclear power continue, chiefly motivated by that country's lack of oil.

## THE GREEN MOVEMENT

By the 1960s concern about future energy supplies was reflected in a greater interest in renewable resources, namely in the increased development of solar, wind, and water power, and in the use of plant and animal wastes. Of course, Frank Lloyd Wright's architecture had embodied the deeper ecological principles of natural building, describing design that works with natural conditions as an organic whole and a living organism. Because it was a living dynamic process, he believed that no house could ever be "finished," but that it continues to respond to its environment and occupants. In his book *The Natural House,* he emphasized the importance of integrity, wherein a house should be integral to its site, integral to its materials, and integral to the life of the inhabitants. In his life's work, Buckminster Fuller created the Dymaxion House and the geodesic dome during the 1940s and 1950s as a call for self-sustaining design. During the 1960s, only solar pioneers such as Dr. George Lof actually lived in one of the nine solar buildings that existed in the world; the others were used as laboratories. Paolo Soleri is one of the first contemporary visionaries to bring what he referred to as sacred ecology together with architecture. He coined the term *arcology* in the 1960s to describe the concept of architecture and ecology working as one integral process to produce new urban habitats. The city of Arcosanti, a project of his not-for-profit Cosanti Foundation, rises dramatically from the basalt cliffs near Phoenix, Arizona. A prototype arcology for five thousand people, it combines compact urban structures with large-scale solar greenhouses on ten acres of a four thousand-acre preserve.

***Fallingwater, Bear Run, Pennsylvania, Frank Lloyd Wright, 1936. Fallingwater is one of the most well known private residences in the United States. Suspended above a waterfall, the house illustrates Wright's belief that architecture should be "organic," or merge with its landscape, respecting the forces of nature. Wrights' beliefs dissented from the "machine" concepts that were recognized as the architecture of his time, and embodied ecological and social principles in early modern architecture. Photo: Scott Frances/Esto.***

One of the most important works of what was to become the green movement worldwide was *Silent Spring,* published in 1962 by Rachel Carson. Carson became a pioneering leader in the fight to save the natural world from the results of industrial and chemical civilization. As a biologist, ecologist, teacher, and writer, she emphasized in her fourth and final book the extraordinary damage being caused throughout the chain of life by the universal use of deadly pesticides such as DDT. Concentrated in the environment's food chains, DDT was found to be toxic and deadly to a wide range of life forms. It thinned the eggshells of many birds–golden eagles and peregrine falcons being most vulnerable–and so threatened the extinction of certain species. Carson was one of the first to inform, alert, and persuade large numbers of people of different cultures that their common natural heritage was in grave danger and that global action was needed. Many species were close to extinction by 1972, when the United States and many other countries finally outlawed the use of DDT. Some species are just beginning to revive, because the poisons require years before leaving the chain of life.

Biologist John Todd, recognized for his pioneering work in the field of solar aquatics, an environmentally responsible family of technologies for wastewater purification and reclamation, established the New Alchemy Institute in 1969. With his principles of ecological design of the "earth as a living machine," he is currently working with municipalities around the United States to build ecologically conscious wastewater treatment facilities.

The Norwegian philosopher Arne Naess wrote in 1972, "The essence of deep ecology is to ask deeper questions; ask which society, which education, which form of religion is beneficial for all life on the planet as a whole." The theory of deep ecology focuses on the exploration of the radical separation between human beings and nature, as well as on other fundamental questions relating to humans and the earth. Deep ecologists feel that traditional environmental approaches apply only "Band-Aids" to a wounded world. The spiritual views of deep ecology are often linked with ecofeminism, which holds that the separation between humans and nature is a result of a masculine consciousness. While it has attracted a great deal of criticism for "too much talk and too little action," deep ecology has nonetheless been strongly associated with the green movement from its beginning.

The oil crisis of 1973 triggered the growth of hundreds of solar homes, especially in the United States, and in 1976, Jon Naar published *Design for a Limited Planet,* a book which reviewed alternative-energy houses. A number of pioneers adopted new energy strategies. Ken Baer built his dome-cluster home in New Mexico with water-drum walls and insulating rooflight "skylids," and the Farallones Institute, Berkeley, with eco-architect Sim van der Ryn created the "integral urban house." In 1974, E.R. Schumacher's book, *Small Is Beautiful,* was published, providing a philosophy for self-sufficiency. In Wales, the Centre for Alternative Technology became a show center and self-sufficient community which popularized "soft" energy and recycling systems. The movement for Intermediate Technology began to develop locally appropriate building techniques and energy systems based on wind, water, biomass, and solar designs for the developing world. Numerous research groups on eco-housing were established and experimental projects begun. Two significant examples are the Ecology House in Toronto and the Rocky Mountain Institute in Snowmass, Colorado. Biosphere II, an ambitious, highly controversial project built in the Arizona desert in 1990, replicates seven of the planet's "biomes," from rainforest to savanna, in an airtight sealed space frame. The systems inside recycle the air, water, and nutrients to maintain the life of 3800 plant and animal species and eight human researchers who are isolated inside. There has also been a revival in earth-covered homes. Architects Sydney Baggs in Australia, Arthur Quarmby in England, and Malcolm Wells in the United States as well as the Underground Space Center in Minnesota have built unique, extremely energy-efficient earth-covered houses.

"The most advanced movement concerned with healthy buildings is that of Baubiologie, or building biology," according to David Pearson, a Gaia architect and author of *The Natural House Book.* Reflecting Goethe's humanitarian philosophy and love of the natural world and the holistic health approach of Rudolf Steiner, Baubiologie has affinities to deep ecology. A different approach to architecture, it combines a scientific with a holistic view of the relationship between people and buildings. The science of Baubiologie characterizes the building as a living organism. Its fabric is compared to skin which, like our own skin, provides functions essential for life–pro-

***Top:** Cyclatron Geodesic Dome, St. Louis, Missouri, Buckminster Fuller, 1960. Forever experimenting with the newest forms of technology, philosopher and architect Buckminster Fuller set out to build more with less in the hope of making efficient buildings available to everyone. The geodesic dome encompasses the greatest amount of space with a minimum of materials and expense. Photo: Wayne Andrews/ Esto.*

***Bottom:** Architect Buckminster Fuller beside the model of his Dymaxion House, 1927. Dymaxion, a word invented by Fuller, refers to an object whose performance yields the greatest possible efficiency with the most current technology. The structure—40 feet high, 50 feet in diameter, and weighing only 6,000 pounds—was constructed around a central axis with a ring at the top. The entire structure could be lifted by a blimp, and carried from place to place. The Dymaxion House had no windows, but light and ventilation could pass through the central shaft. Fuller believed that people could live easily and efficiently in this house without ever growing tired of their surroundings. Photo: UPI/ Bettman Archive.*

tecting, insulating, breathing, absorbing, evaporating, regulating, and communicating. The goal of Baubiologie is to design buildings that meet our physical, biological, and spiritual needs. The fabric, color, scent, and services of a building must interact harmoniously with its inhabitants and the environment. The continuing exchange between indoor and outdoor depends on a transfusive skin to maintain a healthy "living" indoor climate. Professor Anton Schneider, an important pioneer of Baubiologie, established the Institute for Building Biology and Ecology in 1976 in West Germany with branches now in England and the United States.

Baubiologie has reintroduced many traditional and natural building materials and methods. Solid timber frames, clay blocks with lime mortar and plaster, earth buildings with grass roofs–some improved by recent research–are typical in Baubiologie buildings. The materials are handled with particular sensitivity, light and color are consciously incorporated, and all of the paints, treatments, and finishes are organic. Techniques for heating and ventilation by natural systems are combined with older traditions, such as the German tile oven. Baubiologie seeks to site the building and design the interior to recognize our link with nature and improve our spiritual well-being. It teaches a gentle art of building in a way that brings balance and harmony to people, buildings, and nature. Health and ecology are interwoven in natural architecture of all kinds and many recent pioneers, inspired by the vision of Gaia, draw on spiritual awareness as well.

*Gaia: A New Look at Life on Earth,* the book that inspired the Gaia movement, was written by James Lovelock in the mid 1980s. It describes the Earth and all its life systems as an entity–the ancient Greek Earth goddess Gaia–which has the characteristics of a living organism and is self-sustaining. A building or home should be a place of comfort and health, a place where we feel in harmony with ourselves and all of life. "This sense of belonging which is the source of true well-being is fundamental to this vision of ecology with its concept of our planet as 'Gaia'–a living entity seeking, like the Greek Earth goddess, always to create and sustain life. Far from being masters of nature, we are an integral part of Gaia."[4]

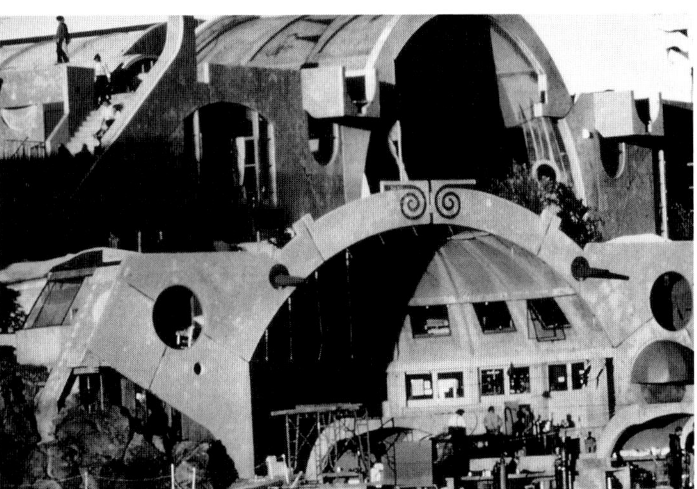

***The Foundry (foreground), the Vaults (center, background), and East and West Housing (on either side of Vaults) at Arcosanti. The Foundry's apse-shaped structure uses the angle of the sun to control the amount of shade in the space, making the outdoor studio comfortable in all seasons. Passive solar design in the East and West Housing make use of the desert sun and breezes to modify the indoor climate. Photo: Ivan Pintar, courtesy of the Cosanti Foundation.***

In 1987, the Montreal Protocol on Substances that Deplete the Ozone Layer, an international agreement, was signed by nations around the world to phase out substances destructive to the ozone layer. In 1990, an amended protocol was accepted in London by ninety-three nations (including some countries such as China and India who were not part of the original agreement) agreeing to phase out five key chlorofluorocarbons (CFCs 11, 12, 113, 114, and 115), carbon tetrachloride, and nonessential uses of the fire-extinguishing halon gases (Halons 1211, 1301, 2402) by the year 2000 and methyl chloroform (MC) by 2005. Hydrofluorocarbons (HCFCs), proposed as interim substitutes (even though they attack the ozone layer, albeit more slowly), are to be used where no other alternatives are found to exist, yet they are to be phased out by 2020 where feasible, and by 2040 at the latest. The 1990 agreement also established the Montreal Protocol Multilateral Fund to help developing countries finance the transition from ozone-depleting chemicals.

The industrialized world remains primarily dependent on non-renewable resources. As of 1994, over 90% of the world's energy needs are provided by fossil fuels–40% from oil, 33% from coal, 18% from natural gas, 4% from wood, 2% from waste material, and 1% from nuclear power. The consumption of the world's stock of fossil fuels has been primarily the responsibility of industrialized countries, particularly the United States. The people of the United States make up 5% of the world's population, but they are responsible for 30% of the world's energy consumption. Most of the population of the so-called Third World consume only 10% of the world's energy. The average American uses twice as much energy as the average European, and thirty times more than the average Indian.

The Earth Summit, a popular name for the United Nations Conference on Environment and Development, took place in Rio de Janeiro, Brazil, in 1992 and was attended by delegates from over 175 countries. Regarded as the largest summit gathering in history, more than one hundred heads of state attended the Conference. Long in planning, the Earth

Summit took on more importance with the ending of the Cold War, as there was widespread pressure to redirect money from military expenditures toward the poorer nations of the world. A whole range of environmental concerns was addressed at the Conference, including biological diversity, the depletion of the ozone layer, loss of forests, and global warming and climate change. Important treaties were written during the conference, scheduled to be signed in 1993. The lack of official attendance on the part of the United States, widely criticized by American environmentalists, reflected the deficit of environmental concern in the Bush administration. Questions remain about which countries, including the U.S., will sign the completed treaties.

Energy sources coined as "alternative" in the 1960s are no longer radical. Progressively entering the mainstream, renewable resources are technologically reliable and economically feasible. The market forces of products have begun to change. There must be a greater emphasis on the education of owners, architects, engineers, and other building professionals in the technologies that help them design projects utilizing renewable resources. For the moment, our failure to adequately do so is one of the major obstacles of the green movement. The pioneers discussed in these pages have created a strong foundation for a new mainstream architecture–one that is being developed by today's building professionals.

The moment we are born, we begin the physical process of growth, decay, and death. Some believe that the life of our earth reflects these processes. Others believe that the life of earth is infinite and will naturally heal itself of our mistakes. There is no argument, however, that the way in which the relationship between people and their environment is conducted forever alters the course of both. A sensitive and educated awareness of history and ecology will help us to regenerate both our environment and our quality of life.

***Top: Biosphere II is the world's largest enclosed terrestrial ecosystem. It is located in the Sonoran Desert, midway between Phoenix and Tucson, Arizona. Photo: C. Allan Morgan, courtesy Lamont-Doherty Earth Observatory of Columbia University.***

***Bottom: Underground Gallery, Cape Cod, Massachusetts, Malcolm Wells. Photo: Malcolm Wells.***

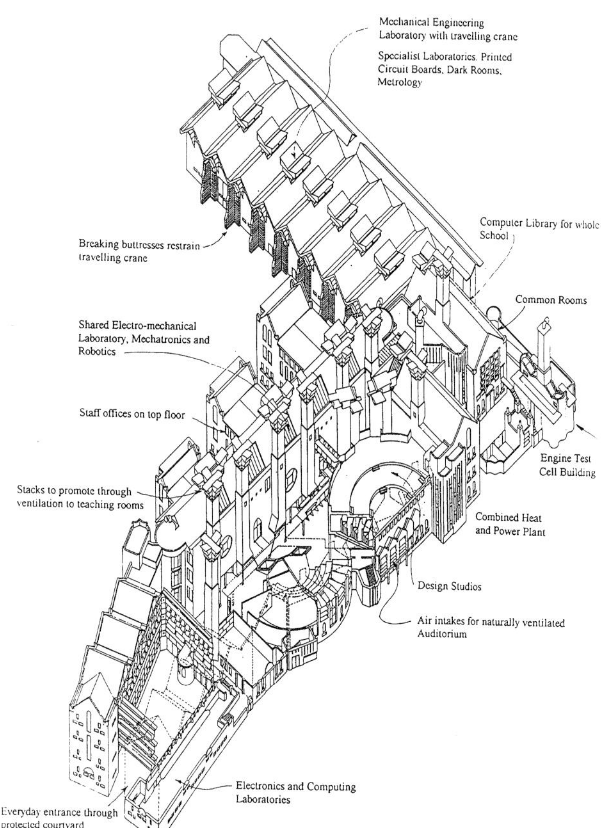


***Top:* The School of Engineering and Manufacture at Leicester Polytechnic in England, designed by Short Ford & Associates of London, provides 1,000 students and faculty with auditoriums, classrooms, offices and laboratories—about 10,000 square meters of space—90 percent of which is vented without mechanical assistance. Although heating laboratory buildings is easy, cooling them can be difficult because the thermal energy generated by heavy machinery and continuously running computer equipment creates about 80 watts of heat per square meter—double that of a typical commercial building. Photo: Peter Cook.**

***Bottom:* Axonometric showing exterior view of laboratories at the School of Engineering and Manufacture at Leicester Polytechnic. A series of eight "Victorian Gothic" vent stacks, exhaust ducts, high ceilings, and innovative double-wall insulation provide engineering students with a living laboratory for energy efficiency. Drawing: Short Ford & Associates, London.**

## ENVIRONMENTALLY CONSCIOUS ARCHITECTURE AROUND THE WORLD

Sophisticated building design solutions to ecological and social concerns have, in this decade, begun to enter the mainstream of American architecture for a variety of reasons that include creative initiatives, available technology, and the recognition that they are, in the long run, good business. Because of the plentiful availability of cheap resources in the United States, initiatives to address energy efficiency and resource conservation, two primary aspects of ecology conscious architecture, were often undeveloped or unrecognized. By contrast, more limited and expensive resources in other parts of the world encouraged ingenuity in building design. In Germany, for example, the law requires sophisticated energy efficiency and recycling measures to be implemented into building design and product manufacturing.

In some cases, American architects, engineers, and building professionals have looked to building technologies developed outside of the United States for new ideas. Foreign countries, in turn, import the expertise of American designers and specialists to assist them. Also, research and technology in the area of resource conservation in this country is on the rise. For example, sophisticated technologies developed by NASA for space exploration have provided research that some commercial building designers are incorporating into their work through unique partnerships. In all countries, the concern for ecologically responsive design and its necessary role in the quality of human life, coupled with the advanced technical capability for communication among individuals around the world, is playing a lead role in establishing a fundamental environmental consciousness in building and community design.

### *Environmentally Conscious Communities*

The resources of a community–energy and water, transportation and roads, access to schools, hospitals, and food supplies–will establish much of a building's ability to respond to ecological and social concerns. Historically, each of the largest cities in the world grew from a community based primarily on its plentiful supply of resources. Transportation played a significant role in the development of all cities, whether a city grew as a medieval center where foot travel was dominant, or began as an agricultural community in a pre-industrial civilization reliant on horses and carts. Communities with ports and harbors accommodated the international trade of natural resources, and cities like Venice became world powers largely because of access to rich resources from faraway places. Cities in the United States such as Boston and New York flourished because of their access to ports, and communi-

*The Netherlands International Bank (NMB) Headquarters, designed by Architects Alberts & Van Huut (Amsterdam) was envisioned as organic, integrating art, natural materials, sunlight, plants, energy conservation, water, and low noise. The 538,000-square-foot building is broken into ten low-rise buildings with sloped façades that are arranged into irregular S-shaped plans. Photo: Sybolt Voeten Architectuur.*

*The buildings incorporate gardens and courtyards interspersed over 301,280 square feet of underground parking and service areas. NMB's energy bill is one of the lowest of any office building in Europe Photo: Jan derwig Architectuur.*

*One of the first public parks to feature native habitats of Taiwan, the Botanical Park at the National Museum of Natural Science will be located on a 15-acre urban site in Taichung. Seven of Taiwan's botanically unique ecosystems are to be replicated including the coral atoll, monsoon rainforest, and the Orchid Island Forest. Designed by the American firm HOH Associates, the architectural focus is a 30-meter-high passive glasshouse containing a tropical rainforest exhibit. Photo: HOH Associates.*

***Under the leadership of architect and three-term Mayor Jaime Lerner, the city of Curitiba, Brazil, has become a model of environmental sustainability. A bus-based transit system draws 28 percent of the city's car owners daily, the park system provides 50 square meters of green space per inhabitant, 70 percent of the households recycle their waste, and a vast array of educational environmental programs for children and adults have been created. The Open University of the Environment (above) is located near an abandoned quarry and provides continuing education for adults. Photo: Susan Di Guilio.***

ties with access to rivers also developed. During the rapid expansion of the railroad in the United States, cities rapidly sprang up across the countryside. And with the regular use of private automobile transportation, the scale of city development changed entirely. Like Los Angeles, travel in most American cities is difficult without a private car. "The quantity of carbon dioxide released by a typical car travelling ten thousand miles a year will need some two hundred trees to absorb it," according to Robert and Brenda Vale in *Green Architecture.* "A million trees will cope with the carbon dioxide emission from five thousand cars. However green a city appears, the city of a million trees organized around car travel can only be considered ecological if its population does not exceed about twenty thousand, estimating one car to every four inhabitants." Suburban living, an outgrowth of automobile transport, developed as an American phenomenon that has spread to include countries all over the world. Fast rising population, the dependence on fossil-fuel-burning transportation, traffic jams, and the isolation from involvement in public life are all factors that diminish the quality of life in suburban centers.

For hundreds of years community leaders, architects and urban planners have tried to create utopian communities. In England, the planned city of Milton Keynes provided a grid of roads with local housing located in some grid squares, with major shopping and city centers in others. In the United States, Frank Lloyd Wright's conceptual Broadacre city, where residents were to own an acre of land that would provide their food, gave its population the opportunity to be self-sustaining. Architect Buckminster Fuller proposed building a giant geodesic dome to shelter midtown Manhattan from pollution. In *The Death and Life of Great American Cities,* published in 1961, author Jane Jacobs attacks modern city planning: "Extraordinary governmental financial incentives have been required to achieve this degree of monotony, sterility, and vulgarity. Automobiles are often conveniently tagged as the villains responsible for the ills of cities, but the destructive effects of automobiles are much less a cause than a symptom of our incompetence at city building." This significant book looks at the sociological details of what makes lively communities work, such as parks, sidewalks, human interaction, and diversity. The work of such planners as Lewis Mumford, who advocates the concepts of decentralization, was by this time used as the basic guideline in schools of planning and architecture, as well as in Congress and city halls. Le Corbusier's plan for the Radiant City had an immense impact on our cities. "It was hailed deliriously by architects, and tells nothing but lies as to how the city works," says Jacobs.

In the 1990s, urban planners are creating "sustainable" communities, communities that provide for the individual, family, and community quality of life along with the appropriate resources necessary to sustain them. For planners like Peter Calthorpe and Doug Kelbaugh, "the solution to suburban alienation is the creation of 'pedestrian pockets,' small communities located on a light rail line that links them to each other and to urban centers that incorporate a mix of housing, shopping, facilities, employment, and green areas within walking distance of each other." The work of Andres Duany and Elizabeth Plater-Zyberk, as illustrated at Seaside, Florida, strives to be pedestrian-oriented, minimally dependent on the automobile, diverse, and inclusive of green areas. As resource supplies decrease and population grows, we must recognize the need for the construction of ecologically and socially responsive communities. American urban planners are helping city leaders address existing concerns or planning new communities around the United States and in other countries that integrate aspects of environmental consciousness.

*Top: The community of Seaside, Florida, by Duany & Plater-Zyberk of Miami, was designed from 1978-1983. Site and program were modeled after the components of a small town to provide an alternative to the methods of contemporary real estate development. A small pedestrian community, Seaside includes a downtown commercial district and a conference facility that doubles as a town hall. A portion of the recreation budget is used to create small civic amenities around town. The private buildings, subject to the provisions of the Master Plan and Zoning Code, are individually commissioned to provide for a varied character of architecture which is sympathetic to regional vernacular. Photo: Duany & Plater-Zyberk.*

*Middle left:The river town of Haymount,Virginia, combines wetlands and hilly terrain with buildable areas surrounded by parks. Designed in 1989 by Duany & Plater-Zyberk, the town layout is a grid based on that of Leesburg, Virginia. Four square blocks, which straddle the main streets, enclose the common parking required by the higher density building of the main street. Linear blocks, which provide the rest of the community fabric, accommodate individual homes. Additional squares are provided for civic buildings, with at least one per neighborhood. The grid accommodates natural landscape and blends with the original landscape at the periphery. Drawing: Duany & Plater-Zyberk.*

*Middle right: Designed in 1988 by Duany & Plater-Zyberk, Kentlands, Maryland, an original farm site, is surrounded by conventional suburban office parks, townhouse subdivisions, and strip shopping centers. The evolving scheme provides pedestrian access to the center of town from each of the four neighborhoods. Photo: Duany & Plater-Zyberk.*

*Bottom: Bamberton, British Columbia, a new town designed around an old industrial site, is planned as a series of environmentally sensitive and pedestrian-oriented neighborhoods that will serve residents of all incomes and ages. Issues ranging from streeet layout and building materials to waste management and sewage treatment have been addressed to foster an ecologically sustainable energy-efficient habitat. Designed in 1992 by Duany & Plater-Zyberk, the town is expected to take about 20 years to build. Drawing: Duany & Plater-Zyberk.*

Chapter 2

# *Defining Environmentally Conscious Architecture*

## *Pioneering American Practitioners*

This chapter defines the notion of "sustainability" within the context of unique visions and architectural achievements and explores landmark principles in ecologically and socially responsible building design. In their own words, pioneering leaders in the United States discuss their personal views, projects, and the current state of environmentally conscious architecture.

The word "sustainable," according to *Webster's 10th New Collegiate Dictionary,* is defined as follows: "Of, relating to, or being a method of harvesting or using a resource so that the resource is not depleted or permanently damaged." "Sustainability" is one of the most significant concepts of this decade, influencing the design of global government policy, economics, energy resources, technology, manufacturing, community planning, and architecture. The concept of sustainability was first identified in *Our Common Future,* a book written by the former Prime Minister of Norway, Gro Harlem Brudtland, published in 1986.

Over the past two decades, environmentally responsible design has been in the process of being defined worldwide. Environmentally conscious building design is a complex and sometimes controversial subject, including issues of available technology and information, economic and legal requirements, and the personal views of key players. Resulting less from right and wrong solutions than from a full exploration of complex subjective issues, "sustainable" design not only respects natural resources, but also embraces human, cultural, and historical distinctions.

Sustainable architecture has been substantially defined by the pioneering approaches of architects and designers who often work in conjunction with their visionary clients, design team consultants, and engineers. Practitioners are faced with number of difficult questions. Should a designer choose synthetic materials that are recyclable rather than utilize a limited natural resource material, or does he/she believe that properly managed natural materials are ultimately the only truly "sustainable" material? What energy resources are self-sustaining and into which kinds of mechanical systems should they be integrated? These questions have more than one answer, and the particular requirements of each project will be called upon to answer them.

The design trailblazers on these pages have played an important role in defining what has come to be known as "sustainable" design during the 1990s with much more than their architectural projects, namely by influencing international and national government policy, technology, and manufacturing. In addition to this handful of innovators, thousands of world leaders and individuals have brought their visions of sustainable design together in an unprecedented message of unity. The guidelines illustrated here toward defining environmentally conscious architecture are a result of not one, but many important sets of principles. The dedicated efforts of environmentally conscious leaders around the world coupled with scientific data, technology, and communication have played a vital role in changing international policy, reinventing global manufacturing methods, increasing the velocity of changing environmental legislation, vitalizing renewable resource technology, and creating a viable economic base for environmentally conscious decision making in the public and private sectors.

### ROBERT BERKEBILE

As founding chairperson of the American Institute of Architects' Committee on the Environment, Robert Berkebile shaped a partnership with the U.S. Environmental Protection Agency, manufacturers, and environmental groups to create the criteria, methodology, and database of information that have become the *AIA Environmental Resource Guide,* a comprehensive and continually updated publication about the ecological impact of architectural decisions. EPA Administrator William Riley believes that "this effort will change the way we design our cities." Berkebile is a founding member of the Union of International Architects Road from Rio Working Group and co-chairperson of the Scientific Advisory Group on the Environment. Through these and numerous other activities, he has become a leader of an international effort by architects to develop the information that will be needed to create healthy buildings and communities.

"The design, construction, and operation of our cities has been a major factor in the degradation of our environment," says Berkebile, "and a more holistic approach to planning and community building can improve the economic and social vitality of our society as well as restore the environment." Toward this vision, he is contributing his time to participate in national demonstration projects and investing the spirit of his firm's work to create buildings and communities as pedagogy.

### *Defining Environmentally Conscious Architecture*

Berkebile thinks that most of the attempts to label ecologically conscious design as "green" or "sustainable" are limiting. Citing Peter Ellyard, the Australian futurist, he says that "sustainable" implies survival, when we should instead be focused on thriving. "This labeling," points out Berkebile, "is symptomatic of our tendency to simplify, reduce, and label before understanding the complex systems we are modifying. Vitruvius had it right–firmness, commodity, and delight, but if he were alive today, he would surely be among the first to point out that commodity must be informed by the needs of a rapidly expanding population with shrinking resources."

According to Berkebile, each design decision must be an act of restoration and renewal, contributing to the social, economic, and environmental vitality of the individual and of the community. "It has become clear that if we care about our children's future, we can no longer be satisfied with reducing the environmental impact of our designs."

It's also clear to Berkebile that as we're willing to invest in creating and maintaining communities through a more holistic, inclusive design process, the quality of the product improves dramatically. This approach requires more attention to restoring or strengthening connections which our culture has weakened or severed during the last century, connections to individuals, races, cultures, nature, ecology, and economy. If we embrace rather than shirk the diversity and interdependence of all life with our designs, we find the outcome can move far beyond efficiency and performance. The result can touch the heart, elevate the spirit, and inform us of the potential for celebration and community building at every scale.

### *Background*

Since building his childhood tree houses, Berkebile has been an environmental designer. His interpretation of beauty and good design were redefined after the tragic collapse of the Kansas City Hyatt Regency Hotel in 1981. "As Project Architect, I found myself questioning every aspect of my life as I spent a long, painful night on the rescue team removing more than 100 dead guests and over 200 seriously injured," remembers Berkebile. "The unanswered question was, What was the real impact of our design on those we intended to serve and on their neighborhood, the community, and the planet?"

Following the Hyatt experience, Berkebile became the founding chairman of the AIA's National Committee on the Environment in order to create a partnership with corporate America, environmental groups, and the construction industry to create a new methodology for the approach to building design and construction in the United States. The results so far include publication of the *Environmental Resource Guide,* national teleconferences on green design and technology, the international sustainable design conference in Chicago in 1993, and numerous national demonstration projects mentioned below.

### *On the State of Ecological Architecture*

Berkebile expresses his opinion about the current state of ecologically conscious architecture by quoting Einstein: "We shall require substantially a new manner of thinking if mankind is to survive." He thinks that our nation is just beginning to wake up and explore the problems and the potential for a new manner of thinking, but that we are far from a new level of consciousness, both as a profession and as a society. "The inertia of business-as-usual has created obsolete governmental policy, land use laws, public safety codes, infrastructure that ignores or attempts to overpower natural systems, and tax and economic policy that encourage our short-sighted take-use-waste behavior." says Berkebile. "At a worldwide level, there are increasing examples of these barriers falling away in the presence of the evidence of better alternatives resulting from good design."

### *Architectural Projects*

As a founding partner in the Kansas City firm Berkebile, Nelson, Immenschuh, McDowell, Berkebile

*The $16 million William Deramus III Education Pavilion at the Kansas City Zoo opened its doors in December 1995. The 71,500-square-foot building features ecological technologies such as building orientation design and materials that maximize solar benefits, a highly energy-efficient HVAC system combined with super insulation, high-performance glazing, and state-of-the-art control systems. Photo: S.J. Swalwell/ Architectural Photographics, KCMO.*

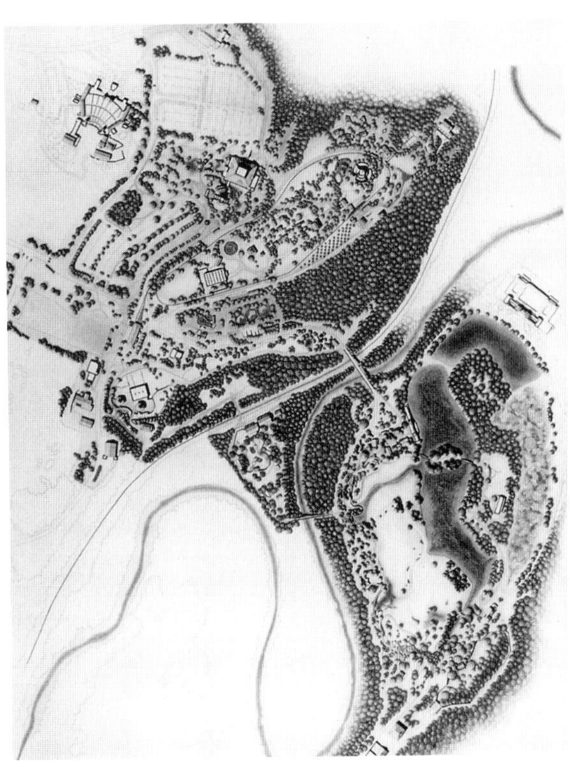

*Kansas City Zoo Master Plan. As concept designers, master planners, and managing architects for the Kansas City Zoo's $55 million redevelopment and expansion from 80 to 180 acres, BNIM Architects developed sustainable design guidelines that were incorporated by all of the firms that participated in the project. The guidelines included requirements in the areas of site development, landscaping, building materials, indoor air quality, building ecology, and resource efficiency. Drawing: BNIM.*

is working to bring the principles of restorative design to many current projects in the United States and Canada. Some of their environmentally concerned projects are highlighted here.

KANSAS CITY ZOO
*Kansas City, Missouri*

A 180-acre zoological garden completed in 1995, the Kansas City Zoo provides the public with an opportunity to experience environmental education in a uniquely direct way. As part of the planning process, BNIM developed a series of sustainable design guidelines that were utilized by all firms that participated in the massive project.

In addition to the master plan, BNIM was commissioned to design two of the new major exhibits developed to represent the wildlife and culture of the world's continents. BNIM's Australia and Africa are both innovative experiences in interpretive exhibits, combining animals, actors, film, native plants, and authentic architecture, allowing total immersion into the culture of the two continents.

EARTHWORKS UNDERGROUND ENVIRONMENTAL RESOURCE CENTER
*Kansas City, Missouri*

EarthWorks is the new environmental sciences education facility of Kansas City's Learning Exchange, a local education reform institution. This innovative

*Earthworks Underground Enviromental Resource Center, Kansas City, Missouri. Completed in 1996, this new 42,000-square-foot, $2-million environmental sciences education facility for third and fourth graders was built inside a massive complex of caves. Photo: BNIM.*

***C.K. Choi Building for the Institute of Asian Research, University of British Columbia, Vancouver. As sustainable design consultant to U.B.C. and Matsuzaki Wright Architects, BNIM Architects established environmental criteria for the design, construction, and operation of the building. The selection of regional materials minimizes embodied energy and is designed for longevity. Photo: Mike Sherman.***

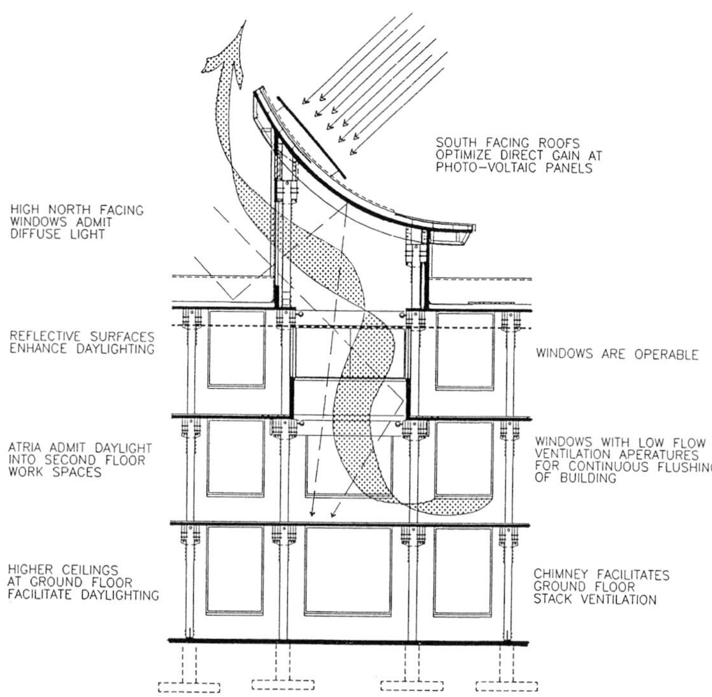


***Section, C.K. Choi Building for the Institute of Asian Research. Features of the building include energy efficiency through natural daylighting, photocells and occupancy sensors, ventilation, preheated hot water, and anticipated photovoltaic technology. Composting toilets, graywater recycling, and rainwater collection contribute to water conservation. Drawing: Matsuzaki Wright Architects.***

facility for third and fourth graders was built inside a massive complex of caves used for a variety of commercial developments. The "by-product" space acts as a tool to reinforce the concepts of reuse and recycling. Similarly, materials used in the project will contain a high percentage of reused, recycled, and recyclable materials.

C.K. Choi Building for the Institute of Asian Research
*Vancouver, British Columbia*

The Institute for Asian Research is a research center located on the University of British Columbia campus. At the outset of the project, the University hired BNIM to work with building users and Matsuzaki Wright to collectively establish criteria for the Institute's design, construction, and operation. In an effort to restore a remaining piece of Douglas fir forest, the design of the three-story facility began with a reduced footprint. The 30,000-square-foot educational facility was constructed of reused materials from campus demolition projects and incorporates extensive daylighting and natural conditioning—it has no air conditioning or boilers, composting toilets, and constructed wetlands for wastewater treatment.

National Resource Center
*Bozeman, Montana*

The National Resource Center is one of four benchmark green building projects funded by Montana State University and the National Institute of Standards and Technology (NIST). In Berkebile's opinion, the Resource Center moves far beyond current sustainable building technology. "In fact," he says, "they told us when we presented the concept that the project far exceeded the scope of the other three buildings." At this writing, the design concept has been completed and is in the client's hands. Some of its unusual features include natural conditioning, passive solar energy for daylighting and most winter heating, and groundwater and night flushing for most summer cooling. This particular region of Montana has a diurnal effect in that the air cools at night and is very dry. The building will therefore be opened at night, and through a power system and a natural ven-

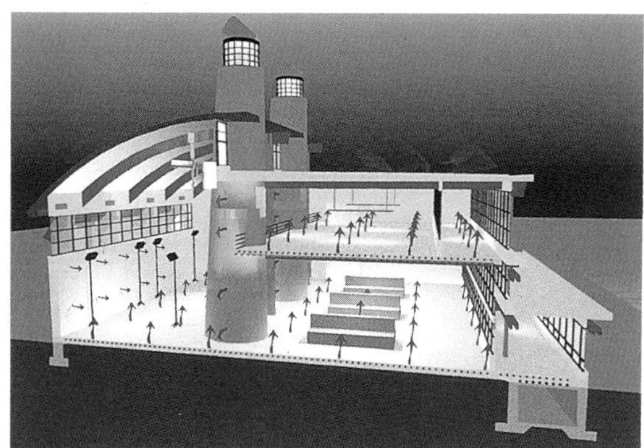

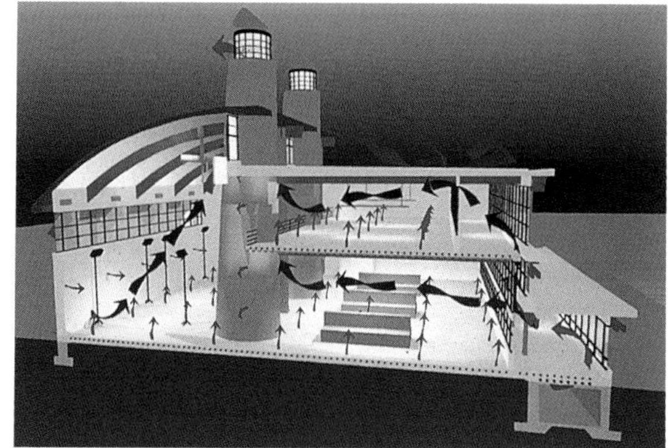

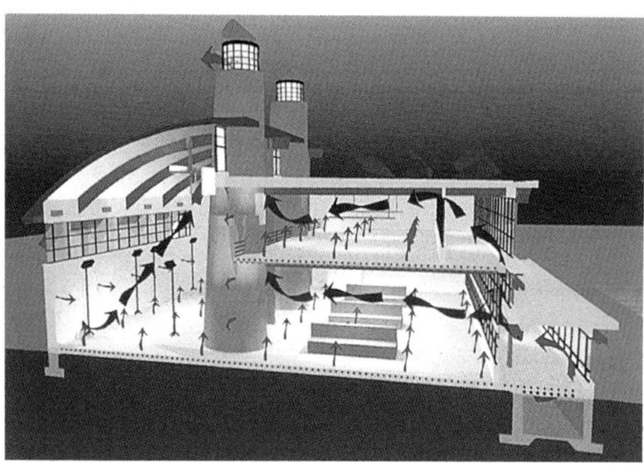

*With construction anticipated in 1997, the Montana State University National Resource Center was funded by the National Institute of Standards and Technology in order to create a new benchmark for sustainable design. BNIM Architects recruited a team of nationally recognized experts with a complete range of disciplines. Diagrams clockwise: winter day heating diagram, summer day cooling diagram, summer night cooling diagram, winter night heating diagram. The particular region of Montana has a diurnal effect that cools the air at night and the building is to be opened at night for 100% natural ventilation, or "night-flushing." During the summer, for example, the surfaces become cooled at night, releasing coolness into the building during the day. Drawings: Berkebile Nelson Immenschuh McDowell Architects.*

tiliation system, the surfaces become cooled to, in turn, release coolness in the building during the day.

One feature that Berkebile feels captures the excitement of the project in particular is a device that NASA calls a "fuzzy photon collector," which was designed on paper for use in moon colonies, which would have been located below the ground surface. Far more efficient than fiber optics, it collects daylight energy, concentrates it into a four-inch column, transports it through space, and then redistributes it inside the facility. Berkebile approached NASA, and asked if they could develop the prototype to function in the design of the National Resource Center. Not only did NASA agree, but their engineers claim that the technology is both sound and affordable.

## *Outside the Architectural Practice*

In addition to the architectural projects of his firm, Berkebile is working on a number of demonstration projects in conjunction with the AIA's Committee on the Environment, the National Parks Service, the Departments of Energy and of Defense, Canadian Provincial Governments, and the National Science Foundation to develop sustainable guidelines for their commissions. In addition to the *Environmental Resource Guide,* the committee has organized national teleconferences on green technology, the international conference on sustainability in Chicago in 1993, and demonstration projects that include a team of national advisors to work with the city of Atlanta, Georgia to help it become the Solar City. The following demonstration projects represent some of the projects that Berkebile has helped to carry out. The AIA's Committee on the Environment has assisted with the design of a number of sites to demonstrate ecologically conscious energy efficient solutions. These are projects which require raised funding, and much of the work is not compensated financially.

### Greening the White House
*Washington, DC*

Berkebile, along with a team of over 100 experts on environmental design, developed recommendations for the sustainability of the White House and Old Executive Office Building complex. The team focused on strategies to improve the efficiency, quality, and durability of the buildings, as well as the health and productivity of their occupants. Specific areas addressed in the recommendations include energy and water efficiency, resource conservation and reduction of waste stream volumes, and improved indoor air quality. President Clinton announced the implementation of these recommendations during his Earth Day address on April 21, 1994. The restoration work currently underway should be completed by 1996.

***During the relocation of Pattonsburg, Missouri, which was devastated by severe flooding in 1993, the residents decided to rebuild as a national model of sustainable development. With the American Institute of Architects, BNIM conducted a series of community-wide design workshops in which residents worked directly with designers to plan the future of their town. Construction of the relocation is underway, with a total cost of $12.5 million coming from federal, state, and private sources. Drawings: Berkebile Nelson Immenschuh McDowell Architects.***

### Town Relocation
*Pattonsburg, Missouri*

Devastated by the great flood of 1993, the city of Pattonsburg chose to relocate to higher ground. In designing their new community, the residents of Pattonsburg decided to redevelop as a national model for sustainability. Funded by a federal assistance grant, BNIM conducted community-wide design workshops in which residents worked directly with designers to plan the future of their town, incorporating sustainable technologies to improve the social, economic, and environmental vitality of their community.

The resulting design includes constructed wetlands for stormwater management, reuse of buildings and materials from the existing town, the creation of a Sustainable Economic Development Council and a Charter of Sustainability, the adoption of Covenants and Restrictions for Sustainability, and a variety of energy-efficiency and renewable energy measures such as the utilization of photovoltaic shingles. Construction is expected to be completed in the summer of 1996.

Art Center College of Design
Library
1700 Lida Street
Pasadena, Calif. 91103

Sustainable Grand Canyon Initiative and Proposed Greater Grand Canyon Partnership
*Grand Canyon, Arizona*

The Grand Canyon as a living laboratory provides an incredible opportunity for public education about the interconnectedness and interdependence of man and nature. So far, the park has received 5 million visitors; by the year 2020, visitation is estimated to be 7 million. Clearly, sustainability has become a critical issue in the maintenance and development of the site.

Six Native American groups have sacred cultural ties to the Canyon, in addition to the concessionaires, developers, and other local interests with their own sets of concerns. In September of 1994, the Sustainable Grand Canyon Workshop brought together national and regional environmental leaders from a variety of disciplines with representatives of government, utility, and community interests, private developers, and Native Americans. The goal was to encourage access to the park while creating a "sustainable" vision for the future as part of the site's 75th anniversary celebration. Fundamental ecological principles of land preservation, waste reduction and reuse, energy efficiency, and pollution prevention formed the basis for bold new initiatives that respect the environment while supporting a strong regional economy.

Energy-Efficient and Environmentally Sensitive Department of Defense Showcase Facility—The Pentagon
*Alexandria, Virginia*

This project is the first and most prominent Department of Defense showcase facility in a program to promote the implementation of efficiency technologies in the nation's 500,000 federal buildings. Berkebile helped facilitate a planning process that included today's leading experts in resource and energy efficiency technologies. The team's recommendations for the $1.2 billion restoration are organized into six sections: energy; building ecology; water; landscaping and grounds; materials, waste, and resource management; and cultural and behavioral change.

Solar Atlanta
*Atlanta, Georgia*

The Department of Energy, the Turner Foundation, and the city of Atlanta invited Berkebile to help facilitate a highly ambitious project that begins Atlanta's transformation into the premier sustainable city. The project seeks to coordinate existing projects and community desires with a new cadre of private and public projects to develop green industries as well as green development and redevelopment. Initiated late in 1995, the effort will continue through the Olympics in the summer of 1996.

## *Suggestions for Professionals*

"Architects and designers frequently ask for 'the list' or 'the book' on sustainable design," says Berkebile. "With mixed emotions, we usually provide the design program and goals for a requested project along with a list of resources that our office calls 'Bob's Top Dozen.'" Berkebile keeps a running list of about 100 publications, keeping the top 12 current. According to Berkebile, *In Context*, a quarterly journal published by the Context Institute, is the most useful journal publication available on sustainable communities.

### Bob's Top Dozen

• *Beyond the Limits,* Donella Meadows, Dennis Meadows, Jorgen Randers.

• *Earth In Mind: On Eduction, Environment and the Human Prospect,* David Orr. (Island Press: Washington, DC.) 1994.

• *The Ecology of Commerce,* Paul Hawken.

• *Environmental Building News: A Bimonthly Newsletter on Environmentally Sustainable Design and Construction.* (West River Communications: Brattleboro, VT) 802-257-7300.

• *Environmental By Design. Volume I: Interiors. A Sourcebook of Environmentally Aware Material Choices,* Kim LeClair and David Rousseau. (Hartley & Marks Limited: Vancouver, BC) 1992.

• *Environmental Resource Guide. American Institute of Architects Committee on the Environment.* 1995. 1-800-365-ARCH.

• *GREBE: Guide to Resource Efficient Building.* Center for Resourceful Building Technology, 1993. P.O. Box 3866, Missoula, MT 59806. 406-549-7678.

• *Guiding Principles of Sustainable Design.* National Parks Service, Department of the Interior, 1993. Stock #024-005-01132-3 from U.S. Government Bookstore, 201 West 8th Street, Pueblo, CO 81003. 719-544-3142; 719-544-6719 fax.

• *In Context: A Journal of Hope, Sustainability and Change* (quarterly). P.O. Box 11470, Bainbridge Island, WA 98110. 206-842-0216 or 1-800-IN CONTEXT.

• *A Primer on Sustainable Building,* Rocky Mountain Institute. 1739 Snowmass Creek Road, Snowmass, CO 81654. 303-927-3851.

• *State of the World–1996,* Lester R. Brown et al. A Worldwatch Institute Report on Progress Toward a Sustainable Society, 1776 Massachusetts Avenue, NW, Washington, DC 20036-1904. 202-452-1999.

• *Your Natural Home: A Complete Sourcebook and Design Manual for Creating a Healthy, Beautiful, Environmentally Sensitive House,* Janet Marinelli and Paul Bierman-Lytle.( Little, Brown and Company: New York) 1995.

However, Berkebile feels that it is most useful to go and visit other projects in order to discover first-hand both what worked and what didn't. "By seeing the building, talking to the owners, the designers, and the users, we usually get to the solutions much faster." He suggests that selecting the best projects and focusing on their particular features will help professionals understand and evaluate the types of solutions that can be integrated into their own ecologically conscious buildings. For Berkebile's projects, the most significant factor has been adding more diversity to the design and engineering team, including them at the outset, and taking enough time to know the place, its ecology, culture, and economy before exploring design concepts.

### *Closing Remarks*

"Designers often seem to be paralyzed by what they perceive their knowledge or ignorance to be. Ecologically conscious design is less about what the individual knows or thinks he knows, and more about approaching the design with a totally new consciousness and the willingness to rely on the collaborative energy of all of the participants."

## RANDOLPH CROXTON AND KIRSTEN CHILDS

Croxton Collaborative, the firm of architect Randolph Croxton and interior designer Kirsten Childs, brought environmentally conscious office design to the forefront of the architecture business with the completion of two major projects in New York, the Natural Resources Defense Council and the National Audubon Society Headquarters. Working also in conjunction with the American Institute of Architect's Committee on the Environment in a leadership capacity, the achievements of Croxton and Childs have caused the professions of architecture, engineering, building construction, business, and real estate to take new notice of ecological concerns in building projects throughout the United States. The Audubon House has been featured on network television and prominently published in nearly every professional journal, the *New York Times, Newsweek, The Wall Street Journal, Time,* and *Newsweek,* to name just a few. Croxton's achievements illustrate how ecological and human concerns make sense and contribute to the bottom line.

### *Defining Environmentally Conscious Architecture*

"At the core of every strong environmental concept, there is an ability to do more with less," says Croxton, who describes the Collaborative's projects as high-performance designs that take simple human needs into consideration. Establishing environmental priorities among the entire project team, implementing real-world applications, focusing on demonstrated reliability and market availability, and seeking to go beyond code compliance limitations are just some of the ways that they define their environmentally informed projects. Through their work, Croxton have carved a path toward creating architecture that is healthy for its occupants as well as the environment, and that uses all of its resources to the fullest extent. If one word could summarize their architecture, it would be "optimization," says Croxton. "There are enhanced levels of energy efficiency, indoor air quality, pollution and CFC avoidance, solid waste management, water conservation, visual comfort, light quality, thermal comfort, and an enhanced awareness of time of day, seasons, and orientation to the sun, achieved within an overall market rate budget." These qualities, together with the commitment to carry them through, define environmentally conscious design.

### *Background*

Randolph Croxton and Kirsten Childs founded Croxton Collaborative, a leading architectural, interior design, and facilities planning services firm that specializes in high-performance environmentally informed design, in 1978. The recipient of the profession's highest award for design excellence, the AIA National Design Award, Croxton Collaborative is recognized internationally for its leadership in environmentally conscious architecture. The Collaborative's early work with two of the most influential environmental organizations in the United States, the Natural Resources Defense Council beginning in 1986, and the Audubon Society starting in 1989, finely tuned Croxton and Childs' value-directed approach to design. In 1995 they joined Pei Cobb Freed in the effort to turn the integrated design criteria for the American Association for the Advancement of Science's new building in Washington into a reality.

### *Architectural and Environmental Consulting Projects*

NATURAL RESOURCES DEFENSE COUNCIL
*New York, New York*

Located in lower Manhattan, the 25,000-square-foot headquarters of the Natural Resources Defense Council occupies the top two and a half floors of a twelve-story building. Completed in 1989, the NRDC headquarters was noted at the time as the most energy efficient office renovation in the country. The local utility company, Consolidated Edison, monitored

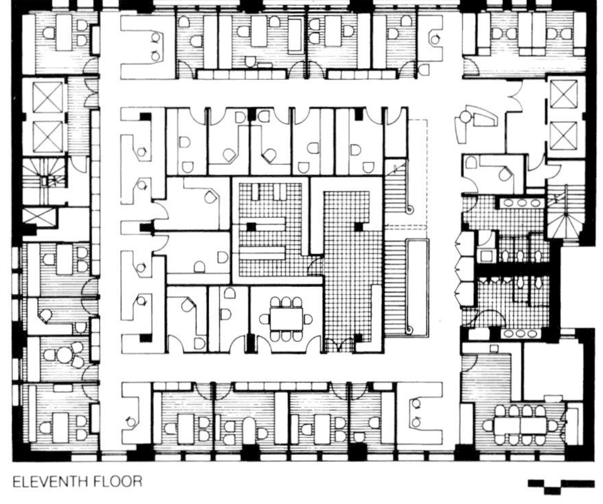


*Natural Resources Defense Council Headquarters, New York, floor plan and section perspective at stair. The 25,000-square-foot offices completed in 1989 incorporate energy-efficiency through natural daylighting, occupancy sensors, energy saving apppliances, increased building insulation, and windows with low-emissivity film. Materials and finishes are non-toxic, and bicycle parking is provided to encourage the staff to use non-polluting transportation. NRDC's annual energy/maintenance savings over a code-compliant model amounts to $45,000 for 30,000 square feet of space. Skylights, original to the 1915 building, were upgraded with insulated glass and low-emissivity film. Wool carpet with tackless application was used instead of nylon materials and glues, which offgass. Light color latex paint was used to reflect illumination, and reduce the use of toxic materials. Drawings: Croxton Collaborative, Architects.*

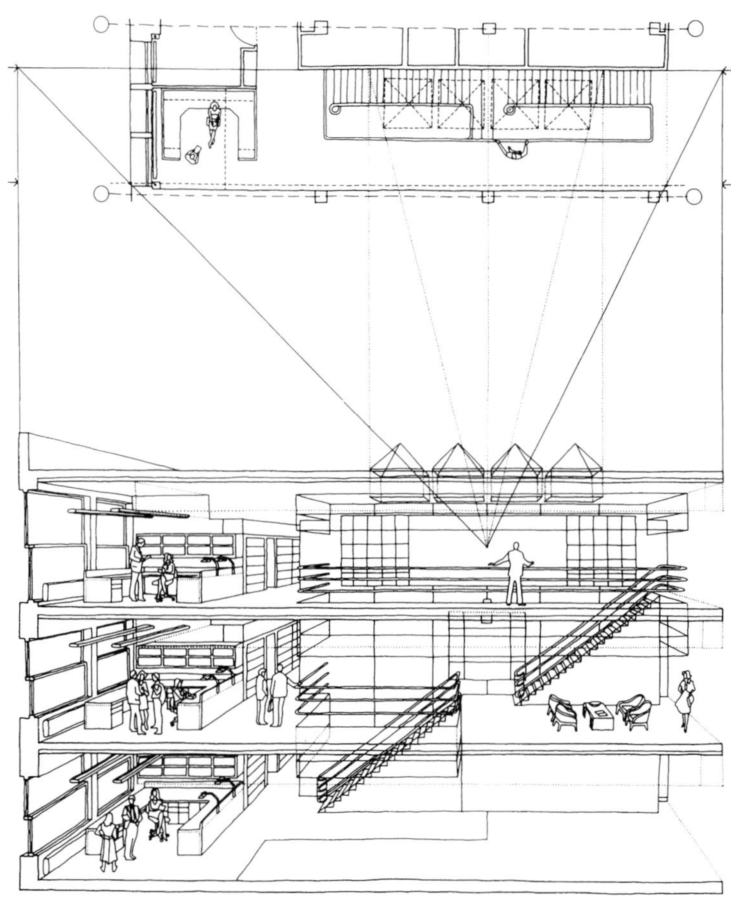

PLAN AND TRANSVERSE SECTION OF STAIRWELL AREA

NRDC's energy use as a demonstration project, providing the non-profit organization with a grant of $100,000 for its energy saving features.

Strategies included more natural light to reduce the artificial lighting and heating loads; windows with low-emissivity Heat Mirror™ film to reduce heat gain; efficient low-wattage fluorescent lamps for ambient lighting, coupled with energy- saving electronic ballasts and occupancy sensors; wall insulation increased to R-ll and roof insulation increased to R-30; and air changes at 6.8 times per hour instead of the standard requirement of half that amount.

#### National Audubon Society Headquarters
*New York, New York*

Completed in 1992, the National Audubon Society Headquarters, located on Broadway in New York City, occupies five and a half floors of a 97,000-square-foot century-old building. One of Audubon's most ambitious features is a recycling system consisting of four chutes that separate high-quality paper, mixed paper, aluminum and plastic, and food. The material is directed to the basement where it is collected for recycling. The unique features of the building include non-toxic materials and furnishings, a high air-exchange rate of six times per hour that mitigates indoor air pollution, and ample natural light with low-wattage fluorescent lighting activated by motion detectors. Increased insulation levels and Heat Mirror™ windows help to reduce the heating and cooling loads, so that a reduced size non-CFC gas-fired system saves the Audubon Society nearly $40,000 per year. The project is reviewed as a case study in Chapter Five.

#### New England Aquarium
*Boston, Massachusetts*

The New England Aquarium's mission has shifted from one of passive presentation to active involvement in aquatic conservation. Their new focus has prompted plans to double the current Aquarium size and address issues relating to regional waters and shores. In their work for the Aquarium, Croxton Collaborative is exploring the use of specific "green" technologies in the areas of systems controls, glazing, water quality, insulation, and low impact materials.

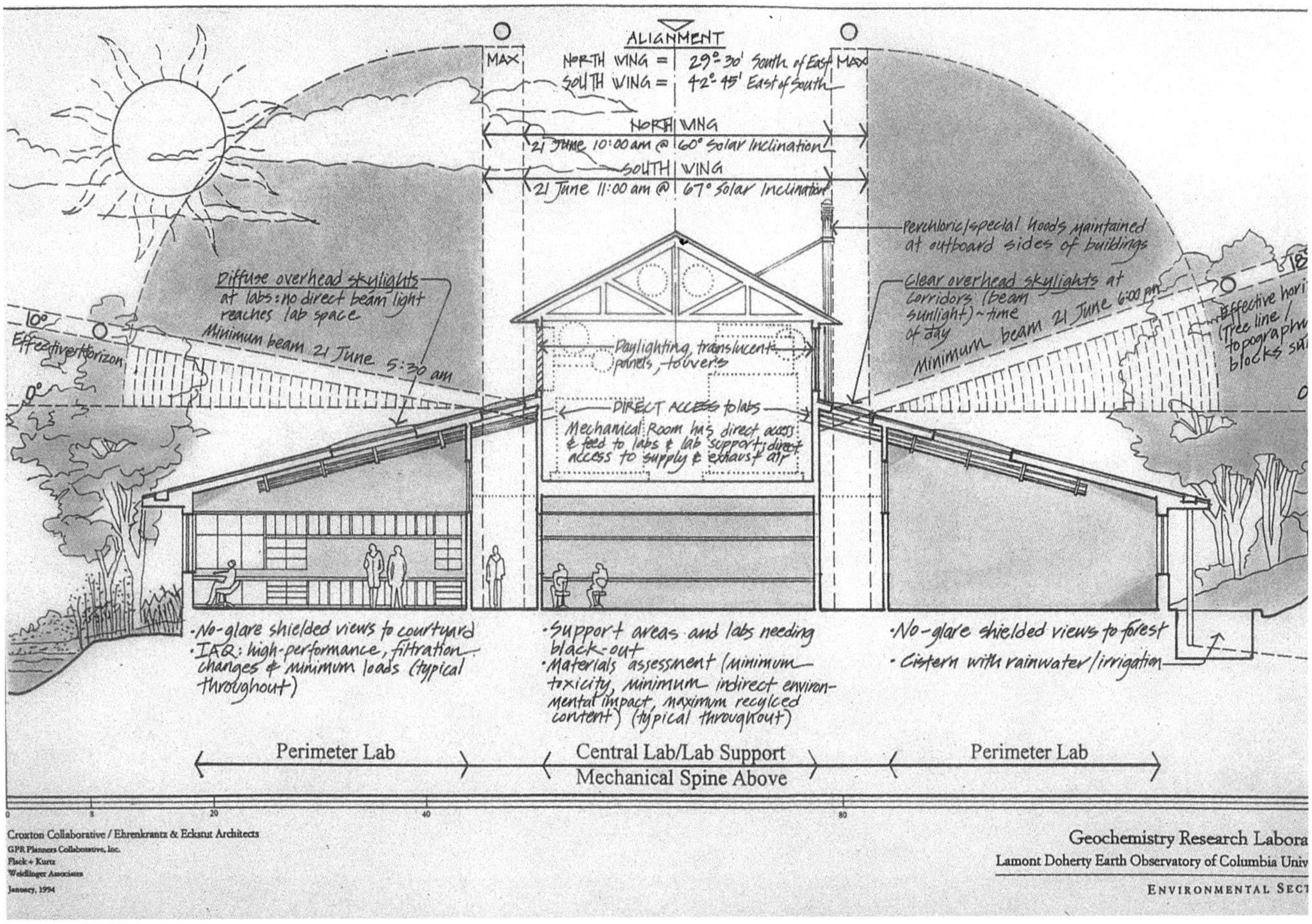

ALIGNMENT
NORTH WING = 29°-30' South of East
SOUTH WING = 42°-45' East of South
MAX MAX
NORTH WING
21 June 10:00 am @ 60° Solar Inclination
SOUTH WING
21 June 11:00 am @ 67° Solar Inclination
Perchloric/special hoods maintained at outboard sides of buildings
Diffuse overhead skylights at labs: no direct beam light reaches lab space
Minimum beam 21 June 5:30 am
10° Effective horizon
0°
Clear overhead skylights at corridors (beam sunlight) ~ time of day
Minimum beam 21 June 6:00 pm
Effective horizon (Tree line / topography blocks sun)
Daylighting, translucent panels, louvers
DIRECT ACCESS to labs
Mechanical Room has direct access & feed to labs & lab support; direct access to supply & exhaust air
•No-glare shielded views to courtyard
•IAQ: high-performance, filtration changes & minimum loads (typical throughout)
•Support areas and labs needing black-out
•Materials assessment (minimum toxicity, minimum indirect environmental impact, maximum recycled content) (typical throughout)
•No-glare shielded views to forest
•Cistern with rainwater/irrigation
Perimeter Lab
Central Lab/Lab Support
Mechanical Spine Above
Perimeter Lab
Croxton Collaborative / Ehrenkrantz & Eckstut Architects
GPR Planners Collaborative, Inc.
Flack + Kurtz
Weidlinger Associates
January, 1994
Geochemistry Research Labora
Lamont Doherty Earth Observatory of Columbia Univ
ENVIRONMENTAL SECT

LAMONT-DOHERTY EARTH OBSERVATORY
*Palisades, New York*

The Geochemistry Research Facility at Lamont-Doherty, Columbia University, is the first U.S. government "Green Demonstration Building." The selection of the Croxton Collaborative/ Ehrenkrantz & Eckstut Architects team represents a recognition of the firms' future-directed knowledge of environmental design and technologies related to land-use and habitat restoration, blended nature-driven/energy-driven systems design, and resource conservation. This project will conserve massive amounts of energy while meeting the demands of a sophisticated, internationally recognized facility.

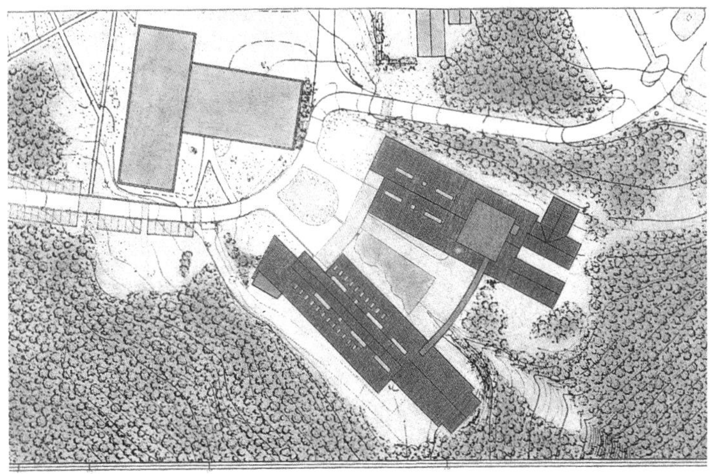

***Lamont-Doherty Earth Observatory, Palisades, New York. The Geochemistry Research Facility at Lamont-Doherty, Columbia University, is the first U.S. government "Green Demonstration Building." Ease of maintenance and deliberate planning for future technology change-out is incorporated into the design, together with low-toxic, environmentally conscious building materials. The facility, which combines a fully-renovated building with a new building, incorporates state-of-the-art laboratories, seminar classrooms, and a 200-seat auditorium. Drawings: Croxton Collaborative, Architects.***

VERIFONE COSTA MESA
*Costa Mesa, California*

VeriFone, an international corporation that manufactures electronic verification equipment, completed their new administrative, manufacturing, and distribution center in 1993 with Croxton Collaborative and associate architect Robert Borders. The renovated 80,000-square-foot facility presented some difficult

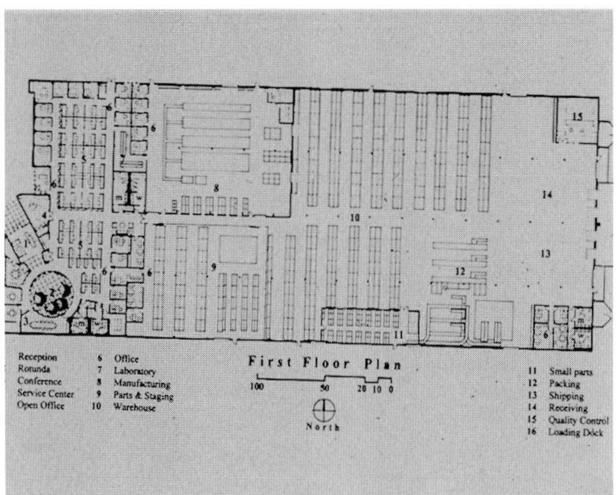


***VeriFone Administrative and Distribution Center, Costa Mesa, California. At VeriFone, the design of a dramatic public rotunda space that is shared by all of the staff incorporates and articulates natural light. This essentially windowless 78,000-square-foot facility, designed in conjunction with Robert Borders & Associates, was tailored to the activities of each space. Various types of skylights and efficient artificial lighting were specified, the air supply is doubly filtered to provide clean indoor air, and materials were selected to mimize maintenance, maximize resource conservation, and reduce toxicity. Studies are underway and a grant from Southern California Edison is anticipated to quantify increased worker productivity in the new facility and compare statistics to an unrenovated comparable facility owned by VeriFone. Photo: Marshall Safron. Drawing: Croxton Collaborative, Architects.***

challenges; it was originally located near a highway, had no windows, and a budget of $38 per square foot.[1]

Maximum use of natural light was a key strategy, as it provides 100% of the lighting in the manufacturing area during most of the day, and marks the time of day in all of the shared public spaces. Of particular concern was the air supply, which is doubly filtered to provide clean indoor air. The HVAC system is free of chlorofluorocarbons.[2]

### Home Box Office Headquarters
*New York, New York*

HBO in New York asked Croxton Collaborative to provide them with an environmental performance record for their offices. Croxton's resulting Environmental Master Plan Report addresses the following range of environmental criteria which have been identified through a process of examination, testing, and energy simulation:

*Indoor air quality, comfort, and related environmentally sensitive operational procedures and monitoring.*

- Energy efficiency potentials developed through tracer gas testing and DOE.2.1 analysis and investigation of existing systems.
- Habitation, operation, maintenance, and renovation protocols for an ongoing environmentally sensitive community.
- Guidelines for environmental characteristics of generic building materials, products, and finishes for future renovations and repairs.

Croxton's report presents a precise model of how the HBO Building performs and, most importantly, provides the tools for an assessment of energy and envi-

**HBO ENERGY BREAKDOWN**
**ELECTRICAL**

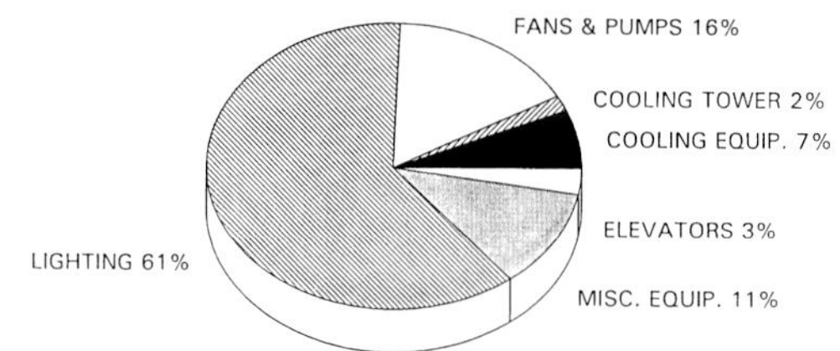

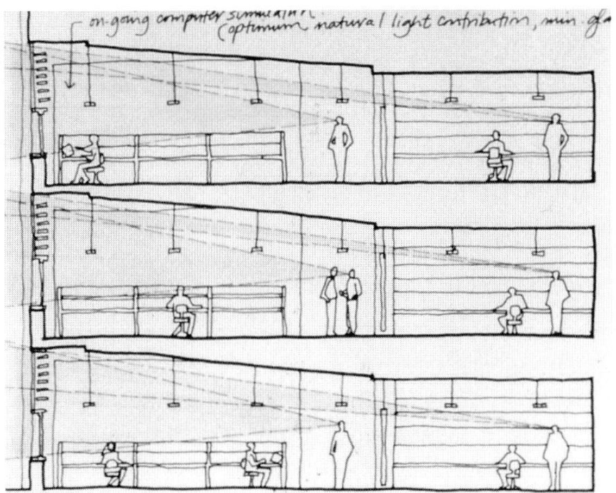

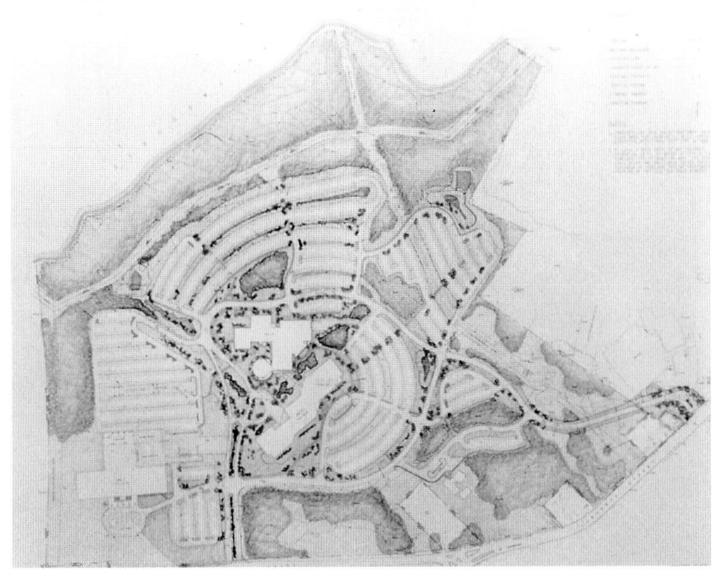

***Unum Life Insurance Company of America, Portland, Maine, site plan and section. New on-grade parking areas and a new internal ring road minimize paving on the site. Wetland impact and deforestation of the site is reduced by the location of swales and roadways, and by reducing existing eroded and heavily graded areas. Vegetated swales handle both stormwater and snow storage, providing a bio-remediation process that enhances water quality and water velocity control. The initial phase of the project calls for a new office building on a site on which two buildings exist, and the second phase completes 100% consolidation of the corporation on one campus. All buildings will be linked by multiple level interior bridges, improving personnel communications and efficiency, and accommodating movement of disabled personnel. A central skylit atrium, containing common conference areas as well as vertical circulation, reinforces staff communication. Drawings: Croxton Collaborative, Architects.***

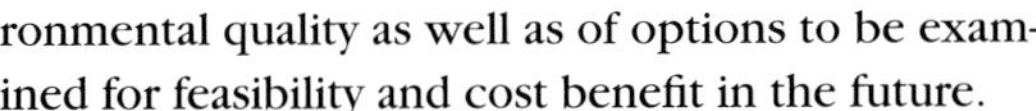

ronmental quality as well as of options to be examined for feasibility and cost benefit in the future.

UNUM LIFE INSURANCE COMPANY OF AMERICA
*Portland, Maine*

This project represents a new threshold in sustainable site and landscape planning. The creation of planned internal links between all buildings on campus along with a low-maintenance, high environmental performance site plan are key features.

## *Outside the Architectural Practice*

Croxton Collaborative is sought by organizations, universities, corporations, and individuals around the world for its ability to integrate technical environmental concerns with contextually sensitive and economically feasible design. Projects produced by the Collaborative like those discussed above represent the cutting edge in environmentally conscious architecture.

Yet both Randolph Croxton and Kirsten Childs are dedicated to addressing environmental concerns far beyond the scope of their architectural projects. Croxton served as International Union of Architects (IUA) and American Institute of Architects (AIA) representative to the United Nations Commission on Environment and Development in New York in 1991, and at the Earth Summit in Rio de Janeiro in 1992, continuing as Chairman of AIA/ACSA Research Council for the AIA. Childs received a degree in design and arts in Edinburgh, Scotland, and came to the United States in 1969 from the London firm of Yorke Rosenberg Mardall. Since acting as pilot space coordinator for the AIA's Greening of the White House project, Childs lectures often to professional groups in the United States and Canada to teach other building and business professionals about environmentally conscious design. Her contributions to the Natural Resources Defense Council helped earn it the first Interiors Magazine Award for Socially Conscious Design.

## *Suggestions for Building Professionals*

Croxton and Childs offer many suggestions for achieving ecologically and socially responsible design. Firstly, look to achieve energy conservation and efficiency, deal with direct and indirect environmental impacts, indoor air quality, and resource conservation. "One of the simplest ways to achieve these goals and create a nearly immediate impact is with lighting," says

Childs. She suggests working with local utility programs that can help assist you.

Croxton believes that it is critical to get an environmental commitment from every member of the project team. "The architects, the client, the mechanical engineers, the structural engineers, the contractors, and everyone else involved need to be able to illustrate their commitment and be involved from the outset of the project for it to be successful." Also, if you're an architect not familiar with environmental criteria, you might consider an environmental consultant who can help to orchestrate the effort. You will benefit from the services of special consultants for landscaping, energy, lighting, and materials. Childs recommends consulting with the AIA's *Environmental Resource Guide,* to which they both contributed information.

## SUSAN MAXMAN

Architect and president of Susan Maxman Architects since 1985, Maxman's approach to design involves a deep respect for the human aspects of a project, the site, and its natural resources. "The construction industry continues to have a major environmental impact," says Maxman, "generating at least 20% of the nation's solid waste, consuming more than 11% of U.S. energy, and producing 30% of the country's greenhouse gases." Once Maxman began to understand the role that architects could play in minimizing energy consumption by designing in a way that promoted stewardship of the environment, she determined that their next challenge would be to design an environmentally sensitive building. Since that time, environmental building concerns have been at the center of all of Maxman's projects. Her clients include individuals and organizations, as well as community, regional, and U.S. federal government.

### *Defining Environmentally Conscious Architecture*

When Maxman thinks of the definition of environmentally conscious architecture, she immediately recalls the Native American adage, "We do not inherit our land from our ancestors, we borrow it from future generations." Maxman believes, "If what we do is governed by this attitude, we as a society will contribute greatly to the well-being of future generations. If what we do is tempered by an understanding of its effect on the balance of life on this planet, we will be able to meet the needs of the present generation without sacrificing the ability of future generations to secure their needs. If informed choices are made with this in mind, professionals will design in a way that conserves rather than consumes, that supports rather than destroys, that mitigates rather than exacerbates the effect of man on the natural environment."

For many years, Maxman has been most interested in indigenous architecture. According to her, indigenous architecture respects climate, site, culture, and region, having evolved out of a necessity that demanded the most efficient and simple solutions for shelter. This type of architecture "did not have the luxury of importing materials from across the globe," explains Maxman. She particularly likes the fact that these structures were ingeniously constructed from limited resources. Montezuma's Castle is Maxman's favorite example of sustainable architecture. "It merges beautifully with the spectacular natural setting in which it is placed. The way in which it is sited allows the winter sun to warm its spaces yet shades it from the hot summer sun." Further, "Adobe wall construction was the appropriate choice for the dry desert climate. There is an elegant simplicity about this structure that says these 'architects' found the appropriate response to their design problem."

### *Background*

Susan Maxman Architects has always practiced what Maxman would call sustainable design. "We'd rather rehabilitate existing structures than build new, and we have the utmost respect for the natural setting when asked to place a foot print in it." Maxman believes that architecture is about people and her first consideration in the design is about how people feel in their buildings. However, once committed to promoting energy efficient buildings that show environmental sensitivity on all levels, she began educating herself and her office in the ways in which they could implement energy conservation in their design practice. They collaborated with Greg Franta and Nancy Clanton, both experienced energy analysts, on the Humane Society project. "We learned a tremendous amount from them," says Maxman, adding that "We are most fortunate in Philadelphia to have the outstanding landscape architecture firm of Andropogon to share their knowledge with us about ecological landscape design, and Don Prowler, who is the current President of the Passive Solar Industry Council, is a frequent collaborator with us on energy efficiency." Susan Maxman Architects attends seminars and does a great deal of reading. "There are many sources for the dissemination of this information," says Maxman. "The *Environmental Resource Guide* published by the AIA was a great help early on."

## *On the State of Ecological Architecture*

Maxman sees positive signs for the continued growth of a more sensitive and appropriate approach to the design of the built environment. "Several years ago when I first began speaking about this issue, few architects had ever heard of sustainability." Later, the Earth Summit in Rio brought international attention to environmental issues. The 1992 AIA National Convention in Chicago was a watershed for sustainable design in that it brought the issue to the forefront of the international architectural community. Tens of thousands of architects from over one hundred countries were represented at this event. They helped to author and signed The Declaration of Interdependence, a document that outlines a commitment to practice architecture that responds to the principles of sustainability. Currently, Maxman sees a trend whereby more and more clients are demanding an environmentally conscious approach to solving their design problems. The National Park Service was the first to require a knowledge of sustainable design for all design professionals pursuing work with their agency. Many other federal agencies have followed suit. "I do believe that these principles will be mainstreamed into the practice of architecture," says Maxman, and "hopefully, in the not too distant future, we can drop the phrase 'sustainable architecture,' as all architectural pursuits will embrace this approach to design."

## *Architectural Projects*

Susan Maxman Architects' most extensive environmentally responsible project to date, the Women's Humane Society in Bensalem, Pennsylvania, represents a giant leap for the firm into the realm of sustainability. The firm received the NESEA award for this project, and it is reviewed in detail as a case study in Chapter Five.

### Women's Humane Society Headquarters
*Bensalem, Pennsylvania*

A 24,500-square-foot facility built on a difficult eleven-acre site, the Women's Humane Society is located just outside of Philadelphia in Bensalem, Pennsylvania. The new animal shelter includes administrative offices, a veterinary clinic, and kennels clustered on buildable areas of the site, freeing the remaining wetlands for the creation of a wildlife refuge.

The Humane Society project incorporated recycled non-toxic materials and wetlands conservation. Energy-efficient HVAC systems and lighting produce a savings of over $40,000 annually. The headquarters is featured as a case study in Chapter Five.

### French Creek State Park and Forest District 17 Office Building
*French Creek State Park, Elverson, Pennsylvania*

Working closely with design team members and energy consultant Don Prowler, SMA utilized a beta version of ENERGY 10 software for energy analaysis

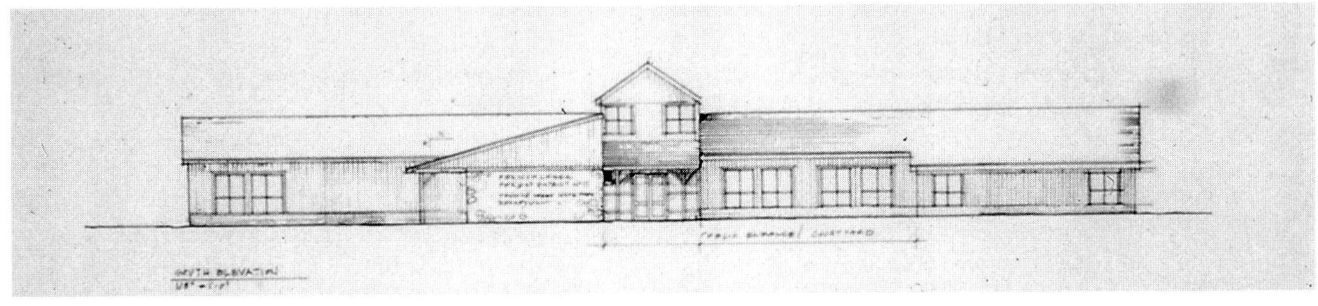

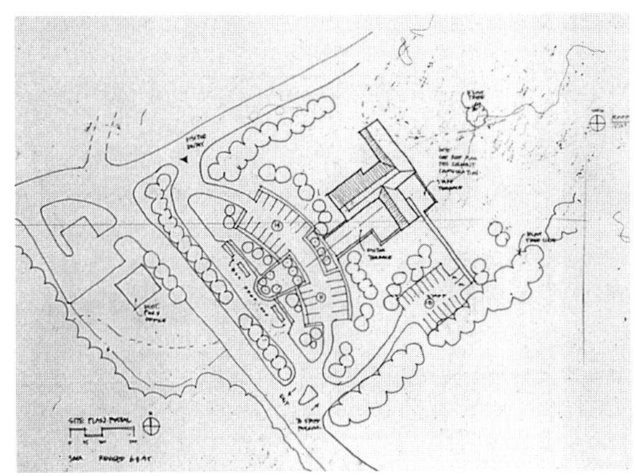

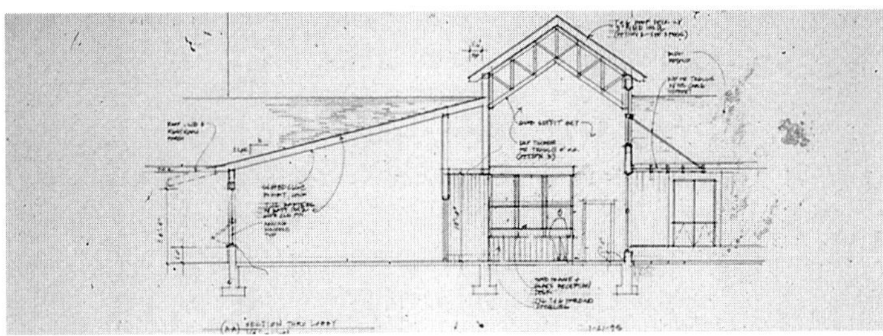

***French Creek State Park and Forest District 17 Office Building, Elverson, Pennsylvania, elevations. The new facility for the Pennsylvania Department of Environmental Resources will be a 9,200-square-foot one-story office building and visitor's center located in the 13,000-acre state park in Berks County. The project is in the design development stage. Drawings: Susan Maxman Architects.***

of the design. The software utilizes an hourly method of calculation but is more user friendly and suited to smaller projects than DOE 2. ENERGY 10 first generates a "shoebox" of typical construction techniques followed by another with optimal energy savings features. "Our goal was to make our project with an actual site and program outperform the idealized energy effficient 'shoebox,'" says Maxman. "We looked at features such as solar orientation, insulation, daylighting, glazing, mechanical and electrical systems, and by integrating energy efficient features we are close to our goal."

By using perimeter and clerestory glazing and optimizing depth of offices, much of the lighting needs for the building will be supplied by natural light. North-facing glazing takes advantage of the diffused northern light from this direction. This light is ideal for offices where fluctuations in lighting levels are not desirable.

A number of options were explored for the mechanical system, including an oil-fired furnace with DX cooling; air-to-air heat pumps, and ground-source heat pumps. Ultimately, the ground-source heat pumps were selected because of their efficiency (SEER 15). This system utilizes a series of wells outside the building through which water for heating and cooling is pumped. The temperature of the earth in the wells is a constant 55°F. The temperature of the water that returns to the building is naturally cooled in the summer or heated in the winter through contact with the well water. The system's other advantage is a utility company (Metropolitan Edison) rebate, which will help to reduce the additional cost to the building owner. SMA has proposed that the design setpoints during occupied hours be reduced from 78% to 80% for cooling and from 75% to 70% for heating. Cooling and heating capacity is diminished on the most extreme days, but by downsizing the equipment it works more efficiently, saving on operating costs and initial equipment cost.

The siding material for the building posed an environmental problem for the design team. The park standards call for wood-lap siding, a product typically made from Cedar or Redwood, both typically harvested from old-growth forests. As an alternative, SMA proposed two solutions: to utilize salvaged siding from existing park structures scheduled to be demolished, or to use fiber cement siding. The cement fiber siding is applied like wood siding but will not burn, decay, or be subject to insect damage. While cement is a relatively energy intensive material, the life of the siding is a minimum of 50 years, and the manufacturer of the product is within 50 miles of the project site. Wood flooring and some furnishings may also be retrieved from the demolished structures and reused.

The roof decking material (Homasote Easy-Ply) is comprised primarily of recycled newsprint and also spans up to four feet, allowing the number of roof joists to be half that of conventional construction. The roof joists themselves are open web members with a wood top and bottom chord and steel web members. The wood members are from small diameter Southern Pine. Upon demolition of the structure, the trusses can be easily disassembled and the steel web members and wood chord salvaged and recycled or reused.

### Seneca Rocks Visitors' Center
*Monongahela National Forest, Elkins, West Virginia*

The reconstruction of Seneca Rocks Visitors' Center represented an opportunity to illustrate the Forest Service's commitment to conservation of the spectacular natural resources that exist in the Monongahela National Forest. The conservation ethic is a story told in every facet of the design of this new facility, from the choice of subject matter for the exhibit to the actual siting and construction of the center. The building is designed in a way that conserves energy, natural resources, and the natural environment in which it is placed.

The former Visitors' Center was located in the flood plain near the confluence of two streams, Seneca Creek and the north fork of the south branch of the Potomac River. Throughout the region, construction in flood plains as well as filling to elevate buildings have reduced the capacity of flood plains to do their work. There is no more vivid case of this than in the Midwest, where the Mississippi and Missouri rivers have regularly flooded many communities. Thus, the design team strongly recommended to the Forest Service that the center not be built in its former location, but relocated to a lobe of higher ground southwest of the old Visitors' Center, above the 100-year-old flood plain.

The Forest Service was quite amenable to the relocation. During a preliminary archeological investigation of the site, it became apparent that 7,000 years ago, Native Americans found this to be the proper location for settlement. The site has been declared a national historic landmark and the building was relocated to the rim of the lobe where an early 20th-century farmstead previously existed. Extensive archeological investigation has taken place revealing some very significant findings. In fact, this is thought to be the most important archeological site in West Virginia and the vicinity. This exciting discovery will become the highlight of the Visitor's Center exhibit.

Care was taken in the location of roads and foot paths so that they cause the least disturbance to existing vegetation and archeological findings. A major

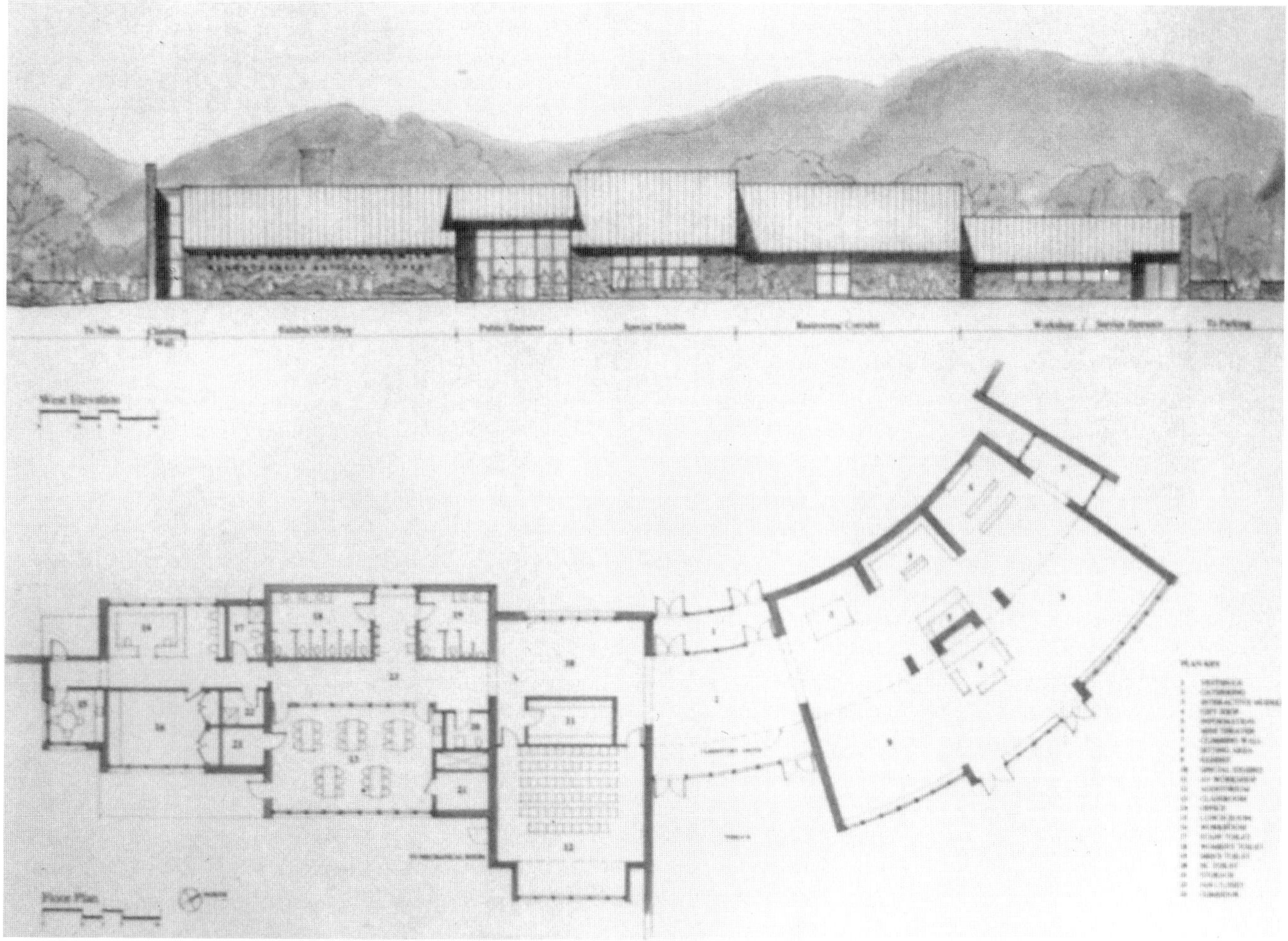

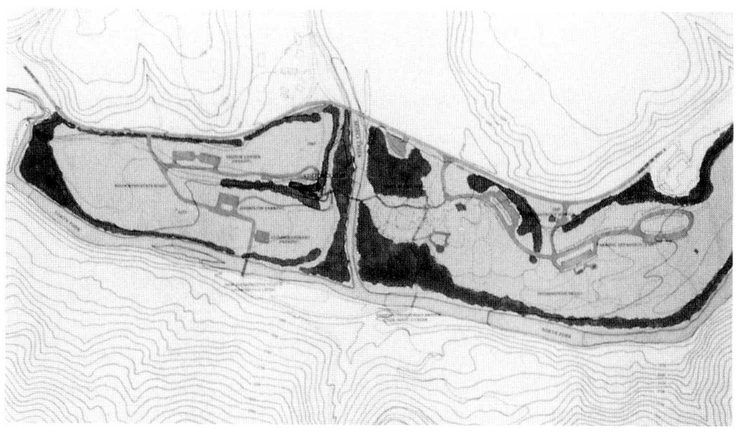

***Seneca Rocks Visitors Center, Monongahela National Forest, Elkins, West Virginia. The Center is designed in such a way that it becomes a part of its site. For the building to become part of the landscape, the choice was made to clad its exterior in river rock found at the site. The interior of the building will be clad in various species of hardwood timbered from the Monongahela Forest. Drawings: Susan Maxman Architects.***

effort will be made to restore the riparian corridor, remove some of the parking lots from the floodplain, and restore native vegetation to extensive areas of existing lawn. An interpretive trail with a pedestrian bridge will link the Visitors' Center to the rest of the site across Seneca Creek.

Visitors will pass through the front doors of the building to be greeted by a spectacular view of Roy Gap. Since visitors come to Seneca Rocks to see the view and not the building, the building's purpose is to provide shelter and enhance the visitors' experience without detracting from the natural setting. Building materials used will be locally available and, as often as possible, manufactured within the region. Local stone and hardwood will be used extensively throughout the structure, making the energy saved in their transport costs significant. Materials with recycled content will be specified whenever possible.

Designed in a way that minimizes to the greatest extent the use of energy, the building will be insulated well beyond code requirements. Glazing will be fine-tuned for each orientation, and whenever possible daylighting strategies will be used to reduce the need for artificial lighting. Occupancy and day-lighting sensors will be specified throughout the facility. The building served as a Beta Test for National Renewable Energy Lab's New Energy 10 program, which models the energy performance of a building during its design.

### *Outside the Architectural Practice*

As President of the American Institute of Architects in 1993, Maxman extended the ecological challenge to the thousands of professionals represented by the organization and created a forum for one of the strongest concerns that the organization's 56,000 members have ever shared. Since the formation of the AIA's Committee on the Environment (COTE Committee), the largest majority of professionals ever to join a single cause within the AIA have joined COTE Committees around the country, creating educational programs and environmentally conscious projects. "The 1993 AIA Conference, in conjunction with the UIA World Congress of Architects, was an opportunity to bring this concern to the forefront and develop a theme on sustainable design," says Maxman. Attended by thousands of architects and other design professionals from around the world, the conference provided numerous seminars, workshops, discussions, and lectures on sustainable building practices and ended with the signing of the Declaration of Interdependence. At the conference, the Interprofessional Council on Environmental Design (ICED), a coalition of architectural, landscape architectural, engineering, and planning organizations representing thousands of professionals committed to sustainable design, unified hundreds of thousands of professionals toward environmental consciousness in their practices.

"The most significant contribution that I have made to sustainable design activities outside of my practice was during my tenure as President of the American Institute of Architects," says Maxman. During her presidency and the year and a half preceding it, she had the opportunity to speak to fellow professionals as well as others about the need to address the issues of sustainable design in the creation of the built environment. When she began, few professionals had heard of sustainable design. Now, most architects are aware that they can make a difference in the quest for a sustainable lifestyle. She has lectured often to her fellow professionals, students, and other groups as diverse as Demand Side Management Conferences, sponsored by utility companies, and the Association of General Contractor's Convention, where she was keynote speaker. Maxman served on the Eco-Efficiency Task Force of the President's Council on Sustainable Development and represented the architectural profession at the Earth Summit, which brought together architects from around the world to develop an agenda for sustainability that was presented at the World Congress of Architects and the 1993 American Institute of Architects convention in Chicago.

### *Suggestions for Professionals*

Maxman will continue to write articles and lecture until sustainable design is universally practiced. She advocates changes in the architectural curriculum at schools of architecture across the country and believes that until an attitude toward sustainable design is integrated into our schools, we cannot successfully become a profession that contributes to the sustenance of life on this planet. As a starting point, "There are many continuing education courses that are offered periodically that help to begin to sensitize design professionals to the issues of sustainability," recommends Maxman. The American Institute of Architects has a Committee on the Environment that provides quite a bit of source material as well as seminars on the subject. By becoming a member of this committee one can access a tremendous amount of information on sustainable design. Also, by subscribing to the *Environmental Resource Guide* one can develop a strong baseline for the practice of sustainability. There are several periodicals that one can subscribe to that provide useful information, such as the newsletter *Environmental Building News.* Local utility companies are often great resources of information on energy efficiency. "Read and listen and begin immediately to practice it no matter how small the gesture," says Maxman, "for anything that is done to promote environmental sensitivity is better than nothing."

### *Closing Remarks*

"I hope that in the very near future there will be no need for the label 'environmentally responsible architecture,' or for the term 'green architecture.' I hope that all design professionals will incorporate in their practices the principles of sustainability, and that nothing less will be acceptable to them and to society as a whole. I believe that the practice of sustainable design is merely a responsible and appropriate approach to the problems that we are asked to solve. Its practice is no great mystery. There is no need for great training or heroic endeavors. All that is required is the will to create the built environment in a way that causes no further harm or degradation to the natural environment."

Jeremy Green 1995

## WILLIAM McDONOUGH

Many of the early and influencial ideas regarding current ecological architecture and design in the United States can be traced back to philosopher, innovator, and architect William McDonough. Internationally recognized for his architectural and related contributions in Ireland, Germany, Poland, France, and the United States, McDonough's ideas and professional accomplishments continue to establish groundbreaking trends in environmentally conscious architecture, business practices, product manufacturing, and public policy. While his architectural projects reflect his approach to ecological and socially responsible practice, they tell only part of his story. It is the concepts behind his architecture that stimulate his private, public, and corporate clients, students, and colleagues, along with thousands of others around the world who view themselves as environmental leaders and closely review the impact of their daily decisions on the natural resources of the Earth.

In January of 1993, McDonough was the subject of a CBS Special Report by journalist Dan Rather. "He seems to have a powerful effect on people," says a friend. Slightly embarrassed by the enthusiastic attention, McDonough is willing to accept it if it stimulates others to think differently about the environment.[3] Herman Miller's Miller SQA Facility in Zeeland, Michigan, completed in 1995, is reviewed in Chapter Five as a case study.

### *Defining Environmentally Conscious Architecture*

William McDonough introduced the concept of "sustainability" provided by the World Commission on Environment and Development to the forefront of the architectural profession with his publication of the revolutionary Hannover Principles. The office of William McDonough Architects was commissioned by the German government in 1992 to develop design principles for the EXPO 2000 World's Fair to be hosted in Hannover, Germany, under the theme, "Humanity, Nature, and Technology." "The first question we asked was, Does the world even need another world's fair?" says McDonough. Explaining further, "Do you know how wasteful past world fairs have been? In the end our decision was to support the exposition but to make its purpose instructive." The purpose of the Hannover Principles was to inform the international design competitions for EXPO 2000 of the guidelines that must be considered by designers, planners, government officials, and all others involved in setting priorities for the built environment. At the World Urban Forum of the Earth Summit in Rio, Hans Monninghoff, the Director of Environment for Hannover, and William McDonough, a U.S. representative for the American Institute of Architects, officially announced the Hannover Principles.

According to the Hannover Principles,

> Germany is the twelfth most populated country in the world with the fourth highest gross national product, the sixth highest rate of greenhouse gas emissions, and the fifty-seventh largest sized country. Most of Germany is in the temperate forest biome and up to 50% of the country's trees are damaged by acid rain. The wooded areas are strictly managed and nothing less than an optimum level of biodiversity is encouraged. Toxic effluents and heavy metals threaten the air and water.

The pressure created by Germany's environmental concerns has fostered some of the most innovative

THE HANNOVER PRINCIPLES

1. **Insist on rights of humanity and nature to co-exist** in a healthy, supportive, diverse and sustainable condition.

2. **Recognize interdependence.** The elements of human design interact with and depend upon the natural world, with broad and diverse implications at every scale. Expand design considerations to recognizing even distant effects.

3. **Respect relationships between spirit and matter.** Consider all aspects of human settlement including community, dwelling, industry and trade in terms of existing and evolving connections between spiritual and material consciousness.

4. **Accept responsibility for the consequences of design** decisions upon human well-being, the viability of natural systems, and their right to co-exist.

5. **Create safe objects of long-term value.** Do not burden future generations with requirements for maintenance or vigilant administration of potential danger due to the careless creation of products, processes, or standards.

6. **Eliminate the concept of waste.** Evaluate and optimize the full life-cycle of products and processes, to approach the state of natural systems, in which there is no waste.

7. **Rely on natural energy flows.** Human designs should, like the living world, derive their creative forces from perpetual solar income. Incorporate this energy efficiently and safely for responsible use.

8. **Understand the limitations of design.** No human creation lasts forever and design does not solve all problems. Those who create and plan should practice humility in the face of nature. Treat nature as a model and mentor, not an inconvenience to be evaded or controlled.

9. **Seek constant improvement by the sharing of knowledge.** Encourage direct and open communication between colleagues, patrons, manufacturers and users to link long term sustainable considerations with ethical responsibility, and re-establish the integral relationship between natural processes and human activity.

The Hannover Principles should be seen as a living document committed to the transformation and growth in the understanding of our interdependence with nature, so that they may adapt as our knowledge of the world evolves.

and conscientious environmental practices on the planet. Environmental regulation, emission controls, product manufacturing, and mandatory recycling affect every aspect of business as well as the daily lives of all German citizens.[4]

The Hannover Principles created by McDonough represent an early model of "sustainable" design. In them, McDonough offers the definition of sustainability provided by the World Commission on Environment and Development as "Meeting the needs of the present without compromising the ability of future generations to meet their own needs." Further, McDonough states, "Designing for sustainability requires awareness of the full short- and long-term consequences of any tranformation of the environment. Sustainable design is the conception and realization of environmentally sensitive and responsible expression as a part of the evolving matrix of nature." The Hannover Principles were assembled in this spirit after extensive consultation with representatives from the design, environmental, and philosophical communities. They remain a universal landmark in the history of sustainable design.

McDonough continues to examine and redefine the aspects of sustainability. During a talk at the Guggenheim, where he told the story of the reinvention of the manufacturing process for a Design Tex fabric collection that bears his name, he referred to Thomas Jefferson's view of natural resources by saying, "Sustainable design simply means to me that no one can desecrate the land they own or occupy to debts greater than those that can be paid during their own lifetime, because if they could, then the world would belong to the dead, and not the living. So the question is, how does the world belong to the living? And it's not just the "natural rights" of human beings that must concern us; it's also the rights of nature itsself."

## *Background*

Born in Tokyo, McDonough says his years in the Far East opened his eyes to the limits of natural resources--food, power, and water supplies. "Growing up principally in Hong Kong before the pipeline from China, during the drought season we had four hours of water every fourth day," he remembers. After living in diverse parts of the world such as Hong Kong, Montreal, and France, his undergraduate studies were completed at Dartmouth College and he received a Master's Degree in architecture from Yale University. While studying at Yale, he designed and built the first solar-heated house in Ireland. "When I came to the U.S., I was taken aback," he recalls. "I realized that we were not people with lives, but consumers with lifestyles." All of McDonough's work is dedicated to reminding us that we are, in fact, people with lives. The following three fundamental trademarks outline McDonough's approach to design:

1. Waste = Food
2. Utilize Current Solar Income
3. Respect Diversity

One of the original founders of the American Institute of Architects Committee on the Environment, the architect and innovator represented the American Institute of Architects at the Preparatory Committee (Prep-Com) hearings in New York and at the Earth Summit in Rio in 1992. McDonough serves as an advisor to the President's Council on Sustainable Development and was the lead designer in the Greening of the White House, a proposal done at the request of President Clinton and Vice-President Gore. McDonough met with former Soviet President Mikhail Gorbachev to discuss using the Hannover Principles as a starting point for cleaning up Eastern Europe, and in April of 1995, mayor Bill Campbell declared Atlanta, Georgia, a Solar City as a result of McDonough's convincing words.

McDonough is also interested in energy protocols in China that involve solar-hydrogen power for zero-emission buildings and transportation and researching photovoltaics. He has worked in association with friend Jaime Lerner, the mayor of Curitiba, Brazil who has been celebrated for his implementation of innovative ecological and social programs. As an honorary board member of "The Natural Step," being introduced into the U.S. from Sweden, he is working with educators, philosophers, economists, chemists, and companies on several environmental education programs creating a pedagogy of natural systems to develop in the United States. "We're really focused on American projects because it's problematic to go oversees and suggest to people what they should do, when we're not even doing it here," says McDonough. "If they're interested in what we've got, let's have the right stuff, because otherwise it's hypocritical."

His lectures in great demand, William McDonough often speaks to groups that include universities, corporations, communities, architects, and city planners. In the end, McDonough does not want to be known as an environmental architect, but as an architect who redefines the making of things in an ecologically intelligent and socially just way, towards producing architecture and objects at their highest level of design.

## *On the State of Ecological Architecture*

McDonough's outlook is a somber one. "I have great fear for the movement because I'm not quite comfortable yet that beyond the general enthusiasm surrounding this issue, we're really in a position to claim any form of victory at any level." He is, however, enthusiastic about some accomplishments that have been made. For example, he is optimistic about his fabric collection, which he considers revolutionary "because it essentially resulted in the creation of a "zero-emissons" process, where the water going out was better than the water going in."This restorative agenda is at the center of McDonough's approach to design. "It's not enough to simply slow down deterioration of natural resources," he emphasizes.

McDonough is concerned that "current so-called sustainable architecture will repeat the pattern of the 1970s where, as Einstein once said, no problem can be solved with the same consciousness that created it." According to McDonough, the solar effort of the 1970s failed because "it wasn't beautiful, ultimately it didn't work, and often didn't even cost out. This is a huge failing of the fundamental criteria of design." Solar architecture also failed in ecologically intelligent criteria, even though it utilized available solar income. The materials used were energy intensive and didn't have an energy balance. Regarding photovoltaic technology, McDonough says he is terrified because "we must be careful not to replace something as persistently toxic as nuclear material with something as heavily toxic as gallium arsenide or cadmium telluride, on assemblies that are so energy intensive, it would take those collectors 12 years or more to pay back the energy required to even make them." Concerned about "green" and "sustainable" being used as marketing tools, he worries about the deep ecological impact of what some call "sustainable" choices, such as recycled plastic countertops. McDonough sees such products as "a soup of petrochemicals, heavy metals, persistent toxins, UV stabilizers, anti-oxidants, catalysts, and dyes which in a fire would create dangerous fumes, and are being used to justify wasteful packaging." McDonough agrees with his friend, Paul Hawken, that buildings and products are either destructive or restorative, and that sustainability is just a neutral concept. "We really need a fundamental change in consciousness. We are looking at the deep, underlying design of all of this, and we're excited about the potential for redesigning design itself."

## *Architectural Projects*

"McDonough is an outstanding architect in the traditional sense of creating beautiful, functional buildings, but his views extend to a much more profound level that includes the relationship and the design arts to deep ecology," says pioneering energy physicist Amory Lovins, co-founder of the Rocky Mountain Institute in Colorado. McDonough + Partners is currently completing a proposal to study the implementation of photovoltaic power for the Atlanta Braves stadium in

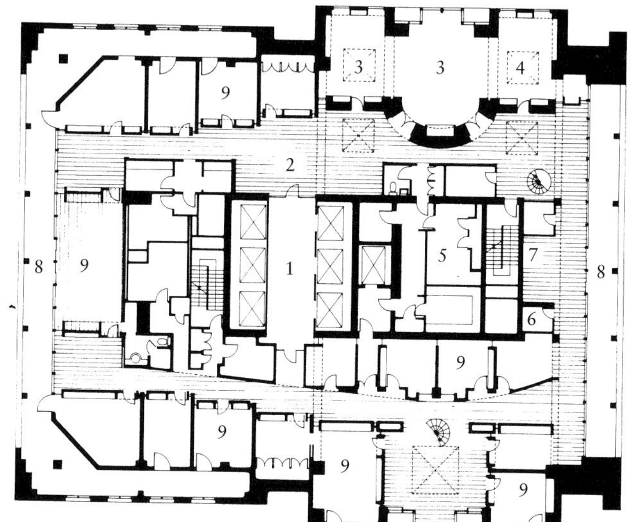


***Heinz Family Offices, Pittsburgh, Pennsylvania. McDonough incorporated lesser known sustainably harvested woods crafted by the Woodworker Alliance for Rainforest Protection. The design of the 12,000-square-foot Heinz family offices was configured as an open-air village and was completed in 1994. Photo: Durston Saylor. Drawing: William McDonough + Partners Architects.***

1. Lobby
2. Reception
3. Conference room
4. Library
5. Mail room
6. Kitchen
7. Staff lounge
8. Roof terrace
9. Office
10. Solarium

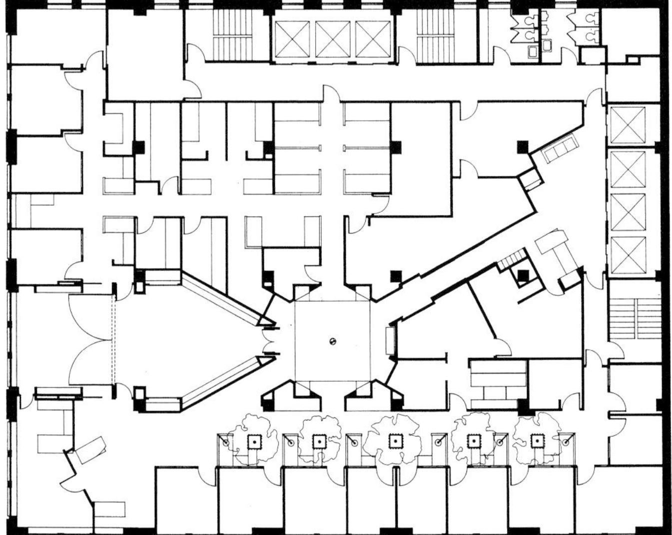

***Environmental Defense Fund Headquarters, New York. This 1985 project brought international attention to American ecological design, introducing strategies of addressing concerns by using non-toxic materials, CFC-free systems, and energy conservation to the commercial office sector. Photo: Peter Margonelli. Drawing: William McDonough + Partners Architects.***

Georgia.[5] "We're studying the spread between three cents per kilowatt hour for gas-fired generators and thirteen cents per kilowatt hour for solar photovoltaic power. We're doing things like inviting all sorts of manufacturers to come and consider creating new kinds of roofing and parking lots that absorb water, and implementing tree-planting urban forestry programs, all of which will create jobs."

In Charlottesville, McDonough is thinking through a hydrogen bus mass transportation program with the same technology that is now being used in Vancouver. "How do we make a building that collects more energy than it requires, and is a net power exporter?" asks McDonough. This is the nature of the commission for the addition to the School of Architecture at the University of Virginia at Charlottesville. "How do we make buildings that purify water, creating better quality water than they receive?" McDonough is working on projects in the United States and abroad in order to answer these questions.

### Environmental Defense Fund
*New York, New York*

The design of the Environmental Defense Fund Headquarters in 1985 brought international attention to William McDonough's progressive architectural design and construction which introduced environmental concerns such as the use of non-toxic materials, CFC-free systems, and energy conservation to the commercial office sector. The project was driven on one side by a socially concerned client and on the other by an architect concerned with respect for human and natural resources. EDF challenged McDonough with the task of protecting the occupants from becoming sick from poor indoor air quality. "We decided that it was our job to find the materials that wouldn't make people sick when placed inside a building," says McDonough. "And what we found out is that those materials weren't there. After working with manufacturers to find out what was in their products, we discovered that the entire system of building construction is essentially in need of reconsideration, even if only in terms of effects on health."

### Frankfurt Child Care Center
*Frankfurt, Germany*

In the design of a day-care center in Frankfurt, Germany, the interaction between teachers, children, and parents with the center is of paramount importance. "During the design process, the engineers wanted to automate the entire building, like a machine," says McDonough. "They asked what would happen if the children forget to close the shades and get too hot? We told them the children would open a

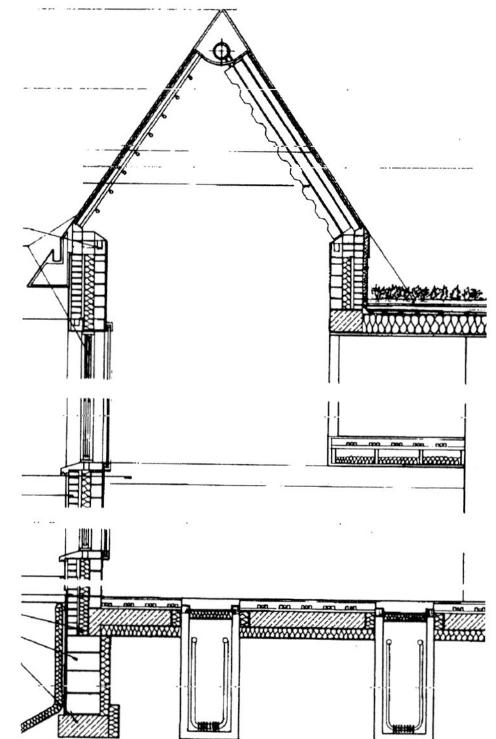

***Frankfurt Child Care Center, Frankfurt am Main, Germany. The design of the Frankfurt Child Care Center evolved from "reflection on how a building could become like a tree." The building relies on daylighting as a primary source of illumination and passive solar heating. The three connected buildings in the complex are linked by a serpentine stone wall that provides thermal mass. Fresh air enters through the air-to-heat exchanger that recaptures 80% of the heat and distributes it through the spine. Each of the twin peaked roofs has aluminum framed superglazed skylights with copper solar collector and moving insulating shutters. Drawings: William McDonough + Partners Architects.***

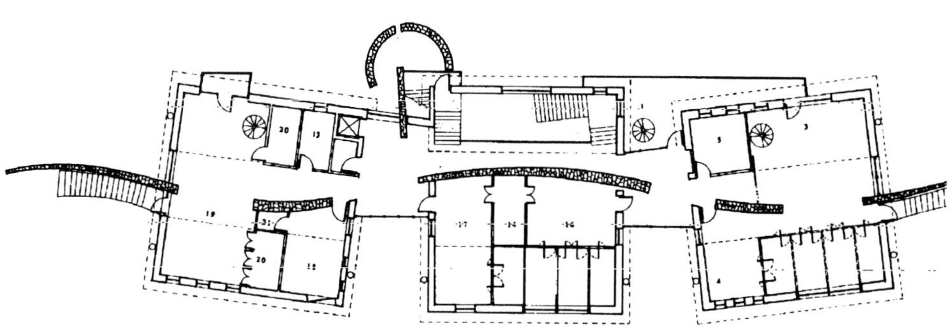

1. Entrance
2. Multi-function room
3. Gathering space
4. Small gathering space
5. Nurses office
6. Sleeping room
7. Kitchen
8. Pantry
9. Toilet
10. Toilet
12. Washroom
13. Custodian
14. Closet
15. Toilet
16. Activity room
17. Parents/ community room
18. Office
19. Multi-purpose room
20. Equipment room
21. Closet

window. The engineers wanted to know what would happen if they didn't open a window? We told them in that case, the children would probably close the shades. Then they wanted to know what would happen if the children didn't close the shades. Finally we told them that the children would open and close windows and shades because children are not dead but alive." Recognizing the importance for children to see what the sun is going to do that day and interact with it, McDonough enlisted the help of the teachers to get the idea across. Now both children and teachers spend ten minutes in the morning and at the end of the day opening and closing the building and all love the idea.

The design incorporated a greenhouse roof with multiple functions: illuminating the space, heating both air and water, cooling, ventilating, and providing shelter from the rain. Since the building contained solar hot water collectors, McDonough asked that a public laundry be added to the program so that parents could wash clothes while waiting for their children at school. Because of advances in glazing technology, the architects were able to create heating and cooling systems that require no fossil fuels. Fifty years from now when fossil fuels are scarce, there will be hot water for the community, a social center, and the building will have paid back the energy "borrowed" for construction.

### Wal-Mart

*Lawrenceville, Kansas*

In 1993, the completion of Wal-Mart chronicled a historic moment in environmentally conscious design in the United States. While the end of the1980s and early

1990s marked a trend in educational and not-for-profit organizations wanting to work in buildings that practiced what they believed in, the growth of economically viable environmentally responsible design began to attract the corporate sector soon after. The design of an environmental store for Wal-Mart in Lawrence, Kansas, in collaboration with its regular store architects, BSW Architects, is one of McDonough's best known projects. The 122,000-square-foot "Eco-Mart" incorporates natural daylighting that reduces utility use by more than 50 percent. Constructed of wood instead of steel, Wal-Mart saved thousands of gallons of oil in constructing the building. The roof design uses sustainably harvested timber from the forests of James Madison and Zachary Taylor in Virginia and a forestry project in Oregon. The air cooling system utilizes non-ozone depleting elements instead of CFC's, reducing its ozone-damaging effects. Were the company to decide to close this store, it is made in such a way that it can be converted to apartments instead of becoming obsolete. Wal-Mart is planning to construct more environmental stores in the future.

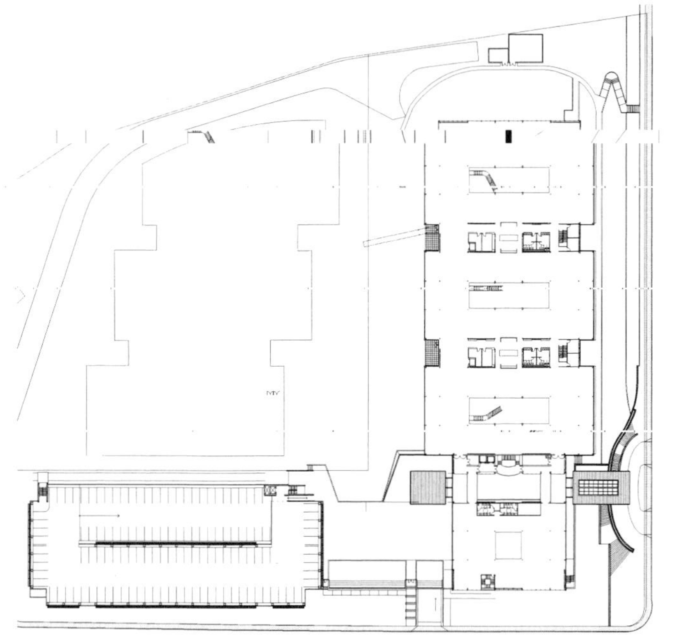

***Corporate Campus, San Bruno, California. The new corporate campus will be ventilated with 100% outside air, daylighting will be used throughout, and the grass-covered roof will collect stormwater. Photo and drawing: William McDonough + Partners Architects.***

McDonough's design for Wal-Mart is not without controversy. Wal-Mart, as a large-scale consumer goods store with huge parking needs, was recently denied permission to build a store in Vermont by one community. McDonough admits that when he was approached by Wal-Mart, he was not sure he could work with them. "I explained my thoughts about consumers with lifestyles," said McDonough "and that we needed to be in a position to discuss the store's impact on small towns. Three days later they called us back to ask if we were willing to discuss the fact that people with lives have the right to buy the finest quality products, even under our own terms, at the best possible price? We said, yes. But we have yet to fulfill our concerns about the bigger questions of products, their distribution, and the full effect of Wal-Mart on communities." McDonough believes that large retailers should be steered toward using their distribution systems to provide not only general products but also locally produced goods without packaging to pedestrian-scaled communities.

### Corporate Campus
*San Bruno, California*

Among McDonough Architects' projects currently in development is a new corporate campus in San Bruno, California. "We're really excited about this project because it's based on humanistic principles," says McDonough. Provisions have been made for the building to be ventilated with 100% outside air at night for flushing, cooling, ventilation, and fresh air delivered to every individual at his or her desk. Daylighting will be used throughout, and the roof–which will be made of grass–will collect stormwater, thereby sparing the town's stormwater system. Because it will use diurnal energy flows, energy consumption will be cut dramatically. At night, the building will cool down because of the way all of the systems have been integrated. Additionally, the corporate campus is designed in such a way that it can be converted into housing should the need arise in the future. "The breakthrough," states McDonough, " is that we've done it all at conventional prices."

EUROSUD CALVISSON
*Nîmes, France*

Eurosud Calvisson was commissioned as the first ecologically "sustainable," high-technology transcultural education center and business environment for multinational companies that want a presence in Europe. The conceptual master plan for this multimedia development center includes approximately 200,000 square meters of office space.

***Eurosud Calvisson Center, Nimes, France. Phase I of the business and educational multimedia center includes a teleport, an international technical university, a hotel, a communications satellite, and software development offices. Photo: William McDonough + Partners Architects.***

## *Outside the Architectural Practice*

William McDonough + Partners relocated from New York to Charlottesville, Virginia following McDonough's appointment as dean of the University of Virginia in September of 1994. As dean, McDonough has watched the faculty and students incorporate ecological and social concerns with the curricula of architecture, architectural history, urban planning, and landscape architecture. Since he also teaches at the University, his influence extends to students in his own classes. He is especially gratified to see a new generation of students excited about environmentally conscious architecture and design.

At the University, McDonough lives with his family in a house designed by Thomas Jefferson, one of the ten pavilions on The Lawn. At a recent lecture at the Guggenheim Museum in New York, McDonough talked about what Jefferson had wanted acknowledged on his gravestone: that he authored the Declaration of Independence, the Statute of Virginia for Religious Freedom, and "fathered" the University of Virginia. "Jefferson honored the significance of the making of things with great respect." Noting that democracy in the United States was designed to provide freedom from a remote tyranny, McDonough believes that "environmental degradation is also a form of remote tyranny of one generation over another. If Jefferson were alive today, he would call for intergenerational Declarations of Interdependence to acknowledge the importance of world interelationships to the environment."

Concerned about urban sprawl, McDonough is working with a number of cities in the United States who want to put his ideas into action. With large scale retailers like Wal-Mart, McDonough is focussing their urbanism and distribution of product-service typologies. McDonough is completing a proposal in Atlanta, Georgia to implement photovoltaic power for the stadium there at the request of the Atlanta Braves. "We're studying the spread between three cents per kilowatt hour for gas-fired generators and thirteen cents per kilowatt hour for solar photovoltaic power. We're doing things like inviting photovoltaic manufacturers to come, creating parking lots that absorb water, new kinds of roofing, and implementing tree planting urban forestry programs, all of which will create jobs. Elsewhere we're discussing with mayors how to develop a hydrogen bus mass transportation program with available technology such as is being used in Vancouver. In Chattanooga, Tennessee 120 city blocks are being considered for zero emissions zoning. McDonough is also working on projects in the United States in Pittsburgh, Pennsylvania, Cape Charles, Virginia, and Oberlin, Ohio.

***Campbell Residence, Traverse City, Michigan. Situated in a vineyard on the north-facing slope of the scenic Old Mission peninsula, the private residence is sheltered within a grove of deciduous trees. Clerestory windows and skylights allow daylight to penetrate the house, and a massive south-facing stone wall acts as a solar furnace. Photo: Yasuo Oda.***

Aside from his architectural projects, McDonough's approach to design touches many other aspects of environmental concerns, particularly product and textile design. For the architect, the challenge of finding appropriate materials and products extends to creating them himself.

### DesignTex Fabric Collection

"Our society measures productivity by how few people are working; measures prosperity by the depletion of natural capital, resource materials, and energy; and puts billions of pounds of highly toxic material into the air, water, and soil every year," according to McDonough and his colleagues. "It is time to stage what we call 'The Next' Industrial Revolution," he says, "one that measures productivity by how many people are working, releases no highly toxic material into the air, and requires no regulation or vigilance because there is nothing there to destroy anyone or any living system."

Chronicling his role in this revolution is his redesign of the textile manufacturing process for the company DesignTex, which enabled them to produce a high-quality, environmentally conscious fabric. The McDonough Collection is a continuation of DesignTex's collection of fabrics designed by world-class architects since 1991. Several years ago the textile company decided, as did many others, to create an environmental product line. Their product, however, stands out in that they were willing to reinvent the entire manufacturing process. "DesignTex was regularly being asked about the environmental specifications of their products," says Director Susan Lyons. "There was a lot of confusion about the 'right' environmental approach. Aware of the complexity of the project, it wasn't until Bill came on board that we began to understand how much we needed to learn." McDonough explains that the frequent approach to recycling is actually what he and his colleague, chemist Michael Braungart, call "downcycling." Over 90% of packaging and products end up in a landfill or incinerator within two months of their distribution. "We should recycle, but it's not the first thing we should do. Redesign first, then reduce, reuse, and finally, recycle."

McDonough coined the phrase "cradle-to-cradle" to describe his design criteria. He explains the following "Environmentally Intelligent Design™ Protocol" based on pioneering Intelligent Products System for product chemistry developed by Dr. Michael Braungart. According to McDonough,

> There are three kinds of products: consumables, service products, and unsaleable products. If a product wears out and cannot be reused in industry, it should become healthy soil. It should be designed as an 'organic nutrient' and return to an 'organic ecology.' This is the new definition of a consumable. If it does not biodegrade, it should be designed as a service product and should remain in a closed loop industrial system. The producer or industry should effectively lease it, take it back, and direct it into manufacturing cycles. It should be seen as a technical nutrient and remain within an 'industrial ecology.' If a product is ultimately unable to be safely returned to either organic or technical cycles, it is effectively unsaleable and should not be made. "Why would anyone want to make something no one should buy?" McDonough asks.

According to the Environmentally Intelligent Design™ Protocols, the fabric is safe for humans and can become safe food for other organisms when it is consumed. The design team succeeded in creating a fabric that could be produced on a commercial scale, conform to applicable industry standards, and be priced competitively.

In developing McDonough's line at DesignTex, it was decided to start with a fabric that was an organic nutrient. That way, the fabric would be compostable and could operate within a closed loop organic life-cycle. Ramie, a plant similar to linen, was found to be an excellent alternative to polyester. When combined with wool, the resulting fabric transports moisture away from the skin, allowing one to remain comfortable when seated for long periods of time. The patented process is registered under the trade name CLIMATEX® LIFECYCLE™. Future plans include the design of a "technical nutrient" fabric to be recycled in industrial processes.

Having completed the first step of the redesign process, the next step required that McDonough and Lyons address the chemistry of fabric dye. "We knew that the dyes would have to be altered to ensure that it meet our concerns and expected a difficult time from the chemical companies, who guard their patented formulas closely," says McDonough. McDonough wanted a product free of mutagens, carcinogens, bioaccumulative substances, persistent toxins, heavy metals, and endocrine disrupters, so he turned to colleague Michael Braungart and his Environmental Protection Encouragement Agency, an independent environmental research institute in Germany. "We wrote letters to over 60 chemical companies and only one, Ciba-Geigy, was willing to work with us," says McDonough. With the cooperation of Ciba-Geigy, Braungart was able to select environmentally sound dyestuffs and finishes. Over 8,000 chemicals were reviewed and of them, 38 were identified as appropriate for the fabric. The resulting colors are deep and rich. McDonough explains that they are still working on true black which typically requires heavy metals.

For the manufacturing of the fabric, McDonough and Lyons worked with Rohner Company, a small Swiss fabric mill. Under the guidance of EPEA, the mill adjusted its manufacturing process to conform to the established protocols. After many hurdles, some progressive solutions, and careful effluent testing, the results proved outstanding and the process, CLIMATEX® LIFECYLE™ was patented. The William McDonough Collection became available in 1995.[6]

"We worked with some of the biggest companies in the world on this product, and some small ones. Conservative companies and innovative companies both understood what we were doing and they're now part of the team." Before, to be successful in the marketplace a product needed to meet three criteria: technical performance–it performs well and satisfies the purpose for which it is intended; cost–it is sold at the right price; and aesthetic value–people will find it appealing. McDonough describes two new criteria that consumers are demanding: ecological intelligence–it is safe and non-toxic; and ecological justice–it is socially just.

### *Suggestions for Professionals*

"At this point in history, architecture cannot be beautiful unless it is conceived within ecological and social parameters. If you intend to do quality work, you must attend to these questions," says McDonough emphatically.

During what has been called a "Centennial Sermon" that McDonough gave at St. John the Divine in 1993 entitled Design, Ecology, and the Making of Things, he expressed his views of the designer's role in society: "Designers are recognizing their position as leaders in society. If we understand that design leads to the manifestation of human intention, and if what we make with our hands is to be sacred and honor the earth that gives us life, then the things we make must not only rise from the ground but return to it, soil to soil, water to water, so everything that is received from the earth can be freely given back without causing harm to any living system," says McDonough, "This is ecology. This is good design."[7]

### *Closing Remarks*

"We are deeply involved in the planning, the buildings, the products, even the chemistry–in cities and regions around the world. But we have to remember that this is not where the answers about what matters will come from. They will come from a place in the human spirit. So the question is, How does humanity find its rightful place in the natural world? We must employ both new knowledge and ancient wisdom in our efforts to conceive and realize the physical transformation, care, and maintenance of the Earth. Almost every phase of the design, manufacturing, and construction processes requires reconsideration."

## JOHN PICARD

Originally a successful Hollywood construction manager, John Picard is considered by his friends and colleagues a visionary, pioneer, motivator, and futurist. He, on the other hand, sees himself as an ordinary guy who wants to leave his mark on the world. As a professional building consultant, his approach is direct and his opinions about environmental concerns cut straight to the bottom line. With enthusiastic optimism, Picard is full of ideas about how companies looking to build ecologically conscious buildings can implement features like non-toxic materials, solar energy and daylighting, energy efficiency, and sustainable materials. He also describes himself as an environmental *non-building* consultant whose goal is often to implement ideas without creating unnecessary buildings or waste.

### *Defining Environmentally Conscious Architecture*

Picard's view about defining environmentally responsible design is less about labels and more about appropriate scale and timing. "I think we need to understand where we are in time and what we have available." He sees green building as a life cycle, from the creation of the natural resources used in construction to what that structure will be in the long-term future. The toxic concerns of a six-month fetus and the biodiversity of a displaced species in the rainforest are just some of the gauges by which Picard evaluates his projects. "Laying lightly on the land in any way you can" is how Picard defines environmentally conscious architecture. Green building is "not just recycled building materials, not just energy efficiency, but breaking out and going beyond the limits using every available tool."

### *Background*

In his career as a successful builder, Picard renovated some elaborate estates in Hollywood including the legendary Pickfair, originally the home of actress Mary Pickford. Though business was brisk, Picard didn't feel that he was making a valuable contribution to society or to himself. One day, while watching television, he saw a one-minute public service announcement that talked about what was happening to the rain forests and how many species would be extinct by the time the commercial ended. "I suddenly realized that although my life was only two frames in a continuing film of the world, I could make a difference in how the rest of the film ran," he says.

He began by designing his environmental dream house in a quiet West Los Angeles neighborhood. To design and build the house, Picard devoted all his time and thought to the project. The house also required that he invest his own money, since it was so unconventional that no bank would give him a loan. "Those same banks are now paying me for ideas about how to design environmentally conscious branch offices and headquarters," Picard chuckles. Picard's house is constructed of recycled steel–"the cars we drove in the sixties"–and its roof is made of recycled petroleum waste. It is nearly 100 percent solar powered and incorporates energy- and water-efficient systems, air and water purification systems, non-toxic paints and finishes, and a computer that controls appliances, heating, and air conditioning for maximum efficiency, comfort, and security. Visitors from around the country–from school children and neighbors to architectural and building professionals–have come to see Picard's house. According to *Interiors & Sources* magazine, "Picard has become one of the most sought- after environmental building consultants in the country." He founded his firm, $E^2$ in Marina del Rey, California, shortly after moving into his new home in 1990.

***Picard Residence, West Los Angeles, California. The solar-powered recycled steel structure incorporates air and water purification systems. Natural light, which bathes the livingroom during most of the day, helps to reduce energy consumption for lighting. Photos: $E^2$.***

## *On the State of Ecological Architecture*

"Everything we're doing relative to the population and global development has largely been anecdotal and very disappointing," laments Picard. As great as all the effort has been, when the percentage of projects completed is compared to the percentage that need to get underway, we are left with an immense gap. He claims that the only way we can bridge that gap is through the help of tools like the Internet, digital mechanisms, software that replicates structure, or software that replaces hardware entirely. "We're moving toward an information-based society and new architecture will be more selective. The future of interior design and architecture will be less in the real world and more in the virtual world," explains Picard. That is to say that "buildings will be constructed out of bytes instead of bricks, and software versions of buildings will be accessible 24 hours a day on the net, resulting in a reduction of the physical demands forced upon the planet."

Does this mean that we are destined to become virtual people? Picard doesn't think so. "On the contrary, we will have more time to be real people concentrating on a meaningful life." This does not mean, however, that Picard is against new construction, provided an unquestionable need is demonstrated. The savings realized from building environmentally, building less, and building in the virtual world, he envisions, can provide money for meaningful new architecture like museums and cultural centers.

## *Architectural Projects*

With a list of completed structures that includes commercial and residential buildings for Hollywood producers, celebrities, and owners of top Fortune 500 companies in the United States, Picard's projects are full of unconventional architectural ideas, innovative energy- and cost-saving features and mechanical systems, and glamour. $E^2$'s work chronicles the high profile of environmental consciousness in the United States that is beginning to create affordable, innovative, ecological architecture, collaborating with companies like Microsoft, Southern California Gas Company, and Intel.[8] In addition, Picard's firm created the

*Left: Sony Pictures Thalberg Office Annex, Los Angeles. Through the use of natural lighting, occupancy sensors, efficient lighting systems, and a reflective roof coating, energy use was reduced by 50% at the Sony office annex.*

*Right: Sony Child Development Center, Los Angeles. E² acted as environmental consultant, working with architect Steven Erlich to complete the Center. Sony Pictures Child Development Center exceeds environmental standards. Cross ventilation provides passive cooling for the building, requiring mechanical air conditioning only on very smoggy days. Building materials include all non-toxic paints and glues, natural cork linoleum, and recycled wood-chip exposed roof sheathing. Photos: Sony Pictures Entertainment.*

*Environmental Products Guidebook,* which is currently available on 3.5-inch disks, and will be available on the Internet in the future. Picard's work on the Southern California Gas Company Energy Resource Center in Los Angeles is reviewed in detail in Chapter Five. Current projects on the boards include Williams Sonoma, the Pottery Barn, and Banana Republic and Old Navy stores owned by The Gap.

PICARD HOUSE
*West Los Angeles, California*

Completed in 1991 and located on a quiet suburban street lined with pastel stucco homes and tall palm trees, Picard's house is constructed out of recycled steel instead of wood, and the roof material is made out of recycled petroleum waste. The house is almost 100% solar powered and incorporates energy and water efficient products and systems, air and water purification systems, non-toxic paints and finishes, and a computer that controls lighting and appliances, heating and air conditioning, opening and closing of the draperies to maintain interior temperatures, and home security.

SONY PICTURES ENTERTAINMENT
*Los Angeles, California*

Picard's consulting firm, E², was brought in to act as environmental consultant for all aspects of Sony's business after Entertainment Chairman, Peter Guber, saw Picard's house. As a result, Sony has revamped much of the way they do business, in addition to the way they approach construction. For example, photocopying is double-sided, e-mail is encouraged instead of paper, and disposable paper cups are not used.

After Columbia Pictures was purchased by Sony, extensive remodeling was needed at the seventy-acre lot. "Environmental concerns were a priority," says Picard, "and it was a great opportunity to implement energy efficiency and recycled materials for the hundreds of millions of dollars in reconstruction work that was needed. Recycled and non-toxic materials were integrated, and all the energy efficiency profiles went into place."

Acting as environmental consultant, Picard worked with architect Steven Erlich to complete the Sony Child Care Development Center. While child care facilities are among the most tightly regulated building types in the state of California, the scheme for Sony Pictures' Child Development Center is anything but institutional. Crowned with an undulating metal roof, the 9,000-square-foot center exceeds current environmental standards and features spaces with diverse materials, textures, and spatial qualities.

The Center emphasizes natural light, connections between indoors and outdoors, natural ventilation,

***Prince Street Technologies, Cartersville, Georgia. A broadloom manufacturing division of Interface Carpet, Prince Street Technologies opened its 210,000-square-foot production facility in 1995. An 80-foot window facing south with a series of translucent louvres provides natural daylight into the plant. Photos: Brian Gassel/ TVS & Associates.***

and a variety of tactile surfaces. The building is cooled by cross ventilation 95% of the time, requiring back up air conditioning only on high smog level days. A variety of sustainable building materials were used throughout the building, including recycled woodchip exposed roof sheathing, natural cork linoleum, all non-toxic paints and adhesives, and American Douglas fir for windows, doors, and sashes.

E² also worked on Sony's Thalberg Annex office building, reducing energy consumption by approximately fifty percent. On average, Sony has reduced energy use by thirty-five percent in its new buildings. Some of the energy efficient features of the building include natural lighting, occupancy sensors, high efficiency lighting systems, reflective roof coating, window glass, insulation, and building automation systems.

PRINCE STREET TECHNOLOGIES
*Cartersville, Georgia*

Through his work as an environmental consultant for the Energy Resource Center, Picard worked with Interface Carpet to develop product lease ideas which the company has further developed. A broadloom manufacturing division of Interface Americas, Inc., Prince Street Technologies moved to their new 210,000-square-foot energy-efficient, ecologically conscious production facility in 1995. Heralded as the first "green" manufacturing facility in the floorcoverings industry, its features include natural daylight throughout the facility. An eighty-foot window facing south allows daylight to stream into the plant, and shading is controlled by a series of translucent louvers. Instead of utilizing underground piping, the site drainage was designed to direct water across the surface, which allows water to filter through the landscape and aerate before it reaches the natural waterways. Exterior finishes of the building are light in color to reflect sunlight, reducing the overall heating load on the building.

In the manufacturing area, increased air changes per hour provide a healthier and more comfortable working environment. Rooftop air conditioning units use R407 refrigerant, manufactured by Carrier, that contain no ozone-damaging chemicals. Programmable thermostats are utilized for each heating and cooling zone to manage and reduce the overall energy consumption of the mechanical system. Interface's patented antimicrobial, Intersept®, is used on the mechanical equipment air filters, duct liners, condensate pans, fan blades, cooling coils, interior exposed surfaces, and insulation. Paints, ceiling tiles, and fabrics are also specified with Intersept®.

Playa Vista Community
*Playa Vista, California*

Picard was asked to oversee the environmental and digital aspects of Playa Vista, a new sustainable community where Spielberg's Dreamworks Facility is also in the early planning phases. He is charged with the task of bringing in the best architects, engineers, and corporate partners to create a team that is a technology and community alliance. "We are looking at things like creating a private power plant with wholesale and retail power distribution, and expanding and incorporating the evergreen lease idea for energy provision." Picard has been talking with Bank of America, for example, to change the way they handle mortgages. He proposes that they extend them so that the extra money made available can turn a residence or commercial space into a high-performance structure. An environmentally advanced building would quickly pay for the difference, and might even compensate the mortgage more greatly than the standard type of mortgage would have with a standard building.

Playa Vista, a community designed by Andres Duany, in development by Maguire Thomas Partners, is located between Marina Del Rey and Los Angeles International Airport. It consists of 1087 acres of land to be used in the creation of a mini-city of 3,200 housing units and 1.25 million square feet of offices and shops. A large portion of this area is the planned site for DreamWorks, the first new studio to come to Los Angeles in fifty years.

A primary focus of Maguire Thomas is to build a modern, technically advanced community that possesses energy efficient structures and alternative attributes. A commitment to "green" building has been made for all residential and commercial spaces, as well as studio and sound stages. City approval has been given for the project. The community of Playa Vista will be connected by its own computer network that will allow for electronic banking, retail shopping, and service, and physically linked by its own form of transportation including alternative fueled vehicles. The studio will take three years to complete, and the community is projected to be implemented over ten years.

Energy Resource Center
*Los Angeles, California*

The Energy Resource Center includes an 8,000-square-foot exhibit hall capable of accomodating up to 700 people with a dozen specialty rooms that are available for meetings, workshops, demonstrations, and presentations. The Center provides technical assistance, computerized equipment simulations, state-of-the-art audio-visual and teleconferencing facilities, and air quality and environmental permitting assistance. As a state-of-the-art technical center, the Energy Resource Center is also a visual showplace for resource conservation from its recycled building and site and all of its "new" recycled materials, to its educational facilities that demonstrate energy efficient strategies with the most current technologies.

Southern California Gas Company built the Energy Resource Center by working with their existing site. Sections of the existing building were dismantled, and other areas of the building are newly fabricated. The design of the center is entirely dedicated to providing educational information regarding energy efficiency and its environmental impact. John Picard acted as environmental consultant for Southern California Gas Resource Center, together with a team of accomplished professionals. The Energy Resource Center is reviewed as a case study in Chapter Five.

## *Outside the Architectural Practice*

In addition to his building projects, Picard is an enthusiastic speaker who is commited to teaching others about building an environmentally conscious future. He has formed partnerships with many of his clients to create some innovative and broad-reaching programs that will have state and nationwide impact. In addition to its role as environmental consultant, his company worked to help the Southern California Gas Company in Los Angeles collaborate with the carpet manufacturer Interface in Atlanta, Georgia. Having created the "evergreen lease," Interface installs and maintains the carpet, while the gas company pays for the benefits of using it. Picard is also working to develop the concept of the evergreen lease to include energy use.

A big believer in the power of modern technology, Picard is developing new ways of disseminating environmental information through software, virtual reality, and the Internet, and is working to create smart, high-performance buildings with software that will address the impacts of demand-side billing and the sun.

## *Suggestions for Professionals*

Picard enthusiastically offers lots of suggestions. "There are some big hurdles in practicing environmentally and energy-conscious architecture in that implementing untested systems and products can be risky, and building professionals have enough liability concerns and problems to deal with just within the bounds of standard practices. But, look at publications like this book, case studies, read available materials, and go see some of the buildings. For example, not enough people look at Croxton and McDonough's buildings," says Picard. "Pay attention to what these projects have done, get in and talk to those who built them. Many of them are very open and eager to share their experience."

Picard feels that designers need to focus on what they will leave behind. "The minute you grasp that," he says, "you realize it's for your sons and daughters and their sons and daughters. Realize the sense of gratification that comes out of doing work the best way you possibly can. Focus on affecting people at the top, because they're waiting for and need new ideas. Use the Internet, and other things like it. Opportunities are coming forward to publish ideas in a free way, unedited and unscrutinized."

When Picard looks back at his projects he feels one hundred percent proud, and his buildings stand out in terms of economic viability, minimal environmental impact, energy efficiency, and aesthetics. He readily admits that he's made mistakes with his buildings, and will probably make more. Picard thinks that if we're not failing, we're not doing enough. "People don't like to talk about failures, but we should because we learn a lot from them. We need radical new infusions of concept as well as reality."

### *Closing Remarks*

Picard thinks that, above everything, energy is paramount. There are huge institutional barriers toward energy efficiency, and Picard spends most of his time on projects dealing with them. "I think that the underpinning strength in me is that I've been blessed with the relationships that I have. For some reason, I constantly have this sense of hope. Hope to me is key. A lot of people are unhappy and fearful, personally and globally. If people pull together and help the next person, we'll eventually get from two percent of the population to five billion people who actively care about their environment."

## JAMES WINES

Internationally recognized for his philosophical and artistic approach to architecture and ecology, James Wines established his practice, SITE—Sculpture in the Environment—Architects, in 1970 in New York City. Never formally trained in architecture, Wines' background in art history provides the basis for his approach. While working in Europe as a sculptor completing large commissions for architectural contexts, he grew increasingly uneasy with his role as a creator of *accessories* for buildings. A sculptor of buildings, Wines believes that architecture is the ultimate public art. It should ask questions, and reflect the soul of its society. In "Architecture in the Age of Ecology," a February 1994 article Wines wrote for *Earthword* environmental journal, he calls for a "new spirit" in architecture:

> Architecture is desperately in need of a conceptual, theoretical, and philosophical reunion with nature. During the crest of the Modern Age, architects passionately believed that there was a direct equation with the combustion engine and a spiritual vision for the design of shelter. What began as a great socialist and technological vision has become the symbol of oppression and isolation from nature.

Wines has designed numerous projects around the world that focus on human and natural resources. Recognized for the gutsy BEST showrooms that pointed mockingly at American hedonism in the 1980s, SITE's ecological theme projects for cities around the world include a vast array of projects, among them the pavilions at the World Exposition in Seville, Spain, in 1992 including the World Ecology Pavillion; a 62-meter circular plaza at the first Japan Expo in Toyama, Japan; a commemorative bridge in Hiroshima celebrating the links between people and the natural environment; a waterfront park dedicated to world ecology in Windsor, Vancouver, British Columbia; and a 220-meter-long integration of public space and participatory public art in Vancouver, Canada. In the United States, Wines worked with the city of Chatanooga, Tennessee, to create Ross's Landing, a community plaza, and the Aquatorium, a museum designed to demonstrate the value of water in the development of civilization and to underscore the city's commitment to becoming an environmental city. SITE also designed Pershing Square Park for the oldest downtown community center in the city of Los Angeles, California, in 1986.

### *Defining Environmentally Conscious Architecture*

James Wines believes that the most instructive examples of sustainability are those remarkable historic buildings and cities around the world that have survived for more than five hundred years and still remain in productive use. "There is no better demonstration than a structure from the 13th century that is comfortably filled with computers and space-age technology," says Wines. "This would seem to be the bottom line for evaluating sustainable design and also the primary source of research if we expect to find an equivalent longevity for human habitat in the future." The environmental sculptor thinks that the industrial and technological influences that have shaped 20th-century architecture and its mindless waste of resources are predicated on the notion that the Earth is an obstacle to be "conquered," a folly that lies at the foundation of most western religions which place man at the center of the universe and absurdly negate the importance of the natural world. "All of the technology developed to reinforce this belief is based on the illusion of endless fossil fuel and an indestructible Earth," says Wines, "but scientists have pointed out that the Earth's surface and atmosphere have been more radically changed for the worse in the past ninety years than by any other destructive force in the past 60 million years." According to Wines, there must be a radical change of priorities and philosophies in architecture and a return to the Earth as a major source of inspiration.

His belief is that sustainable historic societies, with their small buildings, insulated walls, low embodied energy materials, recycled elements, solar orientation, and minimal environmental impact, were primarily the product of limited technology. "I am convinced that the Egyptians would have rerouted the Nile if they had had access to dynamite and motorized cranes." Nevertheless, he doesn't think that "New York City should suddenly abandon advanced technology, return to mud huts, and build Stonehenge-like monuments in Central Park to worship the Sun God, but a kind of radical change is implied if we are really serious about avoiding an environmental Armeggedon." Wines embraces all of the intelligent steps being taken by environmental action groups and green technology innovators, but is convinced that these efforts will be insufficient without a consensus that supplies the spiritual and aesthetic incentive for change.

### *Background*

In 1974, SITE was working on a book titled *On Energy* which deals with the topic of fading energy supplies and how the disciplines of art and architecture might deal with the functional, social, economic, and aesthetic results of this crisis in the future. It was during this time that Wines became seriously aware of environmental issues. After 1979, when SITE completed Best Products Company's Forest Building, a commercial structure surrounded by trees and vegetation both inside and out, he became increasingly involved in saving landscape, fusing buildings with their context, and looking at architecture as an "environmental sponge" that would absorb and communicate information from its surroundings.[9]

Wines has been awarded fellowships in visual art by the Pulitzer Foundation, Guggenheim Foundation, and the American Academy in Rome; for theater design from the Ford Foundation; for critical writing in architecture by the Graham Foundation and the Kress Foundation; and for architecture and environmental design by the New York State Council for the Arts and the National Endowment for the Arts. As Chairman of Environment Design at Parsons School of Design in New York, he established a full graduate professional degree in architectural criticism in the United States. The focus of Wines' creative work is in the fusion of buildings with the landscape and in advocacy of a new role for all building arts in global environmental protection.

### *On the State of Ecological Architecture*

"The effects of a purely technological program of solutions will be extremely limited, unless accompanied by a strong philosophical motivation," believes Wines. "One major reason that the best historical examples of sustainable architecture have survived the millennia is because of their successful fusion of ecologically sensitive, spiritual content and artistic quality–an essential combination." Clearly, Wines feels ambivalent about the future of sustainability. "Much of the current design activity is focused on remedial solutions, but it still maintains the status quo. It matters little that a few environmentally friendly features are added to a glass skyscraper, when this basic building type lies at the root of the problem. The issue is not a lack of knowledge or available expertise in ecological design. It's a question of priorities. Every 'progressive' civilization is guilty of increasing gross national product at all costs, maintaining employment in obsolete, polluting industries, abandoning intelligence for political expedience, and supporting religious beliefs that encourage over-population. Short of an impending environmental disaster, who will give up what and when?"

### *Architectural Projects*

Wines readily confesses to having sometimes failed to use the principle of sustainable design in his work. "Frankly, I think that today's conventional building practices and restrictive budgets make valid sustainability impossible," continues Wines. "In my experience, if conservation technology was used in the choice of materials, the budget then eliminated such options as solar energy, innovative waste disposal, and easy access to public transportation. If the building merited high marks for climate control, energy efficiency, and minimum environmental impact, it was deficient in the choice of building materials and costs of maintenance." He believes that the one contribution that has characterized all of SITE's environmentally oriented buildings is a special sensitivity to context and the inclusion of regional landscape as an intrinsic part of the architecture.

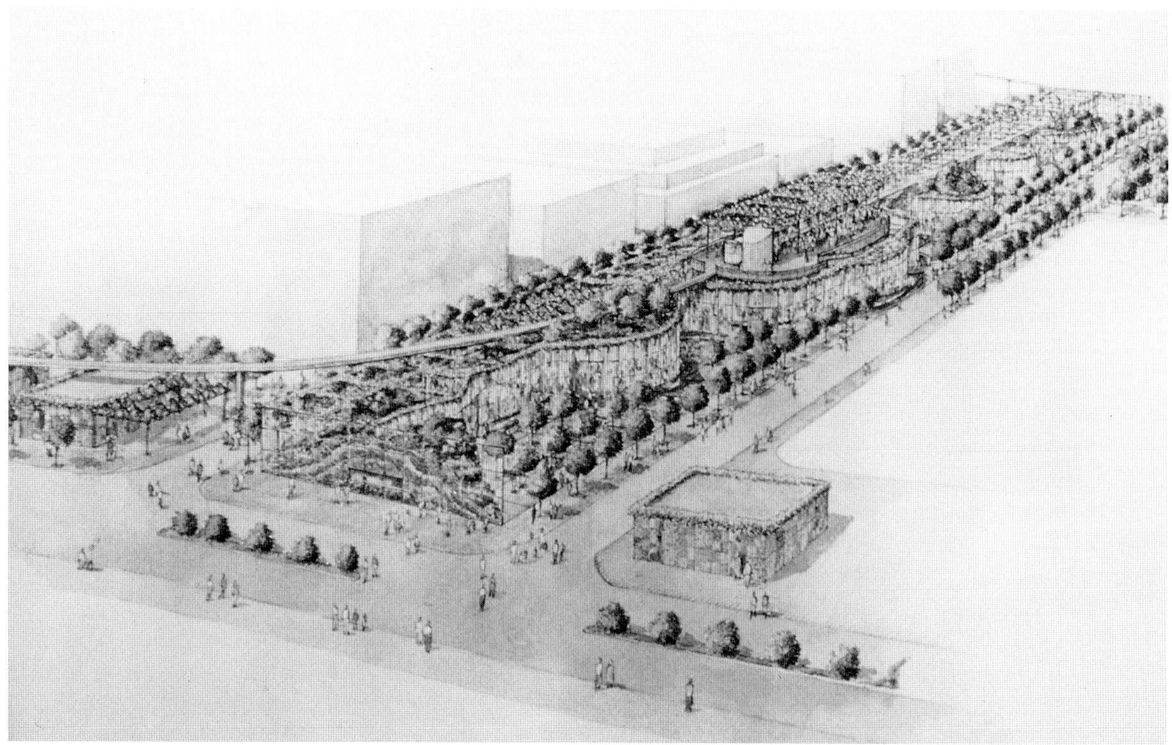

*Avenue Five, Seville, Spain. Built for the World Exposition of 1992, the architecture is composed of a 600-foot-long steel and glass structure that supports a continuous flow of regional water and is completely enveloped by regional landscape. A perpetual motion irrigation and cooling system (right), using only a small pump, is activated by static electricity in the water wall. The system services the entire processional with a periodic mist that cools the atmosphere and provides moisture for the plants. Photos: SITE.*

AVENUE FIVE
*Seville, Spain*

Avenue Five was originally built for the World Exposition of 1992 as a central public space celebrating the Guadalquivír River, where all of the 15th-century Spanish explorers' ships were made. The area around it is presently under development as an industrial park, and the processional itself will eventually house various cultural facilities related to the history of the city and river.

This structure uses innovative technology to create an atmosphere that appeals to its users. The fundamental concept of the processional is based on the translation of climate control into art. The water flowing over glass and the abundance of overhead and surrounding vegetation create a cool sanctuary in the dry, hot environment of Seville. One principal innovation is a massive colonnade of ivy constructed out of seeded volumes of earth in perforated metal sheaths. As the plant life grows, it completely consumes the metal matrix and roots solidify the mass of soil inside each column. The final effect is one of a building that appears to be made out of landscape.

Wines successfully converted all of the environmental technology in Avenue Five into visual imagery, creating a combination of sculpture and architecture, inside/outside relationships, and a magnetic environment where people seem to fuse with the landscape.

***Environmental Education Center, Prince William County, Virginia. The Center is a small solar building that is constructed of low embodied energy materials and harvested lumber, incorporating existing vegetation and designed for minimal environmental impact.***

The deficits, from a sustainable standpoint, are the required maintenance, vulnerable metal structure, and the dependence on a continuous flow of water for climate control. Typically, Seville has plenty of water flowing from its mountain sources, but drought, climate change, or severe rain could shorten the life of Avenue Five.

Environmental Education Center
*Prince William County, Virginia*

SITE is designing a small environmental education center dedicated to recycling in a dense forest flanked on one side by a massive landfill and on the other by wetlands. A living facility showing how discarded materials can be reused in new ways, the structure will be made of recycled materials and many of the sections will contain information units or video monitors describing the step-by-step conversion of waste into construction. This idea of the building as an educational tool will be manifested in a woodland trail system of recycled material walls that start underground in the landfill area, rise to the surface in the form of building blocks made from compressed waste, pass through the architecture as an exhibition wall, and emerge on the other side as vertical wood units serving as metaphors for the surrounding trees. The wall will finally dematerialize into the wetlands, having gone through a complete metamorphosis that

***Ross's Landing Plaza and Park, Chattanooga, Tennessee. Completed in 1992, the waterfront park surrounding the Tennessee Fresh Water Aquarium celebrates regional themes of the river, Indian civilization, local history, and community topography. The plaza riverbed, with a series of lifted landscapes, includes a play area where visitors are invited to interact. Drawing and photo: SITE.***

reveals the transition from how man recycles to how nature recycles. All of the exhibits evolve out of the "walls as passages" concept, which refers to the use of vertical surfaces as a complete inside/outside experience. Ultimately, the building conveys narrative information about the surrounding environment by actually being made of its own context.

### Ross's Landing Plaza and Park
*Chattanooga, Tennessee*

Ross's Landing, an important historic location in Chattanooga, Tennessee, is a riverfront revitalization project that was created by SITE as a microcosm of the entire city and region. The site is articulated by thirty-five longitudinal ribbons of paving, water, and vegetation. To further emphasize the cityscape and landscape metaphor, the ribbons compose a rich tapestry of color and texture in the form of twenty-foot straight-line reflections of the urban grid. The bands are ordered chronologically through the park. Each one is assigned a period of years so that it essentially becomes a time-line history of the founding and settlement of Chattanooga.

### Aquatorium
*Chattanooga, Tennessee*

SITE was commissioned to develop a concept and design approach for phase II of Chattanooga's environmental center six months after completing Ross's

Landing. Expanding on the theme of the aquarium, the Aquatorium serves as an exhibition, research, and recreation building dedicated to the subject of water and people. Its purpose is to explore water, the Earth's most precious resource, in terms of science, culture, education, ecology, and health.[10]

Designed as a circular structure to conform to the crest of the hillside where it is situated, the building is composed of a series of narrative walls that separate the functions of the center–exhibit spaces, study, library, theater, health club, and restaurant. The shape of the Aquatorium is meant to recall the cosmological symbolism of the relationship between water and earth.

The series of lateral walls tell the story of water and civilization by means of structural engineering, natural phenomena, and electronic technology. Also, the divisions create an inside/outside dialogue with the hillsides using an interplay of gardens, small plazas, and earth-sheltered rooms to increase the fusion of building and landscape.

## *Outside the Architectural Practice*

Author of several books and numerous articles, Wines is currently completing a book on environmental architecture in the age of ecology for Taschen Publishers in Germany. He continues to write on ecological issues for *Landscape Architecture, Architectural Record, Interior Design,* and *Art Forum* in the United States, as well as for architectural publications is England, France, Italy, Korea, and Japan.

During 1995, four teams of architects that included Wines, Arup Associates in London, Alsop/Stormer

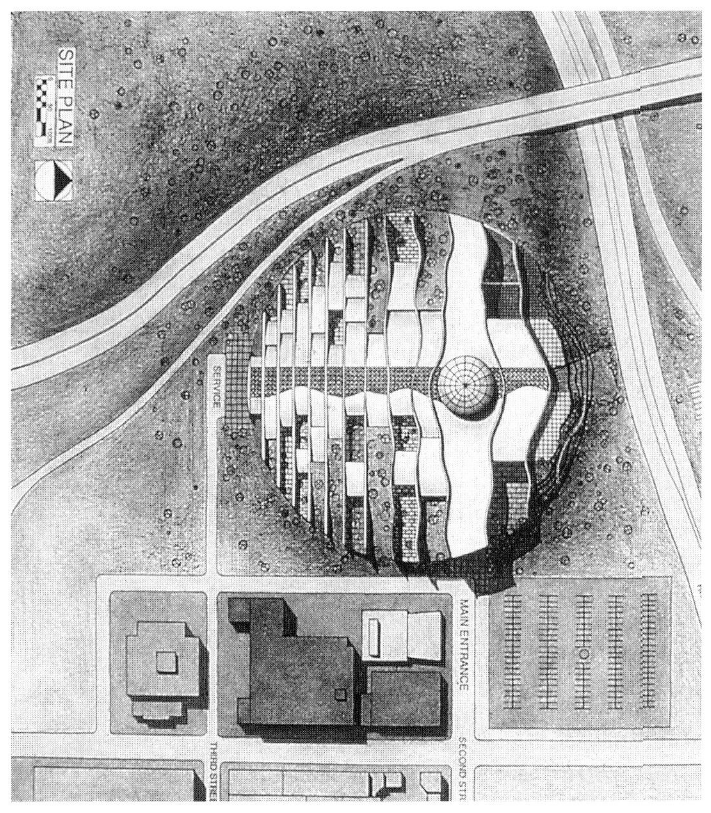


***Aquatorium, Chattanooga, Tennessee. Site plan and model. Ribbon walls divide the functions of interior spaces and integrate the building with the landscape. Drawing and model: SITE.***

***Nuclear Decommissioning Proposal, Trawsfynydd, North Wales. SITE proposed the use of robotic machinery to remove high level nuclear waste, utilizing overhead cranes to perform the process. Existing buildings would remain at their present height, and an impenetrable shield would provide public safety during clean-up. A massive greening project would envelope the reactor in moss, ivy, and regional foliage, and would decontaminate soil, water, and structural surfaces through bioremediation. Drawings: SITE.***

Architects in London, and Ushida/Findlay from Tokyo, submitted proposals for the decommissioning and future use of a recently terminated nuclear power station in Trawsfyndd, North Wales. Sponsored by the British Broadcasting Company and approved by the British Nuclear Electric Company, the proposals addressed a complicated set of requirements and were organized into an exhibition at the Royal Institute of British Architects in London. They later became part of a three-program series on BBC television in England.

Wines has further developed the presentation by including the design of an energy communications center for research and collection of information on solutions for the disposal of nuclear wastes. The introduction to the unresolved issue of decommissioning led to an entire focus of investigation at SITE, which determined that over 400 nuclear power stations must be dismantled in the next thirty years.

### *Suggestions for Professionals*

Wines believes that step-by-step progress toward the cause of "sustainability" is admirable, but too slow to be really effective. "The cancer of industrialization and excessive consumption of resources began gradually and did not reach catastrophic levels until the last two decades. So, it could be hypothesized that the reversal of those trends could take some time. I am convinced that nothing will change until the earth is seen again as the primary focus of philosophical discourse and source of all survival decisions."

Wines offers the following recommendations:

- Make landscape a more intrinsic part of architecture–the building-as-garden and the garden-as-building.
- Radically decrease the size of office buildings and establish a moratorium on the construction of new curtain wall towers.
- Decentralize the work space in favor of the "cybernetic" house, with work/living areas to accommodate computer-age lifestyles and a new concept of the garden city.
- Universally adopt a green technology that is climate- and topography-oriented for each specific location.
- Emphasize public transportation systems and discourage private vehicles.
- Substantially increase government investment in job training and start-up costs for new environmental technology businesses.

### *Closing Remarks*

To summarize, Wines likes noted architect Frederick Kiesler's comment that "What we need are not more and more objects, but an objective."

## SIGNIFICANT ECOLOGICAL PRINCIPLES

In addition to the handful of individual practitioners discussed in the previous pages, many private, public, and not-for-profit organizations, along with individuals possessing diverse professional backgrounds, have banded together in order to promote the education in and concerns of ecological architecture. The following sections represent significant initiatives undertaken by groups in the United States. Landmark efforts toward outlining the principles of "sustainability" have been undertaken in United Nations conferences and government initiatives around the world, and extend to cities and communities such as Seattle, Washington, and Austin, Texas, where green building programs have been implemented. Federal and state laws and building codes will eventually make the ideals of environmentally conscious design a part of required practice. Organizations such as the World Bank are working to integrate "sustainable" concerns into economic issues, redefining all of the elements that are part of the Gross National Product. Self-sustaining practices in a world with depleting resources is a notion that will be fundamental in all aspects of practice by the year 2000. The following principles are significant to the development of defining "sustainability" within the context of building design.

### *Guiding Principles of Sustainable Design*

Published in 1993 by the National Park Service, the *Guiding Principles of Sustainable Design* is a 120-page document that resulted from the work of many groups, among them the American Institute of Architects, American Society of Landscape Architects, Ecotourism Society, National Parks and Conservation Association, National Oceanic and Atmospheric Administration, and Greenpeace. Representatives of these organizations met at a conference in 1991 in the Virgin Islands in order to define the principle of "sustainability."

The document outlines sustainable concerns in the categories of Interpretation, Natural Resources, Cultural Resources, Site Design, Building Design, Energy Management, Water Supply, and Waste Prevention. In it, sustainable design is defined as "the philosophy that human development should exemplify the principles of conservation, and encourage the application of those principles in our daily lives." Bioregionalism, a corollary concept, is the idea that all life is established and maintained on a community basis and that all these distinctive bioregions or communities have mutually supporting life systems that are generally self-sustaining. A general checklist of sustainable building design objectives from the *Guiding Principles* is as follows:

- Use the building (or nonbuilding) as an educational tool to demonstrate the importance of the environment in sustaining human life.
- Reconnect humans with their environment for the spiritual, emotional, and therapeutic benefits that nature provides.
- Promote new human values and lifestyles to achieve a more harmonious relationship with local, regional, and global resources and environments.
- Increase public awareness about appropriate technologies and the cradle-to-grave energy and waste implications of various building and consumer materials.
- Nurture living cultures to perpetuate indigenous responsiveness to and harmony with local environmental factors.
- Relay cultural and historical understanding of the site with local, regional, and global relationships.

Also, the design should:

- Be subordinate to the ecosystem and cultural context of a site.
- Reinforce or exemplify appropriate environmental responsiveness.
- Enhance appreciation of the natural environment and establish rules of conduct.
- Create a rite of passage into special natural or cultural environments.
- Use the simplest technology appropriate to the functional need and incorporate passive energy-conserving strategies responsive to the local climate.
- Use renewable indigenous building materials to the greatest extent possible.
- Avoid the use of energy-intensive, environmentally damaging, waste producing, and/or hazardous materials.
- Strive for "smaller is better," optimizing use and flexibility of spaces so overall building size and the resources necessary for construction and operation are minimized.
- Consider constructability, striving for minimal environmental disruption, resource consumption, and material waste, and identifying opportunities for the reuse and recycling of construction debris.
- Provide equal access to all with physical and sensory impairments.[11]

### *Declaration of Interdependence for a Sustainable Future*

The principles that form the basis for the Declaration of Interdependence for a Sustainable Future were adopted at the AIA/ UIA (International Union of Architects) World Congress of Architects: Design for a Sustainable Future in Chicago in June of 1993. The AIA alone represents 56,000 practicing architects in the United States with participating members in Chapter COTE (Committee on the Environment) Committees, and the UIA represents thousands of architects around the world. Additionally, the Interprofessional

Council on Environmental Design (ICED), a coalition of architectural, landscape architectural, engineering, and planning organizations representing thousands of professionals, developed a vision statement in order to create a team approach to sustainable design. The ICED statement declares that "the ethics, education, and practices of our professions will be directed to shape a sustainable future. To achieve this vision we will join as a multidisciplinary partnership." The AIA/UIA Conference brought thousands of world leaders and professionals together for the purpose of sharing ideas and making a commitment to sustainable design. The declaration states that the members of the UIA and AIA are committed to:

• Placing environmental and social sustainability at the core of practices and professional responsibilities.

• Developing and continually improving practices, procedures, products, services, and standards for sustainable design.

• Educating the building industry, clients, and the general public about the importance of sustainable design.

• Working to change policies, regulations, and standards in government and business so that sustainable design will become the fully supported standard practice.

• Bringing the existing built environment up to sustainable standards.

The concern for environmentally responsible design has, more than any other cause in recent professional history, unified practicing architects for the purpose of meeting the commitments put forth in the declaration. AIA COTE members, under the leadership of dedicated professionals, have brought experts together from around the country to propose sustainable solutions for national monuments such as the White House, the Pentagon, and the Grand Canyon. *The Environmental Resource Guide* (ERG) published by the AIA is an important and regularly referenced source for sustainable building information, containing materials on such subjects as embodied energy, cradle-to-cradle analyses, case studies, and materials.

### *President's Council on Sustainability*

In June of 1993, President Clinton named the President's Council on Sustainable Development in order to help craft national policies encouraging economic growth, job creation, and environmental protection. The Council was established to explore and develop policy that "meets the needs of the present without compromising the future." Meeting quarterly, the 25-member Council was appointed by the president and is comprised of individuals representing the interests of environmental groups, business and industry, charitable foundations, governmental and private sectors with experience in matters of sustainable development, and those individuals with expertise concerning the appropriate use and appreciation of lands, facilities, and natural and cultural resources.[12]

The primary goals of the Council are to:

• Develop specific policy recommendations for a national strategy for sustainable development that can be implemented by public and private sectors.

• Respond to the recommendations in Agenda 21, the comprehensive international policy declaration nations of the world signed as a pledge to global environmental action, and contribute to the U.S. plan to be submitted to the United Nations Commission on Sustainable Development, the international commission created at the Earth Summit to help ensure implementations of Agenda 21.

• Sponsor projects that demonstrate and test the viability of the Council's recommendations and that encourage comprehensive approaches.

• Establish links with other non-governmental organizations within and outside the United States.

• Recognize outstanding sustainable development achievements through an annual presidential award.

• Educate the public about the far-reaching opportunities in sustainable development.

### *The Living Machine*

Since 1969, when they founded the New Alchemy Institute on Cape Cod, biologist John Todd and environmentalist and writer Nancy Todd have been recognized as world leaders in the restoration of pure water, bioremediation of wild aquatic environments, food production, and urban design. Currently involved in numerous projects with cities around the United States, the Todds discuss the principles of biodiversity in their book, *From Eco-Cities to Living Machines: Principles of Ecological Design:*

The Emerging Precepts of Biological Design

1. The living world is the matrix for all design.
2. Design should follow, not oppose, the laws of life.
3. Biological equity must determine design.
4. Design must reflect bioregionality.
5. Projects should be based on renewable energy sources.
6. Design should be sustainable through the integration of living systems.
7. Design should be coevolutionary with the natural world.
8. Building and design should help heal the planet.
9. Design should follow a sacred ecology.

### *Gaia House Charter*

The design principles of the Gaia House further help to define the principles of environmentally conscious commercial architecture. In the mid 1980s, *Gaia: A New Look at Life on Earth,* the book that inspired the Gaia movement, was published. Its author, James Lovelock, described the Earth and all its life systems as the ancient Greek Earth goddess Gaia, an entity which has the characteristics of a living organism that seeks to create and sustain life. A Gaia building or home is a place of comfort and health, a place where we feel in harmony with ourselves and all of life. "This sense of belonging, which is the source of true well-being, is fundamental to this vision of ecology with its concept of our planet as 'Gaia.'" In *The Natural House Book,* British author and Gaia architect David Pearson outlines the principles that make up the Gaia House Charter:

Environmentally conscious design is known by many names. Whether it is called "sustainable" design or development, green, ecologically or environmentally responsible, renewable, socially responsible, self-sustaining, or even restorative, it is the significance of the principles therein that are most important. The understanding and respect for each set of principles, and the endeavor to carry them out within the context of scientific information, available products and materials, and code requirements presents every building professional with a set of complex challenges. These challenges can be simplified by striving to respect all resources–nature, humanity, culture, history, economy, beauty, and quality–in a practical and inspirational way.[13]

***Designed by Ocean Arks International, the Lake-in-the-City scheme is designed to integrate water creatively. This section detail illustrates proposed water purification and heating systems integrated into an urban environment. Drawing: Reprinted from From Eco-Cities to Living Machines, courtesy of Ocean Arks International.***

## The Gaia house charter

**Design for harmony with the planet**

- Site, orient, and shelter the home to make best and conserving use of renewable resources. Use the sun, wind, and water for all or most of your energy needs and rely less on supplementary, nonrenewable energy.
- Use "green" materials and products – nontoxic, nonpolluting, sustainable, and renewable, produced with low energy and low environmental and social costs, and biodegradable or easily reused and recycled.
- Design the house to be "intelligent" in its use of resources and complement natural mechanisms, if necessary with efficient control systems to regulate energy, heating, cooling, water, airflow, and lighting.
- Integrate the house with the local ecosystem, by planting indigenous tree and flower species. Compost organic wastes, garden organically, and use natural pest control – no pesticides. Recycle "greywater" and use low-flush or waterless toilets. Collect, store, and use rainwater.
- Design systems to prevent export of pollution to the air, water, and soil.

**Design for peace for the spirit**

- Make the home harmonious with its environment – blending in with the community, the building styles, scale, and materials around it.
- Participate with others at every stage, using the personal ideas and skills of all in order to seek a wholistic, living design.
- Use proportions, forms, and shapes that are harmonious, creating beauty and tranquillity.
- Use colours and textures of natural materials and natural dyes, paints, and stains to create a personal and therapeutic colour environment.
- Site and design the house to be life enhancing, and increase the wellbeing or the vital life force, *ch'i*, of its occupants.
- Connect the home with Gaia and the natural world and the rhythms and cycles of the Earth, its seasons, and its days.
- Make the home a healing environment in which the mind and spirit can be free and flourish.

**Design for health of the body**

- Create a healthy indoor climate by allowing the house to "breathe", and use natural materials and processes to regulate temperature, humidity, and air flow and quality.
- Site the home away from harmful EM radiation from power lines and also away from negative ground radiation. Design to prevent the build-up of static and EMF from domestic equipment, and to avoid interference with beneficial cosmic and terrestrial radiation.
- Provide safe and healthy air and water, free from pollutants (radon especially), with good humidity, negative ion balance, and pleasant fragrance from herbs, materials, and polishes. Use natural air flow and ventilation.
- Create a quiet home, protected and insulated from external and internal noise, and a pleasant, sound-healthy environment.
- Design to allow sunlight and daylight to penetrate, and thus rely less on artificial lighting.

Chapter 3

# *Renewable Resource Technologies*

## THE FORCES OF FUEL CONSUMPTION AND POPULATION

Most buildings are connected to the grid and get their power from coal-, nuclear-, or natural gas-powered plants. With the possible exception of buildings in the Northwest and other regions where hydroelectric dams supply the bulk of the power, this is not in the long run sustainable. Ideally, a green building would get not just its daylight and heat, but also its electricity from the sun or other renewable energy sources.

—*Rocky Mountain Institute Primer on Sustainable Building,* 1995

It is clear that the growth of environmental consciousness is an inevitable result of an increasing world population with fast decreasing resources. Since the 1500s, the expansion of Europe and the gradual extension of control over colonized areas created a world economic system that benefited industrialized countries. Most of the wealth invested in commerce and industry came from areas with rich natural resources, and the control exercised over these resources underpinned world political and economic forces, resulting in concentrated wealth and poverty. As this precedent continues, more than 70% of the world's population lives outside the industrialized world while accounting for only percent 15% of global personal income. A citizen of an industrialized country has an average calorie intake 40% higher than someone in a Third World country. In Britain there are thirty cars for every hundred inhabitants, in the United States fifty-six. India has one car for every eight hundred people.

Energy consumption per capita varies greatly among nations. The United States contains roughly 5% of the world's population but uses 40% of the world's mineral and 30% of its energy resources. The People's Republic of China contains about 21% of the world's population and consumed 9% of the world's energy in 1990. Each American uses thirteen times as much energy as each Chinese citizen, and twenty-five times as much as the average Indian citizen. Many countries utilize far more energy than they produce and import huge quantities of fossil fuels–primarily oil–to meet their energy needs. Japan, for example, consumed 245 metric tons of oil in 1990, yet it produced less than one million metric tons. In that same year, the nations of Europe produced about 202 million metric tons and consumed 611 metric tons. The United States also relied heavily on oil imports to bridge the gap between energy consumption and production, exceeding domestic production by over 350 million metric tons.

Studies have indicated that at our present rate of oil consumption, the earth contains petroleum resources which will last less than fifty years. Despite volatile environmental, economic, and political byproducts of oil, it remains the world's major source of energy. In 1990, oil provided 41% of the energy derived from the world's nonrenewable resources; coal accounted for 29%; natural gas, 23%; and nuclear energy, 6%. However, the rate of increase of nonrenewable energy use is declining, says the 1991 *BP Statistical Review of World Energy.* After rising at an average rate of about 3 % per year from 1983 to 1989, in 1990 fossil fuel consumption increased only by .2%.

With the concept of sustainable development as an important ethic of the 1990s, available renewable resource technology has entered the mainstream. Reliable renewable resource technology, such as solar photovoltaic technology developed by NASA in the 1950s, remained out of reach for the average American until this decade because of high cost and limited performance. In Europe, where fuel costs are three times higher than those in the United States, the payback for integrating renewable systems in buildings more readily influenced governments, building owners, developers, architects, and engi-

***Los Angeles at night. Photo: Peter Gridley/FPG.***

neers to work with them. Energy performance is the driving force behind the economics of environmentally conscious architecture. In the United States, an energy efficient building can cost the same as a conventional building when the long-term impacts of energy efficiency, waste reduction, and comfort are carefully reviewed. "The high-quality aesthetics, comfort, and performance of an energy-efficient building will translate into higher initial sales prices and rents with lower operating costs," according to *Rocky Mountain Institute's Primer on Sustainable Building.* "Less expensive to heat, cool, and light, green buildings are simply more affordable, healthier places to live. Renewable technology provides the basis for a healthy, self-sustaining, richly individual family, business, government, and civilization–one which gains from working with nature rather than attempting to conquer it."

Building professionals and property owners involved in making critical decisions regarding fuel sources for a potential building should know about renewable resource options. Whether they are importing power from the local utility, or creating a self-sustaining off-the-grid set of mechanical systems, their decision will have immense impact on local, regional, and national ecosystems. Fuel source choices impact air and water quality beyond the boundaries of a given country. In many situations, renewable resources can offer reasonable solutions if long-term costs are carefully reviewed. If going off-the-grid doesn't seem to be a likely solution, check with the local utility to learn from where their power is generated. If you are working to conserve an existing building, be prepared to face difficult decisions regarding the performance and environmental impact of reusing existing equipment. Each situation has its own unique set of concerns and so should be addressed individually. Designing for the long term and phasing in solutions as they become affordable options represent one of the greatest challenges of an environmentally responsible project.

## BIOMASS ENERGY

Throughout history biomass fuel, the first energy source harnessed by humans, has predominantly consisted of wood. Although wood and other biomass fuels account for only 11% of energy used worldwide, they remain the primary source of energy for half the world's population. Biomass energy involves the conversion of organic feedstocks, such as wood or peat, into useful forms of energy, such as heat, electricity, or liquid fuels. The World Bank estimated that this type of energy accounts for 50 to 70% of the total energy used in the developing nations of Asia, and in Africa it accounts for 70 to 90%. Biomass energy presents an attractive alternative because it is readily available in many of the inhabited parts of the world and, when properly managed, its resources are renewable.

Although practical considerations place limitations on the amount of biomass that can be collected and used, if all the energy stored each year in biomass could be made available for human use, it would provide about ten times the total amount of energy consumed by people worldwide.

Biomass energy conversion technologies include combustion, biogas production, waste-to-energy conversion, gasification and pyrolysis, and ethanol fermentation.

### *Combustion*

Energy production from biomass combustion remains the most common technology, but is usually economical only when the raw material is available at little or no cost and when the source is near the site where it is burned. Raw biomass contains less heat energy for a given weight or volume than do fossil fuels. Thus, transportation costs for unprocessed biomass are much higher than those for fossil fuels, resulting in prohibitive costs if unprocessed biomass must be transported long distances. Transportation costs can be reduced if the biomass is first converted into a fuel with a higher energy density. This is done by compressing the material. Wood and its residues, for example, can be converted into dense pellets, cubes, or briquettes. The following biological and chemical techniques have also been developed to convert biomass feedstocks into high-energy solid, liquid, or gaseous fuels that can be transported at a reasonable cost.

## BIOGAS PRODUCTION

Simple biogas-producing devices create anaerobic digestion by decomposing organic matter such as crop residues or domestic wastes in an oxygen-deprived environment. The resulting biogas–a mixture of methane, carbon dioxide, and trace amounts of other gases–can be burned to provide energy for cooking and space heating, or used to create electricity to power other equipment. Since many of the parasites and disease-causing organisms in the wastes are killed by the relatively warm temperatures in the digester tanks, the digested material is sometimes used as a fertilizer or fish feed.

### *Waste-to-Energy Conversion*

In waste-to-energy conversion, municipal solid waste (MSW), which is typically collected and disposed of in landfills at considerable cost, is converted to gaseous or liquid fuels. It has several distinct advantages. Unlike other biomass, MSW must be collected regardless of whether it is used for energy production. The extraction of biogas from landfills converts potentially explosive methane into energy, also reducing the risk that it will infiltrate the air and buildings near those sites. The U.S. Department of Energy estimates that a total of two quads could be produced from MSW each year at current waste-generation rates in the United States.[1] A total of 136 waste-to-energy facilities were operating in the U.S. and Canada as early as 1991, according to the Nation Solid Wastes Management Association (NSWMA). These plants were producing a total of more than 2,100 megawatts of electricity. That same year nearly 100 additional facilities were also in various stages of planning or construction. According to NSWMA, waste-to-energy facilities were handling twenty million tons (16%) of the estimated 185 million tons of MSW generated each year. The U.S. Environmental Protection Agency has projected that by the year 2000, more than 300 waste-to-energy plants will be operating in the United States, handling about a fourth of the nation's MSW.

### *Gasification and Pyrolisis*

Gasification and pyrolysis involve the conversion of biomass to other fuels through the use of heat. In gasification, biomass is heated in the presence of oxygen to produce primarily gaseous fuels. Pyrolysis involves, by contrast, the heating of biomass in the absence of oxygen to produce a mixture of oils, gases, and solid charcoal. Although gases derived from biomass can be used instead of natural gas in the production of methanol, this use of biomass is not cost-competitive when natural gas prices are low.

### *Fermentation*

Some conventional food crops that are high in starches and sugars can also be fermented to produce ethanol–a relatively clean-burning, high-energy fuel. Under favorable conditions sugarcane can produce 1,400 gallons of ethanol per acre per year; corn about 400 gallons; and sorghum about 200 gallons. The commercial production of ethanol requires either a major surplus of food crops or the production of crops to be used specifically for energy. In addition to food crops, other less expensive biomass feedstocks, such as wood and plant wastes, can be used to produce ethanol. However, the two primary constituents of wood and plant wastes–cellulose and hemicellulose–are difficult to convert into ethanol with the techniques available. Consequently, the overall cost of ethanol produced from wood and plant wastes is higher than that from crops.

The environmental repercussions of using biomass as a fuel source vary according to the type of conversion technology. The combustion of biomass produces significantly fewer nitrogen oxides and sulfur dioxides than the burning of natural gas. Liquid biomass fuels like ethanol and methanol produce less carbon monoxide, hydrocarbons, and potentially carcinogenic compounds than gasoline and diesel. Unlike fossil fuel combustion, the use of biomass fuels in a well managed, sustainable production program will not contribute to carbon dioxide levels that cause global warming. If, however, a forest region is indiscriminately cleared for fuel and left with little or no vegetation, then carbon dioxide levels will increase, because the carbon dioxide released into the atmosphere is not recycled by new growth. Conversely, if large, sparse areas were converted to biomass energy plantations, the overall increase in vegetation cover would help to reduce the levels of atmospheric carbon dioxide. Some scientists believe that massive reforestation can provide a partial solution to global warming. Yet improper management of energy farms could create serious environmental problems such as topsoil erosion, depletion of nutrients, soil salinization, and water pollution due to fertilizer and pesticide runoffs. With proper planning, energy farms will be able to provide sustained yields without depleting the land.

Waste-to-energy facilities involve their own set of controversial issues. The facilities produce significant amounts of energy while substantially reducing the volume of landfill. Despite the benefits, some environmental and community groups oppose these plants, claiming that waste incineration of recycled products undermines the success of recycling programs. Opponents of these facilities are also concerned about the potential release of both heavy metals like mercury and cadmium which might be contained in the waste, and hazardous chemicals that are generated during the incineration process and that may be released into the atmosphere. Substantial progress has been made, however, in reducing emissions from incinerators. Some new incinerators burn waste at high temperatures–2500°F–which destroy many toxic chemicals. Scrubbing and filtering systems remove nearly all of the toxic substances and heavy metals, resulting in less than 1% of the amount of dioxin emitted from incinerators since the 1970s.

## GEOTHERMAL ENERGY

Stored in the earth's crust, geothermal energy is heat from rocks and water deep in the earth that are continually heated by the decay of radioactive elements and the intrusion of molten rock known as magma. The stored heat can be extracted and used to warm

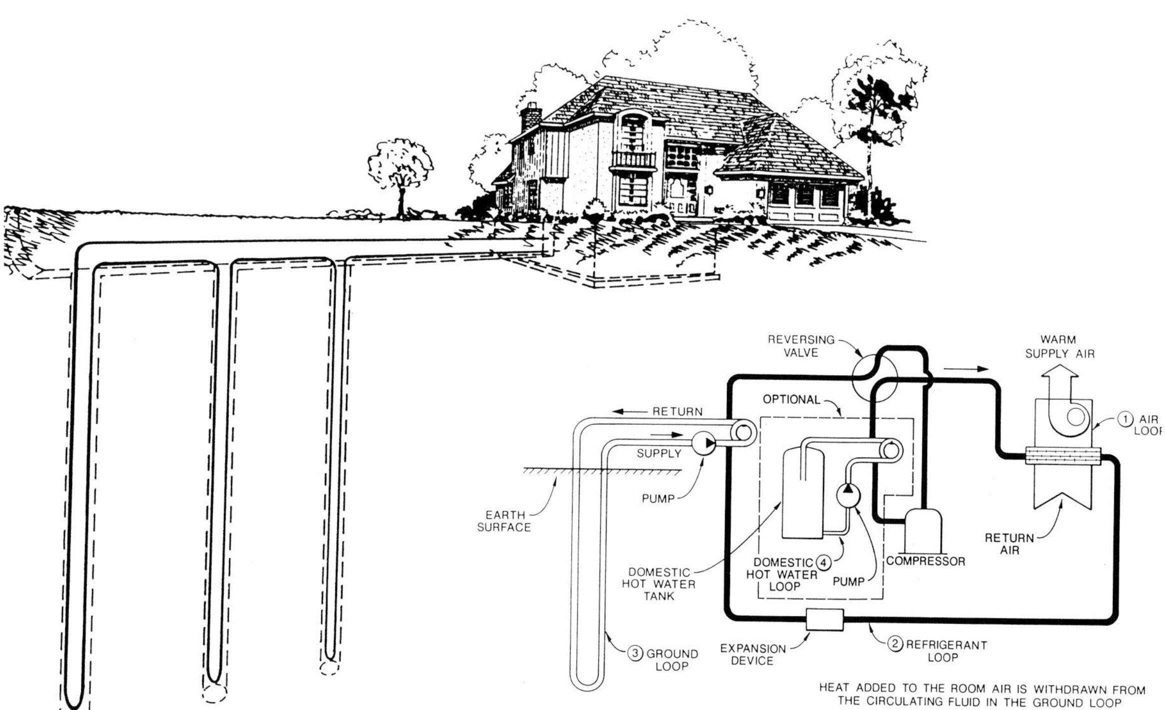


***A vertical ground-coupled heat pump (geothermal heat pump) system transfers heat from or to the ground to the room air. The U-shaped section of plastic pipe is inserted in a drilled borehole measuring 150 to 250 feet per ton in length. In most climates, geothermal heat pumps save consumers hundreds of dollars annually over standard electric technologies, even when their higher initial costs are factored in. Illustrations courtesy Geo-Heat Center, Oregon Institute of Technology.***

buildings or generate electricity. The U.S. Department of Energy has estimated that the total global resource of potentially usable heat contained in the earth's crust to a depth of 10 kilometers is about 100 million quads, over 300,000 times the earth's annual energy consumption. While the potential is enormous, only a small fraction of geothermal energy can be recovered at costs that make it competitive in the energy market.

Hot springs around the world have provided heat for bathing and cooking for thousands of years. Two thousand years ago, the Romans and Japanese bathed in geothermally heated pools. In Iceland, people cooked with geothermal heat as early as the ninth century. In the Middle Ages, several European towns built the first primitive geothermal district heating systems.[2] Direct-use geothermal systems operating at temperatures above 95°F had the capacity to produce 8,664 megawatts of heat in 1994, according to the University of Auckland's Geothermal Institute in New Zealand. Lower-temperature geothermally heated water provides a substantial, but as yet undetermined, amount of energy.

Relatively low-temperature geothermally heated water is now being used for space heating. The Reykjavik Municipal District Heating Service, the largest program of its kind in the world, has tapped geothermally heated water for space heating since 1930, and by 1990 about 85% of all residential buildings in Reykjavik were heated geothermally. Space heating in Reykjavik with geothermally heated water costs less than half as much as space heating with oil.

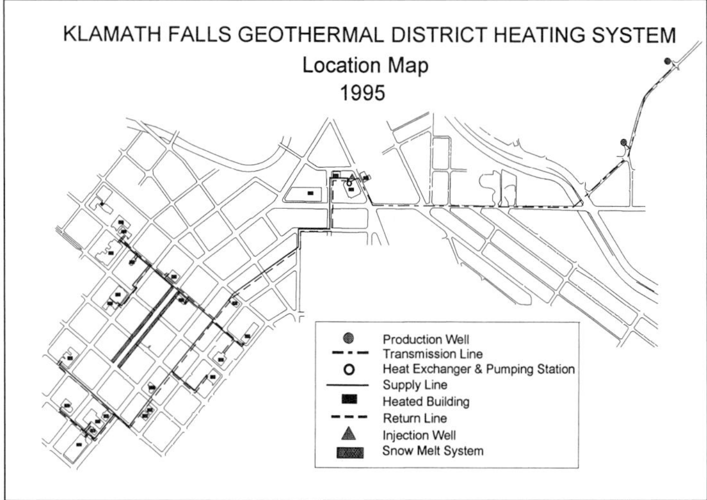


***Klamath Falls geothermal district heating system utilizes two geothermal wells producing 210°F thermal fluids at 1,000 gallons per minute to heat 26 commercial buildings (20,000 Btu/hr) in the downtown area. The cost of geothermal energy to the consumer is approximately 50% of the cost of natural gas. Illustration courtesy Geo-Heat Center, Oregon Institute of Technology.***

Geothermal district heating projects are now providing substantial amounts of energy in Ferrara, Italy; the Paris Basin and Bordeaux, France; and Mons, Belgium.

A 1990 report by the Geo-Heat Center at the Oregon Institute of Technology in Klamath Falls, Oregon, states that geothermal heat is being used directly in about 130,000 individual installations at more than 450 sites in the United States. A geothermal heat pump can "pump" heat from a low-temperature source (such as the ground) to a reservoir at a higher temperature (indoor air). The reverse is true in the summer when heat is pumped from the indoor air and reinjected to the ground. These systems can utilize ground and water temperatures from 40°F to 95°F. The geothermal direct-use resource base (95°F to 300°F) can be used for district heating, space heating, and heating for industry, greenhouses, and aquaculture. In Klamath Falls, 550 homes, 13 apartment buildings, 7 schools, 4 churches, and 2 district heating systems are heated by shallow geothermal wells. About 300 homes in the Moana area of Reno, Nevada, rely on geothermal energy for space heating. In addition to direct use projects, the Geo-Heat Center estimated that more than 110,000 geothermal heat pumps are supplying space heating or cooling in the United States.

The use of geothermal heat from relatively low-temperature resources saved the equivalent of about 4.1 metric tons of oil worldwide in 1990, according to the University of Auckland. Each of four countries–Japan, China, Hungary, and the Soviet Union–had over 1,000 megawatts of direct-use geothermal capacity, led by Japan with 3,300 megawatts (mainly for spas). Over 30 countries on the continents of Africa, Asia, Europe, North America, South America, and Oceania were also using geothermal heat.[3]

The Geothermal Management Company in Frisco, Colorado reported that the world electrical generating capacity from geothermal resources increased from about 3,900 megawatts in 1980 to 5,800 megawatts in 1990, and is expected to grow to 9,000 megawatts by 1995. The U.S. led the world in geothermal electrical capacity in 1990 with 2,770 megawatts. Six other countries–the Philippines, Mexico, Italy, New Zealand, Japan, and Indonesia–each had over 100 megawatts of geothermal electrical capacity, led by the Phillipines with 891 megawatts. Mexico had 700 megawatts; Italy, 545 megawatts; New Zealand, 283 megawatts; Japan, 215 megawatts; and Indonesia, 142 megawatts.

Located about ninety miles north of San Francisco, the geysers in the Mayacamas Mountains provide the most developed geothermal resource in the world. The first plant was built in the area in September of 1960 by the Pacific Gas & Electric Company (PG&E), and by 1990 twenty-six units had been installed by

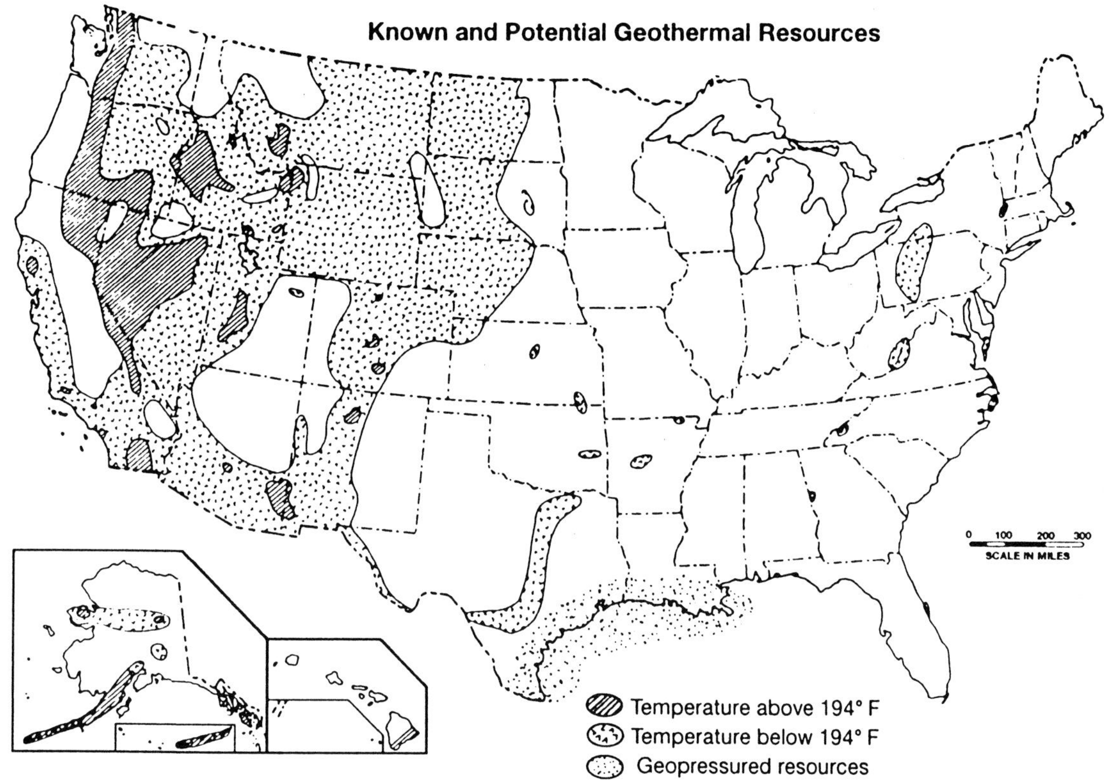


PG&E and other utilities. With a total generating capacity of around 2,000 megawatts, PG&E and other national utility companies provide about three-quarters of the U.S. geothermal total and 35% of the world total. Some other promising geothermal resources in California are being developed. Nine geothermal units with a total generating capacity of 236 megawatts have been installed at Coso Hot Springs in the Mojave Desert since 1987, and six units with a combined capacity of 208 megawatts have been installed in the Salton Sea region of southern California.

The most significant effects of geothermal energy use on the environment are air and water pollution. Geothermal power plants extract large volumes of steam and hot water from a reservoir–as much as thousands of tons per hour at large facilities. Unless adequate steps are taken to control the emissions, a variety of pollutants could diminish air and water quality. Steam from hydrothermal resources contains significant amounts of noncondensible gases–carbon dioxide and hydrogen sulfide–as well as smaller amounts of ammonia, methane, and hydrogen. Modern emission control equipment at geothermal plants, however, can reduce total sulfur emissions by over 90% to a level equivalent to about 1% of the sulfur emissions from a fossil fuel plant of similar capacity.

Geothermal water can contain high levels of dissolved salts and significant amounts of toxic substances such as arsenic, boron, lead, and mercury. Geothermal fluids are typically injected back into the reservoir or disposed of in lined evaporation ponds, avoiding the pollution of lakes, rivers, and groundwater. Reinjection has the added advantage of maintaining the pressure within the geothermal reservoir, extending the life of the field.

An advantage of geothermal energy is that for every ten megawatts of generating capacity, geothermal plants require three acres of land–much less than most other types of generating facilities. Unfortunately, some of the best potential sites for geothermal energy are areas of great natural beauty such as Yellowstone Park, or other environmentally sensitive areas. Several environmental groups have opposed a plan to develop a major geothermal resource on the island of Hawaii near the Kilauea volcano, because they believe that the power stations would destroy the Wao Kele O Puna rainforest, one of the few remaining lowland rain forests in the United States.

The future of geothermal resources will depend on its cost relative to other energy sources and on a variety of political factors. According to Pacific Gas & Electric, geothermal is one of the cheapest sources of energy, second only to hydroelectric power. The United States Department of Energy has projected that, with additional research and development, advanced technologies to extract energy from dry rock and magma could eventually provide vast amounts of geothermal energy at a cost that is competitive with energy from conventional sources like oil and natural gas.

## HYDROELECTRIC ENERGY

Running water's potential as a power source was first harnessed to grind corn in Greece in 1 B.C.The Roman Empire relied heavily on water-powered mills, and the Byzantine general Belisarius is credited with the invention of the floating water mill in 536 A.D. More than 5000 water mills were in operation in Britain 650 years later, and their construction expanded during the Middle Ages.The development of the first hydroelectric power plant in the late nineteenth century ushered water power into a new era.

In modern hydroelectric facilities, a dam or other impoundment is built across a river to capture rainwater and melted snow in a reservoir.The dam contains pipelines or tunnels equipped with valves or gates that can control the volume of water flow.The stored water flows down from the higher level behind the reservoir to the lower water level downstream when the structures are opened, and as the water rushes through turbines and generators near the bottom of the dam, electricity is produced. Generating capacities of this type of hydropower plant depend on the volume of water passing through the dam. In another type of hydropower facility known as a run-of-river plant, the natural flow of the current, rather than the force of water falling from a higher to a lower level, drives the turbines. Run-of-river plants do not store water in reservoirs or significantly alter the river's flow.

***Syrian water wheel. Photo: Dean Conger/National Geographic Society.***

Hydropower production increased nearly sixfold worldwide from 1950 to 1989, rising from 340 billion kilowatt-hours of electricity per year to 2.1 trillion kilowatt-hours. In 1989, hydroelectric power provided around 18%, or one-fifth of the world's energy. In spite of the rapid growth in world hydropower capacity, the growth of coal, oil, gas, and nuclear capacity in industrialized countries has far exceeded that of hydroelectric power. By the end of the 1980s, hydropower accounted for only 9% of the total electricity capacity in the United States and 17% in Europe. In certain countries, however, it has been much greater.At the end of the 1980s, hydroelectric power accounted for over 99% of the total electrical production in Norway; 95% in Nepal; 93% in Brazil; 78% in New Zealand; and 58% in Canada.

"Hydropower is an attractive environmental energy option," according to the *Almanac of Renewable Energy.* "In addition to providing electrical power, dams serve other useful functions.They can provide drinking and irrigation water, reduce the risk of flooding, deepen navigational channels, and create recreational lakes." Hydropower can be ideal for meeting peak power demands, since a plant's output can be adjusted to meet changes in electricity requirements. While major facilities can require large initial investments of hundreds of millions of dollars, these costs are offset over their lifetimes because power generation requires no fuel, hydropower plants typically have lower operating costs than fossil fuel or nuclear plants, and they can continue to provide power for decades.

Compared to fossil fuel and nuclear power generation, hydropower is a relatively clean energy source which produces no greenhouse gases.The U.S. Department of Energy estimated that if fossil fuels were used to generate the amount of energy produced by hydropower in the U.S., the total annual U.S. carbon dioxide emissions would increase about 215 million metric tons, or by about 5%. Globally, the use of hydropower in place of fossil fuels reduces carbon dioxide emissions by over 10%–about 2 billion metric tons per year. Many countries, such as China, are emphasizing hydropower development in their energy and economic plans for the 1990s.Availability of large hydropower resources and environmental advantages are primary reasons for this strategy. China is the world's leading consumer of coal, and coal-fired plants currently produce over 100 million tons of ash and slag each year.Also, the combustion of coal in that country creates high sulfur dioxide and airborne particulate levels, which cause damage to air, water, soil quality, and health.According to a 1995 *New York Times* article, China's heavy reliance on coal, along with its patterns of energy use, will make it the largest

***The 1,368-megawatt La Grande-1 Hydroelectric Power Station east of James Bay in northern Quebec began producing electricity during March of 1994. La Grande-1 is one of seven power plants in Hydro-Quebec's La Grande Complex, which has now a total generating capacity of 14,934 megawatts. In the fall of 1996, this capacity will reach 15,244 megawatts with the commissioning of Laforge-2 power station. Photo courtesy Société d'énergie de la Baie James.***

producer of carbon dioxide by the year 2020. Because of this, it is currently working with the World Bank, Japan, and the U.S. Department of Energy to fund projects that could improve the efficiency of Chinese power plants and develop alternative energy sources[4].

There are, however, huge environmental impacts to be weighed with hydroelectric energy. Large reservoirs created by major projects can inundate vast areas upstream and require the relocation of entire towns. The reservoir for China's planned Three Gorges Project, for example, will submerge over 100 towns and require the relocation of one million people. The project's critics have also claimed that the facility will reduce the scenic beauty of the Yangtze River, damage the river's wildlife and fisheries, and threaten a rare porpoise species with extinction. When requiring substantial deforestation, dams can also compromise efforts to reduce carbon dioxide emissions.

Major dams can also act as barriers to silt and nutrient-rich sediments carried by rivers. Egypt's Aswan Dam has nearly halted the deposition of sediments downstream along the Nile valley and in the eastern Mediterranean Sea. The loss of these sediments has reduced the fertility of Egypt's agricultural land and the productivity of Mediterranean fisheries, while increasing the rate of erosion in both the Nile's river channel and delta. Some dams trap so much silt that the reservoir quickly becomes clogged with sediment. When Soviet engineers designed the Sanmenxia Dam on China's Yellow River, they failed to adequately consider the immense amounts of silt that the river carries to the sea–about 1.5 billion metric tons each year. As a result, in 1964, just four years after the construction of the dam, the silt deposits had nearly filled the reservoir. The Sanmenxia Dam has since been extensively reengineered to allow silt from the river to pass through the dam and continue downstream, yet its reservoir has only one third of its original storage capacity.

Damming primary waterways can also diminish the quality of the water. The moving waters of a free-flow system tend to cleanse and aerate themselves, but the stiller waters of a reservoir can become stagnant. Water captured behind the dam usually becomes warmer, and extensive evaporation at the surface may raise the concentration of minerals in the water, such as salt, as has occurred on the Colorado River.

All of these changes can significantly alter the ecosystem of a river. Warm, stagnant conditions promote the growth of algae. The subsequent death and decomposition of the algae tends to deplete the dissolved oxygen, a result that can harm fish. Reservoirs can damage or destroy fish spawning areas, and dams can act as barriers to the migration of adult fish traveling upstream to spawn and to fish hatchlings traveling downstream to the sea. This problem has been partially overcome by the construction of fish "ladders" that allow the fish to swim past the dams.

In Canada, environmental concerns have prompted conservation groups and Indian tribes to challenge the proposed Great Whale Project, which would divert three rivers that flow into James Bay and flood thousands of square miles of unspoiled wilderness that is home to thousands of animals such as black bears, polar bears, moose, lynx, and vast varieties of ducks and migrating birds. In addition to destroying the wildlife habitat, the disruption of the flow of fresh water into James Bay could increase its saline content, thereby threatening fish, seal, and whale populations there. There are also concerns about the accumulation of toxic mercury, the presence of which was indicated in recent studies. Reservoirs at the nearby La Grande Complex have high mercury levels in both the fish and water supply. Scientists believe that flooded soils and decomposing vegetation release a soluble form of mercury that accumulates in certain fish species. Native Indian tribes also claim that industrial development associated with the complex has interfered with their traditional lifestyle, and caused an increase in social problems such as drug abuse. In response to a lawsuit initiated by Native Indian tribes, a Canadian court ruled in September of 1991 that the Canadian government must conduct additional environmental impact studies to determine whether the Great Whale Project should proceed.

***Annapolis Tidal Power Generating Station, Annapolis Royal, Nova Scotia, Canada. Since 1984, North America's first tidal power plant has produced 30 to 35 million kilowatt-hours of electricity per year. Photo courtesy Rick Winter, Nova Scotia Power Inc.***

## OCEAN ENERGY

Covering 71% of the earth's surface, the oceans are a storehouse of energy. The tropical oceans absorb an amount of solar energy roughly equal to the energy content of the world's entire oil reserves–about one trillion barrels worth. Tides and waves provide another major potential energy source. The total amount of power in waves that break along the shorelines of the world has been estimated at two to three million megawatts, equal to the generating capacity of 3000 large power plants. Some other ocean energy resources have significant potential, such as sea-based wind farms, which could generate electricity at numerous locations. Aquatic plants like seaweed could be cultivated, harvested, and converted into fuels. Differences in the saline content of sea water and fresh water could be used to produce power, although this area of ocean energy research is still in the early stages.

### *Tidal Energy*

Of the different type of ocean energy resources, only the tides have been harnessed for commercial power generation. By the early 1990s, just a few tidal plants were operating worldwide, and together they provided less than one-hundredth of 1% of the electricity consumed globally each year. Research conducted in Japan, the United States, and Europe may soon lead to the development of the first commercial plants powered by the ocean's waves and heat.

Tidal-powered mills were built in the llth century along the coasts of England, France, and Spain. By the mid 19th century, tidal mills were common in parts of Europe, Asia, and North America. As hydropower and fossil fuels provided less expensive sources of energy, tidal energy virtually disappeared by the early 20th century. The world's first and largest tidal electric facility–a 240-megawatt plant–began operation on the La Rance River estuary in northwestern France in 1968. North America's first tidal power plant began producing electricity in 1984. The 17.8-megawatt plant is located on the Annapolis River 100 miles west of Halifax, Nova Scotia, and has produced 30 to 35 million kilowatt-hours of electricity per year. Seawater flows through the open sluice gates into the reservoir behind a 740- foot-long rock dam when the tide begins to rise. When the tide begins to fall, the gates are closed so that the water level in the reservoir remains higher than that outside the dam. The plant reaches a maximum output of 17.8 megawatts when the initial difference between the water levels is eighteen feet.

The British government is considering an 8600-megawatt tidal facility that would be located on the

Severn River estuary in southwestern England. Estimated to cost $14 million and supply 17 billion kilowatt-hours of electricity, the tidal plant would provide 7% of the United Kingdom's energy requirements. A second large tidal facility has been proposed for the Mersey estuary near Liverpool, England. This facility would generate about 1.2 billion kilowatt-hours of electricity per year.

In the former Soviet Union, studies are underway for what would be the world's largest tidal facility–the Mezenskaya Tidal Power Plant–in the estuary where the Kuloy River flows into the White Sea. In this area, tidal fluctuations average about thirty feet, generating about 15,000 megawatts, approximately the capacity of fifteen large coal or nuclear plants. This generating capacity would be greater than the capacity of the world's largest hydroelectric facility, the Itaipu Binacionale on the Parana River along the border between Brazil and Paraguay. "The cost of constructing this facility would be about twice that of building a hydropower facility with equal generating capacity," according to Russian energy specialist Vyacheslav Batenin. "Because Russia has one of the largest undeveloped hydropower resources in the world, as well as large reserves of fossil fuel, it seems unlikely that the country will build a major tidal power plant in the near future."

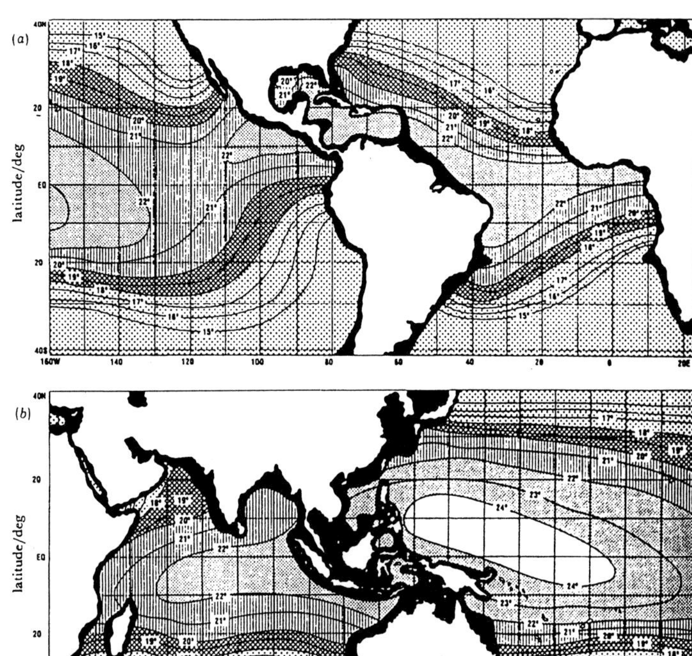


*Global distribution of ocean thermal energy resources.*

## *Wave Energy*

The energy content and size of waves, which are primarily produced by wind blowing across the surface of the water, depends on the duration of the wind and the distance over which it blows. Prevailing winds are westerly in many parts of the world and, as a result, western coastlines often have greater wave-energy potential. The west coasts of Norway, Scotland, and the United States, for example, are favorable locations for wave-energy installations.

The Japanese Maritime Safety Agency began using wave-powered navigation and weather monitoring buoys in 1965 and has installed hundreds of the 70- and 120-watt devices since. The most advanced buoys are equipped with microprocessors to monitor wave pressure and modify the buoys' operation to increase energy extraction. The United Kingdom's first wave-power plant became operational in 1991 on the island of Islay off western Scotland. Like the Norwegian facility, the Islay energy plant is an oscillating water column type (OWC) facility that provided seventy-five watts of power in the first few months of operation. The UK Department of Energy spent around £700,000 to fund the project, which was developed by the Wave Energy Group at Queens University in Belfast, Northern Ireland, and built by Cambridge Engineering Design Ltd. If the plant's performance and reliability is successful, the UK DOE may sponsor the design and construction of a one-megawatt wave-energy station. Another project, designed by researchers at the Coventry Polytechnic in Coventry, England, and Sea Energy Associates in Cheltenham, England, would provide up to two megawatts of electricity and cost an estimated $.12 per kilowatt-hour. Further design improvements could reduce this cost to $.06 per kilowatt-hour.

In 1985, the first two prototype wave-power stations in the world began operation in Toftestallen, twenty miles northwest of Bergen, Norway. One of the stations, an oscillating water column (OWC), generates up to 500 kilowatts of electricity. The second wave-power plant operating at Toftestallen, known as Tapchan, has a generating capacity of 350 kilowatts. The two facilities were designed to produce 1.1 to 1.8 million kilowatt-hours of electricity per year, depending on wave conditions. Tapchan has operated successfully since 1985, while the OWC performed well for three years until its destruction by a severe storm. Kvaerner Brug, the manufacturer of the OWC, has decided not to build any commercial wave-energy plants in the near future because of the high costs. Norwave of Oslo, Norway, the manufacturer of the Tapchan system, is working with the Tasmanian Hydro Electricity Commission to build a one-megawatt power station on King Island in Tasmania, Australia.

Though construction costs are high, low maintenance and no fuel costs will make energy more cost-effective than the diesel generators currently used. Nevertheless, the generators will continue to provide back-up power.

### *Ocean Thermal Energy Conversion*

Power can also be generated by tapping the vast reserve of solar heat that is stored in the ocean's surface waters through ocean thermal energy conversion, known as OTEC. OTEC systems function by using the temperature difference between the warm surface waters and colder water about 2000 to 3000 feet below the surface

In an open-cycle system, warm surface water is converted to steam in a partial vacuum, and the steam is used to drive a turbine. In a closed-cycle system, warm surface water is pumped into a heat exchanger and used to evaporate a liquid with a low boiling point, like ammonia or chlorofluorocarbon. The vapor drives a turbine, and cold, deep water is used to cool and condense the vapor. The resulting liquid is then returned to the heat exchanger, and the cycle is repeated. In a third type, a hybrid OTEC system, elements of both the open-cycle and closed-cycle systems are combined to produce hydrogen through the electrolysis of water or to make other products–such as ammonia or methanol, which can later be transported by pipeline or tanker to shore.[5] Efficient power generation from these systems is possible only when the temperature differential is about 36°F or more.

Ideal sites for OTEC are located in the tropical and subtropical oceans where the prevailing ocean circulation patterns and intense sunlight make the temperature of the surface water much warmer than the waters deep below. These sites can be found in a broad band extending from a latitude of 25°S to 32°N--a region that covers 20 million square miles of ocean. OTEC plants may be built on the shores of coastal locations where the seafloor drops steeply into deep ocean. They can also be constructed as large floating platforms.

French physicist and engineer Jacques Arsène d'Arsonval first proposed in 1881 that temperature differences in seawater could generate power. In 1930, George Claude built and tested the world's first OTEC system on the northwestern coast of Cuba. The early system successfully pumped warm water from the surface and cold water from depths of over 2300 feet to generate up to 22 kilowatts of power. The system consumed more energy than it produced, however, because of the small turbine and low temperature differential. Claude designed a second system that was to be put into use from a cargo ship off of the Brazilian coast. The cold water pipe for the floating plant was destroyed by waves during the installation, and Claude abandoned the project. Then in 1956, a team of researchers proposed that a three-megawatt OTEC be built off of the Ivory Coast. This plant never materialized because of financial and technological concerns that included the installation of a cold water pipe which would have been 2.5 miles deep and 8 feet in diameter.

During the 1970s as energy prices rose and technology improved, France, Germany, Japan, the Netherlands, Sweden, and the United States increased their interest in OTEC power generation. In 1979, the state of Hawaii funded a small system off of Keahole Point that generated up to fifteen kilowatts of net power. A group of Japanese companies built a demonstration facility on the island of Nauru in the Pacific Ocean. The plant produced up to 100 kilowatts of electricity during a one-year demonstration; its average power netted thirty-five kilowatts.

The U.S. Department of Energy continued to develop OTEC technology during the 1980s and 1990s. In 1981, DOE tested prototype heat exchangers off of Keahole Point. The goal of DOE's recent research has been to develop technology for land-based and nearshore OTEC plants capable of generating up to fifteen megawatts of electricity. In cooperation with Pacific International Center for High Technology Research in Honolulu, Hawaii, DOE is

***210 kWe (gross) Open-Cycle Ocean Thermal Energy Conversion (OTEC) Experimental Facility, Natural Energy Laboratory of Hawaii. This facility for the production of electricity and desalinated water has demonstrated that a low-pressure, open-cycle turbine system and a highly efficient vacuum compression system are feasible. In September of 1993, the highest recorded ocean surface temperature at the Keahole Point site was 27.5° C. The system produced 255 kW (gross) electric power. Using 152 kW of electricity to operate the plant, the system operated with 103 kWe of net power. This set a world record for OTEC. Photo courtesy Luis A. Vega, Ph.D., National Energy Lab, Hawaii.***

planning to complete an experimental OTEC facility in the mid-1990s.

Tidal, wave, and ocean thermal systems use no fuel, and therefore produce almost no harmful gases or particulates that are damaging to air or water quality. They may, however, have a significant impact on their local environment.The construction of a tidal barrage or major wave-power facility can change wave patterns, alter the concentration of suspended solids and nutrients in water, and shift the areas of erosion and sedimentation along the shoreline. Regulating tidal flow to maximize power generation could also alter the size of tidal estuaries and wetlands, and thereby interfere with the life cycles of birds and aquatic plants and animals. Engineers calculate that large tidal plants would alter the tidal range at locations hundreds of miles away, possibly increasing the risk of flooding or coastal erosion in wetlands and harbors and along beachfront properties.

Wave-energy systems also can make significant changes in coastal environments.A series of offshore wave-energy devices installed in a continuous line parallel to the coast would tend to reduce the force and size of waves reaching nearby shorelines.Wave-focusing devices would increase erosions in areas where magnified waves reach the shore. Sedimentation would also increase in adjacent areas where wave heights are reduced.

Precautionary measures must be taken to avoid spills of the chemicals used in closed-cycle OTEC facilities.The OTEC plants must also be designed to prevent species of marine life from being sucked into air intakes. Open-cycle OTEC facilities release carbon dioxide into the air during the power cycle, contributing to global warming and air and water pollution. Cold water pumped from the depths contains a high concentration of carbon dioxide, and when this water is brought to the surface, it can release some of the dissolved carbon dioxide, which is then vented into the air.Also, when the warm water is evaporated in a vacuum, it too releases carbon dioxide."Experiments simulating the conditions of open-cycle systems indicate that 38 grams of carbon dioxide would be released for every kilowatt-hour of electricity generated," according to researcher H.J. Green of the National Renewable Energy Laboratory in Golden, Colorado.This emission, in comparison, represents 4 to 7% of the total amount of carbon dioxide from fossil-fuel power plants.

## SOLAR ENERGY

The center of our solar system delivers 5 million quads of energy each year to earth, an amount 16,000 times greater than is currently utilized on the planet. The sun, a continuously renewing source of energy, is the earth's living source of heat and light. Since humankind first created shelter thousands of years ago, builders and architects have sited and designed buildings to take advantage of the sun's heat and light. In the 5th century B.C., residents of Olynthus in northern Greece built a planned community that was carefully designed to be heated and lighted primarily by the sun. In the 12th century, the British Law of Ancient Lights prohibited the siting of new buildings in locations where they would prevent sunlight from reaching existing buildings with windows. In many countries, including ancient Greece, the Roman Empire, modern England, and in cities throughout the United States, daylighting codes were incorporated into extensive building and zoning ordinances.

Solar energy systems contribute to the health and psychological well being of the occupants of a building as well as to the surrounding community. Like a living organism, the solar building continuously seeks the path of the sun.The building becomes a skin that orients its occupants to a universal calendar.The hours of the day and the seasons of the year synchronize the comfort and beauty of the natural world with those inside.

### *Passive Solar Heating*

Solar energy can be harnessed in many ways for the purposes of heating, cooling, and lighting.The term passive solar refers to systems that absorb, store, and distribute the sun's energy without relying on mechanical devices like pumps and fans that require additional energy. Passive solar design reduces the energy requirements of a building by meeting part or all of its daily heating, cooling, and lighting needs with solar energy.

Glass is typically used to collect solar energy because it inherently allows light to pass through the skin of a building without being absorbed or reflected. However, it reflects or absorbs longer-wavelength, infrared radiation in the form of heat. In a greenhouse, for example, sunlight enters through the glass roof and walls and is absorbed by the objects within. It is then converted to heat, which is emitted from the objects in the form of radiation.The radiant heat does not escape through the greenhouse glass, but remains trapped in the building, warming the air inside. Incoming solar energy is typically stored in a thermal mass, such as concrete, brick, rock, water, or a material that changes phases–solid to liquid or vice versa–according to temperature. Incoming sunlight is regulated with overhangs, awnings, and shades, while insulating materials can help reduce heat loss at night or during cold seasons.Vents and dampers are typi-

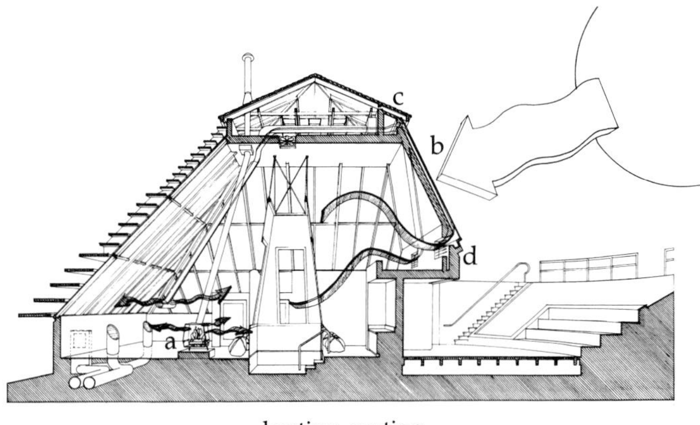


***Spring Lake Park Visitors Center, Santa Rosa, California, Obie G. Bowman, Architect. Spring Lake Park is comprised of a 320-acre flood control district and nature preserve that receives more than 750,000 visitors each year. Custom-designed solar panels clad the southeast elevation, dictating the pitch of the walls. A wood stove supplements the solar heating system. Sunlight heats air trapped between glass and metal on solar panels. Warm air rises into an attic, where the supply manifold blows it into ducts that carry air down into building interior. Photo and drawing: Obie Bowman, Architect.***

cally used to distribute warm or cool air from the system to the areas where it is needed.

The three most common passive solar design systems are direct-gain, indirect-gain, and isolated gain. A direct-gain system allows sunlight to pass through windows into an occupied space, where it is absorbed by the floor and walls. In an indirect-gain system, a medium for heat storage such as a wall located in one part of a building absorbs and stores solar heat. The heat is then transferred to the rest of the building through conduction, convection, or radiation. In an isolated-gain system, solar energy is absorbed and stored in a separate area, such as a greenhouse or solarium, and then distributed to the living space through ducts. In order to additionally conserve energy, insulation is incorporated in the most effective passive solar designs.

In regions with wide seasonal fluctuations in temperature, passive solar heating systems typically require some kind of backup heating. Nonetheless, passive systems contribute significantly to energy savings. Studies show that passive features typically add five to ten percent to the cost of construction, yet the money saved by them generally pays back in five to fifteen years, depending on geographical location and regional energy costs.

### *Active Solar Heating*

In active systems, solar collectors are used to convert the sun's energy into useful heat for hot water, space heating, or industrial processes. Flat-plate collectors are typically used to gather the sun's energy. These are most often light-absorbing plates made of a dark-colored material such as metal, rubber, or plastic, that are covered with glass. The plates transfer heat to a fluid–usually air or water–circulating above or below them, and the fluid is either used for immediate heating or stored for later use. These systems are referred to as active because externally powered equipment such as a fan or pump is used to move the fluid. In residential homes, active solar systems are generally designed to provide at least forty percent of the building's heating needs.

There are two basic types of liquid-based active systems: open loop and closed loop. An open loop system circulates potable water through the collector. When the temperature in the area around the collector falls below freezing, the water may be emptied to prevent damage to the system. In a closed loop system, the circulating fluid passes through a system separate from the plumbing that provides potable water, keeping the two separate because of the antifreezing fluids added to the circulating water to prevent it from freezing. Freezing can also be prevented by emptying the water into an insulated tank. Air-based systems are similar to liquid-based systems, except that a fan instead of a pump provides the circulation. The hot air can be used directly to provide space heating, to heat water, or a large thermal mass which, in turn, provides heat.

Open loop solar hot water systems are sometimes classified according to temperature. Mainly used for heating swimming pools, low-temperature unit collectors warm water up to 110°F. Pool heating systems typically use pumps to circulate the water; storage tanks are generally not needed because the water is in constant circulation. In medium-temperature systems, the temperature rises to 110°F to 180°F for water and space heating in residential and commercial buildings and for industrial process heat. In high-temperature collectors, water warmed to 180°F or more is used for heat and hot water or for industrial processes, such as cooking, washing, bleaching, anodizing, and refining.

One common type of solar water heater called the thermosiphon system uses collectors and circulating water, yet it is actually a passive system since no pumps are involved. In this type of system, the storage tank is installed above the collector. As water in the collector is heated and becomes less dense, it rises into the tank by convection and cooler water in the tank sinks into the collector.

In the late 1970s, high energy prices and resultant tax credits led to the rapid growth of solar thermal systems. Annual shipments of solar collectors dropped sharply between 1986 and 1988, attributable to the expiration of the forty percent residential renewable energy tax credit at the end of 1985. The Solar Energy Industries Association reports that by 1991, a total of about 1.25 million residential solar hot water systems had been installed in the United States–about 1% of the total number of housing units in the country. Solar hot water systems are much more popular in other nations, like Japan and Israel, which are heavily dependent on imported fossil fuels. In Israel, 65% of all homes are currently equipped with solar water heaters, and the government now requires that solar water heaters be installed in all new apartment buildings up to eight stories high. Solar district-heating systems, which use a large number of flat-plate collectors to provide energy for a group of homes or other buildings, can be a more economical heating choice than smaller individual systems. Sweden leads the world in the development of solar district-heating projects, with over a dozen large projects built or planned. The cost of heat from a solar district system large enough to meet 100% of the heating needs of 2,000 homes in Denver, Colorado has been estimated at \$.02 to \$.03 per kilowatt-hour.

### *Solar Cooling*

Passive solar technology can also be used for cooling purposes. These systems function by either shielding buildings from direct heat gain or by transferring excess heat outdoors. Carefully designed elements such as overhangs, awnings, and eaves shade windows from the high-angle summer sun while allowing the light from the low-angle winter sun to enter the building. The transfer of heat from the inside to the outside of a building may be achieved either through ventilation or conduction, in which heat is lost through a wall or floor. A radiant heat barrier, such as aluminum foil installed under a roof, is able to block up to 95% of the radiant heat transfer from the roof into the building. The Florida Solar Energy Center in Cape Canaveral has found that radiant heat barriers are the most cost-effective passive cooling option for hot southern climates.

Water evaporation is another effective method used to cool buildings, since water absorbs a large amount of heat from its surroundings when it changes state from a liquid to a gas. Fountains, sprays, and pools provide substantial cooling to the surrounding areas. The use of sprinkler systems to continually wet a building's roof during hot weather can reduce its cooling requirements by 25%. Transpiration, the release of water vapor through pores in the skins of vegetation, can reduce the air temperature in an immediate area by 4°F to 14°F. Trees provide the added benefit of shading, which can prevent heat gain in buildings. Planting deciduous trees along the south side of a building shades south-facing windows, thereby reducing heat gain in the summer. In the winter, sunlight can reach the windows and heat the building's interior. Planting trees or other vegetation is a highly effective approach to cooling urban environments where unshaded building materials like masonry and asphalt absorb large amounts of heat.

Ice ponds are also an efficient natural cooling source in regions with below-freezing winter temperatures. Ice that accumulates on the surface of a pond during the winter can be extracted and kept in storage for a period of months. When hot weather arrives, cold water can be circulated through heat exchangers to provide air conditioning. The cold water is condensed and provides cool air, which can serve as air conditioning.

Numerous approaches to active solar cooling have been developed as well. One method includes the use of earth cooling tubes–long, buried pipes with one end open to the outside air and the other opening into a building interior. Fans draw hot outside air into the underground pipes, and the air loses heat to the soil, which remains at a relatively constant, cool temperature year-round. The soil-cooled air is then blown into the building and circulated. In active evaporative cooling systems, fans draw air through a damp medium, such as water spray or wetted pads. The evaporation of water from the medium cools the air stream.

Desiccant cooling systems are designed to both dehumidify and cool air. These systems are particularly well suited to hot, humid climates where air conditioning accounts for the majority of a building's energy requirements. Desiccant materials, such as silica gels and certain salt compounds, naturally absorb moisture from humid air. Moisture-laden desiccant materials will release the stored moisture when heated, a characteristic that allows them to be reused. In a solar desiccant system, the sun provides the heat needed to recharge the desiccants. Once the air has been dehumidified with desiccants, it can be chilled through evaporative cooling or other techniques to provide relatively cool, dry air. At the Florida Solar Energy Center, researchers have designed a solar desiccant cooling system that could reduce summer cooling requirements an estimated 65% in Miami, Florida and 95% in Atlanta, Georgia.

### *Daylighting*

As lighting accounts for one quarter of the energy used in commercial and institutional buildings, relying on sunlight to illuminate interior spaces can save large amounts of energy in buildings where users can control lighting levels. Solar energy in the form of daylighting reduces peak energy demand, because natural light is typically most available during summer afternoons when the demand for electricity can be particularly high from air conditioning requirements. Another technique includes light-reflecting panels that follow the sun's path to direct light into the building interior. A daylighting system such as this in Toronto, Ontario, uses eight sun-tracking panels to light 2,000 square feet of top-floor office space.

***Advanced Photovoltaic Systems factory. Photo: Richard Barnes.***

Photosensor systems are also an energy saving feature. They can dim artificial lighting when natural daylighting is sufficient, and increase the artificial lighting when it is needed.

Glazed roof-enclosed courtyard spaces provide a building with both light and heat, although heat gain can be undesirable in hot climates. In this case, special low-emissivity window coatings known as "low-e" can be used to block out particular light wavelengths, control overall lighting levels, or redirect light into a building interior. These commercially available films are particularly effective, allowing visible light to pass through a window while blocking out unwanted heat.

More sophisticated types of coatings that include electrochromic and holographic films are under development. Paper-fine electrochromic films, whose optical properties change in response to a brief pulse of electric current, act as an electronic shutter to dynamically control the amount of light and heat entering a window. The Department of Energy is supporting research to develop electrochromic windows that can switch in less than ten seconds from a light transmittance level of 80% (typical of clear glass) to 10%, the level required to prevent most heat gains. Holographic films that employ the same optical principles and are used in three-dimensional holograms can project outside light onto a particular section of a ceiling deep within a building. Light reflected from the ceiling can illuminate office or living spaces that would otherwise receive little or no natural light. The Advanced Environmental Research Group, a firm based in Davis, California, has developed a plastic holographic coating that can direct light to the same part of a building while the sun's position changes throughout the day.

### *Photovoltaic Energy Conversion*

Photovoltaic technology, one of the most promising and efficient forms of solar technology, directly converts the sun's light into electricity. The beginnings of photovoltaic energy conversion, known as PV technology, can be traced to experiments conducted by the French physicist Antoine-César Becquerel in 1839. While working with an electrolytic cell composed of an electrolyte and two electrodes, Becquerel discovered that he could produce a current by shining light on one of the electrodes in the cell. Heinrich Hertz, a German scientist, observed the PV effect in solids during the 1870s , and the first PV cells were built with selenium–primarily salt–during the following decade. The early selenium cells converted only 1 to 2% of the energy in the incident light into electricity, too complex, expensive, and inefficient to be used as a power source in a world of cheap, available fossil fuels.

***Shown here is the simplest, least expensive solar-powered system for water pumping and storage available to faraway rural areas. Photovoltaic panels (left)--easily transported by donkey, bicycle, or even by foot--power a DC pump which, in turn, pumps fresh, potable water into remote villages. Water is then stored in large containers, such as the two blue vessels seen at right. Villagers take care of their water needs during the day, as the pumps are not powered at night. Research has shown that infant mortality rates have dropped dramatically in areas where these types of systems have been implemented, as the technology makes possible the avoidance of a great many water-borne diseases. Photos courtesy Siemens Solar Industries, Camarillo, California.***

PV technology remained a mere scientific curiosity until the mid 1950s when research on semiconductors led to a breakthrough in the technology. In 1954, a scientific team from Bell Laboratories used the Czochralski process–a method for making semiconductor materials–to produce a PV cell composed of highly purified crystalline silicon. The first silicon cell had a 4% solar conversion efficiency, because it converted 4% of the energy in the incident light into electricity. By the late 1950s, American researchers had developed some experimental solar cells with up to 14% conversion efficiency. While PV technology was used for a few commercial products during the 1950s, it remained generally untapped until the space race between the United States and the Soviet Union led to the first major application of solar cells.

As a power source in space, PV systems were lightweight enough to keep launching costs down, reliable enough to produce power for long periods, and completely self-sustaining. In 1958, the second U.S. space satellite, Vanguard I, carried a small PV array to power a radio transmitter. Since that time, most unmanned spacecraft have relied on PV cells for all or part of their energy supply.

Since 1974, government agencies, utilities, PV companies, and private investors have spent billions of dollars to reduce the cost of PV systems and increase their efficiency. Subsequently, the cost of PV cells fell from $100 per watt in the early 1970s to $4 to $5 per watt in 1990. The market for PV cells has expanded rapidly as their performance and efficiency have improved. In 1980 the PV market netted $85 million, as opposed to $500 million in 1988. According to the Department of Energy, it could exceed $1 billion in 1996. According to consultant Paul Maycock, the amount of PV modules shipped worldwide in 1991 was about 55.3 megawatts, a 19% increase over the previous year. Japan and the United States dominated the PV industry, accounting for 36% and 31% respectively of the total PV capacity shipped in 1990. The market share of European PV manufacturers increased dramatically, from 15% in 1986 to 24% in 1991. The two major current markets for PV cells are consumer products and remote power systems. About half of the solar cells produced in Japan are used in consumer products that require anywhere from a few milliwatts to a few watts of power. By the end of the 1980s, Japanese solar cells were used in more than 150 million calculators, watches, and battery chargers each year. The Chronar Corporation introduced solar-powered landscape lights in 1987, which have since become popular. Chronar and a dozen other companies sold over three million solar outdoor lights from 1987 to 1990. PV cells have become commonly used in numerous consumer products such as cellular telephones, laptop computers, portable radios, and CD players.

In remote locations, PV systems are used to produce electricity, pump water for drinking and irrigation, desalinate salt water, and provide refrigeration. In one major solar electrification project, the French government assisted financing of PV systems to power 550 homes on the island of Faaite in Tahiti, and sponsored a program to install solar-powered pumps and television sets in West Africa. PV-powered television sets bring educational programming to thousands of school classrooms.

In the United States, the most popular remote-power application for PV cells is in navigational aid devices and warning signs, including railroad signals, aircraft warning beacons, and highway signs. Because of their capacity to operate reliably for long periods of time with minimum maintenance, PV systems are ideal for these types of applications. In 1984 the U.S. Coast Guard began converting its lighted buoys, shore markers, and other navigational aids from battery to PV power because of the high costs of purchasing, replacing, and disposing of batteries. By the end of the decade, the Coast Guard had installed more than 15,000 of these systems at a savings of about $5 million per year in maintenance and battery costs.

U.S. government agencies, including the National Oceanic and Atmospheric Administration (NOAA) and U.S. Geological Survey, are using PV power systems as a power source for scientific instruments and environmental sensors. Solar arrays provide the power for radio transmitters that send NOAA's meteorological data from remote weather stations to orbiting satellites, which then relay data and send it back to earth. NOAA has also been adding PV systems to rainfall and river sensors at about 5,000 sites across the country. A U.S. Navy Energy Office survey in 1986 estimated that PV systems could be used for 21,000 remote power applications at 300 Navy facilities. Installing these PV systems would save the Navy a total of $176 million in operation and maintenance costs over the system's lifetime.

In 1991, the Commission of European Communities awarded Siemens Solar a $20 million contract to supply, install, and maintain PV systems in West Africa–in Gambia, Guinea-Bissau, Mauritania, Senegal, and Cape Verde Island–to provide irrigation water for farms in regions which suffer frequent drought and famine. The project, which is reportedly the largest commercial contract in the history of the PV industry, will use thousands of single-crystal silicon modules with a total generating capacity of 640 kilowatts. Siemens will provide 410 systems for pumping, 303 for lighting, 89 for cooling, and 33 for charging batteries over a four-year period.

Photovoltaic cells are made up of semiconductors–materials that conduct electricity better than insulators but more poorly than metals. When negatively and positively charged particles are separated into groups in a semiconductor, battery, or other device, the potential exists for an electric current to flow between the negatively and positively charged regions if they are connected by a conductive material such as a wire. The electrical potential is known as voltage. The material most often used to make PV cells is silicon, one of the most abundant elements in the earth's crust. When sunlight with sufficient energy strikes a PV silicon cell, it can dislodge an electron from one of the silicon atoms in the cell, leaving a positively charged "hole." The freeing of electrons by photons is an essential step in PV energy conversion, but it does not generate electricity by itself. If no other process were at work, the free electrons and holes would immediately recombine without generating an electric current.

PV cells are designed to prevent free electrons and holes from combining in this way. The silicon atoms form a repeating lattice structure in the crystals commonly used for PV cells. Each silicon atom has four valence electrons, the atom's outermost electrons which may form bonds with other atoms. In silicon crystals, each of a silicon atom's four valence electrons is shared, or bonded, with each of four neighboring silicon atoms. The situation changes when a small portion of the silicon atoms is replaced by other elements, such as phosphorus or boron, in a manufacturing process called doping.

Unlike silicon, phosphorus has five valence electrons, and boron has only three. When a phosphorus atom replaces a silicon atom in a PV cell, four of the phosphorus atom's five valence electrons bind with the four adjacent silicon atoms; the fifth remains free and is called a free electron. This free electron becomes part of what is known as the conduction band, in which electrons are able to move freely through the solid crystal and conduct electricity.

Silicon doped with phosphorus is called negative-type (n-type) silicon because the phosphorus atoms give the crystal more free electrons–which carry negative charges–than holes. The free electrons are considered the majority charge carriers in n-type silicon. These electrons are not involved in the formation of bonds and are therefore relatively free to move through a crystal in response to an electric field. Although n-type silicon and other n-type semiconductors contain an abundance of free electrons, they remain electrically neutral, because the total number of electrons in the semiconductor equals the number of protons–positively charged particles–in the nuclei of the atoms that make up the semiconductor.

A silicon crystal doped with boron produces a positive-type (p-type) silicon material. Each boron atom has only three valence electrons to form bonds with the four adjacent silicon atoms when boron atoms replace silicon atoms in the crystal. As a result one of the silicon bonds is missing an electron, leaving a hole. Holes are the majority charge carriers because p-type silicon contains many more of these positively charged holes than free electrons. P-type silicon is electrically neutral, like n-type silicon.

The highly mobile majority charge carriers on one side of the interface, called the p-n junction, are attracted to the oppositely charged majority charge carriers on the other side of the junction when p-type and n-type silicon come into contact. Then, some of the free electrons on the n-side of the junction move over to the p-side, while some of the holes on the p-side cross over to the n-side. The movements of electrons and holes causes the buildup of a net positive charge along the n-side of the junction and a net negative charge along the p-side, creating an electric field. A state of equilibrium is reached when the electric field at the junction acts to repel any additional movement of majority charge carriers across the junction.

The photovoltaic effect is made possible by the existence of this electric field at the p-n junction. When a photon dislodges an electron from an atom on either the p-side or the n-side of the junction in a PV cell, it creates a free electron and a hole. The minority carrier–a hole on the n-side of the junction or an electron on the p-side–is attracted to the junction and may cross over to the other side if the carrier has sufficient energy under the influence of the electric field at the junction. The electric field tends to repel the majority carrier and thereby prevents it from crossing the junction. The final result is that the light-generated free electrons and holes are separated within a PV cell, with the free electrons either traveling to or remaining on the n-side of the junction, while the holes travel to or remain on the p-side. The excess electrons flow from the n-side of the circuit to fill the holes in the p-side, producing an electric current in the process when both sides of the PV cell are connected through an external circuit.

Typically linked together into modules, PV cells do the work of converting light into electricity. A variety of supporting systems, referred to as the balance of systems, are required to make an operational PV system. The equipment includes support structures, connecting wire, and control equipment, in addition to components to convert the direct current (DC) generated by PV cells to alternating current (AC) for use at the site or for transmission to a utility's power grid. Batteries may be used to store solar electricity for use at a later time.

### Single Crystal Cells

The photovoltaic cells most frequently used today are made of pure silicon from a single crystal. The uniform crystalline structure assists the movement of electrons and holes through the cells, making it relatively easy to attain high sunlight conversion efficiencies. In the Czochralski process–the most commonly used method for producing single-crystal silicon–a small "seed" crystal of pure silicon is dipped into a crucible containing molten silicon. As the seed is slowly raised from the crucible, it draws out molten silicon which slowly cools and solidifies into a cylindrical ingot of single-crystal silicon. The ingot is sliced and polished to form wafers, which are later doped with small amounts of atoms such as phosphorus and boron. These wafers are then organized into modules, creating PV cells.

***Polycrystalline cell. Photo courtesy Solarex, Frederick, Maryland.***

Single-crystal silicon cells contain several different parts: an electrically conductive grid on the top surface of the cell to carry the electric current from the cell; one or two layers of antireflective coating to increase absorption of sunlight by the cell; a thin, doped silicon layer called the collector; a silicon base layer doped oppositely to the collector; and an electrode in contact with the base layer to complete the electric circuit.

The high cost of producing single-crystal silicon cells has declined drastically since the first silicon PV cells were made in the 1950s. They are still expensive to produce, and several factors limit the extent to which costs could be further reduced. Single-crystal silicon has a relatively low capacity to absorb light and the wafers must be at least 100 microns (.004 inch) thick to achieve efficiencies suitable for PV cells. Additionally, about 20% of the original ingot is wasted during the slicing of the wafers. Single-crystal silicon is extremely fragile and must be handled carefully during manufacture, packaging, and installation. New techniques that can produce long, thin sheets instead of ingots have reduced the costs associated with producing these cells. The manufacture of silicon sheets eliminates the loss of silicon associated with slicing ingots and polishing wafers.

Gallium arsenide (GaAs), another semiconductive material that consists of the elements gallium and arsenic, has also been used to make single-crystal cells. Although GaAs is costly and rare, it has several important characteristics that make it nearly ideal for PV cells. The range of light wavelengths that a GaAs cell can absorb and use makes it particularly well suited for converting the energy in light into electricity. GaAs crystals are also highly absorptive, so that a layer only a few microns thick can absorb much of the usable light. In comparison to silicon cells, GaAs cells can operate efficiently over a wider temperature range and are more resistant to radiation damage, a characteristic that makes them particularly desirable for use in space. As of 1990, experimental PV cells made of single-crystal GaAs have achieved maximum conversion efficiencies of 26% in unconcentrated sunlight, compared to about 23% for experimental single-crystal silicon cells.

### Semicrystalline and Polycrystalline Cells

Semicrystalline cells are composed of a series of relatively large crystals called grains, with each covering an area of about one square centimeter. Polycrystalline cells are composed of many much smaller grains. Manufacturing techniques for semicrystalline cells and polycrystalline silicon cells are more simple and less expensive than those for producing perfect single crystal cells. In the most common technique for production of semicrystalline silicon cells, molten silicon is poured into a mold and cooled to form a solid ingot, which can then be sliced into wafers.

Semicrystalline and polycrystalline silicon have lower conversion efficiencies than single-crystal silicon, because free electrons and holes tend to recombine at the boundaries between the different grains in the PV cell, thus reducing the amount of electric current that can be produced. Even so, the relatively low manufacturing costs of semicrystalline and polycrystalline silicon have made them popular for PV cells. During 1991, semicrystalline and polycrystalline silicon accounted for about 38% of the world market for PV cells, compared to 36% for single-crystal silicon.

### Amorphous Cells

Materials such as amorphous silicon, cadmium telluride, and copper indium diselenide are also used to make thin film PV cells. Amorphous silicon is by far the most commonly used in commercial thin-film PV modules. The absorptivity of amorphous silicon is about forty times greater than that of single-crystal silicon. Consequently, an amorphous silicon film just one micron thick can absorb 90% of the usable light.

Commercial amorphous silicon modules are made by depositing a series of thin films of amorphous silicon on an inexpensive substrate such as glass or plastic. This process uses very little silicon and is much less expensive than growing and slicing crystalline silicon ingots. Amorphous silicon modules are easy to make in a variety of sizes and shapes, which can accommodate diverse applications.

These solar cells are, however, considerably less efficient in converting light into electricity than crystalline silicon cells, because amorphous silicon contains numerous structural and bonding defects where the free electrons and holes tend to combine. Also less stable than crystalline silicon, the conversion efficiency of amorphous silicon declines about 10 to 20% after its first exposure to light. In spite of the drawbacks, amorphous silicon PV cells are used in many consumer products that require little power. In 1991, amorphous silicon comprised about 25% of the world PV market.

### Concentrator Systems

When a series of PV cells is stacked on top of one another to create multijunction cells, relatively high conversion efficiencies can be achieved. In multijunction cells, each of the different PV cells absorbs light in a particular range of wavelengths and converts it into electricity. Light that is not absorbed into the top cell passes through to the cells below, where it may be absorbed and converted into electricity. Since multijunction cells convert light over a broader range of wavelengths than is normally possible with single junction cells, they have a potential for conversion efficiencies as high as 40%, according to some studies.

Inexpensive lenses or mirrors are used to intensify the incident sunlight by as much as 400 times or more before it reaches the PV cells in concentrator systems. In order to produce a given amount of electricity, concentrator systems need far fewer cells since each cell receives much more solar energy than the cells in nonconcentrating arrays. Due to the thermal and electrical properties of the semiconductors, concentrator PV cells also achieve somewhat higher conversion efficiencies than nonconcentrating cells. As of 1991, Boeing achieved a conversion efficiency of 34.2 percent. This is the highest conversion efficiency recorded for any type of PV device, with a multijunction cell under light concentrated one hundredfold.

Because the lenses or reflective materials used to concentrate sunlight are less expensive than the additional PV cells needed in a nonconcentrating system to produce the same amount of sunlight, concentrator systems can reduce PV electricity costs. Concentrator systems often use smaller individual cells than other systems. Reduced cell size is an advantage because it is typically easier to manufacture small-area, high-efficiency cells than it is to make larger cells of equal efficiency.

However, concentrator arrays do have some disadvantages when compared to nonconcentrating systems. Most concentrating modules must be installed on support structures that track the sun's path through the sky. Sun-tracking equipment can add substantially to the total cost of the system. Concentrating lenses and mirrors are also unable to focus diffuse sunlight and, as a result, these arrays produce little electricity under cloudy conditions. Concentrator systems are therefore only practical in areas with relatively few overcast days. High sunlight concentrations create special problems, though, because the intense light generates heat, and the efficiency and long-term stability of PV cells decrease at high temperatures. Therefore, high-concentration modules must be cooled, either with passive design features, such as metal fins that radiate heat, or with active cooling systems.

### Dye-Based Cells

An innovative PV cell that uses a light-sensitive ruthenium-based dye to absorb incoming sunlight was created in 1991 by Michael Gratzel of the Swiss Federal Institute of Technology and Brian O'Regan of the University of Washington in Seattle. The device is an electrochemical cell in which a liquid electrolyte is sandwiched between two layers of electrically conductive glass that serve as the cell's positive and negative electrodes. The inside surface of the negative electrode is covered with a thin semiconductor layer composed of titanium dioxide particles coated with a ruthenium-based dye. The electrolyte is in contact with the dye molecules, which contain negatively charged iodine ions in solution.

When dye molecules absorb light, they release electrons into the titanium dioxide. This transfers the electrons to the cell's negative electrode, producing an electric current as electrons flow from the negative electrode through an external circuit to the cell's positive electrode. Electrically neutral iodine atoms at the positive electrode acquire the incoming electrons and are converted to negative iodine ions, passing through the electrolyte and transferring their extra electrons to dye molecules that have lost electrons. Both the dye molecules and the iodine revert to their initial state in this process. The neutral iodine atoms diffuse back through the electrolyte to the positive electrode to complete the cycle.

The ruthenium dye molecule has a similar chemical structure to chlorophyll, the molecule in photosynthetic organisms that captures the energy of sunlight. Unlike solar cells which convert sunlight into electricity, however, photosynthetic organisms use solar energy to produce carbohydrates from water and carbon dioxide. According to Gratzel and O'Regan, the dye-based solar cells convert 7 to 12% of the energy in incoming sunlight into electricity. This conversion efficiency is comparable to that of the best available amorphous silicon PV cells, providing a practical alternative to conventional PV cells because the dye-based devices are inexpensive to manufacture and appear to be highly durable.

Photovoltaic technology, an inherently clean source of electricity, produces no noise, acid rain, smog, carbon dioxide, water pollutants, or nuclear waste because it relies on the power of the sun for its fuel. Silicon, the raw material used for most PV cells, is abundant and non-toxic. Some of the other substances which are used in small amounts, such as cadmium and arsenic are, however, toxic. Studies of the PV manufacturing industry and the experience of the microelectronics industry indicate that large-scale production of PV systems has minimal impact on the environment, provided that the processes are properly handled.

The manufacture of PV modules consumes a substantial amount of energy, yet the systems quickly pay back the energy used to make them. According to researchers Wolfgang Palz and Henri Zibetta of the Commission of European Communities, "payback periods are about twenty-five months for crystalline silicon cells, and about fifteen months for amorphous silicon cells." Payback in the United States varies widely depending on the local costs of energy. Remote systems that would require substantial costs for utility hookups produce the most immediate payback periods. In buildings where utility service is provided, independent solar building systems can be connected, providing power from the building to the utility company. Local utilities are required by federal law to purchase the exported power at their market rate, providing the building owner with substantial paybacks.

Since PV systems use only sunlight for fuel, the serious environmental impact of activities such as mining, exploration, production, and transportation, and the hazards of coal, oil, and gas are eliminated. Yet PV power stations do require large amounts of land–about 1 square mile for every 100 megawatts of power produced. However, according to *Almanac for Renewable Energy*, "The total land requirements for PV power plants are comparable to those for a conventional power station when the land used to extract fossil and nuclear fuels is taken into account." Utility companies in several countries are incorporating rooftop arrays on available buildings to provide power without utilizing land surface area. According to one estimate, if the southfacing roofs in the San Diego metropolitan area were covered with PV cells, they would have a peak output of over 2,000 megawatts, a capacity equal to two large power plants. The New

England Power Service Company tested a series of grid-connected rooftop systems during the 1980s that demonstrated the feasibility of generating electricity with these types of systems. Several utility companies instituted programs in 1994 which provide incentives to available public buildings when rooftop arrays are installed that provide additional power to the utility.

PV facilities can also be designed to minimize site disruption so that much of the existing vegetation remains undisturbed. Vegetation which commonly provides necessary passive shading to a building must be carefully designed in order to avoid reducing the efficiency of PV cells in producing power.

Photovoltaic systems offer diverse market products through many companies around the world. When these systems are innovatively integrated into the architecture of a building, the results can be dramatic, elegant, cost effective, and environmentally responsible.

## WIND ENERGY

Wind was one of the world's primary energy sources for transporting goods, milling grain, and pumping water until coal and petroleum gained widespread use. Ships on the Nile River began to seize the wind's energy as early as 5,000 years ago. Windmills were used in China, India, and Persia over 2,000 years ago. The first documented use of windmills in Western Europe was in Yorkshire, England in 1185. Nearly 100 years ago, wind turbines were first used to generate electric power in Denmark. In this century, the total generating capacity from wind in Denmark reached 150 to 200 megawatts, and wind provided nearly one quarter of the energy used there. In the United States, over 6 million small (under 1 kilowatt) mechanical windmills and wind turbines were installed on the Great Plains between 1850 and 1970.

Denmark dominated wind energy development in Europe throughout the past decade, accounting for 80% of the continent's 325 megawatts of installed wind capacity during 1990. During the early 1980s, Denmark imported 95% of its energy. As a result, the development of wind energy resources was encouraged through government subsidies to individuals and businesses that ranged from 15 to 30% of the purchase cost of wind turbines. In the latter half of the 1980s, as the country's wind industry became established, the subsidies were phased out. By 1990, 3,000 wind turbines with a generating capacity of about 250 megawatts had been installed in Denmark. The country set a goal of meeting 10% of its electrical demand with wind energy by the year 2000, a goal which will require Denmark to expand its wind generating capacity to over 1,000 megawatts. In 1991, Elkraft completed the first offshore wind farm in the Langelands Baelt in southern Denmark. Eleven horizontal-axis turbines built on reinforced concrete in 20-foot-deep waters are arranged in two rows 2 miles off of the coast, each having a rated capacity of 450 watts.

Germany, the United Kingdom, and the Netherlands have initiated development programs which will lead the rapid expansion of Europe's wind industry during this decade. Germany is the world's fastest growing market for wind energy. During 1991, the country's total installed wind capacity passed 50 megawatts and is expected to reach 250 megawatts by 1996. Two factors are significant to the growth of wind power in Germany: a German law that requires utilities to pay a premium price for electricity generated by wind farms, and a $240 million wind program sponsored by the German Ministry for Research and Technology (BMFT) which pays wind energy developers a subsidy of $.04 per kilowatt hour of electricity produced. Wind turbines accepted into the program could receive over $.15 per kilowatt hour. As a result of these incentives, over 2000 applications have flooded the ministry.

The United Kingdom has the best wind resources in Europe, having spent over $45 million on research and development between 1977 and 1990. In 1990, with 9 megawatts of generating capacity in place, the government approved nine commercial projects with a total combined capacity of 28 megawatts as part of its Non-Fossil Fuel Obligation (NFFO) Program. The NFFO program implements a 1989 law requiring UK utilities to buy a portion of their power from sources that do not use fossil fuels. Additional contracts for wind energy are expected to be awarded during this decade, with an estimated capacity of 140 megawatts projected. If the proposed NFFO program is approved, the capacity could be significantly higher.

In the Netherlands, home of the traditional windmill, wind energy is making a strong comeback. The country's wind power capacity increased from 50 megawatts in 1990 to 130 megawatts in 1992. The Dutch government first introduced an incentive program for wind energy projects in 1986, expanding it during 1991. The goal of the program is to increase wind power capacity to 250 megawatts by 1995 and to 1000 megawatts by the year 2000. The government allocated over $1 billion for the ten-year program.

Although the Swedish government began sponsoring research on large horizontal-axis turbines in the mid 1970s and funded construction of two multi-megawatt machines during the 1980s, Sweden did not initiate a commercial wind energy program until the 1990s. Under a five-year program, the Swedish energy

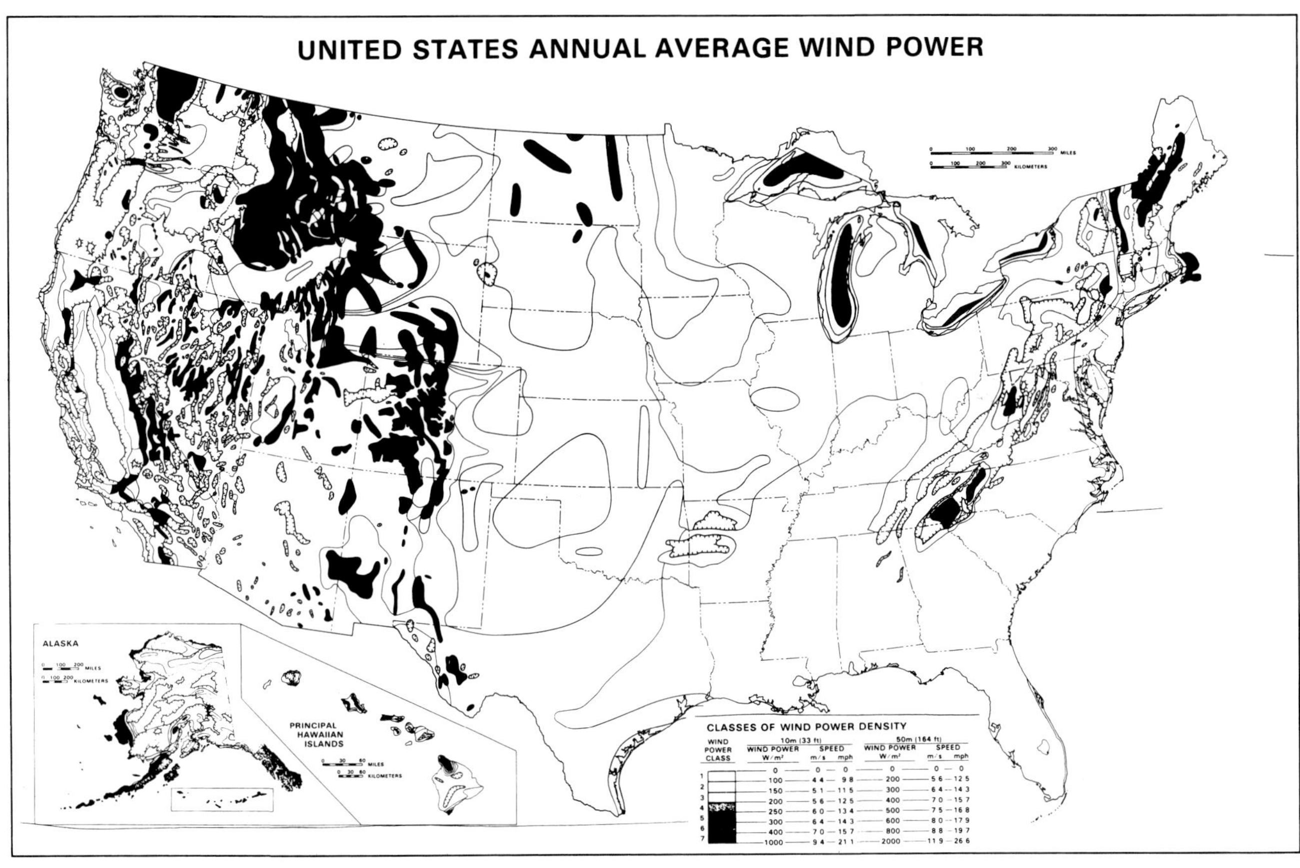


***Courtesy National Renewable Energy Laboratory, Golden, Colorado.***

ministry has allocated $10 million per year to subsidize one-quarter of the cost of turbines with capacities greater than 60 kilowatts. Some turbine manufacturers have estimated that the program could result in the installation of 125 megawatts of wind capacity by the end of the 1990s.

At the Pacific Northwest Laboratory (PNL) in Richland, Washington, researchers used data on average annual wind speed around the United States to evaluate the wind energy potential of each of the forty-eight contiguous states. Categorizing the land area into seven wind categories, they established classes of wind ranging from class 1 (winds averaging less than 12.5 mph) to class 7 (winds averaging 19.7 mph or more). Commercial wind farms have been built only in areas with class 5 or higher according to PNL. Advanced wind turbines, however, are now under development and are expected to make wind power generation in areas with class 3 winds (14 mph).

Pacific Northwest Laboratory considered several scenarios with varying land-use assumptions in calculating the total wind resources that might be developed in the United States. The scenario that they considered most realistic excluded all environmentally sensitive areas (including state and national parks, monuments, wilderness areas, preserves, and wildlife refuges), urban areas, fifty percent of forested land, thirty percent of agricultural land, and ten percent of rangeland. With these exclusions, PNL calculated that the amount of electricity that could be produced in areas with the best wind potential (class 5 or greater) is about 800 billion kilowatt-hours per year, about one quarter of the total amount of electricity used in the United States in 1990. If class 3 areas–those with "good" wind potential–are considered, the total U.S. wind energy potential is over 10 trillion kilowatt-hours per year–more than 3.5 times the nation's electricity consumption. Even though nearly all of the

**U.S. ENERGY CONSUMPTION**

| *State* | *%* |
|---|---|
| Kansas | 38 |
| South Dakota | 37 |
| Montana | 36 |
| Nebraska | 31 |
| Wyoming | 27 |
| Oklahoma | 26 |
| Minnesota | 24 |
| Iowa | 20 |
| Colorado | 17 |
| New Mexico | 16 |

***Sacramento Municipal Utility District Windplant, Montezuma Hills, California. A five-megawatt power plant comprised of seventeen Kenetech Windpower wind turbines, SMUD is the first utility-owned commercial-scale wind energy project in the United States. The turbines pictured here are rated between 300 to 405 kilowatts and operate in wind speeds of nine to sixty-five miles per hour. The plant occupies 4,100 acres in Solano County's Montezuma Hills, yet the Windplant uses less than two percent of this total acreage. While SMUD owns a portion of the land, the rest is privately owned. Sheep graze and crops are harvested in the area surrounding the turbines. SMUD has reduced system-wide $CO_2$ emission levels by 79.3 thousand tons per year, and Nox emission levels by 10 tons per year. Photo courtesy Kenetech Corporation.***

commercial wind development in the United States has taken place in California, the Great Plains and Rocky Mountain States are a much greater resource. North Dakota and Texas have the highest potential for wind energy. PNL estimated that if all the "good" (class 3 or greater) wind resources in North Dakota and Texas were developed, each of the states could generate about 43% of the total amount of electricity used in the U.S. during 1987. Additionally, says PNL, ten other states could generate over 15% of the total U.S. energy consumption.

About a decade ago, the birth of the modern wind energy industry occurred in California with the construction of the first wind farms. In the 1980s thousands of wind turbines were installed in California and wind power generation increased by 200%, from just 6 million kilowatt-hours in 1982 to over 1.2 billion kilowatt-hours by 1986. The California Wind Boom can be attributed to several factors. In the 1970s, California's dependence on fossil fuels increased dramatically and the state had extensive areas of windy, sparsely populated land that was ideal for wind power generation. One of the most important reasons for extensive wind power development, however, was generous state and federal tax credits, available to investors in the state's wind power plants during the early and mid 1980s. Together, the credits totaled 50% of the total investment. In the latter part of the 1980s, California phased out its state tax credits. Investors in California wind farms also benefited from a series of buy-back incentives that the California Public Utilities Commission (CPUC) adopted in the early 1980s. This was done in accordance with the 1978 Public Utility Regulatory Policy Act requiring that power companies buy available power from independent producers at the market rate.

The companies that survived the expiration of tax credits have substantially improved the design and performance of their wind turbines. Recent machines are less subject to breakdowns, and turbine availability–the time a machine is available to produce power–has increased from under 60% in the early 1980s to more than 95% for turbines installed after 1985. Wind turbine design and performance have also reduced costs significantly. The average cost of building and installing a wind turbine in the U.S. decreased from $3,000 per kilowatt of generating capacity in 1981 to as little as $1,000 per kilowatt by 1990. Also during this period, the average annual operating costs for wind turbines fell from $.03 to $.01 or $.015. According to Pacific Gas & Electricity, the total cost of wind-generated electricity at that utility fell from $.5 to about $.08 per kilowatt-hour in 1990. At some of the most efficient sites, the cost is below $.07 per kilowatt-hour, comparable to the cost of electricity from a new coal-fired or nuclear plant.

With the majority of wind turbines located in California, the United States remains the world leader in wind energy production. In 1991, more than 16,000 wind turbines operating in California had a total generating capacity of nearly 1,600 megawatts. Also in that year, wind farms in the state produced about 2.7 billion kilowatt-hours of electricity, enough energy to meet the residential needs of a city of about 1 million people. Three windy mountain passes in California contain most of the wind farms in California: Altamont, Tehachapi, and San Gorgonio. Turbines in the Altamont Pass region near Livermore produced 1.1 billion kilowatt-hours; Tehachapi, northeast of Los Angeles, produced 960 million kilowatt-hours; and San Gorgonio Pass near Palm Springs produced 580 million kilowatt-hours. Almost all of the remaining commercial wind power development in the United States occurred in Hawaii, with 20 megawatts of installed wind capacity in 1990. WindRiver, a joint venture between Iowa-Illinois Gas and Electric and U.S. Windpower–the world's largest wind energy company–announced an agreement to conduct assessments and begin installing wind turbines establishing at least 250 megawatts of wind energy capacity in the Midwest and Great Plain states. U.S. Windpower is also reviewing the possibility of establishing wind farms in the Pacific Northwest, the Northeast, and the Mid-Atlantic.

"Wind turbines create zero emissions, consume no fuel, and are manufactured from commonly used materials like steel and fiberglass," says a Department of Energy report published in 1990. Wind turbines operating in California reduced emissions of carbon dioxide by about 2.7 billion pounds during 1991. The use of wind energy instead of fossil fuels in that state also avoided the emission of about 16 million pounds of other pollutants like sulfur dioxide and nitrogen oxides, responsible for acid rain and smog.

The installation and operation of wind turbines does affect the environment, albeit in minor ways. At an installation site, the natural habitat may be disturbed by necessary activities such as grading the land, pouring the foundations, and building service roads. Also, the spinning blades of wind turbines can be hazardous to birds. While this has been relatively uncommon, the potential danger may prevent siting wind turbines in areas that are critical habitats for endangered or threatened species. Since turbines must be widely spaced to avoid interfering with one another's operation, the technology is considered land-intensive. About ninety-five percent of the land, however, can be used for other purposes, such as farming crops or grazing livestock. In fact, according to AWEA, farmers could earn substantial revenues by leasing wind rights for their property. Wind turbines also produce noise, an issue of particular concern when located near residential or commercial areas. However, the proper design and siting of turbines can minimize the nuisances.

The visual appearance of wind farms is probably the most controversial aspect of the technology. Some residents of communities near wind farms consider the turbines unsightly, detracting from the natural beauty of the landscape. However, as wind energy technology has improved, some long-time opponents have made peace with the industry. A poll conducted by University of California researchers found strong public support for wind energy, even in communities located relatively near large wind farms. The people surveyed were willing to accept wind farms at a closer distance to their homes than any other type of energy facility–biomass, fossil fuels, and nuclear. On average, respondents said that they would not object to a wind turbine at a distance of two to five miles from their homes.

**Chapter 4**

# *The Process: Creating Ecologically Conscious Architecture*

*The thinking that underlies the ecological paradigm is less a linear Cartesian model but rather of the mode that can be better envisioned through chaos theory or by the hologram, embodying ceaseless mutual causality and interdependence.*

—Dr. John Todd, Biologist

The practice of ecologically conscious architecture must embrace an integrated, holistic process. When designing an environmentally conscious building we share the common goal of integrating human and ecological health concerns, yet the process by which each building is created is unique. The commitment and knowledge of the design team who will guide the process; the spirit of the owners who take an active role in the environmental stewardship of their property; the site that will become home to the working and living environment and its micro, local, and regional ecologies; local materials and construction methodologies; and the fuel sources that will be used are some of the primary factors that influence the success of an ecological building. A summary of considerations reviewed in the case studies in Chapter 5 provides a technical list of the ecological issues that must be addressed in a project. Not intended to be followed merely step-by-step, the issues should be approached in an integrated manner with a clear commitment to honoring each human and environmental resource that creates the resulting architecture.

"When designers are assigned a problem, they usually consider three basic criteria: Cost, performance, and aesthetics," says architect William McDonough. "Designers and architects must also ask whether a material or system is ecologically intelligent and socially just. Can something be really beautiful if it destroys the earth or is unfair?" Answering these questions can be complicated and require highly technical knowledge. However, many of the answers are simple, demanding primarily time and a willingness to respond to common-sense concerns. Designers can answer some of the questions through their own research, such as by requesting manufacturing information from suppliers, or by outlining concientious construction methodologies for contractors. Increasingly, architects are working with environmental consultants who can familiarize them with the process of reviewing environmental criteria, saving time and bringing expert opinions to the forefront. Pei Cobb Freed, for example, brought in Croxton Collaborative to design the new headquarters of the American Association for the Advancement of Science in Washington.

Regardless of the project, it is important to keep in mind that appropriate time should be given for weighing ecological considerations. Rocky Mountain Institute's *Primer on Sustainable Building* underscores this aspect: "Sustainable design is front-loaded, the work comes at the beginning and the rewards come later. Early decisions are in many ways the most important, so allow time for conceptual thinking and thorough planning." Additional time should be allotted in the early phases of a project to provide for the integration of design and ecological considerations. Weighing ecological issues adds to the typical agenda of concerns that the architect and client must assimilate.[1]

## GETTING STARTED

### *Profile of the Architect and Project Team*

If you must make design and construction decisions regarding private or public buildings and properties, your choice of architect coupled with your responsible participation with the design team will determine the success of your project. It is important that, in addition to your understanding the professional ability of your architect, you ask, What are this architect's values toward natural and human resources? Your relationship with the architect sets the stage for your working relationship with each of the participants in your project team–be they civil, structural or mechanical engineers, landscape designers, and lighting pro-

ADVANCED GREEN BUILDER DEMONSTRATION

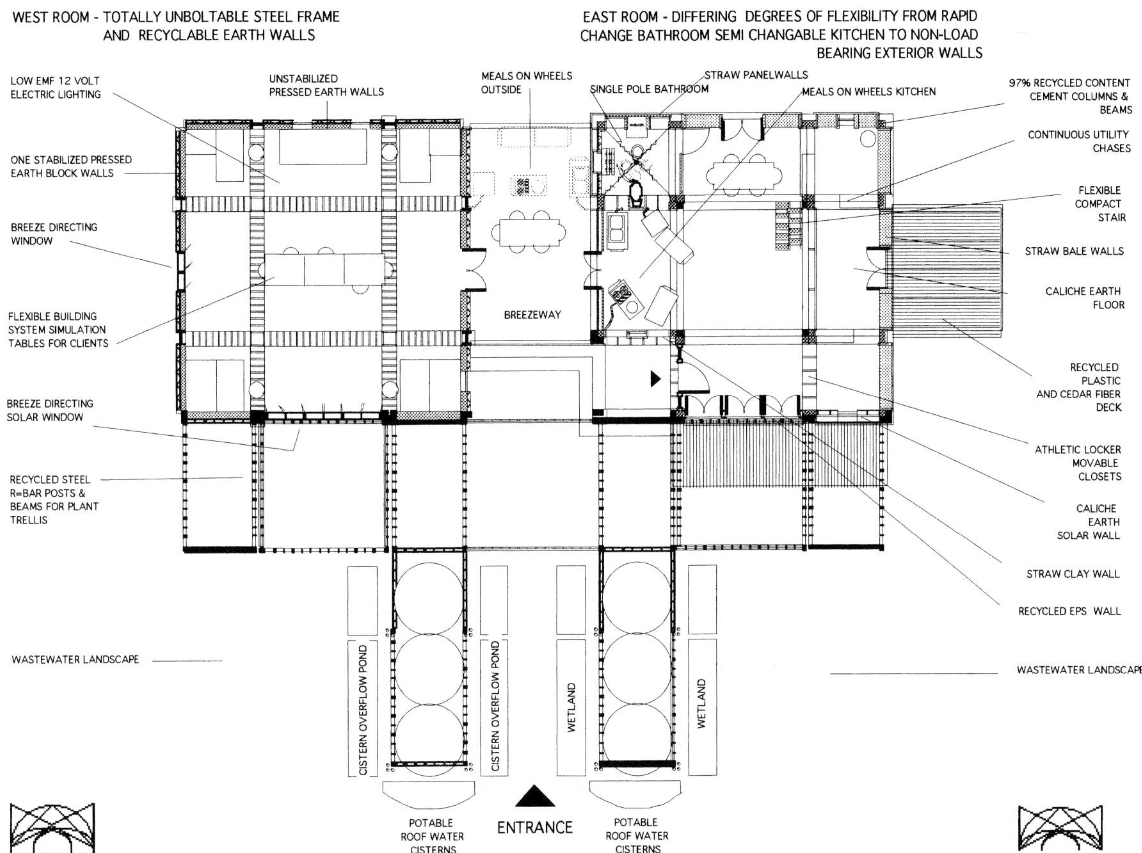

***In 1975, Pliny Fisk founded the Center for Maximum Potential Building Systems, a non-profit education, demonstration, and research organization in Austin, Texas, which he co-directs with his wife, Gail Vittori. At the Center and home of Fisk and Vittori, holism and experimentation are continuing forces that determine the features. The modular building under construction features a full array of technologies—earth walls, straw construction, recycled steel components, on-site water purification, photovoltaic energy systems—in a model of self-reliance and integration at this continuously growing facility. Drawing and photos: Pliny Fisk.***

*In 1988, the National Resources Defense Council undertook a renovation of its Manhattan office space. What resulted was the most energy efficient office in the country at that time. NRDC's project team used a combination of daylighting and energy-efficient technologies to cut energy consumption in half. As much natural light as possible is captured through skylights and windows (shown here, in the office entrance), while ribbons of glass surrounding private offices, open-ended hallways, and an open interior staircase help distribute light throughout the space. Photo: Otto Baitz/Esto, courtesy National Resources Defense Council.*

fessionals; those involved with regulatory aspects such as zoning and code compliance; or the host of contractors and sub-contractors who will physically bring the architecture into being. For the design and construction of a large institutional project, the professionals involved can number into the hundreds. If you are building a home, the number of professionals involved is much smaller, but the types of decisions are the same. Make sure your entire project team understands and commits to an environmentally conscious project and outline the parameters in writing with each. When your needs exceed those of a typical project, some consulting services may be called upon for help.

If you are an architect seeking to create an environmentally responsible building, there are a significant number of good resources that can assist you. You should be prepared to ask a great deal of questions and to do additional amounts of research regarding available materials and systems. Another choice that many architects and property owners make is to include an environmental consultant who can provide ecological research and help to guide the project in relation to ecological concerns. Your project may require the help of other specialists such as energy analysts, lighting specialists, and product consultants. An environmental consultant can help to integrate the information needed from this additional team of specialists.

### *Defining the Project*

It is important to begin with a concise description of the project and goals, both of which the architect should explore with the client. A detailed description of the project outlines its scope, and the goals reveal key ideas and elements that will call for certain design solutions. What are the future user's dreams, needs, and expectations of the project? Has a site already been selected?

Regardless of the size or type of project, choosing an appropriate site is the most important decision any owner can make. Ideally, a potential property owner will consult with environmental experts who can help to review the conditions of the site and to determine its ability to meet the needs of the owner and occupants. Taking the time to carefully review project feasibility in the context of the site can help to uncover the hidden pitfalls that inevitably come with most property, whether they involve land or existing buildings. A home, school, corporate headquarters, or an industrial park will need to meet a unique set of requirements within an ecosystem. Will a building be reused, or will a new one be built? An ecologically concerned architect will ask, Is the proposed project compatible with the site? Is new construction necessary? The spirit and success of the project depends on these basic considerations.

### *Defining Environmental Objectives*

Every project should establish a specific set of environmental objectives that reflect the environmental values the owner, architect, and consultants bring to the project. Historically, innovative individuals and organizations committed to human health and the conservation of natural resources laid the cornerstones for the research and growth of energy-efficient ecological architecture in the United States. The Rocky Mountain Institute, founded by Amory Lovins, is one such model of energy efficiency. With the founding of the New Alchemy Institute in 1969, biologist John Todd has become recognized around the world for his leadership in the restoration of pure water and creation of "Living Machines," a family of

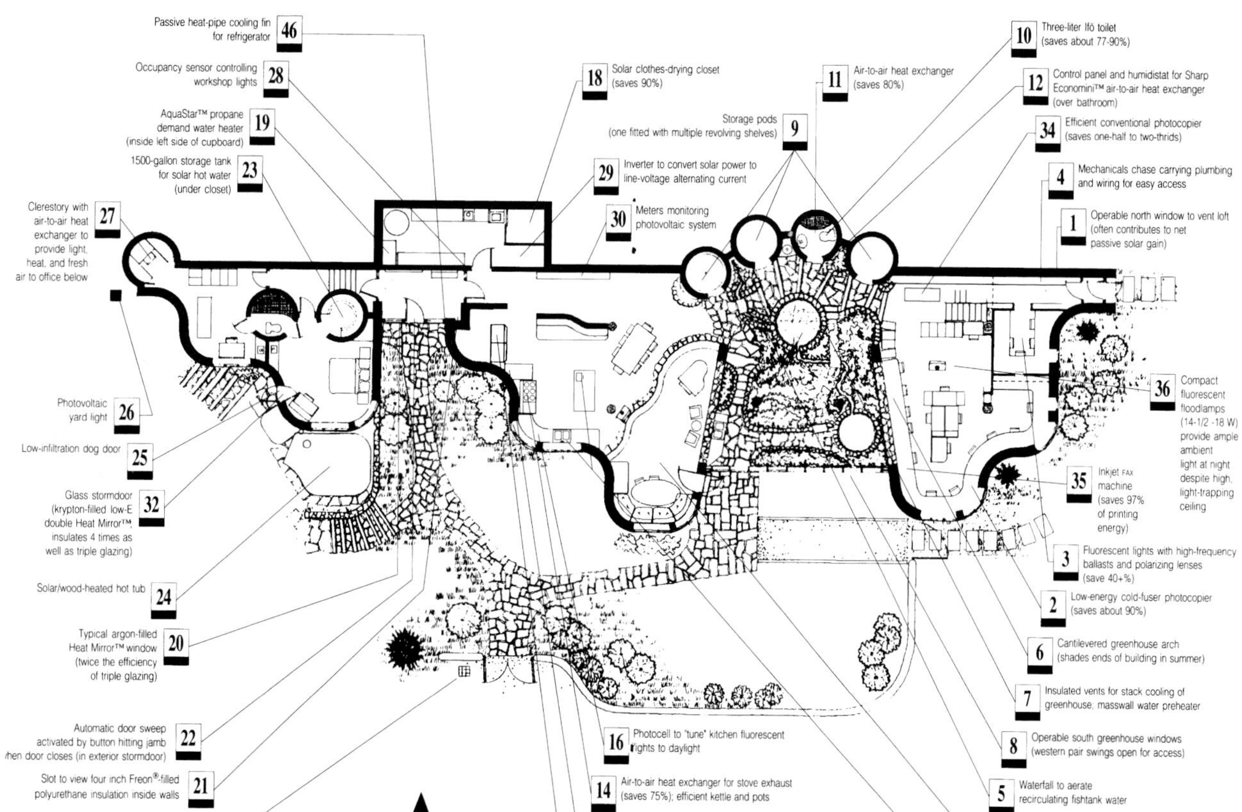


technologies for purifying wastewaters to tertiary quality effluent without chemicals. The Environmental Defense Fund, the Natural Resources Defense Council, and the National Audubon Society are examples of organizations that created landmark architectural responses to ecological agendas initiated by environmentally knowledgeable groups. Each of these individuals and groups actively established an agenda of environmental objectives in order to create a place that would embody their values.

The Hannover Principles were written by William McDonough as environmental guidelines to be integrated into the planning, design, and construction of EXPO 2000, the World's Fair in Hannover, Germany. According to the National Park Service's *Guiding Principles of Sustainable Design,* they exemplify the model of design principles necessary for environmentally conscious design. Environmental criteria established for numerous environmental and design organizations and professional practitioners, the Hannover Principles provided the basis for the "Declaration of Interdependence for a Sustainable Future," which was adopted by the World Congress of the International Union of Architects and the American Institute of Architects in June 1993 (for a more detailed review of these criteria see Chapter Two). These criteria have also been adopted by the

***The Aspen, Colorado headquarters of the Rocky Mountain Institute is a bioshelter, center for energy research, and home of Amory and Hunter Lovins. Designed by Steven Conger, AIA and the Aspen Design Group with owner-builders Amory and Hunter Lovins and completed in 1984, the 4000-square-foot building receives 99% of its heat from passive solar sources and uses a tenth of the electricity and half of the water of a conventional building. The building is open to the public as a demonstration project, and RMI provides energy consulting for building professionals, corporations, utilities and government leaders around the world. According to Lovins, the energy-saving features of RMI cost around $6000, roughly 1% of the construction cost. Savings are about $7100 in utility bills per year, and the payback was less than one year. Drawing: Rocky Mountain Institute. Photo: Robert Millman.***

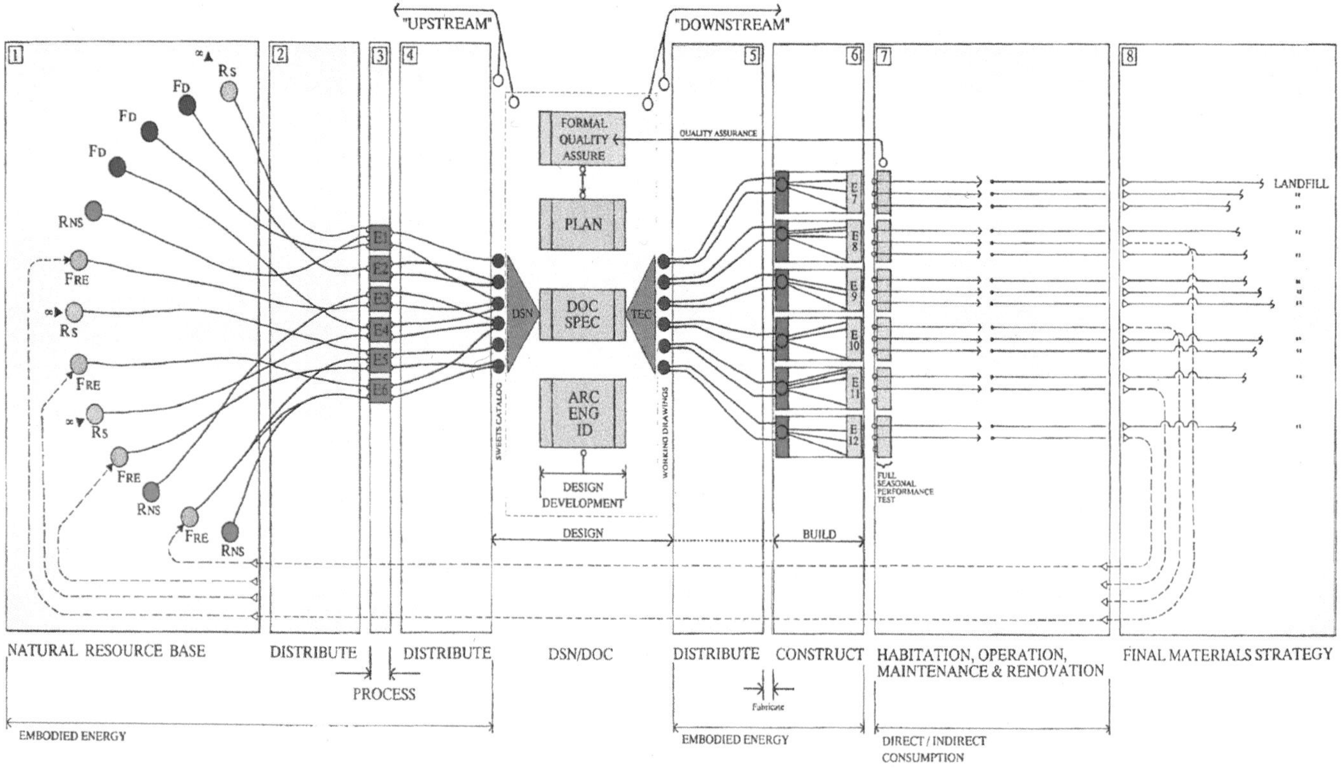


***Materials and energy life cycle chart developed by Croxton Collaborative to illustrate the full life cycle of materials and the energy use within the cycle. Numbered boxes represent (1) the process of obtaining the natural materials that make a product; (2) the distribution of those materials to factories; (3) the manufacturing of the product; (4) the dissemination of product information; (5) the distribution of products to job sites; (6) the construction process; (7) the operation of the completed building; and (8) the disposal or reuse of a material. Drawing: Croxton Collaborative, Architects.***

Interprofessional Council of Environmental Design (ICED), a coalition of architectural, landscape architectural, and engineering organizations that represent hundreds of thousands of professionals in the United States.

Detailed in *Audubon House: Building the Environmentally Responsible Energy Efficient Office* (New York: John Wiley & Sons, 1994), the National Audubon Society with Croxton Collaborative established the following environmental goals for the conservation group's headquarters:

**1. Energy Conservation and Efficiency.** Because of the known impacts of energy consumption by the built environment, energy efficiency was an obvious priority. It was also one of the simplest areas in which significant reductions could be achieved.

**2. Direct and Indirect Environmental Impacts.** This category takes into account impacts associated not only with energy use, such as air and water pollution, but also those associated with the manufacture and use of building products, materials, and systems. Whenever possible, vendors were asked to provide detailed information on manufacturing processes, composition and content of materials, and factory location and conditions so that upstream and downstream impacts could be assessed and minimized.

**3. Indoor Air Quality.** The health and well-being of Audubon House and its occupants were of utmost importance, and the Audubon team set out to create the healthiest and most comfortable offices possible within the other constraints of the project. This goal has both environmental and humanistic dimensions; indoor air quality is the clearly identifiable environmental consequence of a building's construction and operation, and it enhances employee satisfaction and productivity.

**4. Resource Conservation and Recycling.** Whenever feasible, the Audubon team sought to minimize the use of natural resources in general, and of virgin natural resources in particular, by purchasing materials made with recycled content. In certain instances, however, the selection of natural materials was more appropriate. For example, Audubon used the opportunity to encourage sustainable management of forests by selecting sustainably grown rainforest wood. The carpeting that was selected is 100% wool with no dyes. Synthetic carpeting would have involved a more energy-intensive manufacturing process, and the dyes involved were highly polluting. Of equal, if not greater concern was the final disposition of materials–the question of solid waste. Audubon addressed this concern with the installation and implementation of an advanced building recycling system.

**5. The Economic Imperative.** In order to create a project at market rate, Audubon developed a set of financial criteria to parallel the economic ones. Systems and products needed to be economically justified. In other words, the initial cost and premium cost of environmentally appropriate materials versus standard materials warranted serious consideration. Durability and longevity were also taken into account, and aspects such as maintenance records, rebates (if any), cost of installation, and anticipated payback were discussed. The most important guideline, applied to the energy-related systems, was the payback period, for which the Audubon team established a maximum time of five years. This requirement eliminated the choice of a solar photovoltaic (PV) system because it would take more than ten years to pay for itself. However, the team did leave the option open for installing this type of system when the technology becomes more affordable.

## *Design Solutions*

What are the fundamental aspects of the project? What simple solutions can be applied? Architecture that is designed to be in harmony with its surroundings and climate, that uses regional materials, responds to the needs of its occupants, and is built for lasting endurance results in the best possible investment of natural and human resources. For instance, the use of the sun as a source of heat and natural light and the earth as a cooling mechanism enhances the health of the natural environment and the community, the spirit of the architecture, the well-being of its inhabitants, and reduces energy costs. When architect William McDonough was approached by St. John the Divine–the largest cathedral in North America, located in New York City–with the problem of heating the enormous gothic space, he responded, "The building is not a living thing and does not need to be warmed. The challenge is to heat the people, not the cathedral." This approach results in the kind of simple, elegant, and cost efficient solution that is the most important aspect of ecologically conscious design. Although these simple approaches make sense, the majority of homes, office buildings, shopping malls, and industrial parks built in the United States after World War II fail to incorporate them.

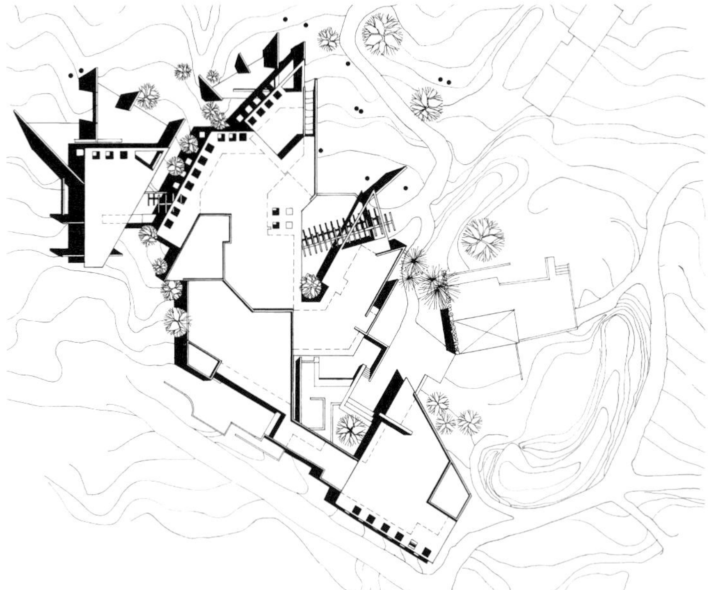

***Arizona Sonora Desert Museum. Architects Line and Space, recognized by the receipt of one of six awards given nationally for environmentally conscious architecture by the AIA/ACSA, designed this museum to to explore the use of tempered microclimates, salvaged materials, and water reuse. The building provides shade, responds to vegetation, and fits appropriately into the terrain. Stone, which makes up much of the building, was salvaged from a nearby elementary school. Graywater is recirculated to flush toilets, and rain is collected for irrigation and used as a source for fountains. Photo and drawing: Henry Tom.***

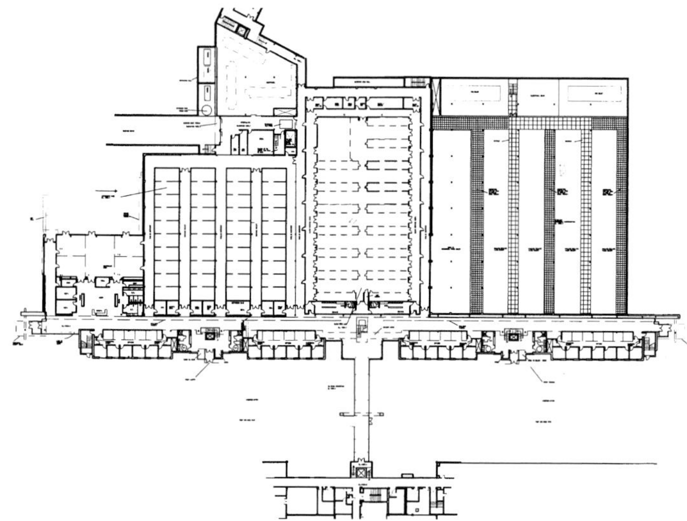

***National Institute of Standards and Technology, Boulder, Colorado (proposed). Architects Henningson, Durham, and Richardson, based in Virginia, and Omaha, Nebraska, were challenged to create the most environmentally stable laboratory in the world, integrating EPA Green Building Standards to the maximum extent possible. Unique features at the NIST Laboratory include temperature control to ±0.01° Celsius, vibration control, high quality clean power, future upgrade capability, and state-of-the-art monitoring equipment. Photo and drawing: NIST Boulder.***

## WORKING METHODS

### *Construction Methodologies*

Beyond the design, specifications, and drawings, the same commitment to environmentally conscious construction is required to ensure that the spirit of the project is carried out. In fact, one needs to be very watchful at this stage. The contractor, as part of the project team, must understand and commit to an ecologically sustainable agenda. In order to make sure this happens, include the additional criteria in the specifications. Working with a contractor who is experienced regarding ecological concerns is optimal, but it may not always be possible. Some will need to be educated regarding these concerns, so be prepared to work collaboratively.

You will also need to establish a protocol for testing, methods, and options. This means that procedures for testing materials and systems, new methodologies, or any need to reconsider choices, be outlined in advance. Protect the natural features and vegetation of the site during the construction process by designating access routes, parking, staging, storage, and work areas. Provide a physical buffer such as a temporary fence between these areas and those that need to be protected. After designing the site to work within the parameters of the surrounding features, make sure that this is carried out. As little vegetation as possible should be cleared. Heavy equipment should be kept to a minimum, and it should always utilize designated access routes. Also designate areas for separation and recycling of materials at the job site, making sure that watershed areas are carefully handled. Many states require prevention of siltation, stream pollution, and loss of topsoil, so be sure you're informed about the laws in your area.

Keep in mind that the materials you have specified should be readily available. Requests for substitutions are common during construction. Before agreeing to any substitutions, be sure that they are absolutely necessary and that they meet the environmental and energy efficiency criteria. The quality of the construction will affect the performance of the building, particularly regarding energy efficiency. For example, make sure insulation is properly installed and that system specifications are carefully followed.

### *Computer Modeling*

The design of energy-efficient buildings depends increasingly on highly sophisticated computer technology which can provide extremely accurate estimates of energy needs and use by simulating real options under varying conditions. The Audubon team incorporated DOE-2, an early model that was developed by the Department of Energy and the Electric Power Research Institute of California, to demonstrate how cost-effective, energy-saving design could perform far beyond code. Run in combination with readily available software extensions, DOE-2 helped the design team calculate the varying conditions of fundamental building components, such as thermal envelope and insulation, the mechanical and electrical systems, and the lighting loads with an array of energy-related factors such as building site and orientation, weather patterns, daylight, glazing, and reflectance of interior surfaces.[6]

Since the development of DOE-2, many other upgraded variations have become available. For further information about computer modeling, see the case studies in Chapter Five. Since new computer software is regularly becoming available, check with publications and organizations such as the AIA, who are working to make updated information available.

## ENVIRONMENTAL ECONOMICS

One of the most significant aspects of the growth of ecology-conscious architecture in this decade in the United States is that it has been developed in such a way that it pays for itself, even in the short run. In Europe, where fuel is traditionally three times more costly than in the United States, a high level of performance has attracted economic incentives like government programs, research, and development of new technologies for many years. In the United States, efforts toward ecological design have been hard fought, requiring unique and individual pioneering successes. The compelling aspects of environmentally conscious buildings that began in the individual research, not-for-profit, and educational sectors have, in the 1990s, produced substantial economic results, causing those in the for-profit sector to pay heed to environmental concerns. Environmentally conscious building design has entered the mainstream of American business because it is profitable, productive, and positive for everyone concerned.

While environmentally conscious buildings require closer analysis to design and build, they cost about the same as conventional ones. Their improved comfort, performance, and aesthetics result in lower operating costs and higher sales prices and rents. Energy-efficient architecture is less expensive to heat, cool, and light, reduces pollution, and provides a healthier environment for its occupants. In the residential housing market, buyers prefer and pay a premium for green homes. According to the *Primer on Sustainable Building,* "Homes in the nation's oldest green neighborhood, the Village Homes in Davis, California, now command $11 more per square foot than nearby homes. Homes in a green development in Sacramento sell for $15,000 more than homes in adjoining subdivisions built by the same developers and builders."

For landlords, reduced water and energy costs allow for a larger profit margin or more competitive leasing. The typical savings of $1 per square foot can provide significant leveraging since brokers can compete for 10 cents per square foot. Business owners have discovered that people like to buy environmentally responsive products and shop in stores built with consideration for natural resources. At Wal-Mart's experimental Eco-Mart, a substantial increase in sales has been reported in the store's daylit sections. NMB, a bank in the Netherlands, attributes its rise to second

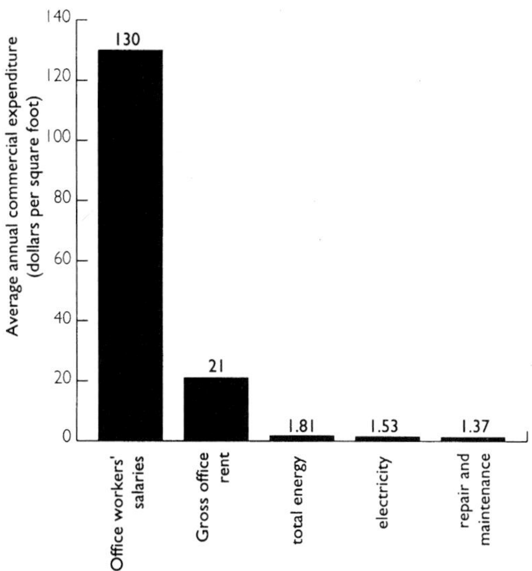


***Copyright 1991, Building Owners and Managers Association (BOMA) International. Reproduced with permission of BOMA International.***

largest bank in that country to a new corporate headquarters, an energy-efficient ecological building complete with indoor waterfalls.

According to a report by Bill Browning of the Rocky Mountain Institute, "A 50% reduction in energy use is relatively easy to achieve, and 80% to 90% is possible with good design." The initial savings to the owner are significant, but the long-term savings in terms of environmental cost are much greater. According to the report, "Reducing an average home's energy use by 80% will reduce its $CO_2$ emissions by nearly 90,000 pounds over its lifetime. Reducing water use by 30% would avoid the creation of more than 4 million gallons of wasterwater during the same period."

A home or building that is less expensive to operate is also more affordable, resulting in increased opportunities for home and business owners. "Many lenders are required to consider protected utility costs as a factor in mortgage qualification. Energy Rated Homes of America, for example, provides ratings that mortgage issuers, including FHA and VA, can use to write energy-efficient mortgages."

"For an employer, the strongest reason to build green has to do with worker productivity. This single argument is so dramatic that it alone is compelling," says the Rocky Mountain Institute's *Primer on Sustainable Building.* "Recent studies illustrate that making a building environmentally responsive can increase worker productivity by 6% to 15% or more." Employers spend an average annual cost of $130 per square foot on salaries, about 70 times more than on utility bills. The increase in productivity reduces the payback period of a green building dramatically. Since

Americans spend 80% of their time indoors, sick building sydrome reflects the highest human cost of non-ecological buildings. According to a study by the EPA, over $1 billion dollars per year is lost in productivity due to building related illness. This figure does not even reflect medical costs, or the cost of long-term health hazards that remain unregulated.

### *Life Cycle Cost*

Since environmentally conscious design often calls for products and systems with a higher price tag than conventional ones, life cycle costing provides the underlying and long-term economic incentives that make ecological projects feasible. The Departments of Health, Education, and Welfare summarized life cycle analysis as the systematic consideration of cost, time, and quality. Life Cycle Costing (LCC) is a fundamental aspect that is necessary in the design of environmentally conscious buildings, total quality management (TQM), and value engineering (VE).

Federal and state institutional building owners have issued mandatory directives to professionals who design their facilities. The National Energy Conservation Policy Act, passed in 1978, requires that all new federal buildings be life cycle cost-effective as determined by LCC methods prescribed in the legislation. The federal government's General Services Division Administration (GSA) has developed elaborate procedures for predicting a facility's total life cycle cost, and cities such as Atlanta, Chicago, and Phoenix require extensive LCC analyses from their designers. In 1977, the AIA issued a formal set of guidelines for architects and engineering consultants. These guidelines present a method for computing the present worth and uniform annual cost for total building costs and recommend techniques for integrating the results into the building process. Regarding mechanical systems and energy performance, a vast number of analysis programs that incorporate long-term economic models are being utilized. The Trane Company developed the first such program, called the TRACE program, which will forecast consumption for alternative fuels applied to various building systems and generate cost estimates for initial investment, utilities, and annual owning expenditures. For further information about LCC, a number of publications and organizations offer detailed guidelines. You can check with your professional organization or review *Life Cycle Costing for Design Professionals,* Second Edition, published by McGraw Hill in 1995.

### *Grants and Rebates*

A vital aspect of environmentally conscious design is that there are readily available funds from a variety of sources to help offset the costs of implementing energy efficient technologies. The National Audubon Society received significant grants to help offset the costs of its energy studies. Through the Energy Plan Act of 1992, millions of dollars in funds were set aside to assist with the construction of federal buildings that are environmentally conscious. The National Institute of Standards and Technology (NIST) is in the process of implementing a ten-year renovation program for its campuses in Gaithersburg, Maryland, and Boulder, Colorado. Part of that program includes the design and construction of new advanced laboratories at both locations, and NIST developed a set of Green Buildings Criteria to be used in guiding this project.[2]

Utility rebates, more easily available than large-scale grants, can provide another source of income to help offset the costs of energy efficient technologies. Local utilities can provide technical assistance in carrying out energy strategies for both commercial and residential owners through lighting technologies, energy efficient appliances, and other systems. The Environmental Protection Agency's Green Lights Program provides technical assistance and continuing newsletters regarding energy efficient lighting strategies. Check with your municipality, which may also offer incentives for resource conservation programs. New York City, for instance, offers cash incentives to landlords who upgrade energy performance and water conservation in their buildings. All over the U.S. and Canada, cities are developing incentive programs to carry out environmentally conscious objectives, modeling their innovative programs after those in places like Austin, Texas. The city of Austin initiated a home energy rating program in 1985 called the Austin Energy Star, designed to give marketing assistance to builders who produced energy efficient homes that exceeded the minimum requirements of the newly adopted CityEnergy Code. The Green Builder program was implemented in the same city through a grant awarded in 1990 from the Urban Consortium Energy Task Force for the purpose of developing a "Sustainable Systems Rating Program." Early development assistance was received from the city's Center for Maximum Potential Building Systems. Austin now funds the entire program, which has established Greening City Construction Guidelines, educational outreach and economic development, a Sustainable Building Sourcebook, and a Demonstration Project Program.

## SITE SELECTION AND DESIGN

The considerations involved in choosing a site underlie every other design decision that will be made in the creation of an ecological building. Ideally, the site

**Life-Cycle Costing Estimate**
General Purpose Work Sheet

**Study Title:** Building Layout
**Discount Rate:** 10% **Date:**
**Economic Life:** 25 years (constant dollars)

| | | | Alternative 1 Describe: sketch | | Alternative 2 Describe: sketch | | Alternative 3 Describe: sketch | | Alternative 4 Describe: | |
|---|---|---|---|---|---|---|---|---|---|---|
| | | | Estimated Costs | Present Worth | Estimated Costs | Present Worth | Estimated Costs | Present Worth | Estimated Costs | Present Worth |
| **Initial/Collateral Costs** | | | | | | | | | | |
| A. Structural | | | 10.74/sf | $472,600 | 9.30/sf | $409,200 | 10.74/sf | $472,600 | | |
| B. Architectural | | | 16.10/sf | 708,400 | 15.20/sf | 668,800 | 15.26/sf | 671,400 | | |
| C. Mechanical | | | 12.40/sf | 545,600 | 12.02/sf | 528,900 | 12.40/sf | 545,600 | | |
| D. Electrical | | | 6.50/sf | 286,000 | 6.50/sf | 286,000 | 6.50/sf | 286,000 | | |
| E. Equipment | | | 0.25/sf | 11,000 | 0.25/sf | 11,000 | 0.25/sf | 11,000 | | |
| F. General Conditions | | | 6.82/sf | 300,000 | 6.42/sf | 282,500 | 6.70/sf | 292,800 | | |
| G. Site | | | 9.00/sf | 396,000 | 8.80/sf | 387,200 | 9.00/sf | 396,000 | | |
| **Total Initial/Collateral Costs** | | | | 2,719,600 | | 2,573,600 | | 2,677,400 | | |
| **Replacement/Salvage (Single Expenditure)** | **Year** | **PW Factor** | | | | | | | | |
| A. Carpeting/Interiors | 8 | 0.466 | 177,100 | 82,500 | 167,200 | 77,900 | 167,900 | 78,200 | | |
| B. Lighting System | 10 | 0.385 | 50,600 | 19,500 | 50,600 | 19,500 | 50,600 | 19,500 | | |
| C. HVAC System | 12 | 0.319 | 193,000 | 61,600 | 184,800 | 58,900 | 193,000 | 61,600 | | |
| D. Carpeting/Interiors | 16 | 0.218 | 177,100 | 38,600 | 167,200 | 36,400 | 167,900 | 36,600 | | |
| E. Lighting | 20 | 0.149 | 50,600 | 7,500 | 50,600 | 7,500 | 50,600 | 7,500 | | |
| F. Roofing | 20 | 0.149 | 58,500 | 8,700 | 63,100 | 9,400 | 58,500 | 8,700 | | |
| G. | | | | | | | | | | |
| H. | | | | | | | | | | |
| Salvage (Resale Value) | 25 | 0.092 | | N/C | | N/C | | N/C | | |
| **Total Replacement/Salvage Costs** | | | | 218,400 | | 209,600 | | 212,100 | | |
| **Annual Costs** | **Diff. Escal. Rate** | **PWA W/Escal.** | | | | | | | | |
| A. Energy-Elect. (computer, etc.) | 1% | 9.894 | 71,500 | 707,400 | 69,000 | 682,700 | 68,000 | 672,800 | | |
| B. Energy-Nat. Gas (heat) | 2% | 10.819 | 15,000 | 162,300 | 13,000 | 140,600 | 13,500 | 146,100 | | |
| C. Maint.-Custodial | 0% | 9.077 | 35,000 | 317,700 | 30,000 | 272,300 | 33,000 | 299,500 | | |
| D. Maint.-Architectural | 0% | 9.077 | 11,000 | 99,800 | 10,500 | 95,300 | 11,000 | 99,800 | | |
| E. Maint.-Mechanical | 0% | 9.077 | 15,400 | 139,800 | 14,500 | 131,600 | 15,000 | 136,200 | | |
| F. Maint.-Electrical | 0% | 9.077 | 8,800 | 79,900 | 8,800 | 79,900 | 8,800 | 79,900 | | |
| G. Maint.-Site | 0% | 9.077 | 4,400 | 39,900 | 4,200 | 38,100 | 4,400 | 39,900 | | |
| **Total Annual Costs** | | | | 1,546,800 | | 1,440,500 | | 1,474,200 | | |
| **LCC: Total Present-Worth Life-Cycle Costs** | | | | 4,484,800 | | 4,223,700 | | 4,363,700 | | |
| **LCC: Life-Cycle Present-Worth Dollar Savings** | | | | — | | 261,100 | | 121,100 | | |

PW – Present Worth PWA – Present Worth Of Annuity (1) Note: Staffing, Insurance, Taxes, etc. are the same for all schemes.

*Reprinted with permission from McGraw-Hill Companies, Life Cycle Costing for Design Professionals by Dr. Stephen J. Kirk and Alphonse J. Dell'Isola, 1995.*

should have clean, uncontaminated water, air, and soil; have access to solar or other renewable power sources; be accessible to public transportation and located near community services; and incorporate the use of existing roads and utilities. Of course, the site should be developed without harm to the environment, with the intent to provide an existing structure for reuse, renovation, or restoration.

Meeting all of these criteria may not be realistic, however. Most importantly, will the proposed project enhance and protect the natural resources it utilizes? The following checklist, from Rocky Mountain Institute's *Primer on Sustainable Building,* provides some helpful guidelines for site selection. Some of the questions will be difficult to answer.

• Is the land suitable for development? First ask, Should anything be developed here? Can the site be developed without damaging the environment?

• Are there better uses for the site? Is the proposed use appropriate? Is it suitable, for example, to convert productive farmland into multiple dwellings or commercial buildings?

• Does the land have cultural, historical, and/or archaeological significance? Does it have a desirable sense of place? How can these qualities be maintained?

• What are the site's natural values? What wildlife, plants, or habitats exist there? Are wetlands present? If degradation by former activity has occurred, can it be restored? If the property is over 5 acres, mapping the area can help to preserve significant areas.

• Is redevelopment possible? Generally, the redevelopment of an urban or suburban site will cause less damage than bulldozing virgin property. An existing infrastructure of roads, utilities, and potential mass transit make a good case for redevelopment.

• Can existing structures be restored, repaired, or renovated? If not, can the materials be salvaged?

•Are clean air, water, and soil present? Has the site been contaminated by past agricultural, industrial, or urban pollution? Do nearby highways, airports, or industrial sites create undesirable sounds and smells? Be sure to test the soil and drinking water before buying.

•Does the site have access to enough sunlight for the building to be powered by the sun? What is the relationship of the site to the climate? How much solar light and heat are available? If electrical access is more than one-quarter of a mile away, can the property rely on renewable resources for ample power?

•Are mass transit, roads, highways, and other transportation options nearby? The answer can have tremendous economic and environmental impacts. Are bike paths available? How far are schools, shopping, the fire station, airport, and hospital?

•What is the topography, geology, and hydrology of the land? How steep is the slope? What happens to run-off? Are soils strong and stable enough to build on? If a septic system is necessary, what's the percolation rate? Is radon a problem? What about flooding or wildfire?

•Are strong electromagnetic fields (EMF) present? Studies of electromagnetic fields remain the subject of great debate. It is a good idea to avoid building within 100 yards of power transmission lines, electrical transformers, and radio, television, or microwave installations.

•How might future development on adjacent lands affect your project? This question can be difficult to answer, but you should try to get as much information as possible, because the quality of surrounding properties will affect yours. Additionally, future development of adjacent lands can affect your quality of water and air, add to pollution and noise, and affect your access to transportation or solar gain.

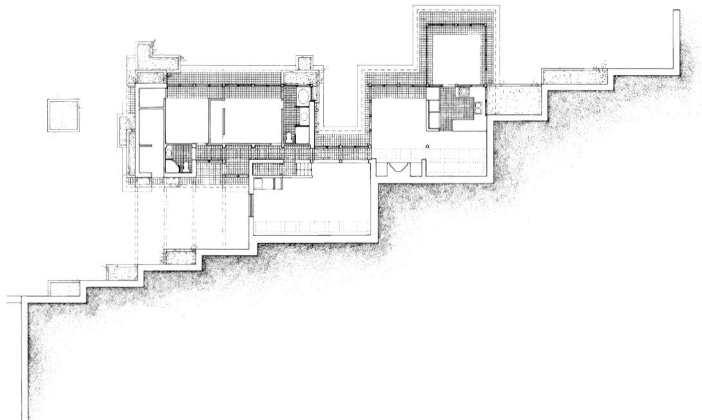

***Moore Residence, Connecticut. Before deciding what kind of house they wanted and where it should be built, the Moores camped out at their property in Northern Connecticut in a small tool shop with a wood-burning stove and propane burner. Architect Alfredo DeVido, designer of passive solar houses for more than twenty years, designed the residence to fit tucked into a knoll. The single story post-and-beam structure is supported by oak timbers that were cut from the site and allowed to weather for a year. Concrete supporting walls are clad in stone, hand-selected by Moore from local fences built two centuries ago. The highly insulated grass roof made up of layers of plywood, absorbent clay panels, gravel, and earth weighs as much as 250 pounds per square foot. The 2,200-square-foot house is arranged along a 60-foot east-west corridor that separates living spaces from garage, entry court, and studio. The central spine is daylit and ventilated by operable skylights. In all, 33 skylights were included, with an entirely glass southern facade facing a pond and and its surrounding clearing in the woods. Heating is provided by a conventional oil-burning forced air system with a radiant heat system that warms the slate floor, and insulation from the earth helps to reduce fuel use. No air conditioning was installed, and according to Moore it is not needed. Photo: Norman McGrath. Drawing: Alfredo de Vido Associates, New York.***

Before embarking on a new project and selecting a site, a potential property owner will gain the most benefit by working with an ecologically conscious architect who can help in the decision making before the final selection and purchase are made. In a case where the site is predetermined, asking each of these questions in the context of the existing site will help to elicit a conscientious ecological response.

Ecological site design seeks to enhance and protect the natural resources and biodiversity of the land. It is a process that requires an inevitable intervention with the environment, but also seeks to respect cultural and historical aspects to the greatest degree. The environmentally conscious approach to site design must take into account a myriad of concerns and address them from initial conception, through assessment and inventory, to detailed design and specific construction processes. In addition to an ecological architect, the latter may require the consulting services of other professionals such as ecologically responsive civil engineers and landscape architects.

The following factors should be considered in the site selection and design process:

**Climate.** Specific climate characteristics should be considered in order to locate facilities for maximum

*Oceanside Water Pollution Control Plant, San Francisco. Designed by Simon Martin-Vegue Winkelstein Moris, Architect (SMWM) with civil engineering firm CH2M for the San Francisco Department of Public Works, the plant combines ecological design criteria for a fragile environment with the presence of potential hazards. The sewage treatment facility, located at the western edge of the Golden Gate National Recreational Area, shares land with the San Francisco Zoo and abuts the National Guard Armory. It is built two-thirds underground, surrounds a man-made canyon, and is concealed from view by a berm. SMWM configured the facility to minimize the footprint, burying a series of innovative egg-shaped anaerobic digestors that take the place of conventional oderous procedures. The roof is designed to carry the weight of drainage rock, ground cover, and trees, plus a 300-pound per square foot live load to accommodate large zoo animals that will run across it. Photo: Jane Lidz.*

human comfort and protection of the site resources and building facilities. The cooling effects, as well as the potential velocity and directions of prevailing winds, should be carefully reviewed. Also integrated into the site design should be the heating, lighting, and power generating ability of the sun, along with its aesthetic affects. What is the annual rainfall, and can it be captured and drained in ways that will protect the soil? Is it a source for primary use–drinking, bathing, and cooking–which can then be recirculated for secondary use–flushing toilets and landscape watering?

**Topography.** In many areas flatland is set aside for agricultural use, leaving primarily sloped lands on which to build. If handled properly, sloped topography can provide visual and sound separation. Protecting the vegetation and soil from erosion are primary concerns; the greater the slope, the faster the land will erode. Reducing the size of the building footprint, eliminating automobiles and parking, keeping soil disturbance to a minimum, elevating walkways, and using point footings for structures are all appropriate ways of protecting the site. Integrating the existing geology of the site will also help to maintain its character and protect both the soil and vegetation. Avoid construction in low-lying flood plain areas or on unstable soils, taking protective measures to address adjacent water ecosystems and habitats.

**Vegetation.** To secure the integrity of a site, it is important to retain as much native vegetation as possible. Sensitive native plant species need to be identified and protected. Existing vegetation should be maintained to encourage biodiversity and to protect the nutrients held in the green canopy. Vegetation is significant because it protects wildlife habitats, nutrients, and soils; enhances visual beauty; offers acoustic and visual privacy; provides a primary source of shade; and, in some cases, provides opportunities for food production or other sustainable products. Protection and restoration of native planting is the fundamental purpose of environmentally conscious design.

**Wildlife.** Sensitive habitat areas should be avoided. By maintaining as much habitat as possible, nearby wildlife is encouraged to remain close to human activity. Creating artificial habitats or feeding wildlife can have disruptive effects on the natural ecosystem.

**Capacity and Density.** Every site has a carrying capacity for development and human activity. A detailed site analysis should determine this capacity based on the sensitivity of site resources and the land's ability to regenerate. The siting of facilities should also carefully weigh the merits of concentration versus dispersal. Natural landscape may be easier to maintain if facilities are carefully dispersed. Conversely, concentration of structures leaves more undisturbed natural areas.

**Visual Character.** Natural vistas should be incorporated wherever possible. Avoid creating onsite intrusions such as road cuts and utilities. By working with the topography, locating small foot-print structures within existing vegetation, and working with the slope of the land, the visual character will reflect the natural and historic character.The existing landscape can be protected by coordinating construction methods and access around it, saving millions of dollars in landscaping costs.

**Natural Hazards.** Sustainable habitats should be located with consideration for natural hazards such as precipitous topography, dangerous plants, animals, or water.The site layout should allow for controlled access to any dangerous areas.

**Cultural Context.** Local archeology, history, and people provide a context into which sustainable design should fit to enhance the potential success of site development. Siting should be compatible with traditional activities such as fishing or agriculture.

**Energy and Utilities.** In any habitat there is the need for systems that provide running water, power, and sanitary waste management. Early in the planning process, identify systems that will work within the parameters of climate, topography, and natural resources of the site. Noise from mechanical equipment and treatment odors should be minimized and mitigated by location and buffering. Stabilizing soils, natural vegetation, and capturing runoff in depressions are ways of regulating storm drainage in a revitalizing manner. Night lighting should be designed to enhance the features of the site and dramatize the nighttime sky. Keep fixtures close to the ground to minimize glare and obstructions to the site and building.

***Arizona Biltmore Hotel, Phoenix, Albert Chase McArthur, 1929. The Arizona Biltmore embodies the spirit of its desert surroundings, perhaps due in large part to McArthur's behind-the-scenes collaborator, Frank Lloyd Wright. Wright's most distinctive contribution to his former apprentice's building was the plain and patterned, pre-cast concrete blocks that form the hotel's most striking component. The rectangular, steel-reinforced blocks were molded on site from Arizona earth and sand, and are decorated with a bas-relief evocative of Aztec and Mayan motifs. The blocks are hollow in the center and arranged back-to-back, thereby providing good insulation and allowing for the inner and outer walls to be constructed simultaneously. Photo courtesy Arizona Biltmore.***

**Site Access.** Access to the site for the purpose of construction, especially for large equipment, should be limited as much as possible to protect the existing vegetation and soils. Material staging and storage, as well as vehicular access and temporary power, must be considered prior to construction.

**Assessing Existing Toxins.** Assess any potential toxins so that they may be addressed as needed.Avoid locating occupied spaces within 100 yards of any power transformers or major connections.Test soil, water, and air for lead, radon, asbestos, and mercury. In existing structures, lead and asbestos must be encapsulated or removed as appropriate.The presence of radon requires appropriate mitigation techniques.

## ENERGY CONSERVATION AND EFFICIENCY

The conservation of energy is one of the most significant aspects of ecology-conscious design."More than 60% of all electricity used and more than 30% of all energy consumed in the United States is used in buildings," says Rocky Mountain Institute's *Primer on Sustainable Design.* According to another study by Croxton Collaborative and physicist Francesco Tubiello, 54% of the energy in the United States is consumed by the built environment.The average American family spends $1500 a year on household energy.At a commercial level, a typical business spends $36,000 a year to operate a 20,000-square-foot facility.The greatest expenses are not immediately apparent–environmental costs such as acid rain, global warming, and oil spills.

Regardless of the type of building, much energy is usually wasted due to less than ideal choices made in design, orientation, insulation and glazing. Even greater waste results from poor choices in heating and cooling systems, appliances, water heaters, and lighting. Designing an energy efficient building that uses fewer fossil fuels makes sense from any point of

view. It saves energy and money, reduces air pollution, helps to protect wildlife, and improves indoor air quality and occupant health. A building that incorporates renewable resource systems such as solar or wind power provides maximum energy efficiency and optimal environmental and human health.

The savings in electricity are staggering. The average power plant is 33% efficient, meaning that saving one unit of electricity means saving three units of fuel at the source. Installing a single compact flourescent lamp can keep a power plant from emitting three quarters of a ton of $CO_2$ and fifteen pounds of $SO_2$, compounds which create acid rain. It also saves \$30 to \$50 worth of energy, and helps to defer hundreds of dollars worth of utility investments in new power plants.

At the beginning of the planning process, a goal should be established to avoid energy-intensive or unnecessary operations. By integrating such features as natural daylighting, passive heating and cooling, and natural ventilation, the quality of the indoor environment is distinctly improved and the energy requirements of a building are drastically reduced. In addition to reviewing the building design and systems, energy conservation can be achieved in numerous creative ways. Food service can contribute to energy conservation by emphasizing fresh, locally available items that limit the amount of energy required for transportation and the production of packaging. Some companies discourage the use of automobiles by locating their businesses within convenient walking distance, providing nearby access to mass transit systems, or putting carpooling incentives in place. To encourage their staff to ride bicycles to work, The Natural Resource Defense Council Headquarters installed indoor bicycle parking in their New York headquarters.

Key to the conservation effort is the design of the building envelope or shell–its walls, doors, windows, and roof–for maximum thermal performance. A well designed building envelope will yield huge energy

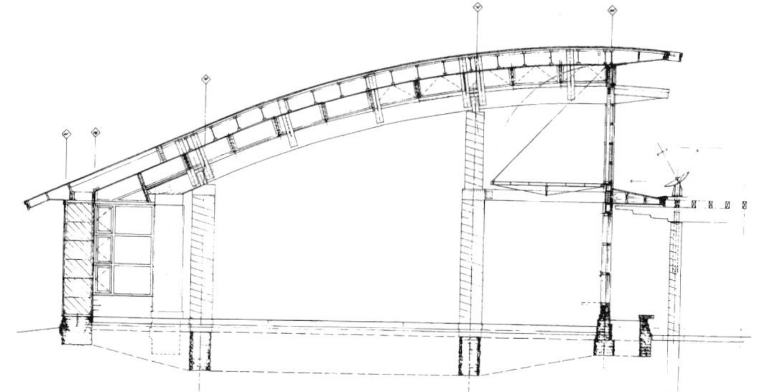

***Real Goods Solar Living Center, Hopland, California, Ecological Design Group, Architects. Real Goods, a leading distributor of products that provide self-sufficiency and energy conservation, asked architects Sim Van der Ryn and David Arkin, Adam Jackaway, and Bruce King to design a showroom that embodied its principles. The 4600-square-foot Solar Living Center features photovoltaic and wind-generated energy. Straw bale construction not only limits straw bale burning that typically emits more than a million tons of $CO_2$ per year, but provides an insulating value of R-65, about three times that of a typical framed wall. Glue-laminated beams of sustainably harvested Douglas fir were cut, milled, and manufactured within 40 miles of the site. The center is a teaching and demonstration facility for the mechanics of renewable resource design. Photo and drawing: David Arkin, Architect.***

savings for its owners. "Each year in the United States, about \$13 billion worth of energy in the form of heated or cooled air–or \$150 per household–escapes through cracks and holes in buildings," according to the American Council for an Energy Efficient Economy. Heat transfer through the building shell occurs in three ways: conduction, infiltration, and radiation. The components of the envelope should be designed to work together as a system to minimize conduction losses and the infiltration of hot air in the summer, and the radiation of heated air in the winter. These systems will vary in the context of diverse climates.

## *Insulation*

Insulation plays an important role in the energy performance of a building. Superinsulation–insulation that maximizes thermal resistance–is cost-effective in

***Top:** Wall cavity is created with screen, then air krete® insulation is pumped through the screening. This is done after all wiring and electrical outlets, plumbing, and ductwork are in place. Existing walls can be insulated by simply making an opening and inserting the application hose down to the bottom of the wall cavity. As the cavity is filled, the hose is withdrawn. Air krete® is free of CFCs, formaldehyde, asbestos, and other carcinogenic fibers; provides a high R-value that remains consistent over time; is inorganic and non-hazardous as waste; and also functions as an effective firestopper and sound barrier. Photo courtesy Palmer Industries, Frederick, Maryland.*

***Bottom:** The Underground Gallery, Cape Cod, Massachusetts. Both sites have been designed and occupied by visionary architect, Malcolm Wells, who has been creating "underground" designs of houses, office buildings, bridges, factories, airports, and entire cities since 1964. Photo courtesy Malcolm Wells, Brewster, Massachusetts.*

many parts of the country in lowering winter heat loss and summer cooling loads. Insulation's efficiency is determined by its R-value, which is the measure of thermal resistance or opposition of material and air spaces to the flow of heat by conduction, convection, and radiation. Architects and builders are familiar with the R-values required by code in their regions, but these requirements should be considered only the bare minimum. California's Title 24 requirements–the toughest in the country–are the guidelines to exceed in order for a building to be truly energy efficient. The payback for optimal insulation will most often justify the additional costs. Indoor air quality and resource use should be closely reviewed in conjunction with insulation. Make sure to investigate the material content of your insulation options, as the manufacture and installation of foam insulations commonly involves the use of CFCs or HCFC's, both of which should be avoided. Some other types of foam insulation offgas formaldehyde or contain harmful chemicals. Fiberglass contains small particles that can cause respiratory irritation when released into the air. Many environmentally conscious designers are specifying air krete®, a cement-like foam which is made of magnesium compounds extracted from seawater and mixed with dolomite and other minerals. It is blown in as a wet foam, and therefore can only be used in vertical applications such as walls, and not in horizontal roof applications. The Audubon Society Headquarters was one of the first commercial scale applications of air krete®.

The ability of porous materials to "breathe" provides a natural insulation process that enhances the building envelope's performance in a temperate climate, as well as its indoor air quality. In addition to lower embodied energy output (particularly for transport of materials) and the reinforcement of local economy, local materials typically incorporated into regional architecture provide time-tested methods of natural insulation. Clay, tile, stone, lumber, and plaster each achieve certain insulation and temperature-lag values that should be incorporated whenever possible.

The earth-integrated building incorporates the natural abilities of surrounding soil and grass to help moderate interior temperature. An earth-covered building will have a stable year round interior temperature as compared with a typical surface-built structure. The soil slows the passage of heat gained or lost to such an extent that it creates a time lag, known as the "thermal flywheel effect," that lasts from 15 to 24 weeks. The heat gained in the summer will reach the building in the winter, thereby creating effective passive heating. Conversely, the cooling effects of the winter climate will impact the building in early summer, resulting in significant passive cooling.

### *Glazing*

In addition to their daylighting and ventilation properties, windows, doors, and skylights are crucial components of the thermal envelope in a building. Advances in window technology in the past decade allow for maximum levels of energy performance, and the higher up-front costs produce impressively short payback periods. Yet even today, twice as much energy is lost through U.S. windows each year as flows through the Trans-Alaska pipeline, according to the *Primer on Sustainable Building.* In 1992, available glazing technology provided R-values 2.2 times greater than standard insulating glass, which has an R-value of 1.83. More recent models achieve R-values of 8 and higher.

"Superwindows"–double or triple-paned windows filled with argon or krypton gas and containing a nearly invisible low-emissivity coating–reflect the most dramatic improvement in window technology. The high insulating values and maximum light transmittance of superwindows offer R-values of 4.5 to almost 12. Superwindows are offered by most window manufacturers and come in varying models appropriate for diverse climates. The new windows also block noise and protect interior finishes from ultraviolet damage. Although they cost 15% to 50% more than standard windows, superwindows save huge amounts of heating and cooling energy, resulting in immediate paybacks by allowing for the downsizing of air conditioning and heating systems in buildings. Also, many utility companies offer rebates to encourage their customers to install high-performance glazings.

The location and design of windows in a building must balance, in addition to their thermal qualities, a number of important factors that include passive systems, light, ventilation, views, and psychological comfort. Heat gain, emissivity, and transmittance of varying degrees can be specified for north-, south-, east-, and west-facing windows. This flexibility captures the ability to accommodate all design opportunities without sacrificing thermal qualities. Computer modeling is often used to assist in the selection of appropriate R-values for different exposures.

The option of individually operable windows in commercial buildings should be thoughtfully considered. In addition to lending a higher degree of psychological control to the occupants in a space, the use of operable windows provides natural ventilation. Open windows, however, can also cause problems which need to be taken into account. Air pollution, dirt, insects, and odors can enter a space; humidity can damage sensitive equipment; noise can be bothersome; security might be compromised; and there can be substantial heating and cooling loss. In some cases, operable vents can provide a less expensive and more desirable design solution than a window. The appropriate use of fixed windows, operable windows, and vents should be integrated with the design and function of each space.

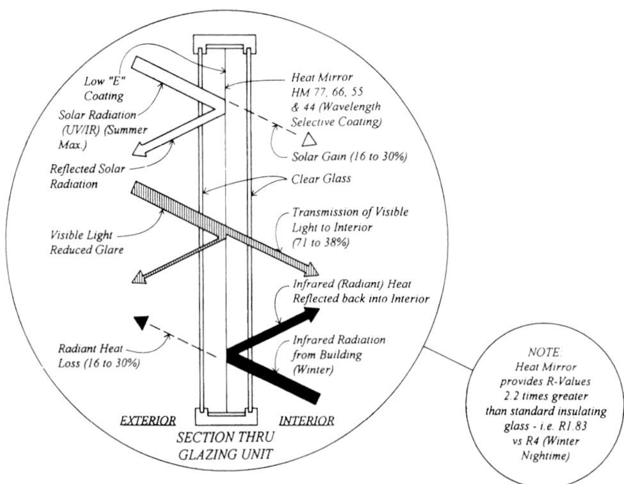


***Heat Mirror technology windows and skylight glazing at Audubon House achieve an R-value of 3.7. Heat Mirror includes a low-emissivity (low-E) wavelength selective coated film that is sandwiched between two panes of glass. It deflects most of the sun's radiant heat outward, keeping the interior cool in summer, and deflects convector radiant heat inward, conserving heat in winter. Diagram courtesy Croxton Collaborative Architects.***

## HEATING, COOLING, AND VENTILATION SYSTEMS

People in the United States spend $25 billion dollars per year to stay cool. In Houston in 1982, residents spent $3.3 billion for cold air, more than the gross national product of 42 African nations combined. Almost 80% of new homes in America are air conditioned, more than any other country in the world. Since fossil fuels are, on average, readily available and inexpensive in the United States, heating and cooling systems have been typically overused and, most often, oversized.

After achieving the best possible integration of climate and site with passive methodologies and optimal building insulation, the next step is to find the most ecologically sound mechanical system that can provide appropriate comfort to the occupants. First, the available fuel sources should be carefully reviewed. What are the long-term ecological, health, and economic consequences of each available option? After looking at scientific evidence, publications like the *Environmental Resource Guide* can provide some necessary information. You may wish to work with an environmental consultant to help answer this question, as all the factors must be weighed in relation to

***West Bend Mutual Insurance Company, West Bend, Wisconsin. The 150,000-square-foot headquarters, winner of the 1992 Intellex Building for Excellence Award, was designed by the Zimmerman Design Group of Wauwatosa, Wisconsin. One of the most significant features of the building is the individualization of air temperature controls through the installation of Personal Environment Modules (PEMs), or Environmentally Responsive Workstations (ERWs), designed by Johnson Controls in Milwaukee. By using slide controls located on a panel at their desks, occupants can individually control temperature and airflow within their own spaces through vents and radiant heaters, which are built into the workstations. In an open office design, the PEMs also provide direct control of task lighting and white noise. A motion sensor turns off the system within the space if the occupant leaves, and turns it on again when he or she returns. Photo: Johnson Controls.***

the specific site conditions. Working with specialized environmental consultants, energy analysts, and mechanical engineers will require additional up-front costs but will enable you to review long-term considerations realistically, resulting in the highest quality, best environmental and economic results.

Can this building be entirely self-sufficient and deliver extra power to the grid? If so, it can provide a service to your community by setting an environmental precedent and contributing a valuable resource. Federal law requires that your utility company purchase power provided by you at a market rate, so economic incentives can also be substantial. Should the building be entirely self-sufficient and off-the-grid? When a utility connection requires a new hook-up at a distance of over 3000 feet, depending on area power costs and quantity of available sunlight, independent photovoltaic power can be cost-competitive, according to the International Solar Energy Society.

How can renewable fuels such as the sun or wind provide necessary power for the building? Computer modeling is often used to help determine the potential design, operation, and cost of solar-powered systems. If renewable fuel sources are not currently feasible, try to make allowances at the time of construction for their potential use in in the future. If fossil fuels must be used, which one is least damaging to the natural environment, and which is most efficient? The environmental and socio-economic impacts of oil–such as embodied energy and potential for environmental devastation in mining, refinining, and transport–are huge. If you are working with an existing oil-fired system in a large facility, a number of difficult decisions will need to be made. As a property owner, you can review a long-term analysis and plan to eventually remove it–with the proper dismantling and material recycling–to install a more efficient system. As an architect, you should assist your client in making a long-term assessment.

During the renovation of the National Audubon Society's 97,000-square-foot New York headquarters, Croxton Collaborative and the Audubon team made the decision to dismantle, recycle, and remove a non-operational oil-fired system and to install a gas-fired heating system. For heating, electricity may be acceptable where electrical requirements and power costs are lower, such as in the south. However, where winters are colder and power is expensive, such as the northeastern United States, electric heat is highly inefficient. There are valid arguments for and against wood as a heat source. Properly harvested wood is a sustainable resource, however burning wood creates air pollution and is sometimes harmful to indoor air quality. Older wood stoves emit significantly greater amounts of particulates than new ones. Wood stoves are sometimes appropriate to provide back-up heat in a home. If you are considering a wood stove, it should be correctly sized and meet Environmental Protection Agency regulations. Furnaces and boilers can operate on natural gas, oil, propane, or coal. Of these, available natural gas, a by-product of petroleum, is the cheapest, cleanest, and most efficient fuel choice. Another fuel alternative is pellet heating technology. Wood pellets, made from wood by-products reclaimed from saw mills and manufacturing plants, burn cleanly and economically, keeping airborne emissions to a minimum and requiring less frequent stove cleaning. Some furnaces today are even equipped to burn shelled corn, which produces from 9,000 to 10,000 BTU per pound.

For cooling, good passive design, insulation, and appropriate system sizing will result in the most efficient systems. Buildings that are earth sheltered, if only in part, gain the benefit of a fairly consistent exterior temperature, which helps to maintain a regulated indoor temperature naturally. Reducing undesirable heat gain can save half to three-fourths of the amount of cooling that would be otherwise required. Natural ventilation, fans, evaporative coolers, and dehumidifiers can also increase the quality and comfort level of the indoor climate. Automated controls and timers can save energy by reducing and increasing cooling during times that a space is unoccupied. Proper zoning, and flexible systems that provide individual occupants with a desired temperature, are all features that add to energy savings. Appropriate interior finishes and furnishings such as window treatments can increase comfort levels and reduce cooling requirements. When mechanical cooling is necessary, try to specify a system that has no ozone depleting chemicals such as CFC or HCFC.

Ventilation has historically provided good quality indoor climate under temperate conditions, with sensitive passive design and use of building materials. The natural diffusion of air through porous materials such as brick, stone, lumber, and plaster creates a breathing "skin" that that can add to air exchange and help to absorb moisture. Passive ventilation incorporates this use of skin which allows air and moisture to pass very slowly through the pores by diffusion. This process filters the air of dust, reducing pollutants and excess moisture. The fresh air inside rises by convection, permeating through the building and either filtering out through the roof and walls or through a roof vent. This Baubiologie principle regulates indoor air quality, humidity, and electrical balance, dilutes and expels pollutants, and works without any powered systems. It is, however, increasingly difficult to achieve because of the trend toward airtight construction with increased insulation and nonporous materials. How air ventilation and energy use are balanced will depend to a large extent on climatic conditions.

Where a controlled indoor climate is necessary, design for the natural flow of air must integrate many facets. As buildings have become sealed for energy efficiency, to prevent warm or cool air loss, air-to-air heat exchangers are increasingly being used in energy efficient buildings. As much as 80% of the temperature differential between incoming and exhaust air can be recovered while preserving air quality. Heat exchange systems can be installed in individual rooms or entire buildings. Newly built low-energy homes in Scandinavia and North America are now typically installing whole-house mechanical ventilation. Active whole-house ventilation systems use air ducting along with the heating system. This type of system delivers fresh, filtered, warm air at floor level to each room and extracts it from ceiling level, while removing moisture, odors, and pollutants. To prevent high concentrations of smoke and oil from accumulating in the system, kitchens are usually ventilated separately. Heat exchangers are used to provide adequate ventilation while maintaining energy efficiency.

***Environmental Education Pavilion, Baltimore, Maryland. RTKL Associates designed an environmental learning center overlooking the Baltimore Harbor where children from the area can learn about the Chesapeake Bay. The $950,000 complex includes a classroom, library, kitchen, gallery, office space, a ship's chandlery, and a 65-foot-tall observation tower, and is constructed of timber framing, wood sheathing, and local stone. The pavilion is oriented to capture sea breezes, and includes a windmill and solar cells to generate electric power and superinsulation. Passive cooling is achieved through ceiling fans, operable windows, and from breezes off of the harbor. Photo and drawing: RTKL Associates.***

## LIGHTING

The illumination of buildings is responsible for 20% of electricity consumption in the United States. Lighting is also the easiest place to make the biggest impact on cutting energy consumption. Currently, new lighting options can cost-effectively save more than half of the energy used in buildings in the United States. Compact fluorescent lamps, solid-state electronic ballasts, imaging specular reflectors, and "smart" light bulbs with built-in controls are just some of the options available. Interior paint colors and finish textures also affect the quality of interior light. White finishes will reflect the maximum amount of light, while soft-textured surfaces will help to reduce glare. Technological advances, utility-sponsored incentives, the Green Lights Program implemented by the Environmental Protection Agency, and product requirements put in place by EPACT legislation in 1992 are some of the catalysts that are changing the lighting industry and drastically reducing the quantity of electrical consumption from lighting.[3]

### *Daylighting*

The first step toward environmentally conscious lighting is the careful consideration of opportunities for natural lighting. Daylighting should be incorporated wherever possible as it will increase the quality of the indoor environment and reduce lighting loads. People have a biological need to see natural daylight. Deprived of it, building occupants are unaware of outside weather conditions or time of day and can subsequently become disoriented, possibly developing strong negative physical and emotional side effects. An analysis of site, climate, fenestration, reflected light, and occupant needs should be closely reviewed. Diffused natural light utilized with pale reflecting materials and supporting systems will result in an optimal lighting design. Photosensoring devices can be used to detect natural light levels, then trigger appropriate levels of supplemental artiificial lighting.

| COLOR | % |
|---|---|
| White | 80 |
| Ivory (light) | 71 |
| Apricot beige | 66 |
| Lemon yellow | 65 |
| Ivory (dark) | 59 |
| Light buff | 56 |
| Peach | 53 |
| Salmon | 53 |
| Pale apple green | 51 |
| Pale blue | 51 |
| Medium gray | 43 |
| Light green | 41 |
| Deep rose | 12 |
| Dark green | 9 |
| Black | 1 |

***Approximate reflectance of paint colors. Reprinted from Eco-Interiors: A Guide to Environmentally Conscious Interior Design, Grayzna Pilatowicz, John Wiley & Sons, 1995.***

### *Artificial Lighting*

The main requirement of lighting is to provide appropriate light to perform a specific task within a given area. Artificial systems should supplement daylight and provide needed light under changing or nighttime conditions. Appropriate application is the most important aspect of energy efficient lighting systems. Typically, good lighting design will include ambient lighting for general background definition, task lighting for individual work, and accent lighting to feature certain areas or objects. Because of continuously changing conditions and the individual needs of occupants, lighting must also be flexible. While New York state energy conservation guidelines call for electric systems to operate at a maximum of 2.4 watts per square foot, some installations have achieved comfortable lighting levels with 1 watt per square foot.

Numerous technical features will enhance energy savings in lighting. Separate circuiting and switching should be provided for different tasks and zones. Light controls should be easily accessible so that occupants can readily make lighting adjustments. Occupancy sensors, dimming, stepped switching, programmable controls, and energy-efficient lamps are recognized for energy credit or rebates with most local utilities, resulting in higher efficiency and lower costs. A review of costs should address initial installation labor and operating costs.

The standard A lamp incandescent bulb is the cheapest lamp to buy and the most expensive to operate. An incandescent bulb uses ten percent of electrical energy to create light, while the other ninety percent creates heat. In the design of a commercial installation, the cost payback of using energy efficient lamps is immediate by resulting in the significant downsizing of cooling system requirements. The multiplier effect refers to the fact that the use of inefficient bulbs not only wastes energy in use, but requires an increased replacement of each lamp, thereby exponentially increasing the amount of energy required in the manufacture of each bulb. Replacing just one of these lamps with a compact fluorescent bulb will save 45 watts of electricity and 157.5 Kwh per year, and prevent the release into the atmosphere of 300 pounds of $CO_2$, 1.4 pounds of $SO_2$, and .8 pounds of $NO_2$ per year.

Energy efficient lamps are now available in a large enough variety of colors and light renditions that they can create equal or better lighting design effects than almost all incandescent lighting. Compact fluorescent lamps (CFLs), which typically use one quarter as much electricity and last ten times longer than incandescents, are dimmable and available in many sizes, shapes, and wattages. CFLs that plug into electronic ballasts–a two-piece fixture–will cost more initially than one-piece CFLs.The CFL in combination with the ballast will last four to seven times longer, and is more energy- and cost-efficient.They can be purchased from most lighting manufacturers.

The tubular fluorescent lamps that are typically used in commercial installations vary greatly in efficiency.The former T-12s use more energy than the new T-8s, which are much more efficient, accurate, and pleasant in color. Continuous dimming electronic ballasts will double or triple the savings of these fixtures.

Halogen lamps are an efficient type of incandescent lighting that provides energy savings for point source illumination. High intensity discharge lamps (HIDs)–a type of halogen lamp–can have a higher efficiency than fluorescent lighting and a life span of 24,000 hours. HIDs were typically used for exterior lighting because of their limited color properties, but are now being used more frequently in indoor applications because of their color improvements.The three main types of HID lamps are mercury, high pressure sodium, and metal halide.

It is important to understand the hazardous waste that is generated in lamp disposal. Even in miniscule amounts, mercury can be highly toxic. Released both as vapor and dust when lamps containing the substance are broken, mercury pollutes the air and water and becomes concentrated in the food chain. Rain can wash the dust into streams and groundwater, spreading it through the environment. Even though the typical amount of mercury in lamps has been reduced by 40% from 1985 to 1995, it remains a concern because its disposal is not uniformly regulated.The EPA has proposed two options for end-users, whom they refer to as generators, for the disposal of fluorescent and HID lamps containing mercury:

Option 1. Referred to as the conditional exclusion. Allows for the disposal of an unlimited number of lamps, if they go to an EPA-approved MSW and the generator keeps record for at least three years of where the lamps were sent.

Option 2. Known as the universal waste option. Would exempt generators of up to 350 lamps per month, but would require others to send lamps to a hazardous waste site or recycler, and to comply with relaxed version of the Resource Conservation and Recovery Act.[7]

"Of the 500 million discarded each year, 60 to 70

***International Institute for Energy Conservation, Washington, D.C., Burt Hill Kosar Rittelmann Associates. The IIEC achieved a 50% reduction in energy costs in their 8,000-square-foot offices primarily through lighting design. Daylighting and artificial lighting made up of T-8 fluorescents, dimming controls, and occupancy sensors combine to achieve a high quality of lighting with a power budget of .8 watts per square foot, among the highest efficiency for lighting design. Photo: Victoria Cooper. Drawing: Burt Hill Kosar Rittelman Associates.***

percent would be covered, affecting 42,000 to 64,000 facilities," says Lindsay Audin, Energy Manager for Columbia University.

The specification of energy efficient lighting reduces mercury waste in several ways. Since the life of energy efficient lamps is longer, fewer lamps result in less mercury. Creating the power for a lamp releases more mercury than is contained in the lamp itself, since much of the power used to create the lamps comes from burning coal which contains mercury. Reducing the number of lamps cuts the need for power generation that releases mercury, as well as the mercury waste from disposed lamps. Lighting efficiency programs, such as the EPA's Green Lights

Program, raise a concern that large amounts of obsolete lamps will be dumped, resulting in a drastic increase of mercury waste. Some states have initiated their own mercury-control efforts, requiring lamps to be placed in hazardous waste landfills designed to contain contaminated run-off. Existing rules allow many lamps to be discarded in the 14 percent of U.S. waste that is burned, creating airborne mercury emissions. Essentially, all of the mercury is reduced during incineration. By 1994, 36 states had approved municipal solid waste plans that addressed mercury run-off. The EPA has concluded that lamp disposal should be handled under its Resource Conservation and Recovery Act. In the meantime, building owners should find out if their local municipal solid waste (MSW) landfill follows an EPA-approved plan. If not, it should be encouraged by contacting your city and state representatives.

## ELECTRICAL EQUIPMENT AND APPLIANCES

Equipment and appliances should be as efficient as possible. In 1987, Congress passed the National Appliance Energy Conservation Act to set minimum efficiency criteria for HVAC systems and a wide range of appliances. When specifying appliances it is important to determine which will be the most effective for a specific use. For example, ceiling fans use little energy and can increase the cooling ability of air conditioning by increasing air flow and creating a "wind chill" effect. A 75° setting can feel like 70°, consequently reducing cooling loads. Conversely, a slow reverse-running fan in winter will prevent warm air from escaping through the ceiling by moving it down into a room.

Less than ten years ago, commercial office equipment wasn't acknowledged as a particular end-use of electricity. Today, it accounts for 30 billion kilowatt-hours per year–a jarring 5% of electricity in the commercial sector–and is expected to grow to 10% by the year 2000. Office equipment is becoming increasingly more energy-efficient, a technical trend which has been encouraged by the EPA's Energy Star Program. Many leading manufacturers are building machines according to the Energy Star criteria without increasing costs or sacrificing performance. Computer equipment which meets energy efficiency standards carries the Energy Star, and includes features such as automatic sleep when the item is not in use.

Additionally, the creative application of equipment such as computers, telephone automation systems, PC networks, and copiers reduces space requirements and increases efficiency by limiting the need for paper flow or personal meetings. For example, the increase of features such as "e-mail" is reducing the use of paper for interoffice communication, and teleconferencing can often effectively reduce the need for meetings. Both features save energy and money, particularly where long distances are involved.

Before specifying or purchasing any electrical equipment or appliances, look for their energy efficiency ratings and estimated annual operating costs. By federal law, every manufacturer has to make this information available to consumers, who will find it printed on black and yellow labels found on every appliance. A helpful publication, *The Consumer Guide to Home Energy Savings,* is updated each year and can be found in most bookstores. It lists specific manufacturer products and indicates their energy efficiency. The embodied energy used to manufacture appliances and the impact to the environment from their disposal should be taken into consideration as well during the selection process. The purchase of long-lasting, high-quality appliances will result in the best conservation of energy. The use of programmable timers or sensors on some equipment can also save energy without decreasing occupant comfort. In these cases day and night operation is controlled by a photocell. In a large-scale installation, sophisticated building automation systems result in considerable energy savings.

After space heating and cooling, water heaters are the biggest energy drain in a typical home. An electric water heater costs twice as much to operate as a gas-fired water heater. Having improved since the 1970s, solar water heaters are another option for saving energy and cutting down on pollution. In larger buildings, cogeneration–the transfer of waste heat from air conditioning or refrigeration condensers–can save huge amounts of energy. Cogeneration can be cost effective for any commercial building that uses large amounts of hot water such as manufacturers, laundry facilities, health clubs, hospitals, or restaurants. According to Rocky Mountain Institute's *Primer on Sustainable Building,* Kaiser Hospital spent $90,000 to install seven cogeneration units in three hospitals, resulting in a savings of about $30,000 annually. The Paradise Hill Convalescent Home in San Diego saves $3,500 per month thanks to cogeneration. In businesses with electric and water bills exceeding $1000 per month, cogeneration warrants serious consideration. The typical payback period is three years.

## INDOOR ECOLOGY

According to a study conducted by the EPA, "Poor indoor air ecology costs tens of billions of dollars

# Indoor pollutants and toxins

| Substance | Biological effects |
|---|---|
| **GASES** | |
| **Ozone ($O_3$)** Unstable, poisonous gas with penetrating odour; protects the earth from dangerous UV radiation. Also generated by photocopiers; exposure of polluted air to UV radiation; appliances with brush-type motors. | **$O_3$** Decays rapidly into oxygen, but even small amounts are serious irritants to eyes, nose, throat, and respiratory tract. |
| **Radon (Rn)** Colourless, odourless, practically inert gas, present in certain geological areas. A serious contaminant which is carried into the home via dust, water, natural gas, and some building materials. | **Radon** inhalation damages lung tissues and long-term exposure is linked with cancer. |
| **COMBUSTION GASES** | |
| **Carbon monoxide (CO)** Colourless, odourless, poisonous gas from incomplete combustion in gas flames, wood, coal and tobacco smoke, vehicle exhausts. | **CO** reduces absorption levels of oxygen, causing headaches, dizziness, nausea and loss of appetite. Those with heart, lung, and circulation disorders are most susceptible. |
| **Nitric oxide (NO) and Nitrogen dioxide ($NO_2$)** Strong-smelling toxic gases from incomplete combustion of gas flames via cookers and boilers. | **$NO_2$** is the most toxic of the nitrogen oxides, affecting the respiratory system. |
| **Sulphur dioxide ($SO_2$)** Pungent gas present in coal and wood smoke, and emitted by paraffin (kerosene) heaters. $SO_2$ was once responsible for urban smogs: now it produces acid rain. | **$SO_2$** rarely occurs at dangerous levels but it can exacerbate breathing difficulties. |
| **Carbon dioxide ($CO_2$)** Colourless, odourless gas. A combustion product of bottled gas heaters. It is responsible for stale and stuffy air in poorly ventilated rooms. | **$CO_2$** Continuous exposure may affect the central nervous system and slow down reactions. |
| **VOLATILE ORGANIC COMPOUNDS (VOCs)** | |
| **Formaldehyde (HCHO)** Binder and preservative with a pungent odour. At room temperatures, toxic vapours are released that contaminate the air. Widely used as a bonding agent and adhesive in timber and plastic products; a preservative in paper products, carpeting, furnishings; a finish for clothing and bed linen. Occurs in combustion byproducts from cooking and heating appliances, as well as in tobacco smoke. Urea-formaldehyde foam insulation (UFFI) foam used prior to mid 1970s is particularly hazardous. | **Formaldehyde** is a potent irritant to skin, eyes, nose, and throat with accompanying headache, dizziness, nausea, and breathing difficulties. It may cause nosebleeds. Suspected carcinogen. Chronic exposure to UFFI vapours causes depression and triggers chemical sensitivity. |
| **Organochlorines** Compounds of hydrocarbons and chlorine, which form the basis of many synthetic chemicals. Found in vaporous cleaners, air fresheners, polishes. Organochlorines are the most toxic and persistent of VOCs. They include **polychlorinated biphenyls (PCBs)**, known carcinogens; **polyvinyl chloride (PVC)**, a plastic that can offgas into stored food; **chloroform** and **chloramines**, both toxic gases. **Chloramines** are released when household bleach and ammonia-based cleaners are mixed together. Other hazardous VOCs include ammonia, turpentine, and acetone in cleaners and solvents; naphthalene in moth balls; chlorine in bleach. | Pungent vapours from **volatile organic compounds** are serious irritants to skin, eyes and lungs; they cause headaches and nausea and damage the central nervous system. All are potentially carcinogenic. **Organochlorine** vapours in solvents, pesticides, and cleaning fluids irritate skin, cause depression and headaches, and may damage liver and kidneys. **Chloramine** can be deadly. |
| **Phenols** or carbolic acids are caustic contaminants found in disinfectants, resins, plastics, and tobacco smoke. Phenolic synthetic resins in hard plastic, paints, coatings, and varnish contain formaldehyde. Never inhale **pentachlorophenol** found in wood preservatives and fungicides. | **Phenols** are corrosive to the skin and damage the respiratory system. |
| **PARTICLES** | |
| **Asbestos** Naturally occurring hazardous fibre mined from calcium magnesium silicate, used in insulation and fire-proofing. Banned in many countries. | Airborne **asbestos** fibres are a serious health risk causing asbestosis and cancers. |
| **Microorganisms** present in dust include disease-carrying bacteria and viruses, plus moulds, spores, and pollen. | **Microorganisms** spread infections and diseases. They also cause allergies. |
| **Metals** Trace elements from lead, cadmium, mercury, aluminium, and copper can be absorbed and accumulate to toxic levels in the body. Lead is present in old water pipes, exhaust fumes; lead and cadmium in paint; mercury in tinned tuna; aluminium is absorbed into food from cookware. | **Lead** and **cadmium** can damage brain and nerve tissues. **Cadmium** can also affect vision. Toxic levels of metals in the body give rise to headaches and breathing troubles. |

***Reprinted from The Natural House Book, David Pearson, Simon & Schuster.***

each year in productivity losses, employee sick leave, and medical costs." However, the highest costs of poor indoor air ecology are long-term health problems and death. Legionnaire's Disease, caused by bacteria growing in poorly maintained HVAC systems, has proved fatal, as well as carbon monoxide poisoning, which takes the lives of at least 500 people per year. As a society who spend most of its time indoors, the quality of indoor ecology is of critical import. More than 50 million people in North America work in offices, spending 90 percent of their time indoors. The air inside a sealed energy-efficient office building often has ten times more pollutants than outdoor air. Sick Building Syndrome, which exists in buildings where at least 20 percent of the occupants experience symptoms of headaches, dizziness, and nausea, is becoming a common problem for as many as one out of five office workers. The major elements of indoor ecology are indoor air quality, electromagnetic fields, noise pollution, and radon.

A recent study indicated that in offices with high comfort levels, productivity is increased as much as 18 percent, translating into significantly increased revenue. Employee absenteeism is about 5 percent, costing $15 per square foot per year. The total cost of HVAC systems, typically $10 to $15 per square foot, can cost an additional $10 per square foot. Considering the long-term costs of maintenance, fuel, and energy use, the payback can be short and effective. Indoor ecology immediately and profoundly affects human health and the bottom line.

### *Indoor Air Quality*

Indoor air quality (IAQ) is the most important element of indoor ecology. In a recent study conducted for the Steelcase Furniture Company, a major manufacturer of commercial furniture, air quality was listed second only to eyestrain as the most prevalent office hazard. Additionally, a study conducted by Building Owners and Managers Association (BOMA) indicated that workspace area temperature and air movement are by far the most common complaints among office workers. Humidity and climate affect emissions and play a leading role in bacterial, viral, and fungal growth. While proper equipment maintenance and management of indoor temperature and humidity help solve the problem, corporations struggle to cut back expenses. The pressure to reduce building costs is great, and so investment in high performance heating, cooling, and ventilation systems can be difficult to justify. However, the cost of not addressing indoor ecology can be greater than dealing with it properly in the first place.[4]

"Indoor pollutants accumulate from four sources: outside air, building materials, HVAC equipment, and people," says a 1995 article from *Interiors* magazine. "Common sources include Volatile Organic Compounds (VOCs), biological contaminants, ozone, carbon monoxide, asbestos, and tobacco smoke." The most dominant VOC–formaldehyde–is present in plywood, particle board, carpets, upholstery, draperies, and urea-formaldehyde foam insulation. In low concentrations, it triggers eye irritations; in higher concentrations, it can affect the lungs and trigger attacks in people with asthma. Formaldehyde is regulated by the United States Occupational Safety and Health Administration (OSHA) as a suspected carcinogen.

Pollutants are most typically a problem when they are too concentrated. The U.S. National Institute of Occupational Safety and Health studied 600 buildings with indoor air quality problems, finding that over half were a result of inadequate ventilation. Another study conducted by Honeywell found that in 90 percent of office buildings, the most significant cause of complaints was the lack of outdoor air. To increase the quality of ventilation, a high number of air changes per hour should be implemented. American Society of Heating, Refrigerating, and Air-Conditioning Engineers (ASHRAE) standard 62-1989 suggests 15 to 20 cubic feet per minute per person in most applications. For optimal exterior air quality, make sure that fresh air intakes are located away from driveways, loading docks, exhaust air ducts, and garbage dumpsters. Good air filtering systems may be utilized to help provide the best quality fresh air possible. A study by NASA shows that by placing an indoor plant every 100 square feet, toxic substances responsible for indoor air pollution can be reduced by 87 percent. According to the report, "Some of the best pollution eaters include philodendrons, peace lilies, spider plants, bamboo, and English ivy. Each of these plants has unique air filtration abilities and none require a great deal of sunlight."

In addition to improving air filtration and ventilation, pollutant sources should be removed whenever possible. A no-smoking policy or designated areas which are separately exhausted will prevent smoke pollution from entering the circulating air. Any areas where toxic chemicals might be handled should be managed with particular care, although the owner's responsible implementation of subsitute materials to eliminate their use will create better results. The selection of non-VOC materials like water-based paints and adhesives, appropriate furnishings, fabrics, and carpeting should extend to nearly every interior specification. The use of non-toxic cleaning products can also contribute significantly to the improvement of indoor air ecology. Every indoor material should be closely reviewed for potential offgassing by asking manufacturers for data regarding their products. By law, Manufacturer Safety Data Sheets (MSDS) provide this kind of information to the consumer. You may find, however, that you need the assistance of a specialist to decipher them. For more about toxicity, see the section on materials later in this chapter.

### *Electromagnetic Fields*

Having been linked to cancer, miscarriages, and other disorders, electromagnetic fields (EMF) directly affect indoor ecology. Electromagnetic fields occur whenever a current runs through an operating appliance or wire. Research is inconclusive regarding EMF, but ecological buildings should respond to the information available. Try to reduce exposure to power lines and transformers, choosing sites at least 100 yards away. Reduce exposure to electrical equipment and appliances in commercial buildings by locating work areas away from areas with concentrated equipment. In residential buildings, televisions and microwaves should be located away from areas where relaxation and sleep are important. Stay 3 to 5 feet away from operating appliances, 2 feet from computer screens, and 3 to 10 feet away from microwaves during their operation. If "twisted pair" wiring is installed, the electrical fields will cancel each other out.

Research also shows that electric fields deplete negative ions. Outdoors in unpolluted places, the air contains 1000 to 2000 ions per cubic centimeters (61 cubic inches) in a ratio of five positive to four negative, providing us with a natural balance and feeling of general well-being. In certain conditions, such as before thunderstorms or when mistral winds are blowing, the negative ions lose their charge and a surplus of positive ions is generated. This imbalance causes tension, irritability, depression, and physical disorders. During the Mistral of France, the Foehn of Europe, and the Sharav of the Middle East, accidents often rise and hospital operations are postponed. Although no consensus among researchers exists, many people utilize negative ion generators to help replenish the ions lost by electrical equipment and to help remove dust, smoke, and some allergens.

### *Noise Pollution*

Acoustics are often overlooked in building design. An ecologically conscious building is typically quieter than a standard building because of downsized HVAC equipment, additional building insulation, and superwindows. Rooms with hard surfaces will create echoes, open windows can permit the entrance of unwanted outside noises, and fluorescent lighting can generate annoying humming sounds. In order to reduce the effects of noise interference, many techniques can be employed. Soft-textured interior surfaces will help to absorb sounds, particularly in areas where large numbers of people work or gather. Plumbing walls should be well insulated and strategically located. Landscaping, such as earth berms or vegetation, can help reduce traffic noise. Water fountains indoors or outside help to mask bothersome sounds and provide soothing background noise. Look for opportunities to buffer and utilize sound to enhance the interior environment.

### *Radon*

Radon, a naturally occurring tasteless, odorless, and invisible gas, can account for up to 50% of all the radiation we receive from natural sources. Radon 222, which occurs from the decay of uranium, is believed to be the second largest cause of lung cancer after smoking. Concentrations can vary drastically, but radon "hot spots" can be found particularly where soil is contaminated by radioactive material. In the 1960s, some houses in Colorado built with materials containing uranium mill tailings were found to be contaminated. Radon was found in Florida, where it infiltrated houses built on uranium-rich, phospate-concentrated reclaimed land. Radon and its particles dissipate in open air, but create a serious cancer hazard indoors. "The EPA estimates that 5,000 to 20,000 additional cancer deaths caused by radon occur yearly in the United States," according to the *Green Encyclopedia,* and that estimate may not fully reflect the impact of radon generated by oil drilling. In sealed buildings with low ventilation, the concentrations are much higher. Extreme concentrations have been found in Finland and Sweden (5000 times outdoor air), and in the United Kingdom and United States (500 times).

Sources of radon can be building materials such as brick, cement, and aggregate made from uranium or phosphate mine trailings. Stone, particularly granite or rocks used as heat stores in solar-heating systems, are another common source of radon. Emissions from these types of materials are thought to be much smaller, however, than those rising from the ground beneath structures in areas where radon is commonly

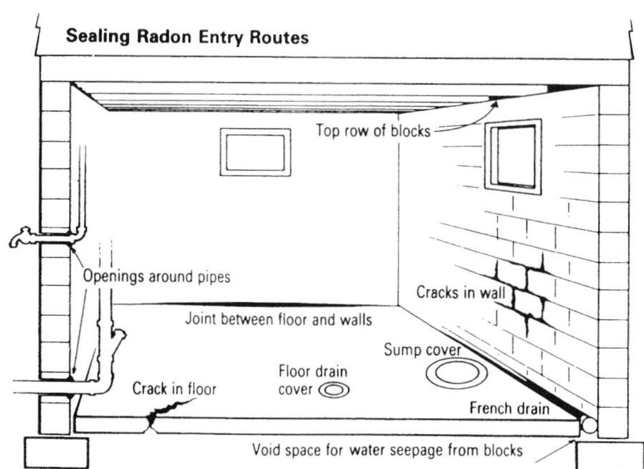


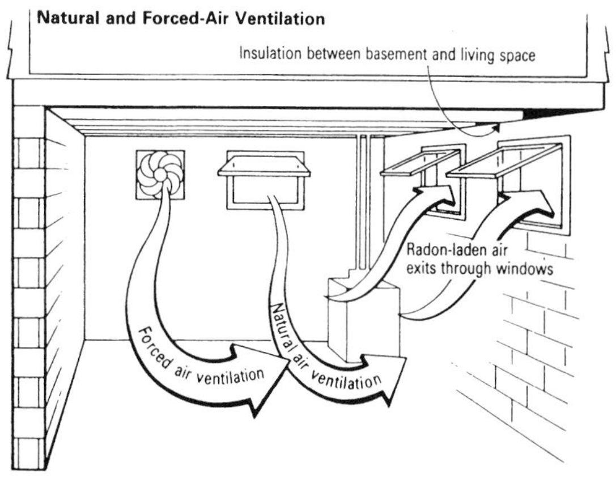

## Responding to pollutants

| Source | Hazards | Action |
|---|---|---|
| **Heating systems** | | |
| Paraffin (kerosene) and bottled gas heaters. | Carbon monoxide, nitrogen dioxide, carbon dioxide, sulphur dioxide. Condensation. | **Do not use.** If unavoidable, use for short periods only. Ventilate well. |
| Gas ranges, furnaces, and water heaters. | Carbon monoxide, nitrogen dioxide, carbon dioxide, sulphur dioxide. Leaks from pilot lights. | Vent all gas appliances to the outside. Replace with electrical models, or choose gas furnaces with sealed combustion chambers. Buy pilotless gas appliances. Have burners regularly serviced. |
| Oil furnaces. | Combustion byproducts; vapours from spillage. | Ventilate to the outside. Replace with electrical heating system, or seal boiler room from house. |
| Wood stoves and fireplaces; coal fires and furnaces. | Carbon monoxide, smoke, benzopyrene. | Have flues regularly swept and checked. Seal chimney cracks. Install air supply direct to fireplace. |
| **Electricity** | | |
| Electrical wiring and appliances (TVs, VDUs, food processors, blenders, mixers, power tools, hair driers, photocopiers). | Low-level electromagnetic radiation. Ozone. | Use less electrical equipment and keep it away from sleeping spaces. Ensure protective wiring and devices are fitted. |
| Refrigerators. | CFCs released from coolant system. | New CFC-free models being developed. Meanwhile use a pantry. |
| Microwave ovens. | Radiation through ill-fitting doors. | Use other fast cooking methods (e.g. pressure cookers). Have ovens checked regularly. |
| Fluorescent lighting (old fitment). | PCBs from rapid start ballasts. | Replace old fitments. Use incandescent or halogen lamps instead. |
| **Water supply** | Lead and other heavy metals from pipes. Nitrates and other trace pollutants and chemicals. Bacteria and radon in showers. | Remove lead pipes and those with lead-soldered joints. Have water tested. |
| **Air** | | |
| Air-conditioning and ventilation systems; humidifiers, heating ducts. | Airborne microorganisms, fungi, bacteria, moulds. CFCs released from some systems. | Maintain comfortable indoor humidity; ventilate to the outside. Have mechanical systems regularly checked. |
| **Construction materials** | | |
| Earth, stone, granite, pumice; concrete, cement, fired bricks, aggregate blocks and tiles made from alum shale, calcium silicate slag, and uranium mine trailings. | Radium, radon. Concentration varies according to locality of source. | Contact local health and safety authorities for information on radon concentrations. Where necessary, seal cracks in building foundations. Increase ventilation to the outside. |
| Plaster, cement, and plasterboard made from phosphogypsum. | Formaldehyde. May contain high levels of radon. | Use natural gypsum plasterboard or lime plaster. |
| Asbestos, insulation, and fire-proofing materials around pipes, boilers, and tanks; roof and floor tiles and boards. | Minute mineral fibres; blue and brown asbestos is more dangerous than white. | Asbestos is now banned in many countries, but is still found in older houses. **Do not disturb or remove flaking asbestos; seek expert advice.** |
| Urea-formaldehyde foam insulation (UFFI) for cavity walls. | Formaldehyde. | Banned in the US. Have indoor air tested. If found, seek specialist advice. |
| **Timber and timber products** | | |
| Pinewood, spruce, and other conifer wood. | Resin vapours. | Use older, recycled wood or other solid lumber. Seal with nontoxic finish. |
| Chipboard, fibreboard, hardboard, particle board, plywood: used in furniture, units, shelving, floor decking, and wall finishes. | Formaldehyde vapours from resin binder, especially when product is new, and in hot, humid climates. | Use solid lumber or "low-emission" formaldehyde boards Buy solid wood or rattan, bamboo, and wicker furniture. |

found. Typically, concentrations in ground-floor spaces are much greater because the gas originates from the soil below and moves upward. Ventilation, flooring material, and construction affect the severity of contamination, as they are designed to inhibit the entry of radon into ground floor spaces. Natural gas and water also contain radon. In the bathroom, radon in the water can be released into the air from showers, creating concentrations up to 40 times higher than in living spaces.

Good ventilation needs to be provided in order to protect occupants from the damaging effects of radon. Protective barriers should be installed underneath ground floors and ventilation under the floor

| Source | Hazards | Action |
|---|---|---|
| Timber treatments. | Lindane, pentachlorophenol (PCP), tributyl tin oxide (TBTO). | Avoid these toxic insecticides and fungicides. |
| **Fabrics and fibres** Synthetics (e.g. polypropylene and polyester used in carpeting, underlays, upholstery, bedding, clothes). | Formaldehyde vapours. Also insecticides, soft plastics, flame retardants, crease and stain repellants. | Avoid synthetic products, especially wall-to-wall carpeting. Use natural, untreated materials such as cotton, linen, wool, burlap. Wash before use. |
| Feathers, down, hair. | Allergies in sensitive people. | Use natural latex pillows, mattresses, and cushions. Protect with close-woven, natural cotton. |
| **Paints, varnishes, stains, removers** Used throughout the home on walls, floors, ceilings, woodwork, furniture. | Volatile organic compounds (VOCs). Toxic vapours and odours in drying: paint removers are the most toxic. Added fungicides and insecticides. Metals. | Avoid petrochemical paints: if you must use them, keep windows fully open and allow plenty of time for the paint to dry before reusing the room. |
| **Adhesives** Adhesives, glues, and mastics: used for wall and floor tiles, furniture assembly, weather sealing, wallpaper paste. | VOCs, notably formaldehyde. Toxic vapours during application and drying. | Use traditional nonchemical glues or water-based acrylics with low solvent content. |
| **Metal products** Cookware, paints, pipes, structural uses, furniture. | Leaching of trace elements into water – lead, cadmium, mercury, aluminium, iron, magnesium, copper. Lead and cadmium are ingredients of paints. Aluminium in cookware can leach into food. Metal furniture springs can distort electromagnetic fields. | Use natural paints Change to stainless steel, glass, or enamel cookware. |
| **Plastics** Foam filling in chairs, mattresses, cushions, and pillows. | Polyurethane: serious fire hazard. | Banned in UK and other countries. Use safe alternatives. |
| Vinyl plastics in floor and wall tiles, electrical equipment, imitation wood panelling, wallpapers. | Formaldehyde and other toxic vapours. Vinyl chloride. | Use natural alternatives. |
| Acrylics used in imitation glass sheets, wrappings. | Toxic vapours. Suspected carcinogens. | Avoid: even small amounts can be dangerous. Use safe alternatives. |
| Soft plastics (thermoplastics) used in numerous household products (e.g. food packaging and storage). | Vapours, especially in hot conditions. Food contaminants. | Use natural alternatives such as cellophane or greaseproof paper. Store food in glass, earthenware, or china containers. |
| **Household maintenance** Cleaners for ovens and carpets, polishes, bleaches, disinfectants, detergents, air fresheners, personal hygiene products. | Formaldehyde. Phenols, vinyl chloride, aldehydes, benzene, toluene, ketones, ammonia, chlorine, lye. All are highly irritant and toxic if swallowed. Aerosol sprays with CFCs. | Use natural alternatives and home remedies. If you must use chemical cleaners, wear gloves and protect skin from splashes. Store in a safe place away from children. Ventilate to the outside. |
| **Pesticides and fungicides** | Toxic – irritants and possible carcinogens. | Practise biological pest control. |

***Reprinted from The Natural House Book, David Pearson, Simon & Schuster.***

should be increased as well. For floors without air-space below, cracks should be sealed and pumps or extractors can be used to expel air outside. The installation of radon detectors will help monitor levels regularly. If radon levels are between 4 to 20 pCi/L, radon levels should be reduced to the lowest possible amount within one or two years; from 20 to 200 pCi/L, radon levels should be reduced within several months; and above 200 pCi/L, levels should be reduced within several weeks if feasible, or a temporary relocation should be considered.

Four major processes are used to reduce radon: soil gas suction, sealing, house pressure control, and house ventilation. Selecting and implementing the right

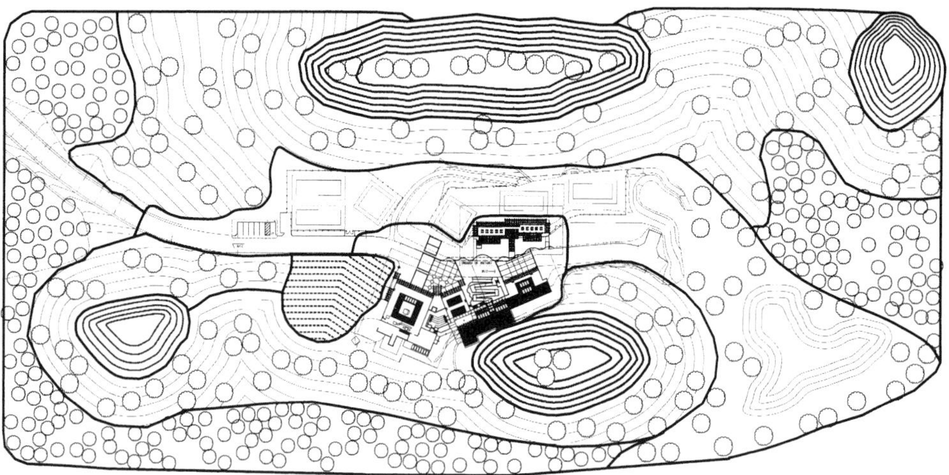

***Center for Regenerative Studies, California State Polytechnic University, Pomona, Dougherty + Dougherty Architects. Completed in 1994, the Center for Regenerative Studies is a learning and living facility where students integrate regenerative technologies into their daily lives by studying technologies dealing with energy, water, shelter, food production, and waste disposal. Features of the buildings include passive solar, solar hot water, solar voltaic, wind energy systems, reclaimed water systems, aquaculture, and environmental agriculture. Cedar, Douglas fir, and copper were carefully selected for long-term durability and appropriateness. The riverfront building is naturally cooled by prevailing breezes that pass over the aquaculture ponds and under the building. Photo: Milroy & McAleer. Drawing: Dougherty + Dougherty, Architects***

option may require the help of a radon reduction contractor. Local building trade associations, realtors, building supply houses, chambers of commerce, and home improvement firms may be able to supply information on contractors in your area.

## WATER CONSERVATION

The Chinese believe that water carries a life force called *ch'i.* In the simplest terms, water makes life possible, as the earliest human settlements–built next to rivers, natural wells, and springs–can attest. The Earth, like the human body, is composed of over two-thirds water. Human beings can survive for weeks without food, but only days without water. In many cultures and religions water signifies creation and regeneration. Bathing, from the ancient Greeks to the contemporary Japanese, is a sacred act. Rivers, streams, pools, waterfalls, cascades, and oceans sustain life, provide transport, and speak to the soul.

Yet as crucial as it is to our survival, the supply of unpolluted water on our planet is finite. The Earth's water is 97% salty, and the remaining 3% of fresh water is locked in glaciers and polar ice caps. The fresh water that we are most dependent on is provided by the hydrologic cycle, in which evaporation lifts purified water from the oceans and land, to have it fall back to the Earth again in the form of rain and snow. Worldwide growth in human population and food production further increase pressure on the planet's water sources. Steel, paper, and textile mills are the most water-contaminating methods of manufacturing, but since they are monitored by law, one can review the available information on their products to avoid any that incorporate highly toxic technologies.

Ecological design should diligently respect water sources. Water conservation should be promoted by specifying low-use water fixtures and appliances and by water recycling systems that limit demand and reduce sewage. To be able to meet the demands of the future, immediate improvements are needed in techniques for conservation, collection, storage, treatment, and reuse. Many municipalities offer rebate programs that offset most of the cost of installing water-saving fixtures. Water conservation includes using water that is of lower quality than drinking water, like reclaimed wastewater effluent, gray water, or runoff from ground surfaces for toilet flushing or the irrigation of vegetation. In the United States, nearly all of our water supply is of drinking quality, yet toilet flushing constitutes the largest use of indoor water.

***Advanced Ecologically Engineered System for Sewage Treatment, EPA, Maryland. After sewage has been screened and degritted, organic constituents are bacterially broken down in an anaerobic bio-reactor. Sewage then flows into aerated tanks, where different bacteria continue the breakdown process. Fluidized bed tanks provide more microbial surface area and exposure to ecological purification processes which involve diverse ecosystems of algae, protozoa, snails, fish, and plants. Accumulated sludges are settled out and removed at clarifier tanks before the waste reaches the marshes. The marshes--the last stage in the natural filtration and cleansing process--yield effluent purity approaching that of drinking water. Photo courtesy Ocean Arks International.***

## *Fixtures and Appliances*

Installing water-saving fixtures is easy, inexpensive, and provides immediate cost savings. The installation of new low-flush toilets, faucet aerators, efficient showerheads, and efficient appliances can cut water use by over 30%, saving an average of $100 per household each year. Numerous models of toilets, shower heads, and faucet aerators provide a large array of features and design options. New low-consumption national standards for plumbing fixtures went into effect in January 1994, and many local codes now require the installation of low-use fixtures. Nevertheless, manufacturers will be allowed by law to sell the older, less efficient fixtures until their stock runs out.

The former standard toilet of 3.5 to 5 gallons per flush is the largest water consumer in the home and office. To conserve water in new construction, the maximum permissible water use per flush is 1.6 gallons according to many municipal building codes. Every toilet manufacturer now provides a number of models that meet this criterion. Before specifying, evaluate the operational noise, solids evacuation, bowl cleaning, and water surface area. Double flush units save water by providing a partial flush for liquid wastes and a complete 1.6 gallon flush for solid waste. A waterless or composting toilet may be appropriate in some environments. Urinals should have a maximum flow rate of 1.0 gpm and be spring-loaded.

**WATER USE IN TYPICAL FIXTURES**

| *Fixture* | *Delivery rate in gallons per minute* |
|---|---|
| Kitchen faucets | 2.5 or less |
| Bathroom faucets | 2.5 or less |
| Showerheads | 2.5 or less |
| Toilets and flush valves | 1.6 or less per flush |
| Urinals and flush valves | 1.0 or less per flush |

Lavatory fixtures should also be spring-loaded and have a maximum flow rate of 2.2 gallons per minute (gpm) at a test pressure of 60 pounds per square inch (psi). Most water systems operate in the 25-40 psi range, but the high test pressure ensures that a conservation device functions over a wide range of pressures. Electronic control devices can be used in commercial installations, but local maintenance people

***Managing an ecosystem to purify water, Boyne River Natural Science School, Shelburne, Ontario, Canada. Following the breakdown of large organic molecules in anaerobic and aerobic pretreatment tanks, wastewater enters these clear cylinders, where organisms growing inside remove soluble plant nutrients. Common organisms found in these cylinders include algae, duckweed, snails, cladocera, daphnia, and flat worms. This is a major step in making the water fit to drink. Photo: Pete Herlihy, courtesy Boyne River Natural Science School.***

should be knowledgeable in their repair.

Shower fixtures should be rated for a maximum flow rate of 2.5 gpm at 80 psi. In public facilities where water use is more difficult to monitor, shower fixtures can have a timed cycle after they are activated by the user. They can also be spring loaded with a chain operator, in which a hand chain-pull device activates the shower only when pulled, and releases by use of a spring, automatically shutting off the fixture.

In kitchen and laundry areas, commercial appliances should be specified as water saving models. Garbage disposals exert a huge load on wastewater treatment facilities, and should be avoided. Composting provides a more useful alternative for food waste.

## *Biological Sewage Treatment*

As an alternative to conventional sewage treatment, biological wastewater systems have many environmental and economic advantages. Though they do not actually save water, they greatly contribute to the conservation of fresh water.

Biological wastewater systems are designed as a microcosm of natural processes. Some systems link wetlands and marshes to purify water, while others treat waste in large solar greenhouses or use algal turf scrubber systems. In a marsh-type system, sewage water passes through a series of wetlands where it is purified by water-loving plants and microrganisms, emerging cleaner than Class 1 drinking water. This type of system is low-cost, low-maintenance, and low-tech, yet it requires a great deal of land. The greenhouse or solar aquatics approach requires much less land. In this system, wastewater passes through a series of tanks and is gradually purified by plants, bacteria, invertebrates, fish, and sunlight.

Biological systems use much less energy, capital, and far fewer chemicals than regular waste treatment plants. They are less expensive to operate, can be an attractive educational feature in a building, and can provide natural habitat, fertilizer, and food. Most buildings are too small to sustain a biological wastewater system. However, biological systems in large facilities, clusters of buildings, subdivisions, and entire municipalities can be highly environmentally and economically effective.

## *Wastewater Recycling/Graywater Systems*

More than 75,000 gallons of wastewater come from each American household every year–not from toilets, but from sinks, showers, baths, dishwashers, and clothes washers. This "waste" can be safely and easily reused. Only treated water should be used for cooking, drinking, bathing, and cleaning clothes and dishes. The wastewater from those uses, also called graywater, can be used to flush toilets and provide water for landscaping. Before using it for irrigation, graywater should be passed through filter systems. Even "blackwater"–sewage from toilets–can be treated and used to water landscape vegetation.

Many plumbing codes have not allowed the use of graywater because of concerns for sanitary conditions, but this is changing. The state of California, for instance, has begun to permit graywater recycling. Typically, separate lines and septic systems must be installed to keep gray and black water apart. In new construction, this is not difficult, but when working with existing systems it can be costly and sometimes not feasible.

## *Rainwater Collection*

Cisterns and catchment basins are ancient methods of meeting a building's water supply needs. Typically, a system of gutters from the roof collects run-off and channels it into a cistern. Ecologically conscious buildings employ these methods of collecting rainwater to reduce the need for treated water. Catchment areas are often designed to look like ponds or marshes. The rainwater collected by these methods is used for landscape maintenance.

Often comparable in cost to drilling a well, rainwater collection systems can be employed within a group of buildings or an entire community. In some municipalities, rainwater may be used as a back-up supply connected to the area's regular water system.

Gravity storage of water should be employed wherever possible, as each foot of elevation of a storage tank provides .433 psi of static pressure.

*Landscaping*

According to the *Primer on Sustainable Building,* an average of 50% of residential water use occurs outside. Much landscaping water is wasted because innappropriate types of vegetation are often specified for a particular region–therefore requiring a higher level of moisture than the local climate typically provides–or because the watering methods are poorly timed and administered. In Oakland, California, a survey of 1,000 homes indicated that those with water-efficient landscape systems used 42% less water, or 209 fewer gallons per day. Refunds of up to 25% of the water tap fee is provided to homeowners and developers who install water-efficient landscaping systems. By 1992, these homes used about 40% less water than their neighbors.

In the arid western section of the United States, the use of water-saving techniques in gardening is called xeriscaping, and it can cut water consumption dramatically. Installing a drip irrigation system to water outdoor vegetation is another way of cutting down on water use. Automatic sprinkler systems should be correctly programmed for maximum water efficiency, while buried moisture sensors can help to determine just how much moisture should be delivered to roots. Rethinking lawns can also help reduce watering requirements. Huge expanses of turf are often the result of insensitive site preparation. Instead, try to work with existing and appropriate types of vegetation, considering the use of additional types of groundcover.

## RESOURCE CONSERVATION

In terms of ecological building design, resource conservation, or recycling, offers the widest variety of options and is perhaps the most complex aspect of the process. First, there are many layers of resource conservation that must be considered. Will an existing structure be reused? If a new structure will be built, what types of materials are aesthetically and economically viable, appropriate for the building type, regionally available, non-toxic, and produced in an environmentally responsible manner? What are the life cycles of each material, product, and system in the building? How durable are they? How much energy is required to produce, transport, and set the material in place? How can the building design make it easy for occupants to recycle waste? What purchasing guidelines can be established? Which maintenance procedures can be set up to assist in resource conservation? In order to answer these questions, one must be knowledgeable about each product, system, furnishing, and manufacturer's production impact.

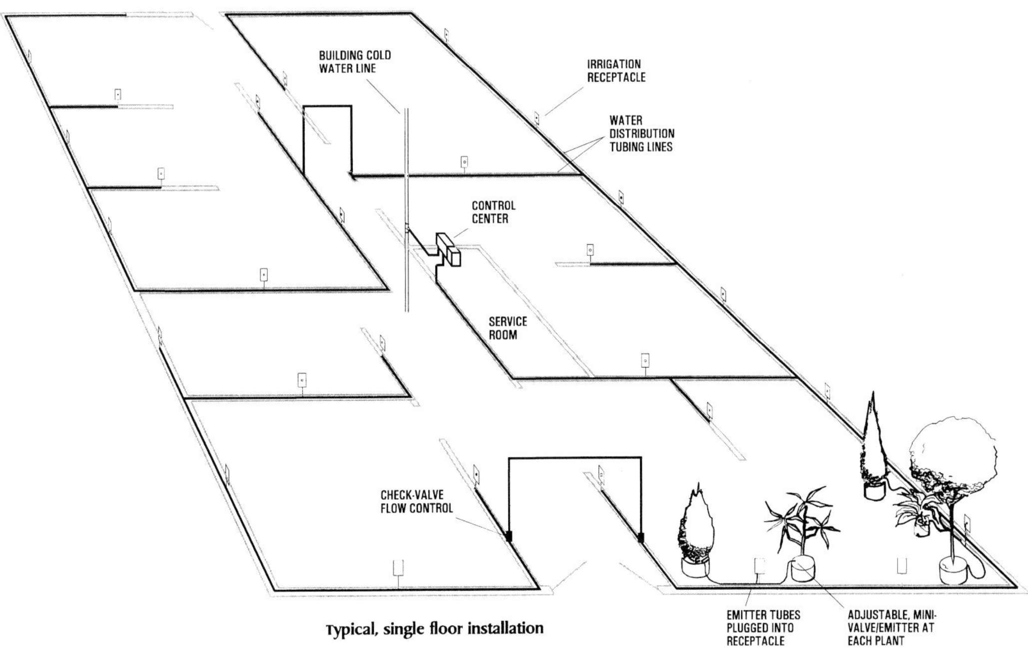


Typical, single floor installation

***Advanced, integrated systems manage planter maintenance, conserve water, and also lower labor costs. Remotely controlled, automated, precision micro-irrigation (APM) systems are used primarily for interiorscapes. The image above shows a typical single-floor APM installation. Container plants are watered through emitter tubes which are plugged into irrigation receptacles located throughout the building. Water pressure and timing are regulated at the system control center, which is programmed to the installation's irrigation requirements. Adjustable control is also provided at each plant to fine-tune flow rates. Illustration courtesy Boca Automation, Inc., Boca Raton, Florida.***

***Chicago's Rookery, built in 1888 by the firm of Burnham and Root, has been renovated several times over the years. The most recent renovation, carried out by McCliere Corp. in 1992, left the building's original ironwork and mosaic floors exposed. The gilded marble, executed by Frank Lloyd Wright in 1907, was also preserved, yet the near right column in the image shows how McCliere left the column partially open so that the original ironwork underneath could be seen. Photo: Nick Merrick/Hedrick Blessing.***

***In their renovation of Washington, D.C.'s Union Station, LaSalle Partners worked with many of the building's existing architectural elements to transform a dilapidated train station into a beautiful, bustling center of commerce. Photo: Carol M. Highsmith.***

## *Working with Existing Buildings*

Building restoration, historic preservation, renovation, and adaptive reuse offer the single greatest opportunity for conservation of embodied energy–the amount of energy required to produce, transport, construct, install, maintain, and dispose of a material–in a building. Environmentally conscious architecture is built to endure and adapt. Architecture that can span centuries by virtue of timeless beauty, quality construction, and enduring materials is truly sustainable.

According to the AIA, the majority of future architectural practice in the United States will involve existing structures. This means that buildings that are crafted to endure can be preserved. Those buildings that are built to meet short-term requirements are likely to present costly problems in the long run. A building that is poorly designed or built and must be removed represents huge waste, an abuse of embodied energy, and the destruction of countless natural resources. Although this seems obvious, short-term building has by far been the norm in the United States. Abandoned strip malls, corporate centers, and vast parking lots must be reinvented at great cost to our natural resources, our communities, and our quality of life. Whenever possible, reuse an existing building's shell. This approach preserves the vast amounts of energy required to manufacture the initial materials and construct and maintain the original building. In addition, these buildings are often supported by an existing infrastracture of public transportation, saving millions of dollars in construction costs and giving new life to the surrounding area's economy.

## *Reusing Deconstructed Materials*

If a decision is made to either remove an entire building or just parts of it, deconstructed materials can be recycled and reused. Rather than simply demolishing an unusable building, review the potential to deconstruct and disassemble it. If reuse is not possible, plan for the disassembled materials to be sorted and recycled. In new construction, using building products made from recycled materials reduces solid waste and saves natural resources. Cellulose insulation, Homosote, and Thermo-ply are examples of recycled products. Materials such as lumber, millwork, plumbing fixtures, and hardware can also be salvaged and reused. Make sure, however, that any reused and recycled materials are free of toxic substances such as pesticides, asbestos, and lead. If possible, avoid the reuse of pressure-treated wood. It includes toxic chemical pesticides that are released when that timber is remilled or burned.

### *Materials and Products*

What criteria determine if a material is environmentally sound? According to architect William McDonough, architects, designers, and building owners have always chosen products based on cost, performance, and aesthetics. "Now," says McDonough, "designers must also ask whether what they are designing is ecologically intelligent and socially just, whether it destroys the earth or is unfair." Only in the past decade have these additional ecological and social criteria come under serious consideration. Less than ten years ago these very questions moved a number of environmental pioneers to research the issue in an effort to provide solutions to practical building problems. Now, thanks to more available data, the task of reviewing criteria is becoming easier. The following list, compiled by environmental architect Paul Bierman-Lytle with editor Janet Marinelli and excerpted from *The Natural Home,* addresses the question of what makes a material environmental.

**Raw Materials Acquisition (Mining, Harvesting, Drilling)**

• Is the raw material in limited supply, or can it be replaced by nature once it has fulfilled its purpose? For example, compare aluminum- and wood-framed windows. Bauxite, from which aluminum is made, comes from dwindling deposits in the tropics. If it is well constructed, a wooden window made with a tree species in plentiful supply will last the fifty years or so it takes for another tree to grow.

• How much energy is needed to mine, harvest, or drill the material? Is that energy provided by nonrenewable fossil fuels?

• How is the surrounding environment affected? Are forests or habitats destroyed?

**Raw Materials Processing and Manufacturing**

• How much and what kind of energy is consumed during manufacturing? The aluminum in the above example is extremely energy-intensive to produce, unlike the wood which requires little fuel to mill.

• What is the manufacturer's environmental impact? How much water is consumed during manufacturing?

• How much air and water pollution is created?

**Product Packaging**

• Is the packaging made of recycled materials? Can it, in turn, be recycled?

• Is the packaging made with materials that are harmful to the environment, such as polystyrene foam made with ozone-depleting chemicals?

**Product Distribution**

• Must the material be shipped long distances or is it produced locally, saving energy that would otherwise be used to transport it?

**Product Installation, Use, and Maintenance**

• Does installation, use, or maintenance result in pollution that threatens human health?

• Does the product contain any toxic chemicals that can affect the indoor air quality of your building?

• Does the product contribute to the building's energy and water efficiency?

• How durable is the product? Will it last a long time, or will it need to be replaced relatively quickly?

**Disposal, Reuse, or Recycling**

• Is the product made with sustainably managed natural or recycled material? Can it be reused or recycled?

• How will it be disposed of after its first-use life is over?

Although there are no perfect products, environmentally preferable ones do exist. Look for materials and products that meet the following criteria:

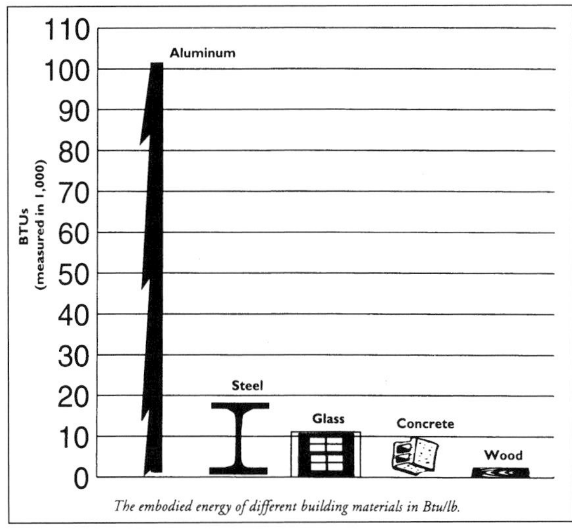


*The embodied energy of different building materials in Btu/lb.*

***Reprinted from A Primer on Sustainable Building, Rocky Mountain Institute, 1995.***

1. They do not pollute the air inside the building, or at least produce less pollution than conventional products.

2. They conserve natural resources. Buying them does not add to the pressure on threatened species or ecosystems or deplete protective ozone in the atmosphere.

3. They are water-conserving and energy efficient.

4. Mining and manufacturing them does not result in excessive air and water pollution.

5. They are recyclable or biodegradable.

6. They are regional or local. Look for local products that meet each of the former criteria. The use of regional products makes sense for many important reasons: it reduces embodied energy use because materials do not need to be transported over long distances; it helps to support local economies; it ensures climatically appropriate solutions for that region; and it expresses the culture of the community.

Since available ecological materials are constantly changing, the environmentally conscious designer needs to respond to environmental and social concerns with as much current information as possible. The subject matter is far broader than this section attempts to address, yet there are many detailed publications available for consultation, some of which are listed in the Appendix. Regarding products, many good resource guides are available in print and computer software.

Following are a number of capsule summaries of commonly specified architectural materials.

**Aluminum.** Strong, lightweight, durable, workable, and recyclable, aluminum is an attractive choice of architectural material. Ranking behind containers and packaging, the building construction industry is the third largest market in the U.S. for aluminum. Nearly one-sixth of the total U.S. production in 1989–16.4 pounds of semi-fabricated and finished items–are shipped to the construction industry each year.

"Virgin aluminum is fabricated from bauxite, an abundant material that comprises about 8% of the earth's crust," according to the AIA's *Environmental Resource Guide.* Aluminum produced from recovered scrap and recycled aluminum rather than bauxite ore saves about eighty percent of total energy consumption. While aluminum has no known negative indoor air quality effects, it is quite high in embodied energy and its fabrication and finishing could produce heavy metal sludges and waste waters. Alternative materials that are less energy-consuming should be specified wherever aluminum's particular attributes are not needed.

**Steel.** Steel, a strong, durable, workable, and readily recycled material, has a wide variety of construction applications. It is significantly used in nearly all construction as reinforcing for concrete, columns, and beams for large scale construction, or as nails for a wood house. "Construction materials are the single largest use category for steel, accounting for more than 11 million of the 84 million tons of steel products shipped in 1989 in the U.S.," says the *Environmental Resource Guide.*

Made from iron, one of the most abundant materials in the earth, steel is usually alloyed with other elements like chromium, manganese, or nickel, depending upon its end use. Iron ores of good raw quality are abundant in many countries and are removed by strip mining. Limestone is also mined for use in the smelting process as a purifying material. Many steel products are made partially or entirely from recycled steel, making it less environmentally harmful than a number of other alternatives. Advances in emission control technology have made steel-making a much cleaner process than ten to twenty years ago. Pollution from the steel-making process has been reduced by approximately ninety percent over the last ten years.

**Glass.** Glass is a transparent, hard, brittle, and chemically inert material singularly capable of providing daylight to the interior of a building while simultaneously protecting it from the elements of weather. The primary raw materials for glass manufacturing are glass sand, limestone, soda ash, and cullet–broken and crushed glass from imperfect trim and waste glass. The use of flat glass for construction accounted for 54% of glass manufacturing in 1991 in the United States. Architects should specify that contractors salvage and reuse glass building products removed during remodeling.

Architects can offer clients increased daylighting without sacrificing energy efficiency thanks to recent technological improvements in the thermal efficiency of glass. Plasma glass, currently under development, will improve energy efficiency in cold climates. Plasma glass units emit incandescent light with about 500 watts of heat–enough to heat the average room.

**Concrete.** Specified almost exclusively as a construction material, concrete has been used for almost 2000 years. The *Environmental Resource Guide* states that following the fall of Rome, the technology of concrete construction was lost until the 18th century. Comprised of three major components–aggregates, water, and portland cement, a binding agent first patented in 1824 by English inventor Joseph Aspdin–concrete is strong, durable, and flexible to form. It is mined from materials typically found in surface mining applications such as limestone, silica, alumina, iron, gypsum, clay, coal, and natural gas. Crushed gravel, rock, and sand is also needed to produce the final product. Concrete can incorporate the use of some recycled materials such as crushed recycled cement, fly ash from industrial furnace operations, blast furnace slag, and waste fines from mining operations.

A stable substance, concrete has minimal indoor air impacts. It can be cleaned with water and requires little or no finish when used as flooring. Architects can use concrete's many positive qualities in buildings, such as fire resistance, thermal mass, and longevity.

**Wood.** There is no natural material more durable, strong, flexible, or widely used than wood. It is used for a variety of construction purposes: structural, formwork, finish materials, interior surfaces, cabinetry, and furniture. The types of woods that are used in these functions make up thousands of diverse products, yet lumber can essentially be separated into two groups: softwoods and hardwoods.

Over 75% of the wood used for building–and nearly all wood used for structural purposes–is softwood. Softwood comes from generally evergreen conifer trees with thin, needle-shaped leaves that produce seeds in cones. In the western United States, the most preferred structural timber is Douglas fir, which grows to well over 200 feet high in the last old-growth stands of the Pacific Northwest. In the eastern United States, various species of pine that are native to the southeastern states are widely used for rough construction. Softwoods are also used for finish products such as moldings, doors, and cabinets. Extremely rot-resistant softwoods, particularly Redwoods, Western Cedar, and Cypress, have traditionally been used for siding, roofing, decking, and a variety of other exterior applications.

Hardwoods are broad-leaved deciduous trees that account for 25% of total U.S. lumber production. Located in the temperate forests of the eastern United States, hardwoods are most often used for decorative purposes such as molding, veneers, paneling, and flooring. The types used are frequently Oak and Walnut, which typically have a more attractive grain pattern than softwoods.

The most widely used softwood and hardwood species come from tropical rainforests and old-growth forests of the Pacific Northwest. Other species, such as Butternut and Cypress, have seriously threatened populations in the eastern forests of the United States. Old-growth forests–those that have never been cut or farmed and include a multilayered canopy with different-aged trees–support significant numbers of plant and animal species. "Timber production in the Pacific Northwest has received a great deal of attention in recent years because the region encompasses the nation's last remaining stands outside of Alaska," reports *Your Natural Home.* "Redwoods and Douglas firs, some the oldest trees in the world, are also home to a number of endangered species, such as the spotted owl." In the United States, only about 13% of the ancient forests in Washington and Oregon remain, and timber cutting still exceeds harvesting.

Tropical woods, known for their outstanding beauty, coloring, grain, and workability, are typically hardwoods that are harvested from tropical rainforests. The rainforests are most concentrated in the Amazon Basin in South America, the Congo Basin in Africa, and the Malay Archipelago in Southeast Asia. More than half the plant and animal species on earth can be found in these forests. Aside from woods, rainforests are the source for many other raw materials–essential oils, gums, latexes, resins, tannins, waxes, and dyes–and provide foods such as fruits, nuts, and spices. Nearly one-fourth of all modern medecines are based on natural chemicals found in these forests, yet only 1% of the plant species that exist in them have been screened for medical qualities. The resources of the tropical forests are exponentially significant, and are disappearing at an even faster rate. Architects should discuss sustainable management with their wood suppliers and encourage building practices that use wood more efficiently.

It is important to remember that while many products are marketed as "green," environmentally responsible, or ecological, it is best to rely on information which has been closely scrutinized by environmental specialists. Using natural resources always exacts a cost, but an acute sensitivity to the reasons for selecting certain materials over others will significantly affect the health of the environment for the better. Consequently, the health of a long-term economy, which can be driven by the availability of resources, will also be positively affected.

One particularly difficult question when choosing environmentally conscious materials is whether they should be natural or synthetic. Many ecological architects have strong and varied opinions about this. Which is better, choosing a "sustainably-managed," naturally occurring material, or a man-made substitute? What are the consequences of such a choice? One may find contradictory answers and choices, even within a single project. The answers will depend on context, availability, long-term durability, cost, and the environmental consciousness of those who make the decisions.

## WASTE PREVENTION

### *Recycling Systems*

After every possible method of resource conservation has been considered in the selection of a site and in the use of materials, existing structures, products, and systems, the next step is to address sorting and recycling.

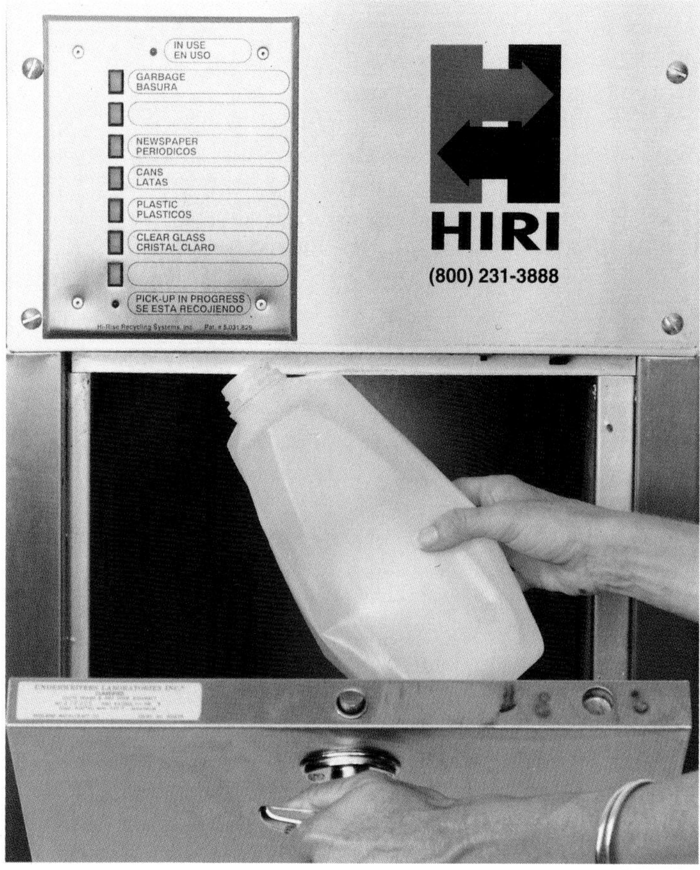


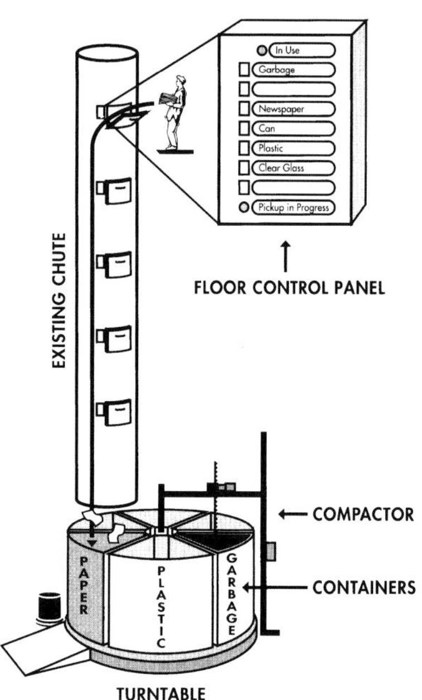


***Recycling systems can be retrofitted or specified in buildings to make recycling easy for building occupants. One simply pushes the button specifying the material, a green light and buzzer indicate that the correct bin is under the chute, and the door unlocks so the trash can be thrown away. The recyclable material travels down the chute and lands in the appropriate bin below. The bins are placed on a turntable that shifts in order to accomodate several types of materials. Photos and illustration courtesy Hi-Rise Recycling Systems, Miami, Florida.***

Sorting and recycling areas should be highly visible and accessible so that building occupants are encouraged to utilize them. Provide ample space for maintenance and pick-up, and make recycling available in high-traffic areas such as pantries and office lounges.

This can be done in numerous creative ways and at varying levels of cost. At the Audubon National Headquarters, a vertical system was installed for the convenience of maintenance and staff to encourage recycling. This choice has resulted in an enthusiastic show of support and increased awareness from everyone in the building. Well-planned efforts toward recycling result in increased maintenance efficiency and a reduction in cost. However, methods of recycling need to be tailored to the specific building and organization. At the Conservation Law Foundation Headquarters in Boston, recycling is handled by maintenance management since the vertical system proved less cost effective.

### *Biodegradation*

During biodegradation, microorganisms break down the components of other living things, incorporating them back into the ecosystem. Biodegradable material includes anything organic. In spite of that industry's contention that they are, plastics have not been considered biodegradable by environmentalists, since they do not break down into organic compounds. Most of the organic components of garbage like paper and food wastes can be eliminated through composting. It is estimated that between 60% and 75% of all solid waste is biodegradable. This percentage is high enough to substantiate the implementation of composting, or anaerobic or aerobic digestion, three types of biodegradation.

Composting, a process familiar to many, breaks down organic waste by mixing it with other materials to achieve a nutrient balance. Large chunks of inert material like wood chips add bulk and provide aeration to the compost pile. Composting requires space on a surface with good drainage, so that the mineral-rich runoff created by the decomposing material can be collected and redistributed to the process. After 50 to 60 days, the compost pile produces high quality soil nutrients and reduces the bulk of the original material by as much as half.

Offgassing of ammonia and carbon dioxide, as well as offensive odors, are unpleasant byproducts of composting. These, however, can be managed to some degree with filters. According to the National Park Service's *Guiding Principles of Sustainable Design,* "a typical small-scale composting operation for a community would cost about $250,000 to maintain."

Anaerobic digestion is used extensively around the world for processing paper, landscape, food, animal, and even human waste. It is a wet fermentation process which converts solid waste into three useful products: biogas—an energy-rich gas stream comparable to natural gas that can be used to offset the cost of energy utilities; a high-quality, solid organic fertilizer for landscaping and farming; and a diluted liquid fertilizer that can be used in drip irrigation as an additive in plantings.

Like anaerobic digestion, aerobic digestion is accomplished with microorganisms. However, air is brought into the treatment process to ensure plenty of free oxygen, which speeds the process of decomposition (about 20 times faster) and reduces the need for space. The systems do not typically produce offensive odors, and can therefore be located near occupied areas. High quality effluent can be produced with a reasonably small filter for irrigation and recycled toilet flushing water. According to the National Park Service which operates five of these types of plants, the best plants for harsh environments are fabricated from durable low-maintenance materials, are designed to use the fewest parts, and are consistent in effluent quality. The Park Service also reports that these plants can be quickly and easily installed and put into service, as they are completely assembled and warranted by the manufacturer. In addition, a good manufacturer provides technical and monitoring services at a reasonable cost for at least one year following initial startup.

*National Public Radio, Washington, D.C., Burt Hill Kosar Rittelmann Associates. Burt Hill Kosar Rittelmann Associates provided architectural, engineering, and interior design services for NPR's 152,000-square-foot broadcast facility and corporate headquarters. Thermal and lighting comfort and a high level of indoor air quality and acoustic performance were key elements of the design solution. HVAC systems required replacement, and CFC refrigerants were recovered from the equipment and recycled; the new systems are the most environmentally benign available. Interior finishes and furniture systems were selected to minimize the use of formaldehyde and other toxic chemicals. Photo: Maxwell McKenzie.*

## MAINTENANCE

After a building has been built, it must be properly cared for to ensure a healthy environment. Each product and system must be regularly cleaned and maintained, and environmentally conscious architects can help owners establish appropriate guidelines for doing so. For example, regular check-ups and cleaning of HVAC ductwork will keep energy efficiency and building ecology at optimal levels. Cleaning agents should be non-toxic and biodegradable to avoid environmental damage during their production, use, and disposal. Guidelines can also be established by the purchasing department of an organization with the assistance of an environmental consultant to help new building owners and occupants continue to be environmentally responsive. Audubon established a limit in cost premiums toward office supplies, allowing for a 10% increase in the purchasing allowance of a product that is environmentally conscious, such as 100% postconsumer waste papers. What follows is a sample of their corporate guidelines:

1. Purchase products with a high degree of recycled content, preferably postconsumer. An overall goal would be the purchase of at least as much recycled material as waste collected for recycling at Audubon, in order to help stimulate recycling markets.
2. Whenever possible, purchase recycled paper that has not been bleached. Chlorine bleaching releases dioxins, which are known human carcinogens.
3. Use rebuilt cartridges for laser printers and copy machines, or buy laser printers that do not require cartridge replacement.
4. For bulk purchases, develop a certification process that takes into account the full life-cycle impacts of the materials involved.
5. Avoid the purchase of mixed-material goods such as paper and plastic combinations, unless the component materials can be separated easily. Mixed materials are difficult to recycle.
6. Use grease pencils instead of felt markers, which emit VOCs.

**Chapter 5**

# *Case Studies: Buildings in North America*

## BODY SHOP U. S. HEADQUARTERS

*Wake Forest, North Carolina*

---

**Environmental Architect:** Design Harmony, Inc., Raleigh, North Carolina, Gail A. Lindsey, AIA, Cheryl Walker, AIA
**Architect of Record:** Clearscapes, P.A., Raleigh, North Carolina, Steven D. Schuster, AIA, Thomas Sayre
**Electrical Engineer:** Campbell and Associates, Greensboro, North Carolina, Dan Campbell, P.E.
**Mechanical Engineer:** Piedmont Air Conditioning Company, Raleigh, North Carolina, Edward L. Kelly, P.E., *President*, Stephen D. Bulluck, *Construction Manager/Designer*
**Plumbing/Fire Protection Engineer:** Triangle Engineering Associates Raleigh, North Carolina, Joel M. Hobby, P.E.
**Structural Engineer:** Lysaght and Associates, P.A. Raleigh, North Carolina, Chuck Lysaght, P.E.
**General Contractor:** Clancy and Theys Construction Company, Raleigh, North Carolina, Bill Macdonald, *Project Manager*
**Daylighting Consultant:** Wayne Place, Ph.D. Raleigh, North Carolina, North Carolina State University School of Design, Raleigh, North Carolina
**Lighting Consultant:** Environmental Protection Agency Green Lights Program, Washington, DC
**Solar Industrial Hot Water Use:** Gravely Research Corporation, Raleigh, North Carolina, Ben Gravely, Ph.D.
**Total Area:** Office: 41,700 Square Feet. Warehouse: 112,000 Square Feet. Total Renovation: 153,700 Square Feet.
**Cost of Construction:** Office and Labs: $21.00 per Square Foot. Warehouse: $11.00 per Square Foot. Total: $2,107,457.00
**Date of Completion:** July 1993

---

### *Project Overview*

The Body Shop Headquarters is a retrofit of an existing 153,700-square-foot structure into a 112,000-square-foot warehouse and 41,700-square-foot offices for a company that manufactures and sells environmentally sensitive cosmetics and bath products. The idea of "recycling" an older building was appealing to the owners, whose socially conscious cosmetics company produces naturally based cosmetics and skin care products. A healthy and well lighted workplace, as well as high worker productivity, were strong considerations in the design equation. These considerations directly affected the decision to introduce ecologically conscious design elements such as daylighting, good IAQ measures, and high-quality ventilation. Owners of The Body Shop made the decision to purchase property with an existing building and lots of mature vegetation in North Carolina. After having relocated their headquarters from New Jersey to North Carolina in 1993, The Body Shop plans to include a manufacturing facility and day care center.

#### ENVIRONMENTAL ARCHITECT PROFILE

For Cheryl Walker and Gail Lindsey, the founding partners of Design Harmony, environmentally conscious design is the basis of their practice. Their approach to architectural design is holistic, balancing health, ecology, and spirit. "Directing the firm's energies toward environmental projects was the basis of the business," says Lindsey. "This requires the evaluation of each potential project with respect to how it aligns with our values concerning ecological responsibility." Both say that this approach has paid off, securing them a variety of rewarding residential and commercial projects.

Lindsey and Walker look at every project with respect to five critical issues: siting, energy efficiency, indoor air quality, alternative building materials, and waste reduction. Team building is also an important part of their approach to design. The belief that team building is paramount to the success of each project has led the two architects to create unique partnerships in almost every project. Partnering, according to Lindsey and Walker, "leads to the best use of each member's time and talents, usually yielding the most innovative results." Humor is also an important component of their work style. They believe that for both the architects and their clients, a good sense of humor actually helps yield a more positive outcome.

Having taught at North Carolina State University and Duke University, both women have a strong commitment to the education of laypeople as well as

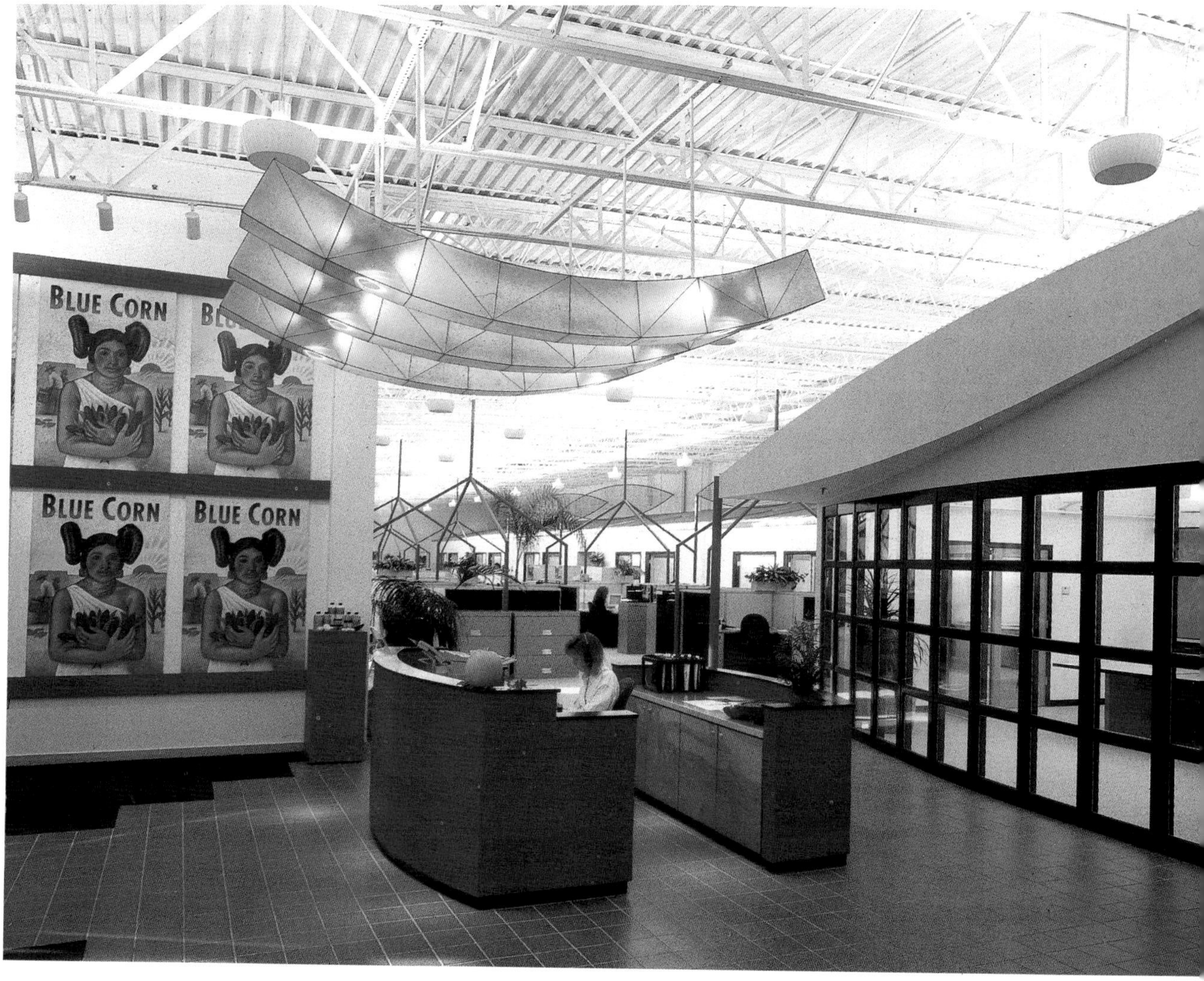

***The reception area receives both natural and artificial light, and has recycled tile flooring. Enclosed offices with clerestories and interior windows admit a maximum amount of daylight into the interior spaces. Photo: Doug Van de Zande.***

***Partial section.***

**LEGEND**

1 - Reused existing high efficiency HPS lights in warehouse, with group re-lamping program

2 - Exposed structure with high reflectance, non-toxic paint maximizes light quality

3- New openings in interior and exterior walls admit more light into mezzanine and warehouse

4- Energy efficient LED Exit Lights

5- Occupancy sensors in offices, conference, training and labs turn lights off when unoccupied

6- Reused existing roof top units with added economizer units increase efficiency

7- Enclosed offices with clerestories and interior windows admit maximum daylight

8- Plants function as natural air filters

9- New daylighting monitors full length of building maximize natural light in office area

10- Full height exposed ceilings with high reflectance paint maximizes natural and artificial light in work areas

11- Indirect, metal halide pendant fixtures

12- High efficiency task lights at work stations

13- Reused workstations from previous facility; low partitions maximize light dispersion

14- Carpet from recycled PET plastics

15- Parking remote from building to improve air quality at operable windows

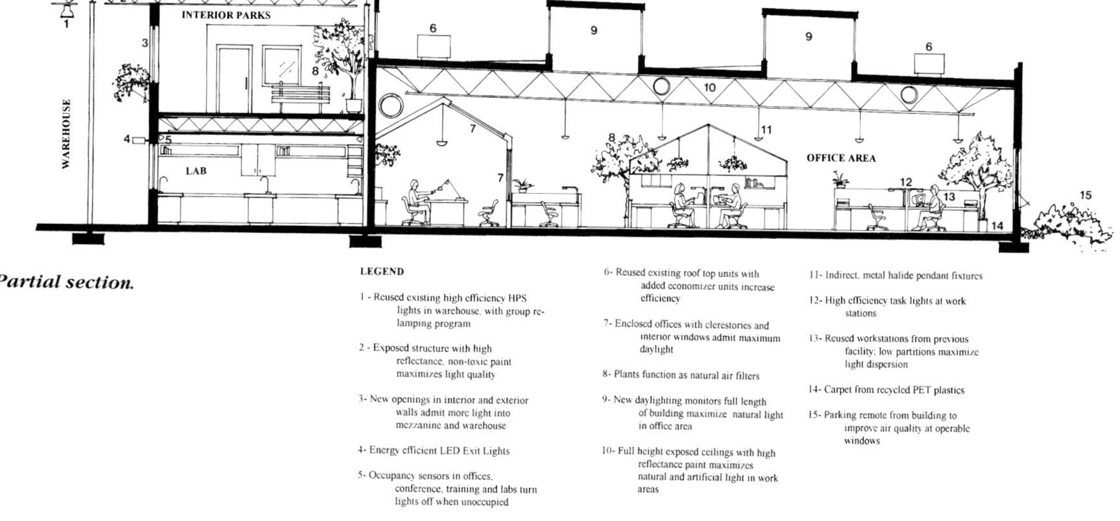

other architects. Consequently, they lecture and consult nationwide on architecture and its environmental impact. Their goal is to educate their profession and the public at large about a design and construction of the built environment that is healthy for people and nature.

### Design Solutions

The most significant practical steps that Design Harmony and The Body Shop took in creating the new headquarters was to work with an existing building and site, reusing as much of both as they possibly could. At the site, existing mature vegetation, parking areas, and an appropriately sized and oriented building yielded outstanding environmental and economic results. New vegetation was added to areas between operable exterior office windows and parking in order to create a visual, acoustic, and air quality filter for the occupants. Within the building, the existing concrete panel structure was reused nearly intact, as were existing functioning HVAC rooftop units. Existing interior office partitions and acoustical tile dropped ceilings were removed and the newly exposed ceiling and joists were painted white for maximum light reflectance. "The elongated E-W building orientation," says Walker, "was excellently positioned to take advantage of daylighting opportunities, and this was a high priority in the design of the interior." The high quality of light not only reinforces the owners' commitment to ecological concerns, but it increases worker productivity as well.

### Environmental Objectives

The Body Shop purchased property that previously housed a fire extinguisher manufacturing plant. One of the first steps in the design process was to develop criteria for their new headquarters with a limited budget and based on a fast-track construction schedule along with the environmental objectives that match their company's concern for social responsibility. The Body Shop retained Design Harmony to outline specific environmental objectives that would lessen their company's impact on natural resources. Together, The Body Shop and Design Harmony established the following objectives:

- Provide for worker comfort, satisfaction, and productivity: This was achieved by incorporating a natural daylighting system which can be accessed by the maximum number of employees from their workspaces. Linear rooftop daylight monitors added at the office wing introduce natural light. High ceilings painted with high-reflectance white paint further increase dispersion of natural light. Additionally, enclosed perimeter offices were equipped with indoor "skylights," giving them the benefit of natural light (see Lighting Systems in this case study). The structure's open, naturally lit design gives employees a visual connection to the outside, an important requirement that often goes unnoticed in most office environments. Where necessary, task lighting supplements natural light.
- Promote resource conservation: Not only were an existing building and site reused for The Body Shop Headquarters, but as many of the existing building components as possible were salvaged and or reused. The team also specified new materials with recycled content wherever it was appropriate.
- Improve energy efficiency: Economizer units were added to existing, reusable rooftop units to increase HVAC efficiency. Energy efficient lighting was specified and daylighting maximized to reduce the building's lighting load. Appliances and equipment were recommended that would reduce the building's plug loads, and solar industrial hot water options were explored and proposed for future construction.
- Improve indoor air quality: Existing HVAC ductwork was replaced and exterior wrapped insulation was used on the newly installed ducts to prevent mold/mildew growth. Ventilation was supplied to labs, offices, and the warehouse at rates that met both ASHRAE standard 62-1989 and local code requirements. Also, low- or non-VOC emitting materials were specified.
- Reduce demolition and construction waste: Alternatives were sought to landfilling building byproducts of demolition and new construction. The team also recycled certain "waste" materials, and the resultant cash was paid back to the owner. Materials that couldn't be recycled were donated to non-profit organizations, which in turn gave tax credits to the owner.

## *Working Methods*

### Project Team

The architecture firm, Design Harmony, whose focus is environmentally conscious design, was contracted by The Body Shop to serve as the environmental architect for their U.S. Headquarters. Clearscapes Architecture, chosen from a selected list of local firms that submitted written proposals and underwent a series of interviews, was added to the team as the architect of record. Clearscapes worked with Design Harmony, provided the construction documents, and oversaw the construction. The contractor was hired together with the architect of record. Design Harmony provided a comprehensive framework in which all team members–owners, architects, designers, and contractors–could evaluate design decisions environmentally.

#### Computer Modeling

Dr. Ben Gravely of Gravely Research Corporation used computer modeling to determine the efficiency and effectiveness of solar applications for the production of industrial hot water. Having assessed The Body Shop's energy requirements for both factory and office space heating, bathroom and shower hot water, and process hot water for factory and warehouse washdowns, Dr. Gravely concluded that TBS had available optimum solar applications–year round hot water for personal and industrial use. Additionally, North Carolina provides tax incentives for solar applications. A solar hot water system was designed by Gravely that could supply 41% of the company's hot water requirements. The owner reviewed Dr. Gravely's proposal, but due to the high initial cost of the sytem, solar industrial hot water use applications will be considered in the future.

#### Construction Methodologies

While traditional construction practices were observed for the most part, The Body Shop team took a number of additional steps to help insure protection of the environment. "Clancy and Theys Construction was brought in because of their excellent work and ability to meet the requirements of a fast track project. They, like many contracting companies, did not have experience working with environmental procedures like extensive recycling, salvaging, or material testing," says Walker. "There was some resistance at first, especially given the time and cost factors involved in many of the decisions. For example, finding someone to come and claim salvageable materials required effort on the part of the architect beyond the typical scope of services, and threatened to slow down the construction schedule." The team worked together sucessfully and slowly overcame this initial resistance.

The site and existing structure were initially tested for potential environmental hazards. The warehouse's existing paint was tested for lead content, while the site was tested for soil contamination. Regarding the disposal of demolition waste products, Design Harmony–the environmental architect–researched alternative recycling options and rebate programs. Habitat for Humanity of Wake County picked up reuseable building materials that were set aside during the deconstruction of the building interior, and a local metal salvager recycled existing metal and pipe.

#### Site Review

Since an existing building was located on the site, the need to alter the original site was minimal. According to the designers, "the original siting provided an elongated east/west axis that was optimal for daylighting opportunities to the building interior." Existing tall trees and mature vegetation provided an attractive ready-made landscape. The owners purchased an easement on adjacent property after learning that the tall pines were to be cut down, to preserve the trees and take advantage of the buffer that they create. Because the existing parking lot was reused, no new paved areas were created. Newly planted deciduous trees between the building and parking lot provide natural "air filtration" of automobile fumes, and further improve the air quality of building intake air at operable windows in office areas. In addition, they provide shade in the summer, permit light to enter the offices during winter, and create better views from the interior.

### *Environmental Economics*

#### Life Cycle Costs

Design Harmony suggested the inclusion of daylighting monitors in The Body Shop Headquarters. While the monitors represented an expensive addition, The Body Shop was pleased with two things: the psychological benefit of providing employees with natural light, and saving energy. Though the daylighting monitors added significantly to the construction cost, the money saved due to the reduced lighting load, reduced HVAC system size, and increased worker productivity more than makes up for the expense. (The calculated payback for the monitors was two years.)

The Body Shop Headquarters renovation was completed with an $11 per square foot construction cost of the warehouse and $21 per square foot cost of the offices and laboratories.

#### Grants and Rebates

The Body Shop Headquarters was eligible for a tax credit for donation of reusable building materials to Habitat for Humanity of Wake County, which used the material in the construction of affordable housing. Donated materials included 15 doors, 5 cabinets, 12 toilets, several fans and other miscellaneous items with an estimated value of $1100. Recycling of existing (mostly damaged) metals from the existing building to K & L Metals, a local metals salvager, netted the owner an additional $835. Reuse and recycling of existing materials reduced the tipping fees required to dump materials in local landfills by $500.

### *Energy Conservation*

#### Building Envelope Insulation

Since the existing building was in good condition and the roof was still under warranty, they were re-used in order to reduce material waste. The designers found it advantageous to remove existing acoustical

***The existing structure was exposed by removing a former ceiling. The exposed roof deck and joists were painted white to increase the level of ambient light from new daylight monitors that provide natural light. Photo: Doug Van de Zande.***

tile ceilings, and to paint the newly exposed joists and roof deck white to increase ambient light from the newly installed daylight monitors. Interior partition walls were removed to open office areas which allowed for maximum flexibility in and daylighting to interior spaces.

### Glazing

Existing double-pane windows and glazing were kept because they were in excellent condition. Also, because the walls were poured-in-place concrete, replacing the windows would have caused substantial damage to the existing structure that had already been deemed worthy of reuse.

### Heating and Cooling

Since the existing heating and cooling units were in good operating condition, all were retained and reused in the Headquarters renovation. Three existing 100%-outside air units were retrofitted with ducted returns to improve heating efficiency. These three rooftop make-up air units were modified to recirculate the plant air and were also retrofitted with economizers. The economizers were added to utilize outside air below 55°F as a means of free cooling. The economizer units use a large amount of already-heated "return air," thus reducing energy consumption by 35%. Energy cost savings with the economizer cycle were estimated at $5700 per year. Gravely Research Corporation, after working with numerous computer-modeled feasibility studies, recommended that solar panels be added to provide industrial hot water for product manufacturing. The future implementation of solar heated hot water manufacturing at this large scale will reduce the use of fossil fuels, cut energy use, and reduce operating costs.

### Lighting

The incorporation of daylighting monitors provides natural light throughout the entire office area, increasing the quality of the interior space and reducing energy costs for artificial lighting. These monitors, which are located along the east/west axis of the roof, were some of the most significant elements which contributed to the design scheme of the building. Feasibility studies were conducted, and the roof monitors were redesigned several times in order to create maximum daylighting and energy efficiency, with a reasonable payback period for their significant cost. In order to increase the ambient lighting available from the newly added monitors, existing dropped ceilings in the office area were removed and the existing ceiling joists and metal decks painted with high reflective white paint. Interior partition walls were removed to create open, flexible office areas, allowing the maximum amount of daylighting to reach all occupants. Offices and conference rooms along the unlit interior perimeter walls were provided with interior "skylights" to allow daylight in while maintaining acoustical privacy.

New T-8 energy efficient bulbs with electronic ballasts were installed in most other locations. The higher cost per fixture was offset by a 15% energy savings with an estimated one-year payback. LED exit lights were proposed for use throughout the building, but in this situation their higher initial cost ($247), when compared to the cost of standard exit lights ($82), outweighed the projected energy savings. Therefore, standard exit lights were installed.

The warehouse's existing High Pressure Sodium lamps were reused, but the lighting layout was modified to provide a lighting level in the warehouse of approximately 45 foot-candles. HPS lights have five times the efficacy of incandescent sources–more than two times that of mercury, and 50% more than metal halide. A group relamping program was proposed by Design Harmony with the assistance of the EPA Green Lights Program and the Alliance to Save Energy in which all fixtures are cleaned and replaced at one time, thus saving human resources and labor costs. Supplemented by natural light and high efficiency task lighting, metal halide indirect lighting was installed in the office area.

## *Air Quality*

### VENTILATION

Existing operable windows on the exterior walls of the offices were retained. Existing HVAC ductwork with interior duct lining, however, was found to be contaminated with dust and mildew, and was thus removed. Cleaning all of the ductwork proved costlier than replacing it, so new ductwork was installed throughout, with exterior wrapped insulation guarding against future accumulations of mold and mildew. In any case the ducts needed reconfiguring to adapt to the Headquarters' more open office plan. The discarded ducts were recycled along with other damaged metals. Laboratories receive separate ventilation and exhaust.

The rates of ventilation are different for each space. The offices receive 1.5 CFMs per square foot; the laboratories, 2 CFMs per square foot; and the warehouse gets the lowest at 0.7 CFMs per square foot. The Body Shop Headquarters met the local and federal code requirements for ventilation.

### MATERIALS TOXICITY

The Body Shop and Design Harmony took several steps that were economically viable to reduce the presence and use of toxic substances. Existing warehouse paint was tested for lead content at a local testing lab, and the lead content was found to be a negligible .01% and .02%. (State standards require mitigation for amounts of lead at 1.0% and above.) The warehouse was repainted with a high-durability, non-VOC paint.

Asbestos was found throughout the building. A costly removal was necessary, and The Body Shop took steps to fully remove it in accordance with federal regulations at the outset of construction. The presence of asbestos should be verified prior to purchasing an existing building, as any abatement procedures in renovation work can be potentially costly. Building professionals should be aware of this, but inexperienced building or lease owners are frequently surprised to learn of the sizeable cost of asbestos removal. In The Body Shop Headquarters, asbestos was found as a component of the mastic which adhered the floor tiles to the concrete slab. All mastic and tiles were removed by the abatement contractor, and a local testing agency provided air monitoring during all aspects of the removal.

Because the previous facility had been a fire extinguisher manufacturing plant, soil and water were carefully tested for contamination. And, even though their products contain only benign natural substances, The Body Shop Corporation worked with the

***Top: View showing front entry of the renovated 1970s building, a former fire extinguisher manufacturing plant.***

***Bottom: The warehouse was painted with a high-durability non-VOC paint. Existing paint was tested for lead content, and asbestos was removed. Existing high efficiency HPS fixtures were relamped and incorporated to light the warehouse area. Photos: Doug Van de Zande.***

local water treatment facility to ensure that any potential spills in the warehouse would not adversely affect the local water supply.

## *Resource Conservation*

### Building Reuse

The Body Shop purchased the former Walter-Kidde Fire Extinguisher Manufacturing Plant, a one-story office and warehouse, for their new U.S. headquarters. The offices and warehouse were carefully reviewed and found inadequate to house the programmatic functions of the new headquarters, which would include ingredient mixing, filling bottles from bulk containers, and product distribution, as well as administrative and product testing functions. The general contractor performed a detailed building analysis and determined that the existing building had no major deficiencies, and that repairs needed to bring the building shell up to excellent condition could be done in the range of $500,000 within the limited six-month time frame. Existing foundations, exterior concrete wall panels, roofing, windows, lighting, HVAC units (with economizer units added for efficiency), and exterior doors were reused in the renovation. The 43.25-acre site was particularly attractive because in addition to having an appropriately sized building and adequate parking for 220 cars, it had extensive mature vegetation. This serves to buffer the headquarters from adjoining industrially zoned properties on the north and west.

The most significant drawback about the existing structure was its lack of natural light. Rooftop daylighting monitors were therefore introduced to create a naturally daylit office environment. Existing high pressure sodium lighting fixtures in the warehouse were redistributed and reused in the warehouse because of their energy efficiency while providing high lighting levels.

### Deconstructed Materials Reuse

A number of existing building materials were removed and donated to Habitat for Humanity of Wake County for use in affordable residential building projects. Some materials were even bartered or sold in order for The Body Shop team to acquire materials for their own project. Among these materials were commercial oak doors, cabinetry, fans, and commercial plumbing fixtures. Recycling and donation of deconstructed materials reduced landfill tipping fees by $500, brought in $835 from recycled metals, and provided a $1100 tax credit.

### Recycled or Sustainable Natural Content

Several materials used in the renovation of the Headquarters contained recycled content waste, including the lobby tiles made from crushed light bulb slag, and some of the carpet made from 100% recycled PET (polyethylene terephthelate) plastic soda pop bottles. The paint used in the 112,000-square-foot warehouse was a zero solvent (non-VOC emitting) paint from Glidden. In addition, existing workstations from the previous headquarters building in New Jersey were relocated, repaired, and reused in the "new" facility. Natural linoleum flooring was suggested for the lab areas, yet because of its higher initial cost, the owners selected vinyl flooring.

### Recycling System for Personnel

The Body Shop employees had been active recyclers in their former headquarters in New Jersey. They voiced to the design team their desire to continue the tradition in their new location, but stated that no special construction was required to accommodate their recycling needs. Body Shop management orchestrated its own recycling system after occupying the renovated Headquarters.

### Purchasing Guidelines

Design Harmony provided The Body Shop with a list of office equipment and appliances that are energy efficient in order to further reduce energy use. Generally, the architects recommended the following:

1. Select the most efficient appliances possible. A good point of departure would be to examine the "Energy Guide" labels found on most appliances.
2. Select computers, copiers, printers, and fax machines that meet the EPA's Energy Star program (the equipment would have an Energy Star label affixed to it) or that come equipped with an "energy saving" button.
3. Purchase an ink-jet or bubble-jet printer over a laser printer. The former are more energy efficient.
4. Consult *The Consumer Guide to Home Energy Savings* for efficiency information on various brands. This publication is updated annually.
5. Consult the Rocky Mountain Institute's *Home Energy Briefs* for information on lighting, miscellaneous appliances, and home office equipment. This publication is available from the Rocky Mountain Institute and costs approximately $2.00.

## *Water Conservation and Quality*

Water conservation was addressed by replacing existing toilets, which used 3-5 gallons of water per flush, with new low-flush models which use only 1.5 gallons per flush. These have not successfully conserved water, since they require more than one flush per use.

The Body Shop initiated a review procedure with Wake Forest Public Utilities to demonstrate that in the unlikely case of a product spill, their facility would not

impose any additional burden on the waste water treatment plant. The Body Shop fills individual bottles with chemically benign bulk products and distributes them from this facility. Product information was given to the town in order to determine any potential impact on the water treatment facility, such as pH balance changes. The Body Shop also maintains a testing lab and regularly monitors products for the presence of bacteria and other problematic chemicals. The town's findings indicated that The Body Shop industrial processes and products would pose no potential negative impact on the waste water system.

## *Materials and Products*

### Criteria

The client requested that non-toxic and recycled-content products and materials be used wherever feasible taking into account the time and budget constraints of the project. Materials, products, and systems were presented on a case-by-case basis and evaluated against standards of performance, cost, and availability.

### Toxicity

Manufacturers' Material Safety Data Sheets, on-site testing, and phone conferences with manufacturers' technical representatives provided the basis for the toxicity evaluation of materials, such as paints, solvents, and sealers.

The issue of toxicity also extends to the maintenance materials used long after the building's completion. With this in mind, concrete cleaners and sealers (for the existing concrete warehouse floors) were tested on site. Products like Sure-Clean, Mean Green, and AFM cleaners and sealers were applied, observed, and compared. In this case, the least toxic products were not used because the owners wanted a "shiny" surface, and the low VOC cleaners/sealers had a more matte finish. In the end, the team settled on Sure-Clean.

### Embodied Energy

Once Wake Forest, North Carolina was selected for the site of the new headquarters, Clancy and Theys Construction then compared the cost, time, labor, and performance involved in the reuse of that building and its components to that of producing or purchasing a new structure. For instance, The Body Shop's former headquarters in New Jersey had office furniture that could be moved and reused. In this case the reuse of existing furnishings, even with transportation issues, made economic and environmental sense.

## *Post-Occupancy Evaluation*

During the two years since the completion of The Body Shop Headquarters, Design Harmony has visited the site a number of times to speak with facility managers and employees about the positive and negative aspects of the design of the offices and warehouse. Employees expressed that the facility is a fun place to work. They particularly appreciate the open work environment, the abundant presence of natural light in the office areas, and the visual connection from workspaces to the outside. Because the building is a single story structure with many existing windows, the addition of the daylighting monitors and high ceilings provides visual access to the outdoors from most work areas. Everyone believes that the full periphery of existing mature vegetation is an important benefit of the design.

The staff also made observations that caused the design team to make some reassessments and modifications. For instance, as originally installed, the daylighting monitors allowed in too much bright light through the south vertical glazed surface. Subsequently, a tinted film was applied to the south-facing monitor to reduce the intensity of and better diffuse the direct sunlight. Second, all of the new HVAC ducts were installed with insulation on the exterior to improve air quality and reduce noise. However, when installed, the team felt that "white noise" might have to be introduced to mask some noise due to air movement through long HVAC duct runs. This has proven to be the case; the Facilities Department is now considering introducing a "white noise" element to mask the noise of the air distribution system.

In addition, the installation of the 1.5-gallon low-flush toilets has not proven successful in conserving water. Because of the low water quantity and pressure, multiple flushes are required. While there are no immediate plans to replace the units, the issue is still under review.

### BODY SHOP U.S. HEADQUARTERS MATERIALS RESOURCES

**Warehouse Paint.** Lifemaster 2000; Non-VOC; The Glidden Company, 925 Euclid Avenue, Cleveland, OH 44115

**Lobby Tile.** "Prominence" tile; Recycled light bulb slag; GTE/ Sylvania Company (sold to Terra-Green Technologies, Inc.) 60 W. Aylesworth Rd., Veetersburg, IN 47918

**Lobby Carpet.** Image "Wearlon"; Made from 100% recycled PET pop bottles; Image Carpets, Inc., 1112 Tuckey Mountain Rd., Armuchee, GA

**Lighting.** 2 x 4 fluorescents T-8 lamps w/ electric ballasts; Reused existing HPS lamps in warehouse; Lithonia Lighting, P.O. Box A, Conyers, GA 30207-0067, (404) 922-9000

**Low-Flush Toilets.** "Allegro" elongated ultra low-flush 1.5 gallons water per flush; Mansfield Plumbing Products, 50 First Street, Perrysville, OH

## ENERGY RESOURCE CENTER/ SOUTHERN CALIFORNIA GAS COMPANY

*Downey, California*

---

**Architect:** WLC Architects, Rancho Cucamonga, California, Larry Wolff, AIA, *Principal,* John Baker, AIA, *Project Architect,* Rick Williams, AIA
**Civil Engineer:** MSL Engineers, LaVerne, California, Mark Lamourex, C.E., *President*
**Electrical Engineer:** RWR Pascoe, Irvine, California, Jerry Andrews, *President*
**Mechanical Engineer:** Mathaudhu Engineering, Inc., Riverside, California, Sukdev Mathaudhu, *President*
**Structural Engineer:** Wheeler and Gray, Los Angeles, California, Paul Weickert
**Landscape Architect:** RJM Design Group, Mission Viejo, California, Larry P. Ryan, *Vice President*
**Energy Conservation Consultant:** California Energy Coalition, Laguna Beach, California, John B. Phillips, *Executive Director*, California Institute for Energy Efficiency, Berkeley, California, Karl Brown
**Environmental Consultant:** $E^2$ Environmental Enterprises, Marina del Rey, California, John Picard, *President*
**Indoor Air Quality Consultant:** Healthy Buildings, Inc., San Diego, California, Simon Turner, *General Manager, Western Region*. South Coast Air Quality Management District, Diamond Bar, California, Andy Abele, *Principal*
**Energy Analysis:** Robert Bein/William Frost & Associates, Irvine, California, Dr. Malcolm Lewis, P.E.
**Exhibit Design:** Display Works, Irvine, California, Nick Snyder
**Interior Design:** Sussman/ Prejza, Culver City, California, Deborah Sussman, *Principal*, Fernando Vasquez
**Lighting Design:** Luminai Souter Lighting Design, San Francisco, California, James R. Benya
**Total Area:** 44,572 Square Feet
**Cost of Construction:** \$7,900,000.00, \$178 per Square Foot
**BTU/Square Foot per Year:** 124,000
**Watts/Square Foot per Year:** 1 Watt
**Date of Completion:** 1995

---

### *Project Overview*

The Southern California Gas Company's new Energy Resource Center located in Downey, just southeast of Los Angeles, is a facility that showcases leading-edge, energy-efficient environmental technologies in its design and construction as well as through the programs presented in its halls. The center was built to serve as a national clearinghouse of information on energy conservation and environmental technology. Completed in the spring of 1995, the building is 80% recycled, with over three quarters of its components having been reused or made from recycled content. "Instead of tearing down an old building and starting from scratch to build a new one, a former Gas Company office complex was dismantled piece by piece, then put back together in a new way," says the project manager for Southern California Gas Company, Tony Occhionero. When the architects or designers couldn't use the materials, they either found other builders who could or sent them to a recycling center.

Environmentally sensitive technologies and building envelope systems are 45% more efficient than California's Title 24 building code requires. In fact, the U.S. Environmental Protection Agency has designated the Energy Resource Center as an "Energy Star Building," a working model of energy efficiency and environmentally sensitive building technology.

The ERC showcases innovations in resource efficient designs, materials, and equipment to help consumers make informed choices about energy consumption and conservation. Its goal is to serve as a one-stop "idea shop" where customers can find the most efficient, cost-effective, and environmentally sensitive solutions to their energy needs. The ERC advances environmental innovation in the technologies it exhibits as well as through the design of its construction. By incorporating the latest in energy efficient lighting, cooling, and architectural design techniques, the ERC minimizes energy, water, and materials consumption in a high-quality, high-performance building.

#### Architect Profile

WLC Architects is a medium-sized firm located in a historic California building in the City of Rancho Cucamonga, California. Rancho Cucamonga is built upon the original Mexican Land Grant of the same name that was founded by the Rains family. The architects were instrumental in the restoration of the original Rains residence, an adobe mud structure that is now a local museum.

Larry Wolff, George Wiens, Robert Hensley, James Di Camillo, and Robert Simons formed WLC Architects in 1977. The firm has received numerous awards for a variety of projects and building types. Most of their work consists of public-oriented spaces and environments, and they have subsequently become recognized as leaders in educational, civic, and municipal design.

The principals have designed a variety of projects featuring sustainable design strategies for public safety facilities, community and civic centers, churches, and schools.

WLC has become a leader in the practice of environmentally conscious design. Their work includes the Environmental Resources Management Center at West Campus Lincoln High School in Stockton, California; Southern California Edison Company's Agricultural Technology Application Center in Tulare, California; the Irvine Ranch Water District's Irvine Gardens Environmental Center in Irvine, California;

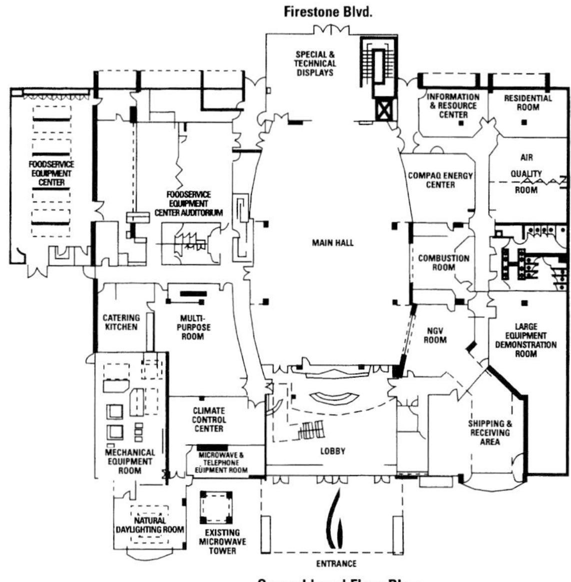


**Ground Level Floor Plan**

*Exterior view at entry of the reconstructed building.*
*Photo: Southern California Gas Company.*
*Drawing: WLC Architects.*

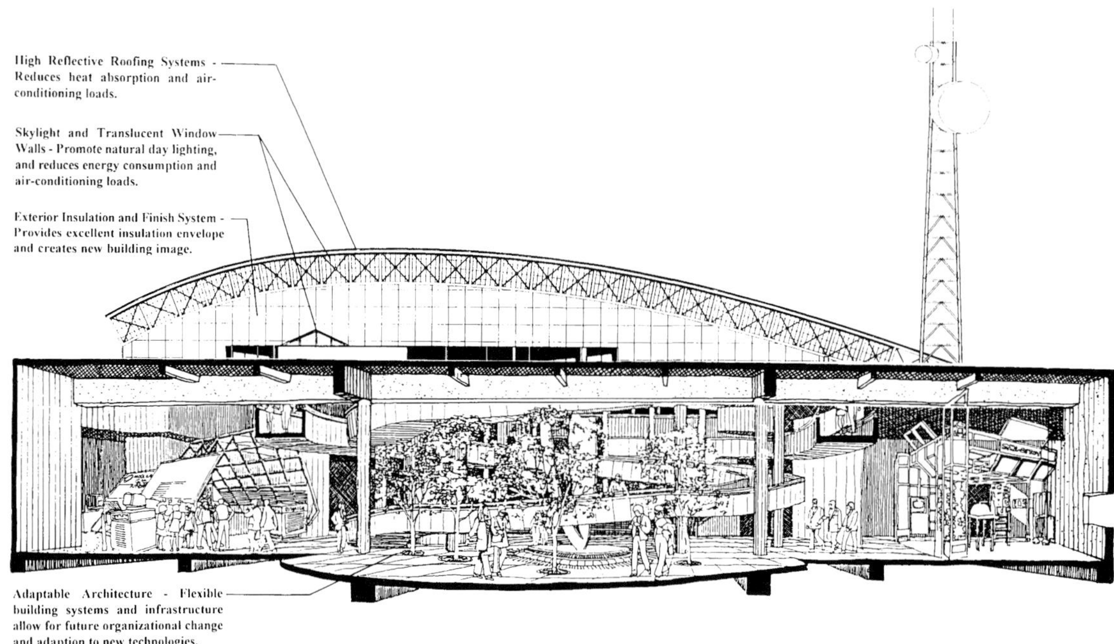


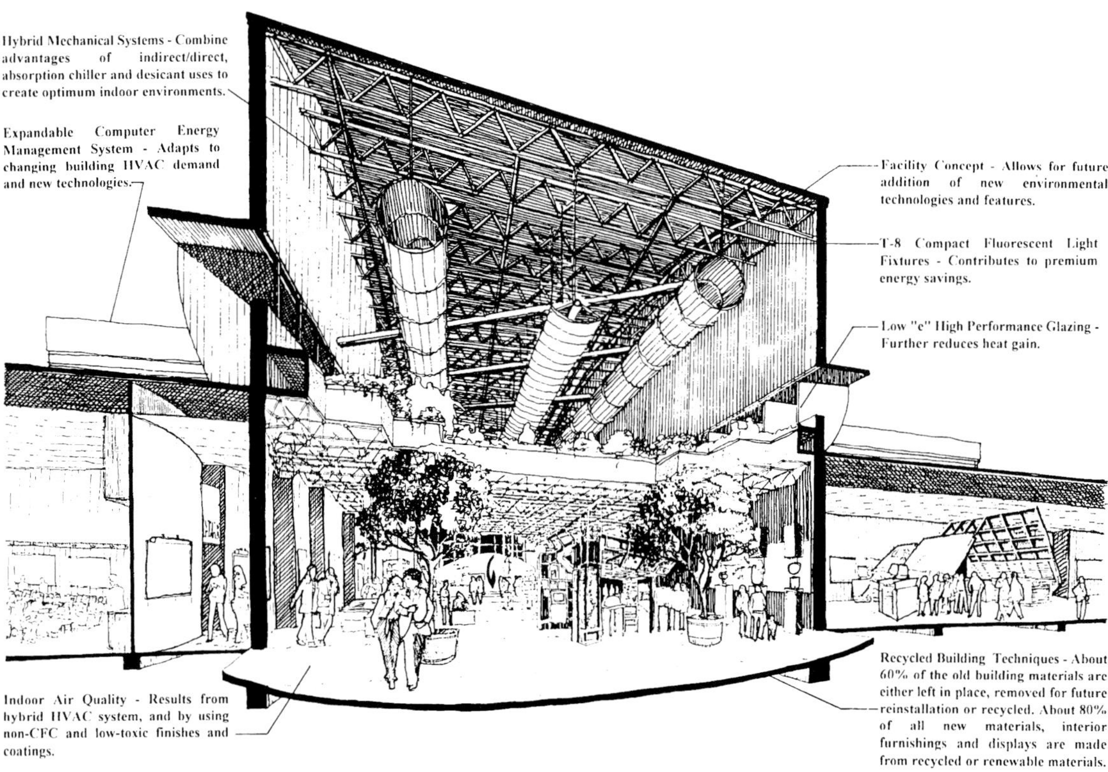


***Section perspectives through the building illustrate primary environmental features. Drawings: WLC Architects.***

*Clockwise: The Food Service Equipment Center permits evaluation of cooking speed, operating costs, and energy consumption; in the Residential Room, builders, architects, and homeowners can review the latest energy-efficient natural gas appliances that exceed building and appliance efficiency standards; the Compaq Energy Simulation Center is home to 21 EPA-designated Energy Star Compaq computers that allow industrial and commercial businesses as well as other equipment specifiers to conduct computer simulations to evaluate energy systems, consult with experts about the latest tools for forecasting energy trends, and access comparable case studies. Photos: Southern California Gas Company.*

and the Azusa Light and Water District's administrative office facility in Azusa, California.

### Design Solutions

As a state-of-the-art technical center, the Energy Resource Center is also a visual showplace for resource conservation–from its recycled building and site and its "new" recycled materials, to its educational facilities that demonstrate energy efficient strategies with the most current technologies. Southern California Gas Company built the Energy Resource Center by dismantling sections of the existing building and newly fabricating others. The design of the center lends itself to the dissemination of educational information regarding energy efficiency and its environmental impact. The Energy Resource Center includes an 8,000-square-foot exhibit hall capable of accomodating up to 700 people with a dozen specialty rooms available for meetings, workshops, demonstrations, and presentations. The Energy Resource Center provides technical help and information, computerized equipment simulations, state-of-the-art audio-visual and teleconferencing facilities, and air quality and environmental permitting assistance. It was designed to provide the building owner with energy information, and to assist over 200,000 customers that include commercial and industrial businesses; facility and plant managers; engineers; architects and designers; contractors; residential, commercial, and industrial developers and builders; manufacturers; energy and environmental organizations; energy management specialists; utility experts; professional and trade associations; technical and marketing professionals; energy supply and service companies; independent power producers; fleet vehicle owners and operators; hotel and restaurant managers; and technical and trade school programs.

The Climate Control Center Room gives commercial and industrial businesses access to the latest information on energy management topics such as alternatives to CFC-dependent air conditioning systems, operating cost comparisons between electrical and gas technologies, and building envelope technologies and their applications. In the Natural Daylighting Room, architects, engineers, and building owners can compare window glazing technologies, their resulting effects on energy consumption, and simulate various lighting conditions. In the Residential Room, designers, builders, and homeowners can test a variety of the latest appliances for cooking, clothes washing and drying, heating, fireplace technology, and building insulation. Other important rooms with dedicated technology information include the Food Service Equipment Center, the Large Equipment Room, the Compaq Energy Simulation Center, the Combustion Room, and the Natural Gas Vehicle Room.

#### Environmental Objectives

As a starting point toward the establishment of clear environmental objectives, the ERC team consulted such sources as the AIA's *Environmental Resource Guide,* detailed research conducted by the architects, the project advisory panel's recommendations, and the *Environmental Project Manual,* a written document containing specific environmental requirements that forms part of the contract with the drawings. The manual includes the owner's Environmental Statement, followed by the Contractor's Environmental Commitment Statement, a summary of environmental work, and a section on Construction Site Recycling Procedures. The following is an excerpt from the Contractor's Environmental Commitment Statement:

The Owner is committed to designing, constructing, and operating the facility with respectful consideration for the environment and the community at large through which the Contractor shall be obligated to participate by means of:

1. Cooperation with local utilities, government agencies, and the consultant to maximize energy efficiency and utilize environmentally safe energy and material sources.
2. Implementation of sound waste management practices through source reduction, recycling, and safe disposal methods. Also, reduction and, where possible, elimination of hazardous substances.
3. Employment of ecological criteria into procurement decisions such as the purchasing of locally manufactured materials to reduce harmful emissions caused by transportation and maximizing the use of post-consumer and post-industrial recycled materials.
4. Encouragment of commuting alternatives by promoting ride-sharing, public transport, and the use of clean fuel.
5. Practice of environmentally sound construction methods, and strict adherence to local, state, and federal laws and regulations concerning environmental protection, pollution control, and noise control and abatement.
6. Promotion of environmental education among the Contractor's and Subcontractor's employees and support from the company in the way of practices and policies.
7. Support for the Owner's environmental consultant.

### *Working Methods*

Using its normal request-for-proposal process, Southern California Gas Company selected their architect. Twenty-four RFPs were sent out, and eight firms submitted responses. From those bids, four were selected for more detailed evaluation. During that period, each finalist assembled his/her design teams. Tony Occhionero, project manager for Southern California Gas, says that WLC Architects was ultimately selected because of its environmental initiatives and willingness to make changes. The contracts let for interior design, exhibit design, and exhibit fabrication were important because every material needed to include non-toxic, recycled, and environmentally sensitive products and content. Sussman-Prejza won the interior design and exhibit design contracts and Display Works produced the exhibits.

#### Project Team

While the method used to select an architect was a standard Southern California Company approach, the process by which the project was carried out was entirely unique. After the architects, interior designer, and exhibit designer were selected, an advisory panel was established in order to bring in outside perspectives. Twenty-eight consultants including energy conservation experts, indoor air quality specialists, advanced lighting professionals, and resource conservation specialists were brought on board to develop the goals of the project. About a year into the project, but still six months away from completion of the final design, environmental consultant John Picard joined the advisory team. "From that point forward," says Occhionero, "John and the others really pushed us to break new ground with this project. The members of the advisory team, along with consultants Healthy Buildings, Inc. (HBI), $E^2$, and Dr. Malcolm Lewis are considered to be leaders in environmental/energy efficiency consulting."

#### Computer Modeling

Not only was computer modeling valuable in the development of the Energy Resource Center, but it continues to be an integral part of the services provided to various industrial and commercial customers in parts of the center. The principal software used in the planning and building of the ERC was DOE2.1E, developed by Lawrence Berkeley Laboratories. It pro-

***Training and a wide variety of computer programs are available to help building owners, architects, and builders create optimum energy efficiency at their facility. Photo: Southern California Gas Company.***

vided a benchmark tool for energy-efficiency and environmental data, and the ERC design team relied on it extensively. An hourly heating and cooling load was calculated using detailed building information, as well as operating economics and life cycle analyses using varying lighting and HVAC system specifications.

As a result, the ERC design team was able to integrate some of the old equipment into its heating/cooling system, maximize sophisticated natural and electric lighting approaches, and get the most out of its building envelope design techniques within the limitations of a recycled reconfigured environment. Mechanical engineering consultant Robert Bein of William Frost & Associates applied the DOE-2.1E model to help compare the gas and electric usage of the new ERC with that of the old facility. Certain assumptions had to be made since the newly recycled, reconfigured facility was significantly larger than the original building complex.

"The Energy Resource Center uses the latest in energy efficient lighting, cooling, and architectural technologies to minimize energy use," says Project Manager Tony Occhionero. Dual-effect gas absorption water chillers are used for space cooling; daylighting controls continuously adjust the amount of electrical lighting to augment natural light; high-performance glazing allows visible light to enter the space while repelling most of the heat; and a comprehensive digital building control system allows all major building systems to be monitored and adjusted. "The new ERC far exceeds the energy-efficiency of the previous

***The new second story parabolic beam is lifted into place. Photo: Southern California Gas Company.***

building, as well as California's Title 24 energy efficiency code for non-residential buildings," says Occhionero. Compared with the previous building, the efforts of the ERC design team and the Southern California Gas Company have resulted in a 45% decrease in source energy use. The previous facility used approximately 224 kBtu per square foot per year, while the new ERC will use approximately 124 kBtu per square foot per year of source energy.

### Construction Methodologies

Southern California Gas Company's construction contract was bid in traditional fashion. After detailed review, Turner Construction was selected–despite the fact that it was not the lowest bidder. "They were selected for two principal reasons," says Occhionero. "Their price was competitive, and they offered the best environmental program. The low bidder had no environmental program and that firm, in fact, tried to talk us out of having an environmental program in this project."

The construction phase involves a number of other important environmental considerations, such as soil protection, dust minimization, preservation of existing land resources like trees, shrubs, vines, and top soil, and adherence to stringent self-imposed noise regulations. The construction contractor was required to make an environmental commitment that was outlined in a contractual agreement that included the following:

1. Environmentally sound construction practices rely on a commitment by the contractor to promote the efforts of the Owner and Architect to create an environmentally friendly structure. Environmental considerations of the contractor will range from site demolition and excavation to managing, recycling, and disposing of solid waste resulting from construction and demolition work.

2. The Contractor should implement a construction and waste demolition program that will successfully divert waste materials from the landfill. This can be economically accomplished with minimal interference by subcontracting a waste hauler that will separate the materials at his/her own yard for redistribution to another end user. Reuse of construction waste materials such as concrete, drywall, wood, steel and others is quite common and can divert significant amounts of materials from the landfill as well as save energy and resources that would have been used in the manaufacture of these products from virgin materials.

3. The Contractor shall submit a statement of its corporate environmental policy and a summary of environmental initiatives as they relate to the project. If an environmental mission statement does not exist, the Environmental Consultant can assist in drafting one.

4. Summary of Work–This section includes requirements for ensuring the most environmentally conscious work feasible within the limits of the Construction Schedule, Contract Sum, and available materials, equipment, and products.

Contractor shall participate in promoting efforts of Owner and Architect to create an energy efficient and environmentally sensitive structure to all subcontractors involved with the Energy Resource Center.

Contractor shall use recycled, toxic-free, and environmentally sensitive materials, equipment, products, and procedures to the greatest extent possible.

Contractor shall protect the environment, both on-site and off-site, during demolition and construction operations.

Contractor shall prevent environmental pollution and damage.

Contractor shall effect optimum control of solid wastes.

Construction site recycling procedures were also outlined in the Environmental Project Manual. Recommendations were outlined within this section for the appointment of a construction waste coordinator and for the handling of materials. Methods of collection of recycled material are described for asphalt, concrete, porcelain plumbing fixtures, ferrous and non-ferrous metals, wood, debris, glass, red clay brick, paper, plastic, lamp ballasts, and any miscellaneous materials. An extensive list of contacts for the recycling and hauling of each of the materials is outlined and regular meetings are specified to track the progress of the recycling effort.

### Site Review

The existing site consisted of nearly 90% parking surface, now down to 58% due to the augmentation of landscaping and building area. Exterior landscaping features include drought-resistant plants such as palm that are native to the region. Bob Goulden, construction manager of the gas company, says that "Some aspects of the site are still being evaluated, such as the possibility of covering the facilities parking lot with a white surface to help eliminate the 'urban heat island effect' created by traditional blacktop surface parking."

To care for the landscape, non-toxic pest control methods such as the use of toads and ladybugs are being implemented. An underground drip irrigation system using reclaimed water and mulches to reduce evaporation is planned for the future.

New outdoor lighting was also provided for security purposes. Low-lying energy-efficient lights illuminate walkways and the parking lot.

**Construction Cost Analysis**
**Energy Resource Center, Southern California Gas Company**

| Project Compariso | | Recycled Building | | | Conventional Construction | | |
|---|---|---|---|---|---|---|---|
| 44,000 SF Facility Size | | Energy Resource Center | | | Convention & Corporate Center | | |
| CSI Division | Item/Description | Cost | Cost Per Square Foot | Percent of Total Cost | Cost | Cost Per Square Foot | Percent of Total Cost |
| 1 | General Conditions | $889,290 | $ 20.21 | 13.16% | $ 1,223,200 | $ 27.80 | 12.55% |
| 2 | Site Work | $452,757 | $ 10.29 | 6.70% | $ 1,046,320 | $ 23.78 | 10.74% |
| 3 | Concrete | $316,384 | $ 7.19 | 4.68% | $ 616,000 | $ 14.00 | 6.32% |
| 4 | Masonry | $31,000 | $ 0.70 | 0.46% | $ 231,000 | $ 5.25 | 2.37% |
| 5 | Metals | $1,029,375 | $ 23.39 | 15.23% | $ 1,591,040 | $ 36.16 | 16.33% |
| 6 | Carpentry | $94,914 | $ 2.16 | 1.40% | $ 316,800 | $ 7.20 | 3.25% |
| 7 | Thermal & Moisture Protection | $388,590 | $ 8.83 | 5.75% | $ 389,840 | $ 8.86 | 4.00% |
| 8 | Doors, Windows & Glass | $318,604 | $ 7.24 | 4.71% | $ 356,400 | $ 8.10 | 3.66% |
| 9 | Finishes | $1,021,494 | $ 23.22 | 15.11% | $ 1,179,200 | $ 26.80 | 12.10% |
| 10 | Specialties | $78,148 | $ 1.78 | 1.16% | $ 127,600 | $ 2.90 | 1.31% |
| 11 | Equipment | $75,270 | $ 1.71 | 1.11% | $ 92,840 | $ 2.11 | 0.95% |
| 12 | Furnishings | $0 | $ - | 0.00% | $ - | $ - | 0.00% |
| 13 | Special Construction | $0 | $ - | 0.00% | $ - | $ - | 0.00% |
| 14 | Conveying Systems | $31,500 | $ 0.72 | 0.47% | $ 79,200 | $ 1.80 | 0.81% |
| 15 | Mechanical & Plumbing | $810,982 | $ 18.43 | 12.00% | $ 1,073,160 | $ 24.39 | 11.01% |
| 16 | Electrical | $1,220,316 | $ 27.73 | 18.06% | $ 1,420,320 | $ 32.28 | 14.58% |
| | **Total Construction Cost** | **$6,758,624** | **$ 153.61** | **100.00%** | **$ 9,742,920** | **$ 221.43** | **100.00%** |
| | **ERC Notes: General Conditions cost breakdown for recycled building.** | | | | | | |
| | On-Site Recycling & Sorting | $5,127 | | | | | |
| | Selective Dismantling | $3,850 | | | | | |
| | Contractor Recycling Management | $7,472 | | | | | |
| | General Conditions | $312,646 | | | | | |
| | Permits | $69,355 | | | | | |
| | Insurance | $79,415 | | | | | |
| | Construction Management Fee | $150,592 | | | | | |
| | Contingency | $260,833 | | | | | |
| | | $889,290 | | | | | |

***Courtesy of Larry Wolff, AIA. 1996.***

## *Environmental Economics*

### Life Cycle Costs

"Every major feature had to be just as financially feasible as it was environmentally correct," says John Picard, president of E² Environmental Enterprises Inc., the environmental consultant on the project. "This technology is available for people to use right now." By expanding its existing facility rather than purchasing new land and building another project, the Southern California Gas Company estimates that it saved $3.2 million.This includes the reuse of $1 million of energy-efficient kitchen facilities used for demonstrations.The Resource Center's state-of-the-art lighting system cost $200,000 more than a conventional one, yet is projected to save $21,000 to $30,000 annually.At a total construction cost of $7.9 million, the architect, Larry Wolff, says that "the green features of the building cannot be detailed in economic terms.There is no precise amount for these features, no estimate of what they save in lower operating costs annually." That sort of economic data is exactly what Wolff has quantified in his recently completed master's thesis at Cal Poly University, San Luis Obispo."At $800,000 or about 10% of the building cost, architectural fees were standard for a remodel, renovation project of this type," according to Wolff. Design costs for new structures are not comparable in the case of ERC, which carefully dismantled an existing structure.

### Grants and Rebates

The local utility, Southern California Edison, gave approximately $17,000 in credits to the Energy Resource Center because of their use of high-efficiency lighting and fan motors.The Department of Water and Power of Los Angeles also provided rebates for the installation of ultra-low flush toilets.

## *Energy Conservation*

Featuring some of the most up-to-date energy efficient mechanical equipment, lighting, and advanced building envelope systems, the ERC is designed to deliver energy efficiency 45% better than California's Title 24 building code requires.Windows that are able to bend light keep the sun's rays from entering

## Southern California Gas Company

Energy Resource Center

**(Site Energy)**

Summary of Energy Consumption by End Use
for EPA Building Star Program

| End Use | base case (MBTU/year) | | | | | proposed case (MBTU/year) | |
|---|---|---|---|---|---|---|---|
| | natural gas | electricity | End-Use | Base | Proposed | natural gas | electricity |
| Area Lights | - | 862 | Area Lights | 862 | 404 | - | 404 |
| Task Lights | - | 201 | Task Lights | 201 | 161 | - | 161 |
| Equipment | - | 471 | Equipment | 471 | 471 | - | 471 |
| Space Heating | 162 | - | Space Heating | 162 | 236 | 236 | - |
| Space Cooling | - | 1,257 | Space Cooling | 1,257 | 933 | 627 | 306 |
| Heat Rejection | - | - | Heat Rejection | - | 37 | - | 37 |
| Pumps & Misc. | - | 18 | Pumps & Misc. | 18 | 33 | - | 33 |
| Fans | - | 355 | Ventilation Fans | 355 | 90 | - | 90 |
| Dom. Hot Water | 129 | - | Dom. Hot Water | 129 | 129 | 129 | - |

***Chart of site energy shows summary of consumption by end use for EPA Building Star Program. Courtesy of Southern California Gas Company.***

the building continually at the the same angle. To reduce heat gain, especially during hot summer days, a reflective paint is used on the roof.

### Building Envelope Insulation

The new exterior walls combine foil-backed fiberglass batt insulation with non-CFC, rigid foam insulation to provide an R-value of 11, reducing the heat gain and loss through the building walls by fifty percent. The tilt-up concrete walls from the former building have an insulation R-value of 7. A reflective roof coating reduces heat absorption between ten and forty percent, dramatically decreasing air conditioning requirements. The ERC's east and west section roof insulation has an R-value of 38, two times more efficient than the average California roof. The center roof section insulation is rated R-30.

### Glazing

Low-emissivity glass windows at ERC reduce heating and cooling needs by allowing light but little heat to penetrate during warm months. The windows are gas-filled and dual-glazed with a Heat Mirror™ sheet. Low-E glass skylights and translucent window walls allow natural daylight to illuminate interior spaces while reducing heat gain. In addition to saving on energy costs, the ERC windows are also an effective sound barrier that help minimize external noise.

### Heating and Cooling Systems

The Energy Resource Center uses both natural gas and electric systems to maximize efficiencies and cost savings. By controlling the peak-load uses of both energy sources, the use of the more energy-intensive mechanical systems is kept to a minimum as are the most expensive peak load volumes. The result is a careful balance of electric and natural gas uses. Part of the ERC system comes from a portion of the original building's system, including two 30-ton, gas-fired chillers and two 7.5-ton gas chillers which are integrated with new equipment. Using the existing air conditioning system significantly reduced new equipment and disposal costs.

The ERC uses a combined system drawing on four different types of equipment:

**Absorption Chiller/ Heater.** The ERC utilizes three 30-ton natural gas-fired double effect absorption chillers/ heaters to serve the majority of the existing building areas on the first floor and the entire second floor in the new center section. These CFC-free chillers reduce electrical demand and keep harmful ozone depleting substances out of the atmosphere. While most electric air conditioning systems still use CFC-based refrigerants, absorption chillers are more environmentally benign in that they use water as the refrigerant. Absorption chiller/ heaters also supply the majority of the Center's heating needs. The chillers are piped to air handling units that feature outside air economizers and variable air volume distribution. One of the units was provided by McQuay International, while the other two are from Yazaki.

**Desiccant Units.** Two dual-wheeled desiccant cooling units from Englehard/ICC Technologies have been installed in part of the building to improve indoor air quality. These units service the multi-purpose room and catering kitchen. By removing moisture, the desiccant units decrease the potential for growth of biological contaminants. The units are designed to intake 100 percent outdoor air when temperature and humidity levels are appropriate. Moisture removal in conventional air conditioning systems typically requires significant energy consumption. The desiccant units reduce conventional cooling requirements in these sections of the building by approximately forty percent.

**Indirect/Direct Evaporative Cooling.** Indirect and direct evaporative cooling serves the new portion of the first floor, including the main hall and lobby. Large quantities of outside air are brought into the space due to its high occupancy levels. Indirect/direct evaporative cooling uses a wetted medium to cool air, both directly and indirectly using a heat exchanger. Although the system operates using solely evaporative cooling for most periods, it is connected to an electric air-cooled condensing unit, which allows for additional mechanical cooling during extremely hot weather. On a seasonal basis, the system, provided by Energy Labs, is fifty percent more efficient than a conventional system.

**Package Units.** Carrier package units for electric cooling and gas heating serve different parts of the building, including the telecommunications and large equipment rooms. These advanced units have a seasonal energy rating (SEER) of 11.0, exceeding California Energy Commission requirements by ten to twenty percent.

All major air handling systems in the ERC use variable frequency drive technology to conserve energy. This varies the speed of the fans depending on cooling or heating demand. Conversion from constant volume to variable air volume (VAV) distribution results in a 75 percent reduction in fan energy requirements. (Fan energy is generally the third largest energy user in commercial buildings, following lighting and cooling.) In addition, one of the drives–called a "clean power" unit–virtually eliminates the need for the costly electronic harmonic filter systems typically required in data processing and other power-sensitive operations.

The make-up air unit (MAU) serves the large equipment demonstration area. When the exhaust fans are working to remove heat from the equipment, the MAU draws in outdoor air to make up exhausted air and maintain appropriate air pressure in the room. The unit employs a gas-fired heater and direct evaporative cooling module, which temper the air in lieu of costly mechanial cooling. A compensating hood, located in the roof above the building's Catering Kitchen and Food Service Equipment Center, acts as a self-contained exhaust and make-up air system, reducing the amount of electrical fan energy required to control kitchen ventilation.

A computerized energy management system optimizes energy use at the ERC by monitoring and controlling the building's heating, ventilation, air conditioning, and lighting systems through an extensive network of more than 230 data-gathering sensors. The system incorporates both equipment from the existing building as well as new equipment.

Though the design team did consider solar energy, demonstrations for heating and cooling could not be economically justified. Solar was also considered for exterior lighting around walkways and the parking lot, but an agreeable sharing of the costs among Southern California Edison, the Gas Company, and the South Coast Air Quality Management District could not be negotiated.

The combination system now in place best fits the ERC goals of blending energy efficiency, environmental sensitivity, and economic advantages. First, there was a desire to reuse as much of the former original office complex as possible. Then, there was an effort

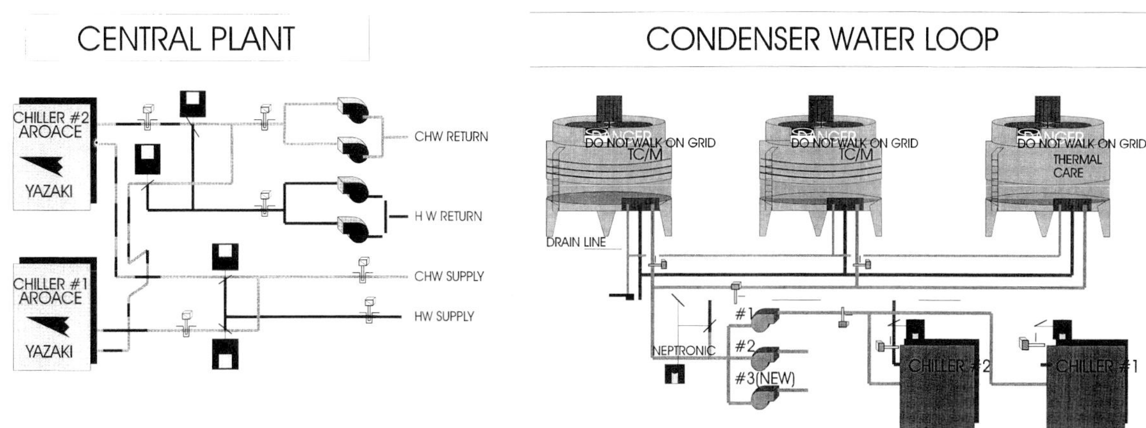


*Left: Central plant configuration. Right: Condenser water loop configuration. Drawings: Southern California Gas Company.*

***View of exterior detail showing shading and windows that provide natural light for the second floor offices. Photo: Southern California Gas Company***

to economically and efficiently augment the old equipment. Finally, the ERC itself serves to demonstrate state-of-the-art equipment with energy-saving and environmental advantages.

### Lighting

Within the constraints of the former building the design team worked to incorporate the greatest use of daylight. This created huge energy savings, as it resulted in the downsizing of the mechanical systems because of the reduced heat output of the lighting loads. The use of natural daylighting and advanced lighting techniques resulted in a reduction of up to 40 percent as compared with the original building.

The design team worked closely with mechanical engineers to incorporate optimal use of the solar orientation of the second story. During days of full sun, natural lighting from the second story reduces electrical lighting needs by as much as 80 percent. Translucent wall sections are strategically placed to allow daylight to saturate interior spaces, creating a soft ambient light in parts of the building. Daylighting controls routinely adjust the amount of electrical lighting used to augment natural light that enters through the high-performance windows and skylights.

Three skylights in the main first floor corridor incorporate a sun-tracking system that uses mirrors, reflective light ducts, and efficient diffusing lenses to create a technologically advanced interior lighting system for daytime use. One Sol-Luminaire skylight can eliminate the use of over two million watt hours of electric lighting per year. The skylights pay for themselves through energy cost savings after two to five years.

The use of high-efficiency T8 fluorescent lamps, electronic ballasts, daylighting systems, and light occupancy sensors reduces electrical energy requirements for ambient and task lighting by 47 percent. The savings is partially offset by a slight increase in heating load during winter months, due to the absence of waste heat from traditional lighting. However, the combined lighting systems and design techniques reduce electrical lighting costs by 41 percent. "Electronic ballasts and T-8 fluorescent lamps provide most of the ambient and task lighting in the ERC. T8 lamps are as much as 25 percent more efficient than standard T-12 fluorescent lamps," says ERC management. "Also, their one-inch diameter allows for the design of smaller, more compact fixtures with improved photometrics. Electronic ballasts increase lamp life and reduce heat normally generated by magnetic lighting ballasts, ultimately lowering air conditioning needs and energy bills."

Duplex/ 8DM light fixtures are used primarily for downlighting and wallwashing, and their shallow recess depth allows them to be mounted in a variety of areas. They are dimmable and use two 26-watt compact fluorescent bulbs. They provide 3600 lumens, nearly equivalent to a 200-watt incandescent lamp. The light fixture consumes only 60 watts when operated at 120 volts.

Occupancy and light sensors are used throughout the ERC. The sensors have a significant impact on energy savings, estimated between 35 and 60 percent. Ultrasonic or infrared occupancy motion sensors, which switch the lights on and off, are installed in all interior spaces of the ERC. In addition, in rooms with windows, ultrasonic or infrared sensors continuously adjust the amount of electrical lighting used depending on natural light levels. Through their energy savings, the sensors have a payback of one to three years. Dimmer switches and occupancy sensors increase efficiency by allowing for individual control or energy reduction when spaces are not occupied.

## *Air Quality*

The Energy Reource Center sought to create maximum indoor air quality through the design and selec-

***Second floor offices receive a combination of natural and artificial lighting, have an open layout of workstations, and exposed structure and HVAC plenums. Photos: Southern California Gas Company.***

tion of systems and materials for the facility. NASA research helped ERC's designers select plants that have the greatest ability to absorb indoor air pollution. In particular, the design team sought to increase fresh air ventilation, and decrease off-gassing by specifying toxic-free products.

At the ERC, one of the educational rooms is dedicated to air quality education and information. In the Air Quality Room, one can obtain information about the effects of major air pollutants, how new advanced gas technologies can be part of the solution to air quality, and programs and services to help building owners address local, state, and federal air quality regulations. Air quality computer simulation programs are available to help assess calculations and expedite the permitting process, and the technical staff provides guidance on the best available emissions technology.

### Ventilation Systems

Healthy Buildings International, ERC's air quality consultant, designed the building's ventilation system. Three air-handling units are equipped with carbon dioxide sensors for control of the outside air dampers, depending on the occupancy loads in the areas being served. The sensors are placed in the return-air ducts of the units to modulate the outside air dampers and maintain carbon dioxide levels below 700 ppm. Airborne particulate levels in the supply air to the building are controlled through the use of twelve-inch-deep box filters and two-inch-deep pleated panel filters in the main air handling units. These help minimize mold and bacteria in the air streams.

### Materials Toxicity

For optimal indoor air quality and minimum off-gassing, the design team opted to reduce the use of toxic products and materials. For example, some surfaces that could be left natural remained unfinished. Some of the non-toxic products that were used include:

- Non-toxic interior paint containing no petroleum derivatives, volatile organic compounds (VOCs), or other organic solvents.
- Non-toxic flooring sealers that provide available economic alternatives to urethanes, lacquers, and var-

***The reception area's recycled wood floor came from a San Francisco warehouse that was condemned after an earthquake. The reception desk is made of recycled tempered glass.***

***Carefully removed prior to construction, electrical conduit was stacked for reuse. Photos: Southern California Gas Company.***

nishes, reducing VOC emissions which react with nitrogen oxides and sunlight to form smog.

• Non-toxic sheet flooring, a durable linoleum floor made from linseed oil.

• Non-toxic carpet and padding adhesives, which eliminate toxic off-gassing while providing a permanently tacky, resilient glue line that withstands heavy traffic.

• Non-toxic tile adhesive that contains no petroleum-based solvents and bonds ceramic, vinyl, parquet, and formica tiles.

• Recycled carpet tiles made with a face fiber of 35 percent recycled, post-industrial nylon with a backing material that contains 2.5 percent recycled material. The backing also contains a broad-spectrum, antimicrobial called "Intersept," which helps keep indoor air healthy by inhibiting the growth of bacteria and fungi.

## *Resource Conservation*

The design of the Energy Resource Center primarily minimized the use of natural resources by decreasing consumption, reusing materials, recycling, and incorporating products that contain post-consumer recycled content and sustainable material sources that do not threaten fragile ecosystems. The first and largest step that they took to do this was to use more than sixty percent of the existing building. Sections of the former building were dismantled and reused.

### Deconstructed Materials Reuse

"The Energy Resource Center is not just using a few recycled products here and there. Instead of demolishing the building, the ERC was built mostly from parts of the former building. It was dismantled and 400 tons of materials were reused," says ERC's Tony Occhionero. Steps were taken to reduce the amount of waste destined for local landfills by recycling hundreds of tons of demolition material. Items separated for recycling include 232 tons of concrete sent to crushers and recyclers, 23 tons of roofing materials, 820 tons of asphalt, 27 tons of drywall, and 57 tons of metal. Craftsman Concrete Cutting sorted and recycled some of the materials, depositing the debris into eight 40-cubic-yard bins provided by local recycling subcontractor Calsan Inc.

Once the former building had been carefully dismantled, recycled, and most of the materials reused, a new structure was built in place of the original. The construction team incurred costs of more than $200,000 for coordination and extra meetings, mostly related to recycling. "We may have paid a premium for our efforts, but we felt strongly about the environmental issues," says Robert Goulden, senior project manager for Southern California Gas Company.

### Recycled or Sustainable Natural Content

The Energy Resource Center is composed of hundreds of innovative recycled products, from non-toxic paints to benches made of recycled plastic. All suppliers of selected environmental materials are required to use recycled, non-toxic, and environmentally sensitive materials, equipment, products, and procedures to the greatest possible extent. Where possible, local suppliers were selected to reduce the transportation distance of materials, resulting in the use of less energy and lower vehicular emissions.

Each "new" material was evaluated for its recycled content or sustainable natural content. Reinforcement bars in the building's structure are made of recycled steel from weapons confiscated by the Los Angeles County Sheriff's Department. The steel from a dismantled navy submarine was also purchased and recycled for the framing, and steel frames from the former Downey facility were reused. The reception area floor is made entirely of Douglas fir beams and posts from an abandoned turn-of-the-century warehouse in San Francisco. The pavement includes scraps of orange polyvinylchloride pipe used by the Southern California Gas Company to transport natural gas underground. Installed in the lobby is a 100% recycled wood floor, reclaimed from a San Francisco warehouse that was condemned after the Loma Prieta earthquake; a wall made of recycled aluminum that was taken from stock once earmarked for military aircraft; and a twenty-foot-long reception desk made from recycled tempered glass from demolished commercial buildings. Broken tempered glass, aviation metal, and car tires were also reused.

***Seen in this exterior view of the entry, the logo of the Southern California Gas Company is comprised of scraps of polyvinylchloride pipe used by the company to transport natural gas underground. Photo: Southern California Gas Company.***

### Purchasing Guidelines

In their Environmental Project Manual, the architects and E² made purchasing recommendations for food service equipment and office supplies. State-of-the-art gas appliances were specified for the kitchen/pantry, as well as an Asko dishwasher, a super-efficient refrigerator, front-loading washing machine, and gas dryer selected by The Gas Company. Final choices of all appliances were made at the time of occupancy to ensure that they would contain the latest in energy efficiency technology.

Energy Star computers and printers were suggested, and in addition to being energy efficient, the former pass rigorous Swedish Emission Standards. Internal fax modems and networking software also enable users to perform paperless tasks. Copy machines with double-sided copying capability and energy saving shut-down options, as well as plain paper ink jet faxes additionally cut down on energy use and material waste.

## *Water Conservation and Quality*

Water-conserving plumbing fixtures and sound landscape management reduce the use of water and

***The scope of work involved in the deconstruction, renovation, and new construction of the center was extensive. Built in 1957, the original building was carefully dismantled only as needed to be integrated into the design of the new facility. With construction underway, sections of the new structure were placed into the existing building. An aerial view of the completed site landscaping and building show the results. Photos: Southern California Gas Company.***

energy and the cost of sewage treatment bills. The plants featured in the landscape are native arid vegetation requiring little water. A drip irrigation system further increases water efficiency. Ultra low-flush toilets use half the water of conventional toilets, and the Department of Water and Power of Los Angeles provided rebates for their installation. In a future renovation, water captured from an experimental roofing system will irrigate planters surrounding the building.

## *Materials and Products*

### Criteria

The architects established that recycled, toxic-free, and environmentally-sensitive materials and products were to be used at the Energy Resource Center. Efficiency ratings for all equipment were obtained from the California Energy Commission, and final selections were made at the last possible moment, ensuring the use of only the most cutting-edge energy-saving technology.

### Toxicity

Paint, flooring sealers, adhesives, and carpeting are the products most likely to offgas and compromise a building's indoor air quality. Not so at the Energy Resource Center, however, because all of these were specified in non-toxic variations. ERC's paint contains no petroleum derivatives, VOCs, or other organic solvents; low-maintenance linoleum flooring is made from linseed oil; carpet padding and office partition panels are treated with Intersept, an anti-microbial agent that prevents bacteria and fungi from diminishing indoor air quality.

### Manufacturer's Environmental Impact

In addition to reviewing MSDS sheets for materials under consideration, the design team reviewed the manufacturer's impact on the environment for each system and product. Energy Labs, manufacturer of the indirect/direct evaporative cooling unit, used a special non-toxic white paint to finish the surfaces of the equipment for energy efficiency. Forbo Industries, the supplier of ERC's non-toxic sheet flooring uses environmentally friendly manufacturing methods and reuses production waste in its own facility. In general, the ERC Environmental Project Manual served as a guide not only for the types of environmentally sensitive materials and equipment that were used, but for how the production processes of each item are environmentally benign.

### Embodied Energy

The most striking example of ERC's concern for the embodied energy of building and construction materials is reflected in their use of an existing building. Instead of demolishing the 1957 office complex, they dismantled it only as needed. Approximately sixty percent of the building materials were either left in place, removed for future reinstallation, or recycled.

### *Post-Occupancy Evaluation*

Still in its first year, the ERC has not yet performed a post-occupancy evaluation at this writing, but their plans to do so involve "commissioning" the energy efficiency consultant. "Commissioning, in its broadest sense, is the structured process of ensuring that the energy-saving systems are designed, installed, and functionally tested and operated so as to meet the original design intent," says Robert Bein of William Frost & Associates. "This concept is relatively new, and is in an early stage of evolution and development. Ideally, commissioning should begin before the structure's design is completed, and the commissioning expert should be part of the project design team from the beginning. In the case of the ERC, this didn't happen, but we are making up for lost ground since entering the project two months prior to completion."

The post-occupancy evaluation was made more comprehensive with the addition of ninety monitored locations around the facility, bringing the total to just under 300. The combination heating/cooling system was fine-tuned in the first six months of operation. Indoor air quality assessments have been completed, and the special consultant for that area reported that there was significant improvement over the first four months of operation, recognizing that the facility began with an acceptable level due to low and non-toxic materials used. In addition, the lighting system was calibrated during the first four months. However, complete evaluation through commissioning takes the better part of the first year of operation of a building.

"It is only through careful calibration, testing, analysis, and integration of the performance of independent systems that it is possible to determine whether the building's energy systems are actually performing as intended," says mechanical engineer Sukdev Mathaudhu. The process also provides data which allows the systems to be modified and adjusted to achieve optimal performance. In addition, there is an important training function for building operators that can best be done as part of the commissioning process. Therefore, the ERC commissioning was structured so it could assure through the long term that the building performs at its best. The commissioning process is completely detailed so the center itself can use the data to help train energy decision-makers who look to the ERC as a knowledgeable business source.

## ENERGY RESOURCE CENTER MATERIALS RESOURCES

**Concrete formwork.** Polystyrene formwork; 50% reduction in concrete use, increased thermal insulation value; American ConForm Industries, 1820 South Santa Fe Street, Santa Ana, CA, 92705 (800) Con-Form

**Reinforcing bars.** Recycled weapons from LA County Sheriff's Dept; Tamco, P.O. Box 325, Rancho Cucamonga 91739 (909) 899-0660

**Plywood.** Oriented Strand Board (OSB); Made from rapid-growth trees, primarily aspen, uses less formaldehyde than conventional applications; Louisiana Pacific, 13850 Central Avenue Suite 500, Chino, CA 91710 (714) 628-2825, (800) 648-9116

**Hardwoods.** Sustainable woods; EcoTimber International, 350 Treat Avenue, San Francisco, CA 94110-1326

**Particleboard.** Medium-density fiberboard, "Medex II"; Medite Corporation, P.O. Box 4040, Medford, OR 97501 (800) 676-3339

**Insulation.** Amofoam-Rcy, recycled Insulation Board; Amoco Foam Products Company, 400 Northridge Road, Suite 1000, Atlanta, GA 30350 (404) 587-0535, (800) 241-4402

**Skylights.** Active daylighting systems; So-Luminaire Daylighting Systems, 444 Quay Avenue 6, Los Angeles, CA 90744

**Flooring.** Stoneware tile; Stoneware Tile Company, 1650 Progress Drive, Richmond, IN 47374 (317) 935-4760

**Adhesives.** Titebond All-Purpose, ES 747; Low VOC, water soluble; Franklin International, 2020 Bruck Street, Columbus, OH 43207 (800) 877-4583

**Flooring.** Marmoleum Linoleum; Made from linseed oil from flax, resins from pine trees, wood flour, jute, and cork; Forbo Industries, Inc., Maplewood Drive, P.O. Box 667, Hazleton, PA 18201 (717) 459-0771

**Carpeting.** Recycled materials, anti-microbial. Evergreen lease arrangement; Interface, Orchard Hill Rd., La Grange, GA 30240 (800) 336-0225

**Paint.** Spred 2000, Lifemaster 2000; Non-VOC, water-based; Glidden Paints, 1900 Josie, Carlton, TX 75006 (214) 416-1420

**Paint.** Cycle II recycled paint; Major Paint Company, 4300 West 190th Street, Torrance, CA 90509 (310) 542-7701

**Bathroom partitions.** Poly-Mar HD, HPDE; 80% postconsumer-recycled plastic; Santana Plastics, P.O. Box 2021, Scranton, PA 18501 (800) 368-5002

## HARMONY: A CENTER FOR THE STUDY OF SUSTAINABLE RESORT DEVELOPMENT

*St. John, Virgin Islands*

---

**Architect:** James Hadley Architect with Wank Adams Slavin Associates, New York, New York, James Hadley, *Associate Partner*

**Mechanical Engineer:** Real Goods, Ukiah, California, Jeff Oldham, *Manager, Renewable Energy Division*. Sandia National Laboratories, Albaquerque, New Mexico, Elizabeth Richards, *Sr. Member, Technical Staff*

**General Contractor:** Stanley Selengut, New York, New York and St. John, Virgin Islands. Nelson Uzzell Construction, St. John, Virgin Islands, Nelson Uzzell, *Principal*

**Energy Consultant:** Sandia National Laboratories, Albuquerque, New Mexico, Gary Jones, *Manager, Renewable Energy Program Office,* Elizabeth Richards, *Sr. Member, Technical Staff*

**Materials Consultant:** U.S. National Park Servic, Denver, Colorado, Bob Lopenske, *Senior Architect*, Sally Small, *Historical Architect*

**Total Area:** 2 1/2-Acre Site. 13,500 Square Feet. 840 Square Feet per Building (6 Buildings). 420 Square Feet per Unit (12 Units).

**Cost of Construction:** $160,000 per Building. $80,000 per Unit. $190 per Square Foot.

**BTU/ Square Foot Per Year:** None

**Date of Completion:** 1993

---

### *Project Overview*

Harmony is an independently powered research resort that overlooks Maho Bay in St. John, U.S. Virgin Islands, and rests on a 2 1/2-acre hillside. Conceived, according to owner, developer, and civil engineer Stanley Selengut, as an "educational experiment blending a luxury vacation adventure with the sustainable development of a fragile ecosystem," innovative construction techniques and a commitment to sustainability earned Harmony *Condé Nast Traveler*'s first annual Ecotourism award. The recipient of numerous prestigious international awards, it is the first luxury resort facility in the world to operate exclusively on sun and wind power. An article in *Forbes* magazine refers to Harmony's architectural features and economics as "good business." Harmony's creator, Stanley Selengut, is a pioneering developer, ecologist, and civil engineer whose practical approach establishes the simplicity and beauty of the resort. The aspect of Harmony that truly sets it apart is Selengut's unique view of architecture and resort operation as "theater."

"Instead of sealing off the elements of nature to protect its inhabitants as does traditional shelter," says Selengut, "the dwellings at Harmony orchestrate intimate interaction with the natural surroundings–iguanas, parrots, orchids, the lush tropical jungle, and the sun—without the discomfort associated with rustic habitats."

Selengut, in collaboration with the National Park Service, established the groundwork for environmental considerations within the context of tourism and hospitality with his first ecologically consious resort, Maho Bay, nearly twenty years ago. Located within a National Park on the north shore of St. John in the Virgin Islands, Maho Bay consists of 114 three-room open-air tent structures that rest on walkways high above the forest floor. Guests share four toilet and bath structures and a dining and activities pavilion. A commissary with manager's residence, kitchen, and office facilities completes this low-impact resort.

Another feature of the resort is that it has no roads. The main boardwalks were built first, and construction materials were then moved by hand along them; no excavation and minimal relandscaping were performed. Maho Bay also takes advantage of natural ventilation, thereby eliminating the need for air conditioning. The rustic character of the resort is based on the outdoor experience, and this generates a conservation ethic. Greater concentration of native bird and plant life is found at Maho than any other location on the island. Completed in the 1980s before the phrase "ecotourism" was ever coined, "Maho Bay quickly blossomed into a profitable enterprise that has earned international respect from environmentalists, economists, and hoteliers," says *Travel & Leisure* magazine.

In November of 1991 a workshop hosted by the National Park Service took place at Maho Bay. The partnership forum included participants from the American Institute of Architects, the America Society of Landscape Architects, the Ecotourism Society, National Parks and Conservation Association, National Oceanic and Atmospheric Association, Greenpeace, local representatives from the U.S. Virgin Islands, private architectural and engineering firms, and ecotourism resort operators. The professional participants brought diverse perspectives and ideas to the topic of ecological and cultural considerations in design. The result was the publication of *Guiding Principles of Sustainable Design,* a National Park Service publication which details many of the important aspects of building within an environmentally conscious framework.

The principles applied at rustic Maho Bay and further developed at the workshop were brought together and incorporated at Harmony to create a resort with sophisticated technologies in a more refined environment. Harmony: A Center for the Study of Sustainable Resort Development opened in October of 1993.

*The first luxury resort in the world to operate exclusively on sun and wind power, Harmony overlooks Maho Bay in St. John, the U.S. Virgin Islands. The open air pavilion is located to provide visitors with a view of the bay, natural light, fresh air and breezes, and lush natural vegetation. Photos: Maho Bay Camps, Inc.*

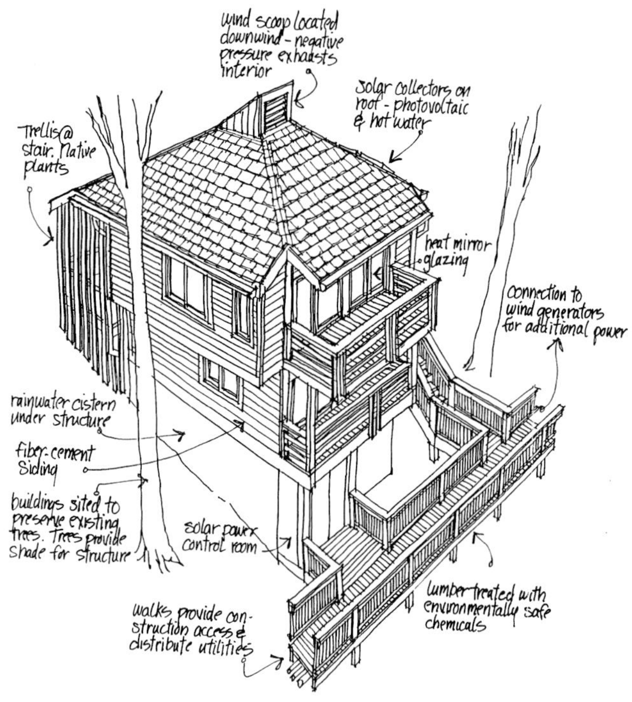


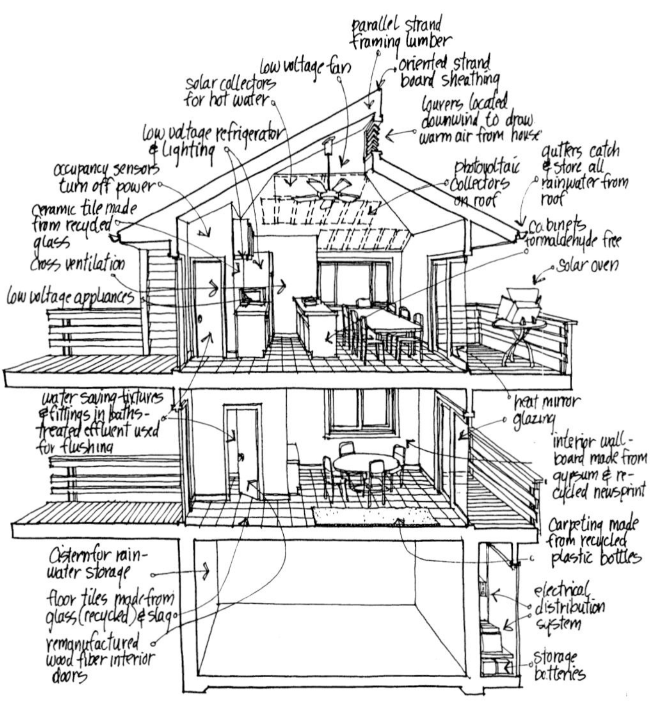


***Significant ecological features of the guest dwellings, which are grouped into two units per building. Drawings: J. Hadley Architect.***

### Architect Profile

Jim Hadley describes himself as "an acknowledged liberal with an interest in community and communities." Raised in a cooperative community established by a group of friends following World War II, Hadley left New York in the 1970s after receiving his Masters in Architecture from Columbia University in order to live and practice in a village community where he could be close to his children during their school years. Hadley's interest in community led him to help develop a farmers market in the town of Nyack, and to organize walking tours of the town's historic architecture.

Stanley Selengut and Jim Hadley first began working together during the 1970s in the planning and design of Maho Bay, and have continued to work together on proposed projects for resorts in Key West, Florida, and Grenada. As an associate partner with Wank Adams Slavin Associates of New York, Hadley recently worked on socially concerned projects that include housing for 135 homeless families, a control center for Metro North Commuter Railroad, a sports medicine center for Mount Sinai Medical Center, and a number of sites for the Phoenix House Drug Rehabilitation Program.

### Design Solutions

Eight of sixteen small structures planned for Harmony have been built and are separated by an extensive system of raised walkways. Rather than dominate the scenery, they are tucked inside trees, and subsequently blend with the tropical surroundings. "We designed the buildings to have a small footprint in order to create as little impact as possible, " says Selengut. "A passive solar cooling design uses a windscoop, cross-ventilation, overhangs, and landscape shading as well as heat-rejecting glazing and heat shields in the exterior walls. The units feature off-the-grid renewable resource energy systems and integrate recycled and renewable natural materials." According to Selengut, Harmony's design illustrates the ways in which a typical house can be sustainable.

One of Harmony's most distinguishing characteristics is the informality of the siting of buildings. Based on considerations of tree preservation, orientation to sun and breeze, and views from guest rooms, siting locations were chosen by the design team at the site. The structures' relatively small footprints allow them to be fit in among the trees, thereby preserving a maximum amount of vegetation and soil. Siting was done by the construction team under strict review by Maho representatives and the architect based on a set of sketch site plans establishing basic orientation and density guidelines.

## Environmental Objectives

In "Some Guidelines for the Architecture of Ecotourist Facilities" (*The Ecolodge Sourcebook*, 1995), coauthored with Patricia Crow, James Hadley succinctly outlines the goals of both Maho Bay and Harmony:

- Minimal impact on the environment
- Conservation of natural resources
- Active and passive environmental education of guests
- Contribution to the local community

"The most important and challenging aspect of designing Harmony was to build in the Maho Bay tradition of minimum site disturbance," says architect Jim Hadley. The project's main goal of maintaining the site's natural beauty was central to every other element in the design and construction of the resort. Selengut recognizes that site is the primary resource of Harmony and Maho Bay. From there stems his notion of site as living theater; natural features choreograph a discerning relationship between the activities and the guests enjoying them. This reverence for natural resources engenders a deep respect in the guests and staff at Harmony, who in return, protect and promote the natural beauty.

"Our goal is to leave as much valuable flora as possible, to restore the habitat to its past glory by plant-

***Top:** To leave as much valuable flora and fauna as possible, dwellings with small footprints were designed to be sited within existing trees.*

***Bottom:** Each visitor unit features recycled and non-toxic materials, natural light and breezes, energy efficient appliances, and walls decorated with woven fabrics and ceremonial masks crafted by tribes in South America and Africa. Photos: Maho Bay Camps, Inc.*

ing native plants and trees that will attract and support native birds and wildlife," says Selengut. On Harmony's pathways visitors are treated to special views of the landscape and wildlife, punctuated by the sound of chattering birds. Harmony's approach not only provides entertainment for the guests, but also serves functional purposes, as with the control of insects through the use of bat houses, which according to Selengut, "host one of the world's best bug catchers."

A recognition of endangered cultures was also part of the Harmony team's environmental goals. The resort features educational programs about indigenous cultures around the world, rooms are decorated with wall hangings and ceremonial masks crafted by tribes in South America and Africa, and walls bear paintings and weavings from Amazon cultures.

## *Working Methods*

### Project Team

"Most architects want to make things bigger," says Selengut, "but Jim understood our approach to resort design." The two then asked Nelson Uzzell, who had been building solar homes in California for many years, to join the team. Selengut also solicited help from the National Park Service, with which he had worked for many years. During a conference on sustainability in 1991, he met officials from the local Virgin Islands energy office who were looking to build a demonstration project. After connecting through the local energy office, Sandia Laboratories provided energy systems assistance while Real Goods, the main designers for the energy systems, provided the equipment.

***Guests monitor their water use and energy consumption and have access to information on renewable energy through a laptop computer provided in each of the units. Photo: Maho Bay Camps, Inc.***

Guests play a significant role in the ongoing project team. Paying tuition instead of room rates, they participate in the analysis of the project and provide suggestions for the future direction of the resort. As part of the routine, they monitor their electricity and water use by using the Toshiba laptop computer which is provided in each room. The high color resolution graphics software monitors the energy available in the building's batteries, helps guests convert current and voltage to watts, provides weather reports and electronic mail, and makes suggestions for further conserving energy. "On a cloudy day, patrons need to think twice before making toast," says *Caribbean Travel & Life* magazine, but Harmony's visitors don't seem to mind. "It's nice to feel like part of a solution," says Anita Evans, a New York musician who was one of the resort's first visitors.

### Computer Modeling

Each unit at Harmony is equipped with a Toshiba laptop computer that helps the visitor monitor energy use. When guests click on House Information, for instance, they can see their daily hot and cold water usage in gallons, as well as their input and output power in watts. An informational and educational tool, the computer also provides such data as current and future weather reports, brief facts on renewable energies, and a description with detailed diagrams of how a solar cell works.

### Construction Methodologies

According to Selengut, the Harmony team not only designed the resort's architecture, it designed the construction process itself. During construction, workers were required to avoid damaging the vegetation and heavy equipment was limited to certain areas. For instance, to avoid disturbing the site, the bulldozer stayed on one narrow service road, building footings were dug by hand, and cisterns were placed under the units close to the road. Walkways were built in the beginning of the process so that workers could traverse the slopes without trampling undergrowth. The walkways, however, were useful for more than foot traffic. The hose that delivered concrete mix long distances without spillage snaked along the walkways, while site plumbing and other lines were fastened underneath. "We purchased solar panels and a wind generator early so we could use them to power construction equipment, which also saved us money on a generator and diesel fuel," says the developer.

In November of 1991, during a National Park Service Workshop and as an outgrowth of the Maho experience, the following guidelines for the development and construction of the resort were established:

- Program all construction vehicle movement.

***Solar panels and a wind generator were purchased early to provide renewable power sources for construction equipment. The construction shed at Harmony houses equipment that was later integrated into the project. Photo: Maho Bay Camps, Inc.***

- Plan construction access and follow future circulation routes.
- Allow site considerations to form circulation where appropriate.
- Reuse site wastewater and compost.

The independently powered construction system was configured and provided by Real Goods International, an American company that specializes in products that promote the use of renewable solar technologies. Its components consist of:

- Trace C-30A Controller
- 30A 2 pole fused disconnect
- Ananda 400A fused disconnect
- Siemens M-75 Modules
- Trace 2524SB Inverter
- Pair 4/0 Inverter/Battery Cables
- Surplus 2V Submarine Batteries

### Site Review

The single most important aspect of Harmony is its site. Natural vegetation and wildlife, Caribbean beaches and seas, warm temperatures, breezes, and consistent sun are the primary resources at Harmony and Maho Bay. Every single design decision that was made took those resources into consideration first. James Hadley feels that the most important and challenging aspect of designing Harmony was to build in a way that would pose minimal site disturbance. Maintaining the original natural beauty of the site as the primary goal of Harmony was central to every other element in the design and construction of the resort. Selengut's notion of the site as living theater established that the natural features choreograph a discerning relationship between the activities and the guests enjoying them. Major pathways as primary movement through the site, special views, or chattering birds, for example, create pleasurable highlights.

Every effort was made to avoid excavation and most of the site remains undisturbed. All of the dwellings are built on piers, and the walkways are raised above the forest floor as well, providing hidden locations for pipes with easy accessibility for maintenance. Large equipment at the site was limited, and footings were dug with hand shovels. Ecological restoration of the site includes native plant landscaping; wildlife management; feral animal control; maintenance of existing relationships between site elements; positioning of structures to enhance perception of the landscape (note that a dispersed site plan allows for more visitor contact with the natural environment); the use of natural barriers for privacy; and utilities and services as part of the interpretive elements of the resort.

***The site and its important flora and fauna were at the center of every design decision that was made at Harmony. In fact, the siting of all major buildings was done on location, rather than the traditional method of locating structures on a site plan. All of the elements were choreographed as "living theater" to allow guests to interact with the site. Photo: Maho Bay Camps, Inc.***

## *Environmental Economics*

### Life Cycle Costs

"It's important to remember that life cycle costing is central to environmentally conscious and responsible design," says Hadley. Together Maho Bay and Harmony receive around 7,000 visitors annually at full capacity and gross $1,000,000 per year. Each unit at Harmony cost about $80,000 to build, including the $6,000 spent for energy equipment and shared walkways. The expense of landscaping was avoided by the practical effort of careful siting and construction methods.

"We net about 25% of gross, translating into an estimated four-year payback, which does not take into account savings for water and electric bills. Through the interest that we've received by creating a conscientious resort committed to preserving ecology, we've probably received $100,000 of free advertising. The notion of nature as living theater left us with money to spend on other necessary items," notes Selengut. "Environmentally responsible design is very profitable for us."

### Grants and Rebates

No financial assistance was received for design and construction, but Harmony attracted interest from the Clinton Administration and was granted technical support from a variety of sources who provided valuable professional services. The U.S. Virgin Islands Energy Office functioned as an energy consultant, providing important energy research data. The National Park Service was a significant partner in the development of Harmony, providing materials consulting assistance. Sandia National Laboratories and Real Goods provided mechanical engineering assistance that was required in order to design the independent energy systems at Maho Bay and Harmony.

## *Energy Conservation*

Harmony is completely "off the grid," and power is provided by the intense Caribbean sun and the reliable trade winds. Low-voltage appliances and the electrical systems are run by solar photovoltaic panels, back-up wind turbines supply power, and the design of the structures features passive solar energy design. Selengut formed an informal partnership with the Virgin Islands Energy Office and Sandia National Laboratories, a research arm of the Department of Energy that supplies Harmony with experimental products like solar ovens and solar ice-making machines. In turn, Harmony's guests provide feedback on the equipment's performance.

***A commercial solar ice maker is delivered to the site. Photo: Maho Bay Camps, Inc.***

*Clockwise: Each unit includes a key-activated power switch located at the entry that connects to everything except the refrigerator and the water pump. When a guest leaves and locks the door, power is turned off as well; each guest dwelling houses eight dry-cell batteries that convert the sun's rays to DC or AC current and store enough power at each unit for three consecutive days of cloudy or windless weather; each kitchen features energy efficient appliances such as a Sun Frost refrigerator and a Burns Milwaukee Sun Oven. Photos: Maho Bay Camps, Inc.*

At the core of each guesthouse are eight dry-cell batteries that convert the sun's rays to DC or AC current. An array of Siemens crystalline silicon photovoltaic panels provide 1100 watts. The system stores enough power to run a refrigerator, microwave oven, a ceiling fan, lights, and a water pump for three consecutive days of cloudy or windless weather. Experimental hardware is used to power refrigerators, solar ice machines, and solar ovens. Each dwelling features a key-activated power switch that feeds everything except the refrigerator and water pump. The key is fastened to a ring that also holds the door key.

Both the AC and DC panels are fitted with a contactor controlled key switch at the front door. When a guest leaves the room, she must remove this with the room key, which drops out the contactor, disconnecting one buss of the panel that has all of the nonessential loads on it. "We wanted to build the project using renewable energy, so we set up a PV construction system." The PV construction system proved to be more reliable than both the grid and generators would have been. There were many days when the grid was down and the crew was able to continue working productively. The system is now providing power to build the next phase of Harmony.

Each of the eight units at Harmony has a 24-volt system and uses the following equipment, designed and provided by Real Goods:

- Room Power Key Lock: When the room key is inserted into the lock to open the door, the room's power is activated. Conversely, when the key is used to lock the door, all power is deactivated, with the exception of the refrigerator.
- Siemens PC-4 Poly framed modules: These solar cells deliver high currents of power under difficult charging conditions, including overcast skies and hot temperatures.
- Ananda APT3 200 Power Center (Per 2 Units): A control center for the resort's photovoltaic and wind energy sources, it provides fuse protection and controls the charge for the entire power system.
- Powerstar UPG 1500 Inverter: Converts low-voltage DC into higher voltage AC, allowing Harmony to use conventional power loads.

***Roof detail of a typical unit with solar panels. The black rectangular panel provides hot water, while the other solar panel sections provide electricity. Photo: Maho Bay Camps, Inc.***

•L-16 Batteries: Offer more power with lower maintenance.

•Cruising Equipment Kilo-Watt Hour Meter: Permits the monitoring of power generation and usage at a glance.

•6 Circuit Square D Type QO Subpanel: Functions as a conventional electrical subpanel.

•Sunfrost RF-4 Refrigerator: In addition to providing highly effective refrigeration, it uses 1/6 of the energy of a standard model.

•Burns Milwaukee Sun Oven: Generates temperatures up to 500°F.

•Shurflo pump, 2.9 gpm at 40 psi: A very efficient low-voltage pump, it runs on battery power and pressurizes domestic water.

•Rocky Creek Hydro 24V Ceiling Fan, controlled by spring-wound timer: Extremely energy efficient, this "Casablanca"-type fan uses 1/4 the power of a conventional fan.

•Wind Baron Neo wind generator shared by both Maho Bay and Harmony: Acts as a charging source by generating 750 watts of power at 30mph winds.

### Building Envelope Insulation

In Harmony's roofing system, Low-E insulation is used between Homasote panels and plywood sheathing with a one-inch air space provided. Strong, effective, and efficient, this material provides high insulating value for its thickness. The foam is made from recycled milk jugs. The foil, also made from recycled sources, creates a surface of 97% heat reflection.

### Glazing

Windows and glass doors have Heat Mirror™ insulated glazing that deflects heat from the sun while admitting natural sunlight.

### Heating and Cooling

No heating or cooling systems are necessary in Harmony's Caribbean climate. The design of each guesthouse features a wind scoop which provides natural ventilation and reflects a design vocabulary in harmony with indigenous architecture on the island. The windscoop faces downwind so that warm air is drawn out through the louvers. The windows in the cottages are positioned for cross-ventilation to take full advantage of St. John's cooling northeasterly breezes. Also, the buildings are tucked between trees that provide shading. As new tent-cottages are built, design improvements continue to be made for better ventilation to lower energy consumption from fans.

Water is heated by a solar hot water system, supplied by a local company, Solenergy. Water used in the bath houses and laundry is not heated.

LIGHTING

Natural daylighting was incorporated by making public areas such as dining rooms and shared walkways open to the elements. At each of the dwellings, multiple glass doors and windows are used. Yet architect James Hadley feels that the exclusion of daylight was actually more important than its incorporation. The Heat Mirror coating that is installed at all of the glass admits natural light while deflecting the heat of the sun, and the preservation of existing vegetation close to the buildings provides passive cooling.

In addition to the use of natural ambient light, energy-efficient fixtures were specified throughout. Occupancy sensors and energy-efficient fixtures and bulbs are found in all of the systems at Harmony. All indoor lighting, provided by Real Goods, is compact flourescent. Each light bulb uses about one-fifth the energy of a standard bulb. When a guest leaves the room, the lights and non-essential appliances are automatically shut down. Harmony is also equipped with an exterior Heath/Zenith solar floodlight that becomes activated when it senses motion. Future plans include replacing light bulbs with halogen-type bulbs, and putting timers on electric switches in bath houses.

## *Air Quality*

MATERIALS TOXICITY

Interior materials were reviewed for off-gassing based on manufacturers' information and industry literature. Sally Small, of the Denver Resource Center of the National Park Service, advised the Harmony team in the area of materials specification. Toxic content was avoided wherever possible due to off-gassing that would adversely affect the indoor air quality. For example, interior cabinets were constructed without the use of formaldehyde adhesives. Non-toxic paints, ceramic tiles adhesive, and pest-resistant recycled content decking and siding was used in place of pressure-treated lumber.

## *Resource Conservation*

RECYCLED OR SUSTAINABLE NATURAL CONTENT

"Harmony is built entirely of scrap lumber, reconstituted paper, glass, plastic, and rubber," enthusiastically reports Selengut. "We chose construction materials from recycled materials. The floor decking is made from 100% recycled newspaper and the siding is a composite of cement and recycled cardboard. It comes with a 50-year guarantee, as do the roof shingles, which are also made from waste cardboard and cement. These shingles look like slate but are lighter and easier to work with." Rafters and floor joists are wood scrap composites; decking is made from a composite of sawdust and bits of plastic; the bathroom tiles are composed of crushed used light bulbs; the insulation foam is made from recycled milk jugs; the ceiling is made from recycled newspaper with vinyl coating; doors are remanufactured wood fiber interior doors; and the white kitchen countertops are made from 70% recycled glass. For Harmony's floors, the team used quarry tiles made from 100% scrap clay and ground brick, along with post-industrial waste from a GTE

***The floor joists that provide the structure for each of the dwellings are made of wood scrap composite that comes from waste and farmed trees. Photos: Maho Bay Camps, Inc.***

*Clockwise: The siding and roof shingles are made of a composite of cement and recycled cardboard; quarry tile, composed of 100% scrap clay and ground brick and post-industrial waste from a light bulb manufacturing facility, is set into place; floor decking, made of 100% recycled newspaper, is laid across wood scrap composite joists. Photos: Maho Bay Camps, Inc.*

light bulb manufacturing facility. The material used for the exterior decking, made of recycled old tires, is excellent for gymnasium floors and around slippery pools and walks. Lumber for the walkways is treated with a new process called ACQ, which makes it rot- and termite-proof. The process uses no chrome or arsenic, so the lumber is less toxic than regular pressure-treated lumber. The ACQ lumber deck and picket fence topped with a plastic lumber railing will outperform traditional materials. The sheetrock is recycled paper and gypsum, and the paint is water-based.

Harmony's furniture is either refurbished or fabricated from recycled materials. The furniture chair cushions are crafted from naturally colored cotton fibers. Bed linens and upholstery fabrics are woven from organic cotton processed without dyes or bleaches. Throw rugs are made from recycled plastic, and doormats from recycled automobile tires.

### Recycling System for Personnel and Guests

Effective recycling has been slow to come to the U.S. Virgin Islands. There are many problems inherent in being isolated by distance and water, and it is questionable whether the energy usage and cost of shipping the collected materials is cost effective. Nonetheless, Maho Bay and Harmony have been instrumental in starting an island-wide aluminum recycling program on St. John, and continue to promote recycling efforts whenever possible. "We collect, crush, and recycle our own glass which is used for backfill. We compost all of our kitchen waste. Paper and plastic cannot be recycled on the island, but we are working with the local government to solve some of these problems," says Selengut. Newspapers are donated to the Humane Society in St. Thomas and also used as protective wrapping at the store.

Some creative on-site recycling–or, rather, reusing–is also practiced. For instance, in the office, used paper is recycled into scratch pads, copying is double-sided, and envelopes are reused whenever possible. Housekeeping recycles old towels into cleaning rags, old sheets go to maintenance, and old blankets go to the store for insulation of freezers. To eliminate waste, a Help Yourself Center is located centrally where guests can leave unused goods like suntan lotion or coffee. Additionally, no disposable items are provided in Harmony's tent cottages and restaurant; glasses, cups, plates, and utensils are reusable, and at the bar, guests are given a 25-cent discount on every refill of beer if they reuse the same mug. In the store, cardboard boxes and egg crates from vendor deliveries are used as an alternative to disposable shopping bags, and customers are encouraged to bring back their gallon plastic jugs for reuse as water carriers.

### Composting

A composter shared by the resort's units turns food waste, newspaper, and cardboard into garden mulch in just two weeks, eliminating the need for the removal of organic waste to landfills. The Composift machine is powered by a small electric gear motor (one kilowatt-hour per cycle) and is designed to both compost and sift.

### Purchasing Guidelines

Harmony extends its commitment to the environment through its choice of products and suppliers. Products whose manufacturers contribute to philanthropic causes are sold in the store and, in turn, those known to originate from endangered plants or animals are not carried or used. The restaurant carries no disposable cans or bottles, instead providing draft beer and sodas; homemade granola is offered in lieu of cereal in boxes; and take-out is not permitted, thereby eliminating the use of styrofoam containers. The kitchen and housekeeping departments purchase supplies in bulk, and the restaurant and store have consolidated their ordering of supplies to reduce traffic and consumption by delivery trucks. The purchase of certain items has even been banned due to their excessive packaging.

***Top:* Bed linens are manufactured from harvested cotton that is dyed with natural colors during its growth. *Middle:* Aluminum cans are compressed into bales and stored for recycling. *Bottom:* Food waste, cardboard, and newspaper are turned into garden mulch in about two weeks. *Photos:* Maho Bay Camps, Inc.**

## *Water Conservation and Quality*

Rainwater is collected on roofs, stored in cisterns underneath the buildings, and filtered before use. At Maho Bay, where guests take solar-heated showers in community bathrooms, shower hours are restricted and no running water is supplied to most tent-cottages. The "luxury" units at Harmony use low-flush toilets and spring-loaded faucets. All of these measures have resulted in extremely low water usage–25-30 gallons per person per day, about a third of what the average person uses in the United States. Wastewater is treated and reused for irrigation. A water retention system is planned at the site for graywater to be used for garden irrigation. Human waste, currently housed in a septic system, will be treated in a small package plant.

## *Materials and Products*

### Criteria

To find appropriate products, the Harmony team consulted the AIA's *Environmental Resource Guide.* "We wrote letters to each of the companies and worked with Sally Small at the Denver Resource Center of the National Park Service to review criteria such as toxicity, embodied energy, and manufacturer's environmental impact." says Selengut. "If anything, it's been tough deciding which products to choose from. We found either recyclable products or renewable products for every element, down to the nails."

All appliances are low-voltage models. The heavily insulated Sunfrost refrigerator uses one-sixth of the energy of a standard model. The barbecue grill is a solar oven that generates temperatures of up to 500°F.

***The pristine beaches at Maho Bay serve as a reminder that water is a critical resource that directly affects the quality of life. Water conservation and quality are paramount in the design, construction, and operation of Harmony. Photo: Maho Bay Camps, Inc.***

### Toxicity

When designing the resort, the Harmony team even took the aspect of maintenance into account. Surfaces at the Center are swept or wiped down, and no electrically powered cleaning equipment is needed. Whatever cleaning products are used are strictly biocompatible. To control cockroaches, the staff uses boric acid powder rather than poisonous sprays that can adversely affect wildlife.

## *Post-Occupancy Evaluation*

Guests are asked to complete a questionnaire prior to leaving the resort. Harmony's management is centered around carefully responding to the suggestions of its visitors, whose repeat business comprises the largest margin of Harmony's revenue. "We're excited about the recognition and awards that Harmony has received, but the most interesting thing that we learned after spending $7000 per unit at Maho Bay and $80,000 per unit at Harmony was that most of our guests missed the rustic hands-on experience of the less expensive solution." As a result, Stanley Selengut is currently working on Estate Concordia, designing and building "eco-tents" that combine the best of both and cost less to build. His approach to the ongoing project expresses his belief that "it is continuously evolving, an important aspect of sustainability."

During the hurricane in the summer of 1995–the hurricane that destroyed most of the island of St. John–Harmony not only structurally weathered the storm, but also maintained full power and hot water while other facilities suffered from power outages. Damage that occured to tents in Maho Bay was minimal and easily repaired.

### HARMONY RESORT MATERIALS RESOURCES

**Railways and walkways.** Timbrex Composite Lumber; Wood polymer composite lumber, recycled plastic and sawdust; Mobil Chemical Company, Composite Products Division, 800 Connecticut Avenue, Norwalk, CT 06856, Kevin Porter (800) 846-2739

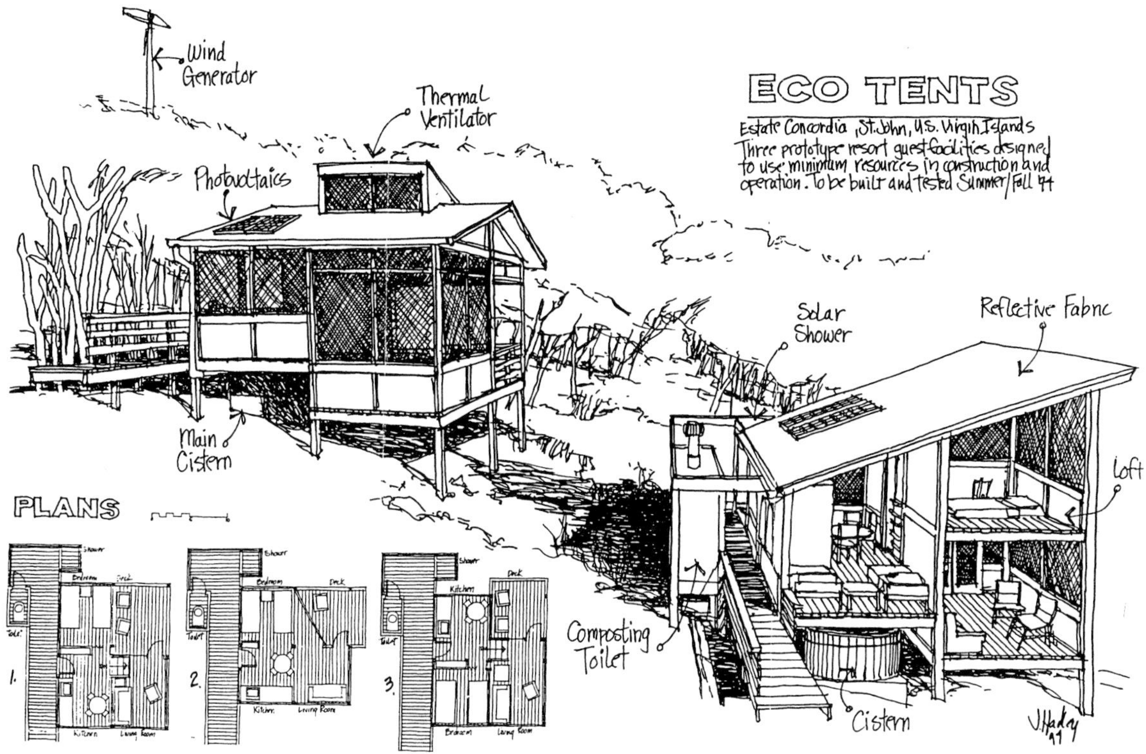


***New Eco-Tents at Estate Concordia combine the best features of both Maho Bay and Harmony, and incorporate more new high-performance, recycled, and non-toxic materials. Drawing: James Hadley, Architect.***

ACQ Preserve; Pressure Treated Lumber; Chemical Specialities, One Woodlawn Green Suite 250, Charlotte, NC 28217, Tom Bailey (800) 421-8661

**Floor Girders.** TJI Joists; Products are made from waste and farmed trees; Pompano Beach, FL 33069, Jeffrey Lieder (305) 946-5111

**Roofing Shingles.** "Southern Slate" roof shingles; Made from cement fibers and recycled cardboard fibers; FibreCem Corporation, 11000-I S. Commerce, Boulevard, Charlotte, NC 28241, Markus Francke (800) 346-6147

**Roofing Insulation.** Low-E insulation between homosote panels and plywood sheathing; Environmentally Safe Products, 313 W. Golden Lane, New Oxford, PA 17350, Peter Held (800) 289-5693

**Roof Decking .** "Easy-Ply" 1 3/8"-thick boards; 100% recycled newspaper, load bearing w/ pre-finished surface exposed above the rafters; Homosote Company, Box 7240, W. Trenton, NJ 08628-0240, Tom Petrino (609) 223-3300

**Windows and Doors.** Solar Cool glazing, high quality units w/stainless steel gears (operate in a moist, humid marine environment; Progressive Glass Technology, 155 Center Court, Venice, FL 34292, David Layman (800) 237-6258

**Exterior Siding.** Hardi-Plank Siding; Moisture-resistant, fire-resistant, rot-proof; James Hardie Building Products, 1225 La Quinta Drive, Suite 218, Orlando, FL 32809, Gabe Ferrazzano (800) 343-5711

**Interior Walls.** Fiberbond Gypsum Wallboard Panels and Dri-Mix Joint Compound Cellulose fiber; From recycled waste paper; Louisiana-Pacific, P.O. Box 2012, Port Hawkesbury, NS BOE-2VO, Canada, Lloyd George (902) 625-3070

**Nails.** Made from industrial remelt; Maze Nails, 100 Church Street, Peru, IL 61354, Roelif Loveland (815) 223-8290

**Floor Decking.** 4-way tongue & groove floor decking; 100% recycled newspaper, 4' x 8' sheets, moisture resistant, treated for termite, rot, and fungus protection; Homosote Company, Box 7240, W. Trenton, NJ 08628-0240, Tom Petrino (609) 223-3300

**Floor Tile.** Softpave tiles; Recycled tire rubber, water permeable, resilient; Carlisle Tire & Rubber Company, P.O. Box 99, Carlisle, PA 17013, John Yaw (800) 851-4746

**Counter and Table Tops.** Craftsman tile; 73% recycled waste glass; Stoneware Tile, 1650 Progress Drive, Richmond, IN 47374, Ken Cloud (317) 935-4760

**Carpet.** Image Broadloom Carpet Throw Rugs; Fiber is 100% post consumer recycled PET polyester; Image Industries, Inc., P.O. Box 5555, Armuchee, GA 30105, (706) 235-8444

**Generation System.** 4 Siemens PC-4 poly-framed modules, 1 Ananda APT3 200 power center (per 2 units)1 Powerstar UPG 1500 inverter, 4 L-16 batteries, 1 Cruising Equipment kilo-watt hour meter, 16- Circuit Square D-type QO subpanel, 1 Shurflo pump, 2.9 gpm at 40 psi, 1 Rocky Creek Hydro 24V ceiling fan, controlled by spring-wound timer, 1 Heath/Zenith solar floodlight, 1 Wind Baron Neo wind generator (shared by the entire project); Real Goods Trading Corporation, 966 Mazzoni Street, Ukiah, CA 95482, Jeff Oldham (707) 468-9292

**Lighting.** Compact fluorescent; Real Goods Trading Corporation, see previous.

**Oven.** Sun Oven–Villager Model; Institutional size for restaurant and bakery use, generates temperatures up to 500°F; Burns-Milwaukee, Inc., 4010 W. Douglas Avenue, Milwaukee, WI 53209, Tom Burns (414) 438-1234

**Refrigerator.** Sun Frost RF-4, 24-volt DC refrigerator/ freezer; Uses 1/6 energy of typical unit; Sun Frost, P.O. Box 1101, Arcata, CA 95521, Kael Balizer (707) 822-9095

## HERMAN MILLER
## MILLER SQA FACILITY
*Zeeland, Michigan*

---

**Architect:** William McDonough + Partners, Charlottesville, Virginia, William McDonough, AIA, *Principal*, Chris Hayes, Kevin Burke, *Director of Design*, Celia Imrey, Loren Abraham, AIA, IDSA, *Director of Research*, Roger Schickedantz, AIA
**Architect of Record:** Ver Burg & Associates, Holland, Michigan, David VerBurg, AIA, *President*, Craig Slager, AIA, *Associate Architect*, James Davis
**Interiors Architect:** Ver Burg & Associates, Inc., Holland, Michigan, Bede Van Dyke, AIA
**Acoustic Engineer:** Shen/Melsom/Wilke, Inc. New York, New York, Mark Reber, Fred Shen
**Electrical Engineer:** Parkway Electric Company Holland, Michigan, Doug Mitchell, Frans Jungslager
**Mechanical Engineer:** Quality Air Heating and Cooling, Grand Rapids, Michigan, Gerry Munger, *Designer*, Bob Powers, Mike McKenna
**Structural Engineer:** Soils and Structures, Muskegon, Michigan, Bill Hohmeyer, Brian Murphy
**Structural Consultant**:Thornton-Tomasetti Engineers, New York, New York, Kirk Mettam, P.E.
**General Contractor:** Owen-Ames-Kimball, *Vice President*, Grand Rapids, Michigan, John Keelean, *Vice-President*, Ron Bieber, *General Superintendent*, Brad McAvoy, *Project Manager*, Ken Nederveld, *Project Superintendent*
**Lighting Consultant:** Kugler Tillotson Associates, Inc., Suzan Tillotson, IALD, *Principal*
**Daylighting/ Materials Analysis:** Environmental Research Group, Charlottesville, Virginia, Loren Abraham, AIA, IDSA, *Principal*
**Glazing Design:** Lakeshore Glass & Metals, Inc., Holland, Michigan, Brad Zeeff
**Landscape Architect:** Pollack Design Associates, Ann Arbor, Michigan, Peter Pollack, *Principal*, Patrick Judd
**Total Area:** Manufacturing/ Warehouse: 240,000 Square Feet. Interior: Street: 13,600 Square Feet.
**Air Conditioned Areas:** (includes Offices, Health &Fitness Area, and Commons): 42,400 Square Feet.
**Total:** 296,000
**Cost of Construction:** $14,382,271
$49.07 per Square Foot
**Date of Completion:** 1995

---

### *Project Overview*

"The CEO of Herman Miller, whom I had come to know well," says architect William McDonough, "was interested in integrating sustainable practices into Herman Miller's furniture manufacturing and selling practices." Herman Miller needed a new manufacturing facility for its subsidiary, Miller SQA (previously Phoenix Designs). Several of Miller SQA's products were made with recycled materials, some of them recycled from previously owned Herman Miller products. It seemed like a natural opportunity for both Miller SQA and McDonough to introduce environmental principles into the manufacturing process, so McDonough suggested that his firm should design the new facility, which would be conceived as an ecologically intelligent building from the start.

The Miller SQA Facility incorporates integral siting of wetland areas, a plan that provides long-term flexibility, and a number of energy-efficient measures. The most significant environmental feature among them is the implementation of daylighting and solar heating. The way in which the two are combined makes the Miller SQA Facility responsive to natural energy flows.

#### Architect Profile

William McDonough established his firm, William McDonough + Partners, in 1981 in New York. Since his project for the Environmental Defense Fund in 1985 in New York City, McDonough has become one of the most highly respected and commissioned architects in the United States for his approach to design and his sensibility of environmental justice. McDonough is covered in greater detail in Chapter 2, Defining Environmentally Conscious Architecture.

#### Design Solutions

Three key concepts guided the design of the new facility: occupant comfort, health, and communication; the integration of the exterior landscape; and maximum use of daylighting. "At the new Miller SQA Facility, attention to the social and physical conditions faced by employees guided the design of the entire project," says McDonough. Miller SQA sought to create a high level of communication between those who worked in the office and those who worked in the plant. McDonough's response was to create a long, open "street" to establish a public "urban" connection between office and manufacturing areas. The entire building is organized along a curved street which offers, as in ancient cities, the most important place for social encounter. The skylit street serves as the main circulation link, and runs nearly the entire length of the facility. The cafeteria, referred to as the "Commons" is also a central gathering place which is connected, like a piazza, to the street. A series of smaller-scale open spaces and bamboo plantings along the street create an environment conducive to spontaneous social and business encounters. "To further engender communal well-being and worker satisfaction," says "McDonough," one large break area is located at the end of each street."

The creation of a work environment which feels like the outdoors was intended to provide a refreshing and productive atmosphere in which to work, and to establish a physical association with the exterior environment. The interior was conceived and

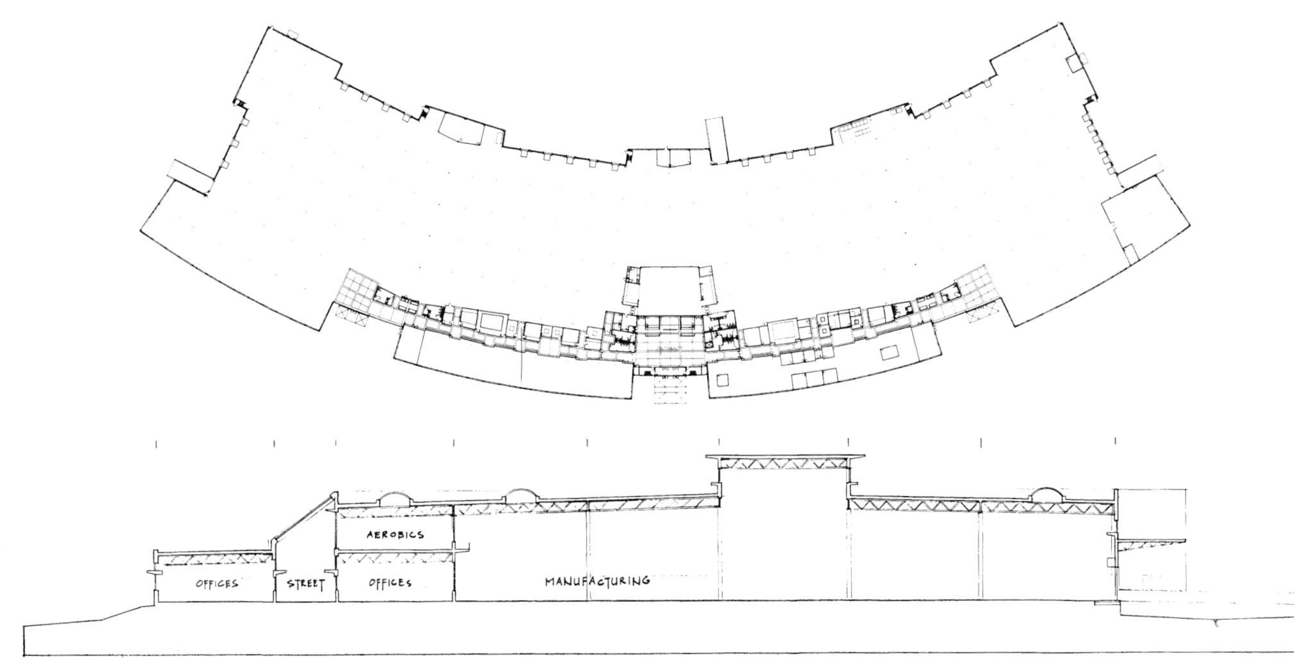


***Integration of the landscape, attention to physical health and comfort, and ease of communication guided the entire design of the Miller SQA Facility. The plans are organized along a curved daylit "street" that runs the full length of the building, encouraging social encounters. Photo and drawings: William McDonough + Partners Architects.***

***The inclusion of amenities like the fitness room and a basketball court contribute to staff health and productivity. Photos: William McDonough + Partners***

detailed to make connections to the natural world, and to introduce its natural light and color into the interior. Linking the building with the landscape was addressed as the context of the site, existing housing, and significant natural features were acknowledged and respected in every way. "Seen from afar, the building and site blend, the view is one of native trees, grasses, and wildflowers," says McDonough. "Closer in, land shape and landscape lead toward the architecture. As one moves closer, through a layered series of woods, hedgerows, and grass fields, and on up vertically past wetlands, lowlands, and uplands, the overiding message is that Miller SQA and the land are physically integrated."

Daylighting was a key element in determining the architecture of the building. Large amounts of carefully modulated daylight provide a pleasing, healthful environment in which to work, and significantly reduce energy costs by reducing electric lighting needs. "Bringing in maximum daylight wherever possible for both the manufacturing and offices allows the building occupants to work in optimum natural light," says McDonough. "The windows and clerestories are oriented toward the south and are operable for fresh air."

### Environmental Objectives

"Living in sustainable architecture is nothing less than an appeal to accept our place in the world, mediated between natural and human purposes," believes McDonough. "We should listen to John Todd's idea that we need to work with living machines, not machines for living in. The focus of architecture should include people's needs, natural resources, clean water, safe materials, and long term durability." McDonough's goal is to design a building that is alive and responsive to its inhabitants. A major aspect of the living machine concept is to allow people to experience cyclical and climatic changes. In a typical modern building, one is sealed in an environment that is completely cut off from the outside. "In this facility, people have easy access to operable windows and multiple views to the outdoors," explains McDonough. "In other words, one goal is to put the occupants of the building in touch with their environment." The design of the Miller SQA Facility seeks to do this at every turn. The design process addressed the various scales of the project, from the regional to the individual, while looking for a design solution which would bridge the two.

The energy savings in the building have far greater consequences than simply the cost savings to the owner. "As a result of the implementation of energy-efficient strategies, the annual energy savings will be 1.718 Gwh (GigaWatt-hours)", says consultant Loren Abraham. This will result in the prevention of the following associated emissions annually:

| *Power Plant Emissions Tons* | *AFBC Conversion Factor* | *Metric* |
|---|---|---|
| CC2 | 1,057.09 Tons/GWh | 1,816 |
| NOx | 1.55 Tons/GWh | 2.66 |
| SOx | 2.97 Tons/GWh | 5.1 |
| Particulates | 1.62 Tons/GWh | 2.8 |
| Coal Waste to land fill | 142.69 Tons/GWh | 245 |

## *Working Methods*

### The Project Team

Herman Miller had a significant facilities management team already in place, including a structural engineer, environmental engineer, landscape architect, and architect of record. Following the initial suggestion that William McDonough + Partners design a new facility for Miller SQA, McDonough proposed to hold a charette at the site that would include all the members of the existing facilities management team. Fifteen people, including most of the principals involved, comprised the project Design Team and worked over a three-day charette to develop a basic scheme for the building. The charette yielded the building's basic geometry as well as the key concepts that would be further developed to help define the project. Upon returning to their offices, William McDonough + Partners led the Design Team and further developed the architectural, landscape, and technical concepts which first emerged during the charette. A booklet was prepared which would represent the fully developed proposal to the Herman Miller Board of Directors regarding the new facility. "A presentation was made to the Board that was accepted in record time—less than 10 minutes," remarks McDonough.

The advanced research department of William McDonough + Partners, led by Loren Abraham, AIA, contributed greatly to the project. "All projects present specific challenges that can't just be addressed by existing research because related technology evolves rapidly," says McDonough. "For this project, we did specific research on paint and carpet, and an especially thorough study of daylighting conditions was completed."

### Computer Modeling

In order to fully complete a study of daylighting and passive solar strategies, extensive computer analysis using several types of simulation software was used. William McDonough + Partners documented the resulting information in a final report which included details of all designs evaluated, the results of the computer simulations, and the various tables and charts displaying the data, supporting conclusions, and recommendations. Of the schemes analyzed or recommended, many included preliminary cost and payback analysis in addition to estimated savings. Other recommendations regarding possible visual problems, required shading and dimming systems, surface finishes, excessive thermal gains or losses, current products and technology, and other related issues were outlined as well.

Space was analyzed individually by computer simulation using AAMASKY1 and SUPERLITE 2.0 lighting simulation software developed by Lawrence Berkeley Laboratory in Berkeley, California. Other analysis tools used were DAYLIT and SOLAR 5.2, both developed by the University of California Los Angeles (UCLA) Graduate School of Architecture and Urban Planning. DAYLIT is a daylighting analysis tool and SOLAR 5.2 is a tool for analyzing passive solar strategies in buildings. AAMASKY1 is configured to run on Lotus 123-Macintosh version. SUPERLITE 2.0, DAYLIT, and SOLAR 5.2 are configured to run on a Macintosh simulating an MS-DOS Operating System via Soft PC 3.1.

Several versions were performed for each of the spaces to evaluate the proposed design as well as other possible configurations and performance specifications. Each of the design configurations was analyzed in a sequence intended to lead to an optimal daylighting and passive solar design solution or to compare various possible configurations. In addition to the iterations listed and documented in the appendices of the report, numerous subiterations were performed to determine optimal glazing specifications and skylight-to-floor area ratios or glazing-to-floor area ratios. The report attempts to analyze probable brightness or visual comfort problem areas, and daylight distribution and uniformity based on the computer simulation findings, standards, conventional practice, and known daylighting guidelines.

### Construction Methodologies

After the initial charette, the project team was already in place. "The Herman Miller facilities management team had worked closely with WM+P over the initial charette, and they would continue to play their established roles, working closely throughout the project. The Herman Miller team proved eager to learn more about ecologically intelligent design, and clearly valued its participation in the project as an opportunity to develop within its own business," recalls McDonough. "Because there was so much communication and general agreement about the special nature of the project from the start, typical construction documents and coordination were sufficient to guide construction of this project."

The issue of soil disturbance during construction was addressed both in planning stages and through-

***Materials, such as the metals shown here, were separated for recycling. Photo: William McDonough + Partners.***

***The integration of the building with the site was a primary objective for the architects. The Miller SQA Facility responds to a harsh climate, preserves vegetation, and water quality, and sustains the creature habitat. Drawing: William McDonough + Partners Architects.***

out the construction process. In addition, many construction techniques were evaluated, such as the use of masonry cleaners to remove efflorescence or floor coatings for manufacturing areas.

### Site Review

Of particular interest to McDonough was the integration of building and site. The Holland/ Zeeland region of western Michigan where the Miller SQA Facility is located has several unusual environmental features. The site's location is in the transition zone between the southern lower peninsula's oak hickory habitat and the northern lower peninsula's beech maple habitat. The climate produces a long, 160-day growing season, but the lake compounds the freeze-thaw cycle, or, in other words, causes more days with melting and nights with freezing. This produces a more harsh condition for both constructed and natural features and facilities. The Black River watershed, within which Miller SQA lies, is primarily within Ottawa County. The site is adjacent to and drains directly toward the river. Water quality resulting from storm run-off is of major importance as Black River is the primary source of surface water feeding Lake Macatawa. Lake Macatawa, in the heart of Holland, is directly tied to the sustenance of animal, bird, and fish habitat, as well as to human social, economic, and environmental quality of life.

At the site itself, neighbors include the very visible new homes in an adjacent subdivision, travelers on highway 196 to the east, and Herman Miller's Distribution Center. "Not so obvious," says McDonough, "is the flora and fauna in the river/ stream corridors, wetlands, and fields. We felt that the goal of the project should include increasing the quantity and quality of habitat. We believed the building should fit within existing human and natural systems and create minimal long-term interruption." For nearly fifty years it has been Herman Miller's policy to maintain fifty percent of all its sites as natural habitat and green space. Within the Miller SQA site, the most dominant influences are topography, occuring as a ridge line falling off more steeply toward the Black River; the farmhouse environs with their cultural history and mature trees; existing wetlands and stormwater surface flows; and existing vegetation in the form of hedgerows, new plantings, and native grasses in lieu of manicured lawn.

All of the site and regional conditions reflect a midwestern landscape of layers. "The objective of the site,

***At Miller SQA, portions of the site were reforested in order to provide shelter and buffer winds, direct windblown snow away from the building, visually screen adjacent homes, and direct stormwater run-off. Photo: William McDonough + Partners.***

like that of the building, is a living landscape, not just something to be displayed," explains McDonough. "The Design Team listened closely to Peter Pollack as we created a facility that can be actively and healthfully used by birds and animals, as well as humans. Landscape is a sequence of horizontal and vertical layers that should be thought of as creating habitat." Horizontally, the layers are additive and move from the existing homes west to new hedgerows and woods, to fields and land forms, and to building and parking. Vertically, the layers progress from the river to wetlands to low-lying lands, and then to uplands where the building is placed.

Project goals included the reforestation of portions of the site in horizontal layers to provide shelter, buffer winds, encourage windblown snow to fall at areas other than at the building, and visually screen adjacent homes, Miller SQA, and Midwest Distribution Center (an existing warehouse) from each other; the buffering and direction of stormwater run-off; and the use of native plants and grasses to create habitat, lower maintenance costs, and provide educational opportunities to employees and area residents.

## *Environmental Economics*

### LIFE CYCLE COSTS

"Life cycle analysis in design implies the study of the entire cycle of material from construction to adaptation of structures which will be built," writes McDonough in the *Hannover Principles: Design for Sustainability.* "Usually, this information is considered part of environmental impact analysis, but we believe it is an integral part of design. Quality of life needs to be implied in the design itself, not legislated by a list of rules."

ANNUAL COST SAVINGS BY AREA AND FEATURE

| *Savings* | *Area* | *By* | *Total Savings* |
|---|---|---|---|
| Lighting | Mfg/Warehouse | Skylights | $39,269 |
| Lighting | Mfg/Warehouse | Roof Monitors | 1,676 |
| Lighting | Offices | Windows/Shelves | 4,712 |
| Lighting | Interior Street | Sloped Glazing | 6,044 |
| Lighting | Wellness Center | Windows | 1,098 |
| HVAC | Air Conditioned Spaces | | 5,180 |
| HV | Non Air Conditioned Spaces | | 30,820 |
| **Total Annual Cost Savings** | | | **$88,799** |

*Above: Daylight monitors in the manufacturing area provide bright indirect natural lighting that, on sunny days, provides most of the lighting needed in the area.*

*Right: A number of glazing treatments provide direct and indirect natural lighting for maximum aesthetic and practical impact. Photos: William McDonough + Partners Architects.*

McDonough refers to this process as optimization. Optimization implies looking at all the data available about the products or systems related to their initial cost, the potential savings in energy and/or benefit to productivity and the health of the occupants and the environment over their life cycle, and then incorporating this information into the design solution. It means having an attitude regarding design wherein one has the intention to "invest," in every profitable sense of the word, in a program that recognizes that there will be a tomorrow.

With the assistance of computer modeling, consultant Loren Abraham determined the following savings based on energy efficient strategies: According to the study, without the energy saving features, particularly passive solar and daylighting strategies, annual energy costs were projected at $585,000 or $1.98 per square foot. The projected costs, with the strategies employed, are $487,000 or $1.65 per square foot, providing a savings of $.33 per square foot per year.

Grants and Rebates

No grants or rebates were available for this project because the local utility has extremely low power costs (around four cents per kilowatt hour) with no peak rates.

## *Energy Conservation*

### Building Envelope Insulation

The Miller SQA team specified a non-CFC expanded polystyrene insulation for the building envelope. Applied by being blown in to the building cavity, this insulation provides an especially efficient R-60 value for the roof and R-20 for the walls. The disparity between the two arises from the fact that the single-story structure contains so many windows. This, however, is mitigated by the glazing the team selected, a low-E argon-filled type that, according to the Design Team, is the most appropriate glazing available on the market.

### Glazing

Technologically advanced, low-emmisivity argon-filled skylights and windows were specified throughout the building. Because of the daylighting strategies and abundance of glass in the structure, glazing in all its forms–windows, roof monitors, and skylights–was of particular importance. A window to floor ratio told the design team how much glass the envelope contained compared to floor area, and conductive and radiant losses were determined by using computer software to arrive at the optimal figure. Miller SQA's glazing contains eleven microscopically thin sandwiched coatings, all of which make for high energy efficiency.

In the manufacturing and warehouse areas, roof monitors provide necessary lighting throughout the day. The ideal slope for glazing at the interior "street" was determined to be forty degrees, providing the best insolation of light and radiation during winter heating months while providing the best overall rejection of thermal gains during summer months.

### Heating and Cooling

Thirty percent of Miller SQA's heating is provided by passive solar heat; the remainder is electrical. The offices are serviced by a centrifugal chiller that uses HFC 134a refrigerant, instead of a CFC refrigerant that is more damaging to the ozone layer. Direct digital controls also serve to dramatically reduce energy costs.

Fresh air chases run on both sides of the "street"–the main corridor of the office interior–to provide fresh filtered air to a series of four-pipe heat/cool fan coil units that are located at the various ceilings throughout the office, cafeteria, and exercise area. Nozzles and grilles stem from these units providing a way to direct air to specific areas when individuals require it. For instance, if an employee is working on the weekend, he/she will simply turn on the closest fan coil unit which conditions the air only in that one area.

***View of the interior "street," or primary walkway, under construction shows the fresh air chases that run the length of the corridor. Completed, the street is bathed in natural daylight and incorporates maximum fresh air.***

***In the manufacturing area, energy efficient lighting, surfaces painted white, and clerestories with electronically controlled exterior blinds that block undesirable glare provide the light necessary for production. Photos: William McDonough + Partners.***

In-floor hot water heating is located at all of the perimeter exterior walls. The system uses only recirculated water.

### LIGHTING

Maximizing solar income–the usage of the sun as a resource–through daylighting is a primary feature of the Miller SQA Facility. Throughout the building, in both office and manufacturing areas, windows and clerestories are oriented for the best possible lighting conditions, as well as being operable for natural ventilation.

A preliminary daylighting analysis of the building performed by Loren Abraham, AIA revealed that an optimum skylight-to-floor ratio (SFR) is approximately 5% of the total floor area. Therefore, an 8' x 8' skylight placed in each structural bay (36' x 36') would result in dramatic lighting energy savings. The skylight, provided by Naturalite, is equipped with a diffuse glazing that is highly efficient and possesses a 46% visible light transmittance.

The clerestories over the manufacturing space integrate solar control devices, such as electronically controlled exterior blinds that block undesirable glare. Nearly all of the occupied spaces receive adequate light from natural daylight, even for task lighting during bright sunlight. The sun control screens provide privacy and greater comfort. A light shelf about seven feet above the finish floor provides shading in the lower portion of the glazing, and bounces light off the ceiling above.

For the atrium glazing, an exterior shading system incorporating slanted louvers reduces the heat buildup inside the space. Ceiling fans help to distribute the warm air.

Artificial lighting is controlled with electronic sensors that dim the electric lighting during times of sufficient daylight. Motion sensors are installed where continuous lighting need only be provided when spaces are occupied. For the interior, highly efficient 400-watt metal halide HID lighting was specified. The

***Right: The Training Room is equipped with continuously dimming fluorescent lighting and motion sensors.***

***Below: View of the entry at night. Photos: William McDonough + Partners.***

***To ensure the best possible indoor air quality, non-toxic materials and high levels of fresh air were incorporated. In the Manufacturing Area, four large air rotation units turn the air over every thirty minutes. Photo: William McDonough + Partners.***

offices are equipped with continuous dimming fluorescent lighting that is either off, turned on to 50% capacity, or all the way to 100% capacity depending on the amount of natural light in the room. The manufacturing area lighting is controlled by a two-step control that measures light by zone and steps back the light accordingly.

## *Air Quality*

Another important aspect to the priority of human comfort, health, and safety, is indoor air quality. In order to ensure the best possible indoor air quality for everyone, non-toxic materials and high levels of filtered fresh air are provided. Because Herman Miller has a conscientious environmental record and has always tried diligently to avoid the use of toxic materials, dust was of more critical concern to them in the construction of the Miller SQA Facility. This concern was addressed to the client's and architect's satisfaction through the incorporation of a two-stage filtering system.

### Ventilation

In the manufacturing area, four large air rotation units with hot water heating coils turn the air over every thirty minutes. Filters located at each intake remove any particles larger than ten microns in size, thereby drastically reducing the hazards, particularly for allergy sufferers. In this two-filter system, the first filter removes the larger particles at 30% efficiency, and the second eliminates the remaining at 60% efficiency. Fresh air is introduced into the factory space at approximately 50,000 CFM after being tempered and filtered to eliminate dust and particulates. Miller SQA receives two times more fresh air per person than was required by code. Through-the-wall supply air transfer fan cabinets service the paint line with filtered make-up air from the main factory space. This provides fresh air to the factory while ventilating the paint line. Where there are extra heating loads, such as with furnaces, spot fan-filtered velocity coolers with multiple air nozzles provide supplementary cooling to workers at their stations.

In addition to the mechanical systems, natural ventilation is used to create air currents through the space. Operable windows along the offices can be opened, weather permitting. The clerestory has mechanical vents above that create a chimney effect to draw warm air out of the building.

### Materials Toxicity

The design team first reviewed reference manuals and MSDS sheets for all materials, paying particular attention to exposure limits and known medical hazards. Known carcinogens were screened out wherever possible, although this is a difficult task where finishing materials are concerned. For instance, in one area the Miller SQA team specified a necessary floor finish that only required one application. Since the finish was applied prior to the building's occupation, any fumes were well controlled by spot ventilation. Another type of finish they considered would have called for repeated applications, even after employees would have been working inside. An ozone-safe refrigerant is used in the chiller to cool the water that circulates through cooling coils in the building.

In-depth studies were also conducted using the material qualification protocols developed by the Miller SQA team in the design stage. Forty different types of paint were evaluated using the criteria of VOC content, toxicity, manufacturing practices, and the site's distance from the manufacturer. American Formulating Manufacturers makes a paint for chemically sensitive people, and this was used throughout most of the Facility. Dry-fall paint, used on the underside of the structure to maximize daylighting, was provided by Benjamin Moore. This type of paint, which is blown onto the surface and adheres to it already dry, is of serious health concern because it is airborne during application. Nevertheless, the type used on the Miller SQA Facility is the lowest of its kind in VOCs and highest in solids; contains no hazardous VOCs; and possesses low volatile or no solvents.

***Exterior details showing masonry that was specified from local suppliers. Photos: William McDonough + Partners.***

The carpet was laid down in tiles and secured with velcro.

### *Resource Conservation*

"Recyclability and recycling of materials is essential and provisions should be made for the disassembly and reuse of all products by the manufacturer," says McDonough. "The recyclability of entire structures must be considered in the event that the building fails to be adaptable to long-term needs." The aspect of resource conservation at all levels is a crucial factor at the Miller SQA Facility. The most visible results include the integration of unclad structural steel and the use of brick as an exterior material. Aluminum uses high levels of embodied energy, and it was only used sparingly. The structural steel system was designed on a 36-foot module which provides maximum flexibility for the rearrangement of office and warehouse space and allows for the easy expansion of future phases.

#### Recycled or Sustainable Natural Content

McDonough is only in favor of using synthetic materials such as plastics when they can be designed and used as part of a closed-loop "industrial ecology." Typically, local or regional materials and products that were produced with sustaining and healthful methodologies were sought out and specified.

#### Recycling System for Personnel

"We recycle *everything,*" says Paul Murray, Herman Miller's environmental director–and this is only a slight exaggeration. Of the twenty-six different materials they recycle, these include corrugated cardboard, office paper, various types of metals and plastics, fabric, newspaper, and foams. Office paper is sold to a toilet tissue manufacturer, from whom Herman Miller then buys the recycled product for its facilities. Polyeurathane foam injected into chairs is also recycled, turned into carpeting and carpet padding by a high-end carpet manufacturer. Fabric scraps are used by automobile companies to create sound-deadening material for their cars. Even sawdust finds a new purpose, used by local farmers who mix it with manure for bedding. In 1991, the company's CEO and Environmental Steering Committee announced the goal of becoming zero-landfill by 1995. While this goal wasn't met, they did manage an 85%-90% reduction, making them one of the top five companies in the U.S. in the area of environmental conservation. In 1994, Herman Miller recorded 20

***Site design that includes careful stormwater management, retention ponds, and nearby wetlands creates a restorative biological process, resulting in better water quality. Photo: William McDonough + Partners.***

million pounds of waste; in 1995, that figure was down to 9 million.

Herman Miller's commitment to the environment runs company wide. Employees volunteer to serve on environmental low-impact processing teams, working together to find ways of making recycling easier and more efficient. Because the employees give up their own time to contribute to this effort, and because recycling also generates revenue for the company, Herman Miller actually celebrates the program with workers, throwing parties during which both refreshments and information on their environmental performance are provided.

#### Purchasing Guidelines

While Herman Miller has no "formal" purchasing guidelines, they share their wealth of conservation experience and information with suppliers to help them lower their environmental impact. This is achieved in a unique way by Miller's Environmental Liaison, whose joint efforts with suppliers have led to such developments as returnable packaging and lower emissions on paint lines.

The company also tries to buy as much as it can from those sources who use material discarded by Herman Miller. In 1994, each employee was given a black leather duffel bag for Christmas. To their surprise, it had been manufactured from recycled leather by a company that had earlier purchased the scraps from Miller. Not only did everyone learn an important lesson about recycling first-hand, but the bags were such a hit that they placed orders for 900 more.

### *Water Conservation and Quality*

A specific example of minimal impact and maximum gain is Herman Miller's stormwater management system, which McDonough has coined a "no-pipe" design concept. Run-off from hard surfaces is directed overland rather than underground. This prevents it from flowing toward a series of sediment basins where silt particles can be deposited and petroleum products and metals begin to be absorbed by plants' natural processes. The quantity of run-off is additionally lessened by evaporation and transport. Retention ponds and non-manicured lawns absorb oil and petroleum from the parking lot, thereby preventing groundwater contamination.

The nearby wetlands provide an on-site habitat that creates a restorative process, providing better water quality leaving the site. Many miles away, the habitat of

***Photos: William McDonough + Partners.***

Lake Macatawa, which is affected by the site run-off, is protected and provided with nutrients.

## *Materials and Products*

All materials and products must be considered in terms of their sustainability; process of extraction; manufacture; transformation; and degradation through proper resource management and biodiversity on both a global and local scale. A material's embodied energy is also important to consider, as well as its characteristics of toxicity, potential off-gassing, finish, and maintenance requirements. Flexibility to meet long-term requirements and long-term durability should also be addressed.

### Criteria

To make every effort to conserve resources, simple criteria were applied to almost every material and product used in the Miller SQA project. Is it needed? Is there a substitute with lower mass and/or lower embodied energy? In most every case, nothing was specified without having been scrutinized for toxicity and its effect on indoor air quality.

### Toxicity

The toxicity of materials was carefully reviewed to protect indoor air quality and the employees from off-gassing effects. The nylon carpeting in the Facility, for instance, has a non-PVC backing.

### Manufacturer's Environmental Impact

Interface, the provider of Miller SQA's carpet, has a recycling plan where they take back their product for recycling after it's worn. Miller SQA also recycles its own furniture by either refurbishing it or deconstructing it for materials reuse.

### Embodied Energy

The building structure was the area where embodied energy was most considered. In the end the design team decided to work with steel. Steel was the most appropriate material with the lowest embodied energy and was procured from a local source, which drastically cut down on transportation, fuel costs, and emissions.

## *Post-Occupancy Evaluation*

A post-occupancy evaluation process was designed for the Miller SQA Facility by Pacific Northwest Labs. Among the elements to be tested are indoor air quality, illness in the old versus the new building, and worker productivity. The study will be funded by the Department of Energy, U.S. Building Council, and Pacific Northwest Labs.

***Embodied energy was the most crucial concern in the building structure. Steel, procured from a local source, was selected by the team as most appropriate. Photo: William McDonough + Partners.***

## HERMAN MILLER
## MILLER SQA FACILITY
## MATERIALS RESOURCES

**Roofing.** Single-ply recyclable membrane; Great Lakes Systems, 2286 Port Sheldon Ct., P.O. Box 108 Jenison, MI 49429-0108

**Exterior and Interior Walls.** Low-toxic masonry; Lamar Bros. Construction, 15595 Ransom St., Holland, MI 49423 (616) 399-1482

**Glazing.** Low-e, argon filled; Lakeshore Glass & Metals, P.O. Box 1945, 11007 Chicago Dr., Holland, MI 49424 (616) 395-8555

**Carpeting and Carpet Padding.** Interface; Ritsema Associates, 2438 28th St. SW, Grand Rapids, MI 49509, (616) 538-0120

**Furniture systems.** Recycled components; Herman Miller, 855 East Main Avenue, Zeeland, Michigan 49464 (616) 654-3316

**Heating/ Air Conditioning Unit and Ventilation.** CFC-free product name; Quality Air Heating/Cooling, 3395 Kraft SE, Grand Rapids, MI 49512, (616) 956-0200

**Lighting controls.** Occupancy sensor system, Product name; Parkway Electric Company, 11598 E. Lakewood Blvd., Holland, MI 49424, (616) 392-2788

## NATIONAL AUDUBON SOCIETY HEADQUARTERS

*New York, New York*

---

**Architect:** Croxton Collaborative Architects, New York, New York, Randolph Croxton, *Director, Architecture*, Kirsten Childs, *Director, Interiors*, Lauren Reiter, *Project Architect*, Jim Van Aken, *Project Manager*
**Mechanical Engineer:** Flack and Kurtz, Inc., New York, New York, Peter Flack, *Managing Partner*
**Structural Engineer:** Robert Silman & Associates, New York, New York, Robert Silman, *Principal*
**General Contractor:** A.J. Contracting Company, New York, New York, Jerome Gannon, *President*
**Restoration Consultant:** Building Conservation Associates, New York, New York, Raymond Pepi, *President*
**Total Area:** 97,000 Square Feet
**Cost of Construction:** $13,900,000; $143 per Square Foot
**BTU/Square Feet per Year:** Modeled at 30,000
**Date of Completion:** 1992

---

### *Project Overview*

In 1992, the National Audubon Society opened its headquarters on lower Broadway in New York City. It has since been recognized as a model of environmental sensitivity because of its successful resource conservation, energy efficiency, and indoor air quality. This building restoration and interior office renovation was unique because of its scale, sophistication, and the extensive environmental research that was incorporated in the design and construction. Croxton Collaborative, Audubon's team of architects and designers, worked closely with Audubon's scientists in the collection and analysis of material specification data. The project team reviewed energy efficiency data with Consolidated Edison, the New York utility company that provided grants and rebates for the installation.

The Audubon Headquarters renovated office space set a new national standard for the environmentally sensitive workspace. At a market cost of $143 per square foot for demolition and construction, the $14 million construction budget was purposefully devoted to high-quality environmental systems rather than to high-cost luxury finishes, fittings, and furnishings. The strategy creates substantial savings. For each $10 that Audubon would have spent on energy, it is currently spending $4, translating into a projected $100,000 savings per year. Advanced mechanical design technologies and sophisticated computer programs have resulted in a five-year payback and savings of at least $500,000.

In the case of the National Audubon Society, however, the success is actually due to a low-tech factor: simple design solutions which are ultimately concerned with the individual, the true resource in any office environment. This is not to say that statistics and cost savings figures are not important in making design decisions. Peter A.A. Berle, President of this not-for-profit organization, believes that the cost-efficiency factor and the human factor are not exclusive of each other. The truth is, in excellent design the two enhance one another. "We hope that Audubon House is not seen as an isolated example of a building created by environmentalists, but as a vehicle for real change in the way building design and construction is practiced worldwide," says Berle. In terms of the scope of interior architecture, the project's sophistication, design, and hard results, the Audubon Headquarters represents the first achievement of its kind in ecologically responsive design. A stellar role model, it provides some of the first performance records, specialized data, and strategies for cost and energy savings from which future commercial tenants and architects can profit. Through this restoration and renovation, the National Audubon Society has created a living example of its mission and values.

#### Architect Profile

When work was done on the National Audubon Society Headquarters, Croxton Collaborative had created one of the most comprehensive environmentally responsible projects ever in its genre. Also architects for the National Resources Defense Council (NRDC), New York, completed in 1988, Randolph Croxton and Kirsten Childs are frequently sought out as knowledgeable professionals regarding ecological sustainability. At NRDC, architect and client together set two basic standards: first, that all selected materials and systems be on the market for at least one year in order to prove their financial and performance viability; and second, that the energy-efficient technologies pay for themselves in three to five years. Randy Croxton and Kirsten Childs are discussed in more detail in Chapter Two.

#### Design Solutions

While the categories of resource and energy conservation, lighting, air quality, and materials can be studied individually, one must look carefully at all of the solutions in relation to each other. Many considerations which fall under the heading of design excellence include simple and conscientiously reviewed strategic placement.

The decision to locate interconnecting stairs at every floor of Audubon Headquarters decreases reliance on elevators, resulting in energy savings and providing increased staff communication and productivity. Locating these stairs at southern windows per-

*The National Audubon Society Headquarters is located on lower Broadway in Manhattan in a "recycled" neo-Romanesque structure designed by George Brown Post, the architect of the New York Stock Exchange. The former department store of glazed brick, cast iron, brownstone, and terra cotta opened in 1891. Photo: Peter Mauss/Esto.*

mits natural light to permeate the center, and further enhances the the visual connection to the outdoors at areas most frequented by the staff. Few building owners and employers understand that a distant view to the horizon and access to natural light relieve stress and increase productivity–especially important to workers who spend large amounts of time at computer workstations.

Further, the decision to locate a conference center at the rooftop and to provide a terrace accessible to all of the staff clearly underscores the Audubon Society's commitment to creating a comfortable and healthy environment for its staff.

### Environmental Objectives

The National Audubon Society clearly outlined environmental goals together with Croxton Collaborative prior to beginning the plans for the new headquarters. Environmental problems related to the built environment were addressed on both local and global scales. The global concerns addressed include climate change, ozone depletion, and loss of biodiversity. On a local and regional level, factors affecting workers and their health were discussed, as was the controversy over hydroelectric development in the James Bay region of Canada. Increasing demand for electricity in the Northeast, including New York, has caused utilities to consider importing hydroelectricity from the Canadian government. Proposed con-

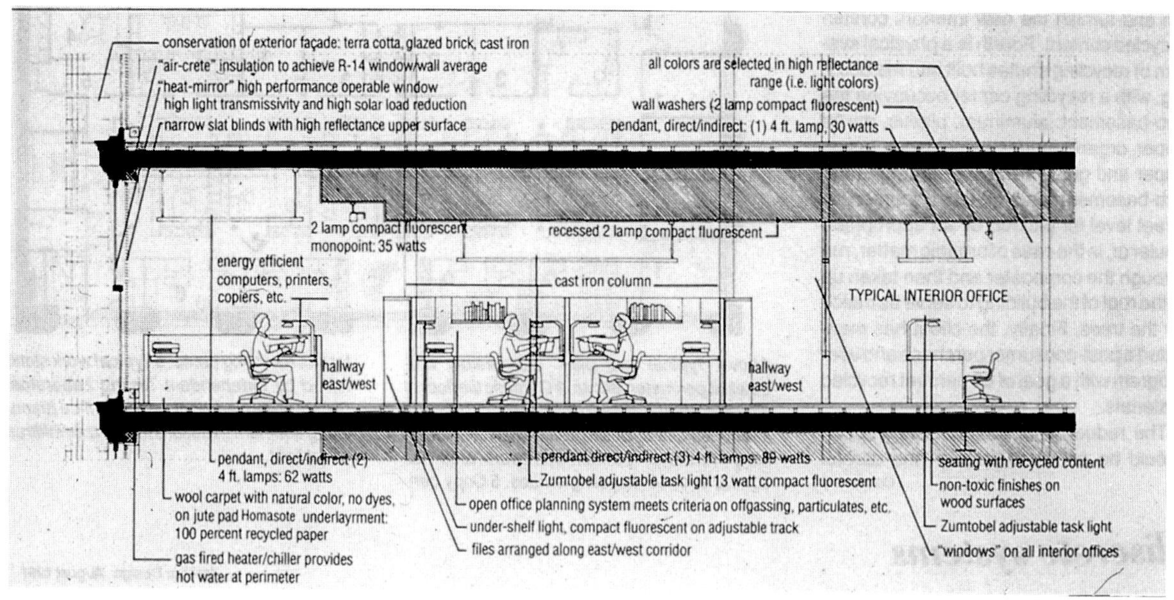


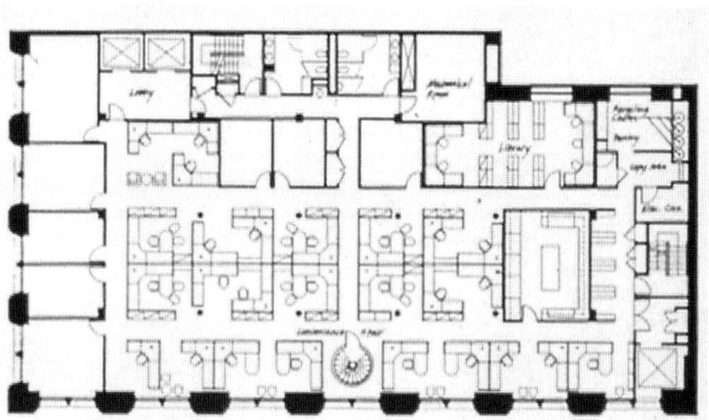
TYPICAL FLOOR PLAN

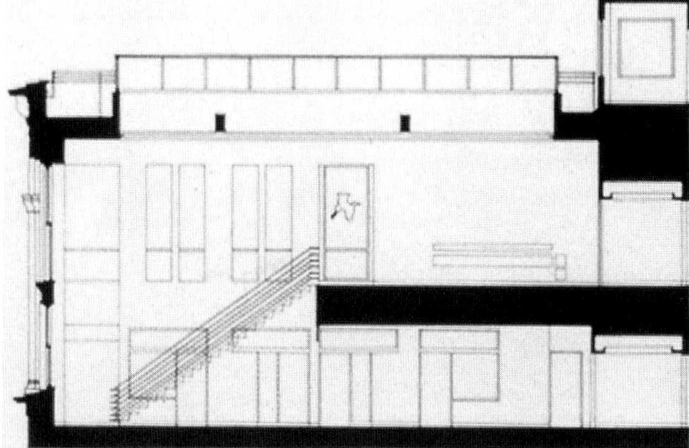
SECTION THROUGH 7TH AND 8TH FLOORS, AND CONSERVATORY LEVEL

***To increase access to natural light, open offices and an interior stair are located along the southern exposure. Private offices have glass clerestories that allow light from the west into the interior workspaces.***

***Located on every floor, interconnecting stairs increase staff communication and provide occupants with an exterior view, thus increasing productivity, comfort, and health. Reliance on elevators is also decreased and natural daylight filters in, contributing to energy efficiency and lighting quality. Drawings and photo: Croxton Collaborative Architect.***

struction of an array of large hydroelectric dams in the unspoiled subarctic ecosystems would destroy the remaining traditional hunting grounds of the native Cree people. Cutting down on the demand for electricity was significant in light of Audubon's opposition to the James Bay development. The effect of CFC's on ozone depletion and global warming also made the elimination of chlorofluorocarbons a priority. Wherever possible, the Audubon team identified direct and indirect upstream and downstream impacts associated with the manufacture or production of each material, product, or system part included in the building process.

## *Working Methods*

### Project Team

The team players for any project of this size and scope might typically include its architects, structural, mechanical, and lighting engineers, additional consultants for restoration procedures and code compliance, construction managers, general contractors, and scores of sub-contractors. For the National Audubon Society Headquarters, the team roles had to be redefined and extended, and expert environmental advice was needed. Teamwork and committment to environmental issues were required of all of the professionals involved. "In searching for professionals to work on the Audubon House, each team member was expected to have a broad understanding of and commitment to environmental and energy issues; a grasp of manufacturing processes; the ability and commitment to conduct research; and above all a willingness to work in an integrated fashion with other team members," says Audubon's President Peter Berle.

The Audubon's chief scientist and staff expert, Jan Beyea, played a key role in the project. Having had extensive training in analyzing chemical components and their effects on human health, the environmental expert was key to the analysis and selection of materials. Many of the choices required difficult judgements and analyses. As an environmentalist, the chief scientist was familiar with reviewing upstream and downstream impacts associated with different products and had special expertise in energy issues. Since the completion of the headquarters, he has had the major responsibility of carrying forward the environmental goals of the project to the daily operation and maintenance of the building.

Both the Audubon's chief scientist Jan Beyea and Croxton Collaborative's Kirsten Childs and Randy Croxton provided critical environmental technical expertise. The environmental expert is in a position to offer advice in key decisions, such as in the evaluation of costs with potential environmental gains, and

***A new penthouse houses the conference center, elevator tower, and mechanical room. The roof garden gives the staff access to the outdoors. Drawing: Croxton Collaborative Architect.***

in the comparison of trade-offs when different issues are at stake. Finally, and most important, the expert helps establish credibility that professional judgements have been made. This is especially important because the subjective judgements are the basis for most of the decisions.

Specifications were written by the architects, engineers, and designers, and the project was then put out to bid.

### Computer Modeling

The use of DOE-2, computer software developed by the U.S. Department of Energy and the Electric Power Research Institute in San Francisco, was an important tool in many of the design decisions made for the Audubon Headquarters. For example, it established the superiority of one model of Heat-Mirror™

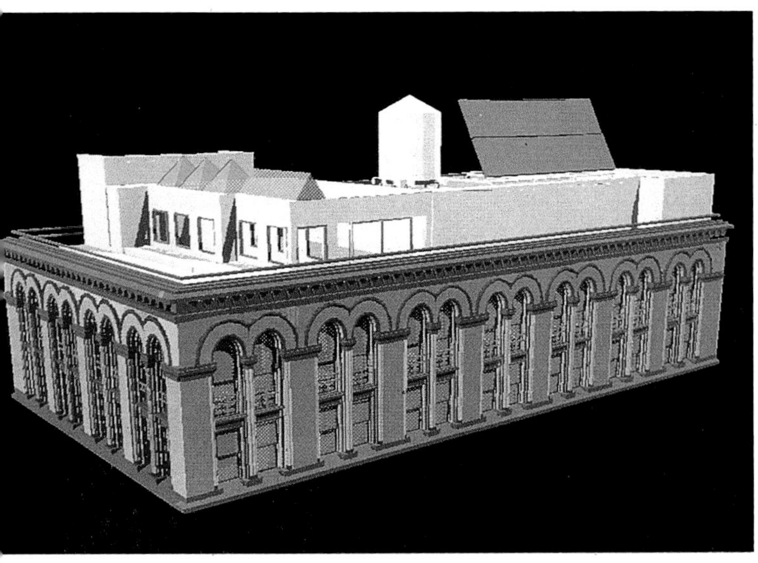

***Using computer modeling methods, the headquarters was designed to accommodate solar energy sources that could be integrated at a later time when the technology becomes cost effective. Photo: Croxton Collaborative Architect.***

over another, and ascertained the benefits of adding a passive solar night cooling strategy to the building's heating and cooling system.

Run in combination with readily available software extensions, DOE-2 assisted the team in calculating the optimum relationship of components, the building thermal envelope and insulation, HVAC systems, and electrical and lighting systems by taking into account complex interactions of variables such as conductive heat flow, solar gain, daylighting, mechanical systems, and occupancy patterns. The software, which simulates the entire building, modeled the complete hour-by-hour performance of Audubon over an entire year. To do this it required input consisting of weather data, utility rate schedule, the building's geometry, materials, equipment, and operation schedules. The output summarized the building's loads and costs, as well as the performance of the mechanical systems and central plants.

At the time of the Audubon project, the cost of the full DOE-2 analysis and the expertise required to analyze the data was high. Croxton proposed a study-grant which led Con Edison, the local utility, to donate approximately $50,000 for the analysis.

## *Environmental Economics*

### Life Cycle Costs

With the help of DOE-2 software, life-cycle cost analyses were performed, incorporating the variable options of energy efficient equipment and materials.

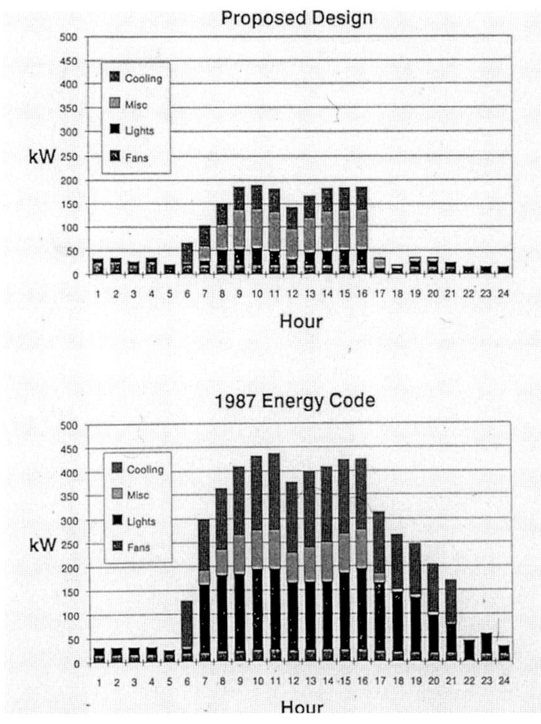


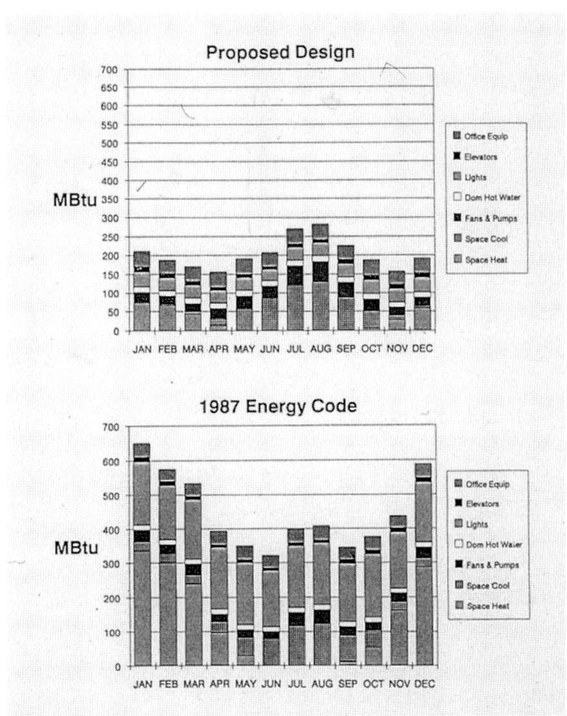

The additional premium cost of the lighting system was about $92,000 over the cost of a typical lighting system, with one fourth of this amount paying for energy-efficient ballasts and controls. The direct savings of electricity is about $60,000 a year. Con Edison, the New York City utility company provided $31,000 in rebates toward the purchase of the lighting equipment. The payback for the lighting system is two and a half years.

An additional premium of $102,000 was paid for the energy efficient heating and cooling system, with a payback period of three to five years. While the heater/chiller saves roughly $18,000 in electricity costs per year, an additional $15,000 is saved due to rentable space which was conserved and included in tenant working space. The heater/chiller unit generates an additional savings of $10,000 for features in the overall system, such as variable speed fans and variable air valve boxes.

#### Grants and Rebates

The local utilities company, Consolidated Edison, provided a grant to the National Audubon Society to help complete computer modeling of energy performance. A computer-modeled solar analysis was also performed with the intent to locate a photovoltaic array at the roof should solar energy become a viable option for the building in the future. A rebate from Con Edison of $72,000 helped to defray the cost for the gas-fired heating and cooling equipment.

Cost effectiveness also plays a significant role in the energy savings of lighting. According to Audubon's Gigi Cooper, $31,000 in rebates was provided from Con Edison to purchase efficient lighting systems. The lighting consumption costs are 20% less than the average use for a building the size of Audubon.

### *Energy Conservation*

Energy performance and savings are the key to the economic viability of the entire Audubon project. Highly efficient insulation, glazing, HVAC, and lighting systems function together to reduce the energy use and environmental impact of this nearly 100,000 square feet of office space over standard construction by more than fifty percent. The building consumes 64% less total energy than it would if it had been built to meet the 1990 New York State Energy Code. This savings protects the environment from the effects of the continually growing demand for energy. According to *Audubon House,* "The built environment consumes over half–54% of the base use in 1982–of the primary energy used in the United States. Based on recent growth rates, it has been estimated that by the year 2020, the appetite for energy demand will double, requiring additional energy sources the equivalent of 40 new nuclear power plants."

#### Building Envelope Insulation

An upgrade of the thermal shell reducing heating/cooling losses includes an increase of wall

***View of a typical floor prior to construction showing the original cast iron structure and window openings. CFC-free cementitious foam was sprayed into sections at the perimeter walls to insulate the building. Photo courtesy of Croxton Collaborative Architect.***

***The reception area and interior stair receive daylight from a skylight and south facing windows. The reception desk is constructed of certified mahogany and maple. Photo: Jeff Goldberg /Esto.***

and ceiling insulation respectively to R-11 and R-30, capacities three to five times the industry norm. While the code of the State of New York requires an overall R-3 insulation factor, Audubon House provides R-12. The roof is insulated at almost three times the code requirement of R-12 with an R-33 factor.

According to the team's research, the two most common types of available insulation are foam and fiberglass. Foam insulation is often a type of plastic typically produced using CFCs or HCFCs, the leading causes of ozone depletion, responsible for over 25% of the global warming effect. Some foam insulations off-gas formaldehyde and other harmful chemicals. Fiberglass contains small particles that can cause respiratory irritation when released into the air.

The choices seemed undesirable until the architects discovered a new product called AirKrete™, a cement-like foam made of magnesium compounds extracted from seawater and mixed with other minerals. AirKrete ™ was air-blown into the cavity walls while wet, creating an R-ll insulation.

### Glazing

To minimize heat loss from windows and skylight, each double-glazed unit contains a two-millimeter polyester rigid sheet that is coated with a reflective transparent "heat mirror." The wavelength-selective shield allows light to penetrate while reflecting solar gain in the summer and retaining infrared heat waves in the winter. The shield protective factor of each window elevation varies, depending upon its particular orientation and exposure to the sun.

Heat Mirror™ technology is a low-emmissivity, or low-e, wavelength-selective coated film with a shade coefficient equal to .41 and a daylight transmittance of 53%. It deflects most of the sun's radiant heat outward, keeping the interior cool in summer, and deflects convected radiant heat inward, conserving heat in winter. Resulting in an R-3.7 insulation factor, the Audubon windows provide insulation equivalent to a standard brick wall. Current available models can provide R-8 or higher. A rubberized thermal break minimizes the transfer of heat or cold, further conserving controlled temperature loss.

### Heating and Cooling

The Audubon team reviewed the potential fuel sources which included electricity, oil, steam, gas, and solar power. Systems and operating costs were evaluated using DOE-2 computer software. According to Croxton, the use of electricity in the Northeast region of the country where winters are cold is expensive and impractical for heating and air conditioning. The analysis of solar power proved this source too expensive. While its payback period was not in accordance with Audubon's economic goals, considerations were made for future installation when solar applications may be available at lower costs and greater efficiency. Fuel oil was more seriously considered, as it is a common source of heating in many commercial and residential buildings in the area. Evaluating the serious environmental impacts of oil extraction, transport, and related activities, the team determined gas to be the most viable option.

Unlike most commercial buildings, heating and cooling are provided by a single source at Audubon. A gas-fired absorption heater/chiller located on the top floor services an air handler on each floor. The system dramatically reduces or eliminates toxic emissions such as carbon, nitrogen oxides, and sulphur dioxides while eliminating CFCs by operating on lithium bromide and water. Additionally, the system radically reduces energy consumption. One measurement of high performance and energy efficiency is the estimated consumption of 30,000 BTUs per square foot per year. This energy requirement compares to 100,000 BTUs per square foot per year, a typical quantity of energy required by a commercial office building. The energy and insulating systems are saving $18,000 per year over conventional systems.

Randolph Croxton says of this project, "We have been characterized as doing environmental design, but what we really do is high-performance design."

One of the necessary tools for a precise analysis was the Department of Energy's DOE-2 computer program. The program measures energy density of a building by factoring the location and size of the building, efficiency of lighting and mechanical systems, and the thermal characteristics of walls and windows. It can additionally reveal the cost effectiveness of varying design options.

### Lighting

"Lighting is the simplest area in which to make substantial energy-saving decisions. If architects or designers were to do only one thing to make a building more energy efficient, I would suggest they look at the lighting design. Lighting represents 30% of all energy used–not only for illumination but also for cooling costs," says Kirsten Childs, Interior Design Director for Croxton Collaborative. Natural daylight was incorporated wherever possible. Instead of locating private offices at all perimeter walls, as is the com-

***The gas-fired absorption heater/chiller located on the top floor services an air handler on each floor. Operating on lithium bromide and water, it dramatically reduces toxic emissions such as carbon, nitrogen oxides, and sulfur dioxides and eliminates CFCs. Photo: Croxton Collaborative Architect.***

***Open offices with interconnecting circular stair located near a window. The combination of arched windows that admit natural daylight, energy efficient lamps and fixtures, white ceilings that reflect light, and low workstation partitions provides high quality interior lighting. Photo: Otto Baitz /Esto.***

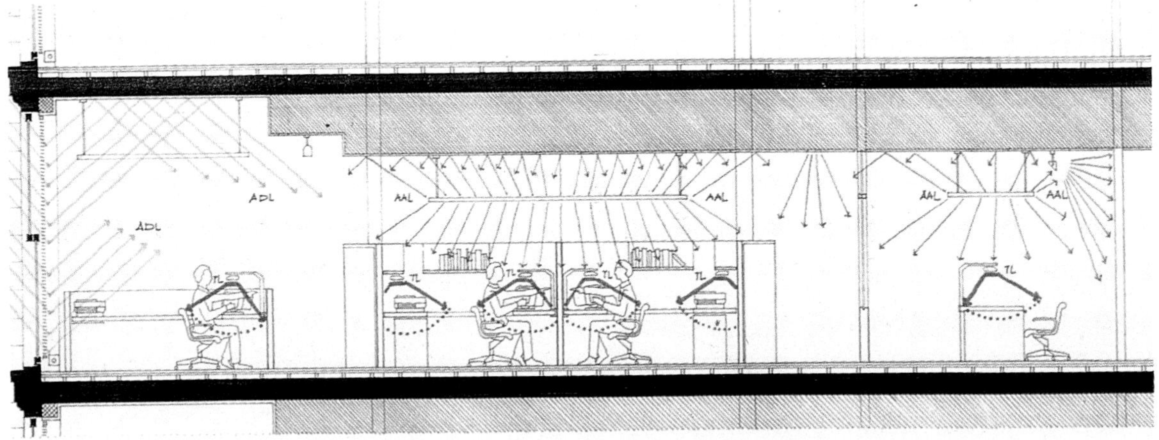


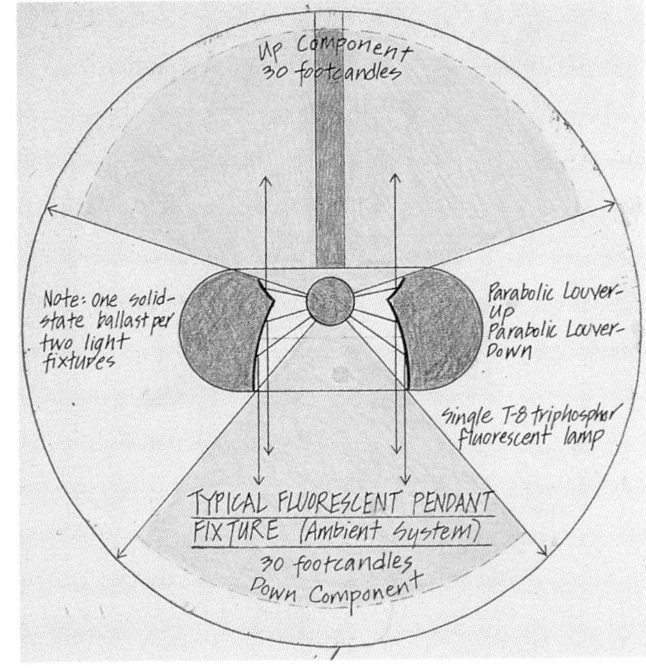


***Above: Section drawing showing daylighting and artificial lighting patterns.***

***Right: Fluorescent fixture diagram. Drawings: Croxton Collaborative Architect.***

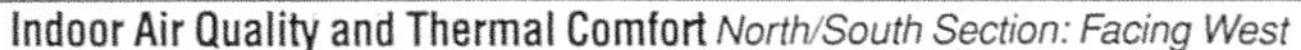


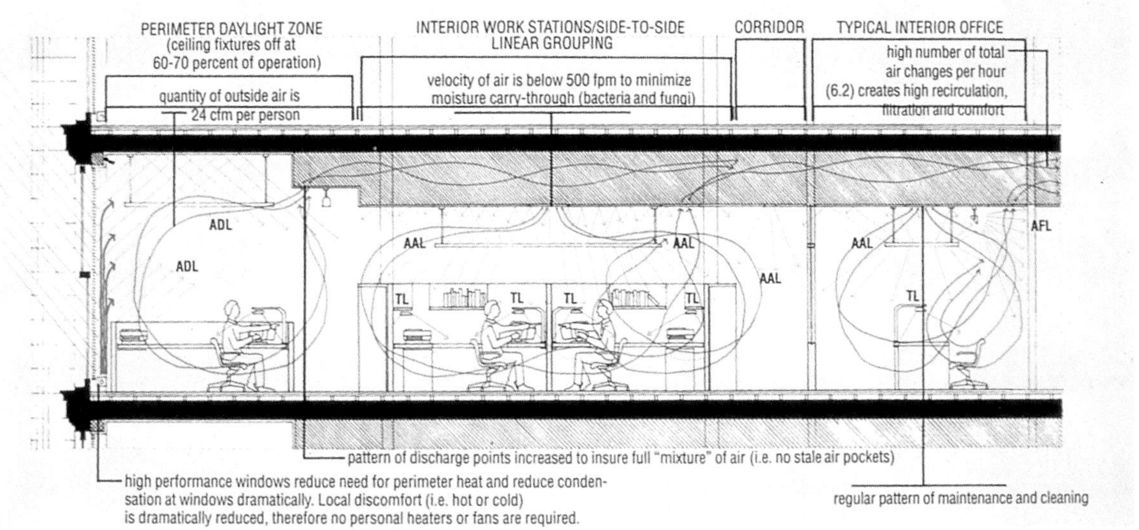


***Section drawing illustrates air ventilation and circulation with light and heat source patterns. In order to minimize moisture carry-through (which increases the potential for bacteria and fungi), the air velocity is below 500 FPM. Drawing: Croxton Collaborative Architect.***

mon practice, the architects located open workstations and connecting stairs at south-facing windows in order to allow daylight to reach central public areas. This design choice also allows the staff to enjoy a visual relationship with the outdoors. Interior walls incorporated partially glazed walls to further permit daylight into the interior areas where private offices were located at windows.

Where artificial lights were necessary, several layers of design elements were incorporated into their design. Office lights, controlled by heat sensors, are activated when a person enters a room and turn off six minutes after the room is vacated. Photoelectric cells allow perimeter lights to dim in accordance with natural light entering the windows. All lighting fixtures at the National Audubon Society Headquarters are fitted with recently available T-8 fluorescent tube lamps that feature a tri-phosphor coating, which gives the light a warm color that replicates daylight. Since T-8s have electronic ballasts, they pulse 20,000 times per second, eliminating any perceptible flicker. The system provides 30 foot-candles of ambient light, increasing to 70 foot-candles where task lights are employed.

## *Air Quality*

### Ventilation Systems

The air-handling system at Audubon balances psychological well-being with operating efficiency. The architects increased the flow of outside air within the offices to circulate 26 cubic feet of air per minute per person, which is substantially higher than the national standard of 5 cubic feet per minute (since upgraded to 20 cubic feet per minute per person). Also, new operable windows were installed. While operable windows can contribute to the loss of energy efficiency, they have a positive effect on individual well-being. Croxton believes that "people feel trapped if they can't open windows." Since private offices have individually controlled heating/ventilation/air conditioning systems, fresh air can be substituted for heat or air conditioning if desired.

Duct systems were redesigned to allow for easy access for maintenance. Proper care diminishes the possibility of moisture carry through, which can create proliferation and spread of harmful molds and bacteria. Exterior fresh air intake vents were placed at a location near the roof, maximizing the potential for entry of the cleanest possible fresh air. Too often, the vent is located near the mechanical systems room at or near street level, or often near loading docks and hazardous exhaust fumes.

### Materials Toxicity

The presence of toxic chemicals in building and finish materials and furnishings, combined with poor or average ventilation, typically contributes to Sick Building Syndrome. Recent research has revealed that the U.S. business industry loses $60 billion dollars per year in loss of work and medical costs due to this problem. Research of toxics which outgas into the air was performed by the architects and verified by the scientific staff of National Audubon Independent

***Private offices incorporate operable windows with low-emissivity film between two panes of glass. Photo: Jeff Goldberg/Esto.***

Testing Laboratory. Data were utilized to examine many of the individual materials and products specified.

Office maintenance procedures also affect the Audubon Headquarters' air quality. Purchasing guidelines were established for environmentally sound cleaning supplies and interior plant maintenance. For instance, carpet cleaning mixtures were tested over many months to determine which was least harmful to the environment. Typical cleaners made with ammonia or isopropyl alcohol have significant upstream impacts, but steam cleaning does not work well with wool carpet. After testing over ten formulas, a mild soap that removes loose dirt was found to be satisfactory, but a benign stain removing formula has yet to be discovered. For the building facade, experiments were performed to find an environmentally sound cleaning process to remove graffiti. One cleanser listed propylene glycol monomethyl ether (PGME), which is indicated in the toxicology handbook as an irritant and central nervous system depressant that is potentially hazardous to workers. Its use was avoided once the team found a product with no hazardous chemicals at all.

Further information regarding materials toxicity is covered under the section on materials.

## *Resource Conservation*

### BUILDING REUSE

Resource conservation was addressed at every level in the National Audubon Society Headquarters project. First came the decision to reuse an existing building. The Audubon Society Headquarters is located in a "recycled" neo-Romanesque structure of glazed brick, cast iron, brownstone, and terra cotta designed by George Brown Post, the architect of the New York Stock Exchange. The building, originally a department store which opened in 1891, and land were available

***Left:* The existing building's historic, handcrafted brownstone and terra cotta were cleaned and restored.**

***Below:* Materials diagram. Photo and drawing: Croxton Collaborative Architect.**

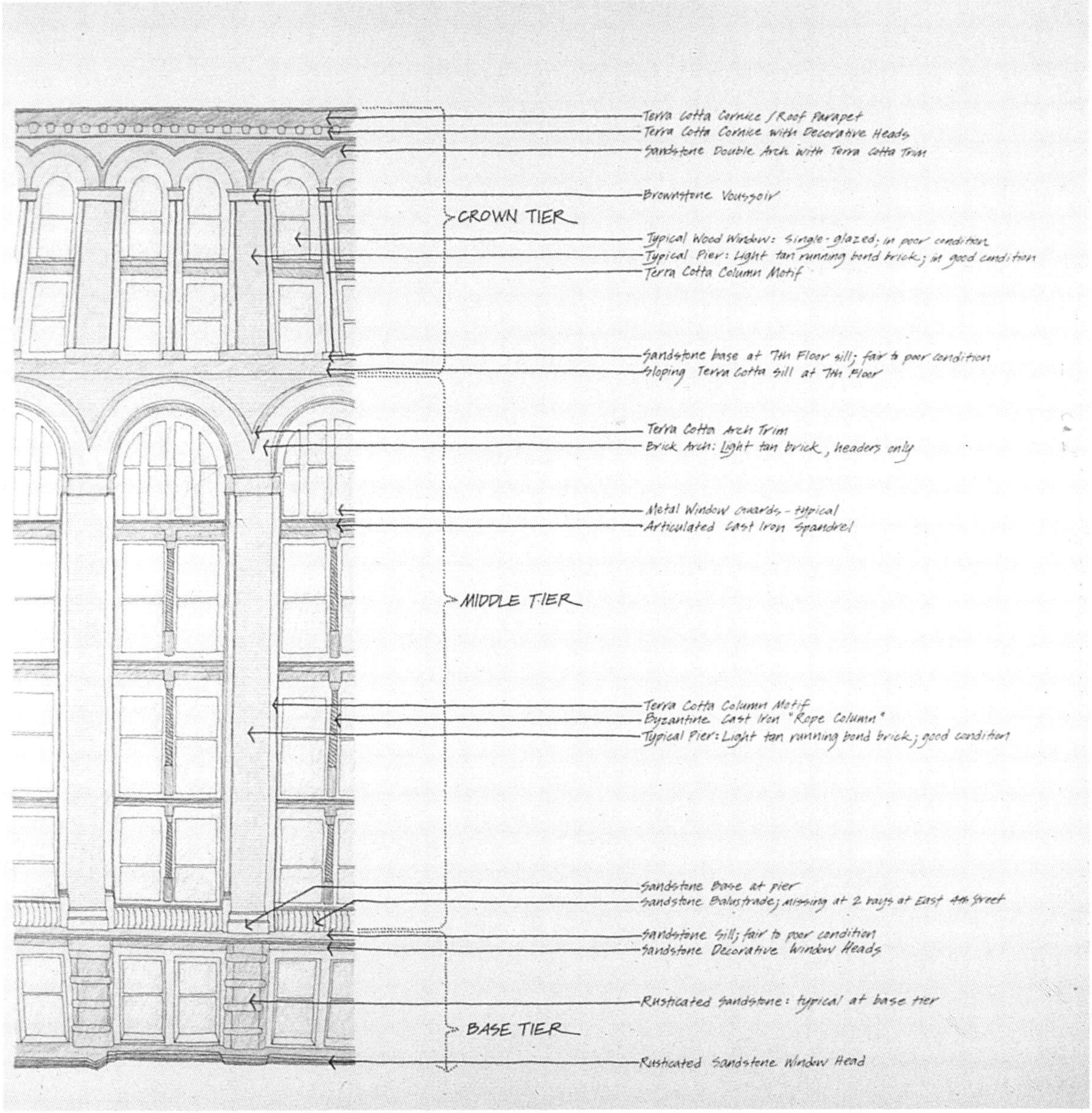

Terra Cotta Cornice / Roof Parapet
Terra Cotta Cornice with Decorative Heads
Sandstone Double Arch with Terra Cotta Trim
Brownstone Voussoir
CROWN TIER
Typical Wood Window: Single-glazed; in poor condition
Typical Pier: Light tan running bond brick; in good condition
Terra Cotta Column Motif
Sandstone base at 7th Floor sill; fair to poor condition
Sloping Terra Cotta Sill at 7th Floor
Terra Cotta Arch Trim
Brick Arch: Light tan brick, headers only
Metal Window Guards - typical
Articulated Cast Iron Spandrel
MIDDLE TIER
Terra Cotta Column Motif
Byzantine Cast Iron "Rope Column"
Typical Pier: Light tan running bond brick; good condition
Sandstone Base at pier
Sandstone Balustrade; missing at 2 bays at East 4th Street
Sandstone Sill; fair to poor condition
Sandstone Decorative Window Heads
Rusticated Sandstone: typical at base tier
BASE TIER
Rusticated Sandstone Window Head

for $10 million, slightly more than the value of the land alone. The choice to recycle an existing building rather than construct a new one resulted in a savings of 300 tons of steel, 1000 tons of masonry, 560 tons of concrete, and the preservation of irreplaceable historic craftsmanship, as well as the embodied energy and the costs and consumption of new materials.

### Deconstructed Materials Reuse

In the second step of resource conservation–salvaging demolished materials–masonry and concrete were crushed to make new roadbeds, steel and aluminum were recycled, and wood frames and the water tower were shredded for garden mulch. The metal from the existing heating unit was also cut down and taken as scrap metal.

### Recycled or Sustainable Natural Content

The third step of resource conservation is exhibited in the "new" materials and products specification for the Audubon Headquarters, which includes as much recycled material as possible. The manufacturing history of every specified material, system, and product was carefully studied by the architect. Wallboard containing recycled paper and partially recycled gypsum core was used. Existing columns above the ceiling were fireproofed with recycled cellulose, and the public lobbies incorporate floor tile with recycled glass. Because plywood, which is typically used as underlayment for carpeting, outgasses toxic formaldehyde, fiberboard of recycled newsprint was substituted instead. Kirsten Childs worked with the Rainforest Alliance Smart Woods Program to specify woods certified as harvested through sustainable programs.

***Steel deck is cut and separated for recycling. Photo: Croxton Collaborative Architect.***

### Recycling System for Personnel

Further methods of resource conservation include the incorporation of a permanent recycling system for bottles, cans, aluminum, mixed paper, and white paper. The commitment to resource conservation extends to employees, who follow a conveniently planned regimen. Every floor includes a staff lounge outfitted with recycling chutes for redeemable metal and plastic containers, mixed paper, high-quality paper, and organic garbage, which includes paper towels used to clean up coffee spills. The paper is shredded and, along with the other organic materials, redistributed to the soil in the rooftop terrace garden. The chutes terminate in large moveable bins at the basement of the building. There, they are picked up and carted for recycling. Additionally, computer paper and newspaper is separated at each workstation.

### Composting

Composting, which should be implemented in 1996, is one of the most unique aspects of the recycling effort. Various models were tested at Scully Science Center, an Audubon facility on Long Island in New York State.

Small or easily broken food scraps and soft paper will be collected in the recycling chutes or by maintenance staff. The food waste is held in refrigeration in the recycling room. After enough has accumulated, it passes through a grate into one of four vessels, each with a 40-pound capacity. In order to minimize bad odors from the decaying material, the vessels are enclosed. The Audubon team selected an aerobic composting system, which supplies a steady flow of air to the reactors, promoting growth of bacteria which break down waste. Each reactor is separately ventilated and the exhaust passes through a biofilter to remove potential toxins and odors. This kind of system, the same that is done in backyards, is faster and more odor-free than anaerobic composting, a system that does not utilize air.

The aerobic process can be approximately divided into two stages. To begin the composting process, compost starter and wood chips are added to the food waste with air and water to bring the temperature to 140°F. Initially, compost will be purchased and later Audubon will be able to start with its own compost.

In this first stage, the waste decomposes rapidly. If necessary, fertilizer may be added to provide nitrogen. The reactors are enclosed with insulation to maintain the temperature. After at least three days at 140°F, the waste contents are sterilized. In the second stage, the compost is cured in the reactors over a three-month period, and the smaller organic particles turn into a rich compost. Less active management is needed in this stage. At the end of the process, the finished compost will be transported to planters on the building's rooftop.

### Purchasing Guidelines

As is required in the operation of any business, equipment and supplies from pencils to computers must be purchased for the staff. Audubon has established guidelines which encourage their employees to reduce consumption and buy environmentally sound supplies and materials. The guidelines are as follows:

1. Purchase products with a high degree of recycled content, preferably postconsumer. In order to help stimulate recycling markets, an overall goal would be the purchase of at least as much recycled material as waste collected for recycling at Audubon.
2. Whenever possible, purchase recycled paper that has not been bleached. Chlorine bleaching releases dioxin, a human carcinogen.
3. Use rebuilt cartridges for laser printers and copying machines, or buy laser printers that do not require cartridge replacement.
4. For large purchases, develop a certification process that takes into account the full life-cycle impacts of the materials involved.
5. Avoid the purchase of mixed-material goods such as paper and plastic combinations, unless the component materials can be separated easily. Mixed materials are difficult to recycle.
6. Use grease pencils instead of felt markers, which contain VOCs.

A 10 percent limit was set on cost premiums for "green" purchases in accordance with an economic imperative. Due to the rapidly declining prices of these products, an increase of no more than 1 to 2 percent is expected.

Because the Audubon Society publishes and sends out huge amounts of environmental information to educate members and the public, an organization-wide analysis of its publications and mailings is being performed in order to create standards to reduce environmental impacts. Already, most of the printed material is published on recycled paper, using soy-based rather than petroleum-based inks. Elimination of "glassine" windows in envelopes and the use of paper with higher postconsumer content is in the planning stages.

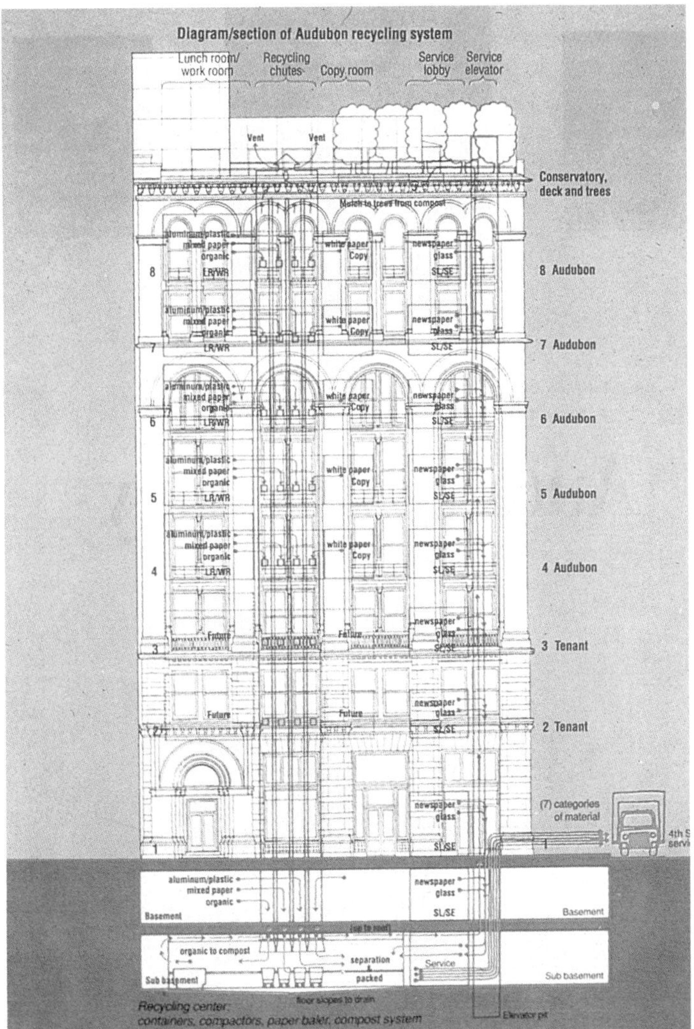

*In the building's recycling system, organic material, paper, cans, and plastics are dropped from chutes located in the personnel lounge on each floor. The material is collected for recycling in bins located in the basement. Drawing: Croxton Collaborative Architect. Photo: Jeff Goldberg/ Esto.*

Finally, guidelines will be set in place to encourage workers to reduce their contribution to waste and promote environmental habits. Tasks like reusing one-sided printed paper and using double-sided copying, circulating memos rather than sending out copies, sharing newspapers and magazines, refusing excess packaging when shopping for lunch, and bringing reusable coffee mugs and dishes can significantly reduce the total office waste stream.

### *Water Conservation*

Low-flush toilets and automatic shut-off faucets in Audubon's restrooms help to reduce water use.

### *Materials and Products*

#### Criteria

Before materials and products could be selected for the Audubon Headquarters, they needed to be tested and analyzed. This is one of the most time consuming and daunting stages in designing and building an environmentally sound building. Numerous criteria were established for the specification of each material at the Audubon:

1. Toxicity: Minimization of toxic content is a primary objective.

***Reception area. Photo: Jeff Goldberg/Esto.***

2. Manufacturer Environmental Impact: The manufacturer who employs methods which result in maximum resource conservation (recycling) of all resource materials and minimum upstream and downstream environmental impact is preferable.
3. Embodied Energy: The product should require a minimum of inherent energy in its transport and manufacturing.
4. Performance: Each material or product must have been on the market for at least two years or longer in order to illustrate a successful track record.
5. Economy, aesthetics, and comfort.

Each material, product, and system was carefully studied for its technical contents, manufacturing history, and performance record. Office furnishings were tested for the presence of formaldehyde, and paints with minimum volatile organic compounds were applied to walls. All carpets, paints, wall coverings, floor finishes, and furniture systems were carefully reviewed to reduce the presence of toxic elements such as formaldehyde, other VOCs, and harmful chemicals found in common construction materials which affect indoor air quality.

The nature of all of the findings is complex, and, as a result, difficult trade-offs needed to be made. At Audubon, the criteria were prioritized to help in making decisions. The Audubon team gave indoor air quality first priority because it affects the building users more directly and because information on chemical composition was generally more readily available than data on manufacturing processes or disposal. However, when the team could identify particularly dangerous trade-offs in the upstream and downstream effects, exceptions were made. For example, polyvinyl chloride (PVC) plastic emits highly toxic chemicals when incinerated, thus its use was avoided wherever possible.

#### Toxicity

Establishing a material's toxic chemical content by knowing the quantity of chemicals, the rate at which they off-gas and can be transmitted to building occupants, and their health hazard potential is not an exact science. The Audubon team reviewed Material Safety Data Sheets (MSDS) as a first step to determine the presence of harmful chemicals in products. MSDS sheets provided by the manufacturer upon request list the names and amounts of major chemicals found in a product. The information was checked against the International Agency for Research on Cancer list of carcinogens and a number of handbooks on toxicology. The MSDS information was supplemented with data from manufacturers when further information was required.

The lack of available information from manufacturers made general research on product types a pivotal requirement in the decision-making process. Although MSDS sheets can be made available, certain expertise is required to interpret the scientific data. For example, widely available environmental research on plastics helped the chief scientist to rank them as follows:

- Polyethylene, polypropylene: Benign
- PET and Polystyrene: Intermediate
- ABS: Questionable
- Polyvinyl chloride (PVC): To be avoided

Toxic solvents and alkyds such as benzene, xylene, and toluene found in many common building products such as oil-based paints can enter the bloodstream and cause respiratory problems, allergic reactions, and liver damage. Chemicals used in the production of fabrics, carpets, and pressed woods used in furniture systems include formaldehyde, diphenol ether, and styrene, all of which are believed to cause numerous health problems, including suppression of the immune system.

In the end, lead-free water-based latex paints were employed, as were wool/nylon blend formaldehyde-free carpets installed over 100% natural jutepad on homosote underlayment. All furniture under consideration was tested by an independent laboratory for the presence of formaldehyde.

### Manufacturer's Environmental Impact

While the determination of toxicity is indefinite and complicated, the manufacturer's environmental impact is even more difficult to measure. The Audubon team reviewed the upstream and downstream effects of each product's manufacturing process and the manufacturer's general environmental records. They also relied on research included in the American Institute of Architect's *Environmental Resource Guide.*

### Embodied Energy

The energy expended in the extraction and processing of raw materials, their manufacture, transport, and construction is known as embodied energy. The process of calculating embodied energy was too costly and time consuming to undertake, so the Audubon team instead applied a general set of comparisons concerning the inherent energy of each product. For example, a product being transported a great distance to reach a processing plant or building site requires more embodied energy than products traveling a shorter distance. Therefore, products using local or regional manufacturing processes and materials are more desirable than those traveling long distances. In another example, using recycled materials preserved embodied energy in two ways: first, discarding materials results in a complete loss of embodied energy for that product, and second, the energy required to create virgin material is always greater than that required to recycle it.

The Audubon team again used the AIA *Environmental Resource Guide* to help determine the quantities of embodied energy in each material and product. The single decision to retrofit an existing building resulted in the greatest savings of embodied energy.

## NATIONAL AUDUBON SOCIETY HEADQUARTERS MATERIALS RESOURCES

**Sub-floor.** Recycled newspaper content; Homasote Company, Box 7240, West Trenton, NJ 08628 (609) 883-3300

**Dry-wall board.** Recycled newspaper content; Gold Bond Building Products, 2001 Rexford Road, Charlotte, NC 28211 (704) 365-7300

**Wall insulation.** AirKrete; CFC-free cementitous foam; Palmer Industries Inc., 10611 Old Annapolis Road, Frederick, MD 21701 (301) 898-7848

**Windows.** Low-E Heat Mirror™, 2 Layers 1/4"glass w/ polyester film; Southwall Technologies, 1029 Corporation Way, Palo Alto, CA 94303 (415) 962-9111

**Carpet padding.** 100% natural hair and jute; Dixie Manufacturing Co., P.O. Box 59, Norfolk, VA 23501 (804) 625-8251

**Floor tiles.** Recycled glass; GTE Engineered Ceramics, 135 Commerce Way, Portsmouth, NH 03801-3200 (603) 436-8900

**Paint.** Spred 2000, Lifemaster 2000; The Glidden Company, 925 Euclid Avenue, Cleveland, OH 44115 (216) 344-8140

**Countertops.** Recycled plastic; Santana Solid Plastic Products, P.O. Box 2021, Scranton, PA 18501 (800) 386-5002 or (717) 343-7921

**Furniture systems.** Recycled components; Herman Miller, 855 East Main Avenue, Zeeland, MI 49464 (616) 654-3316

**Heating/Air conditioning unit.** Gas-fired lithium bromide; CFC-free; York International Corporation, 420 Lexington Avenue, Suite 2520, New York, NY 10170 (212) 949-1800

**Lighting controls.** Occupancy sensor system; Osram-Sylvania, Inc., 1 Jackson Street, Wellsboro, PA 10901 (717) 274-8350

## PAULK RESIDENCE

*Seabeck, Washington*

---

**Architect:** James Cutler Architects, Bainbridge Island, Washington, James Cutler, FAIA, *Principal,* Bruce Anderson, *AIA, Project Architect*
**Structural Engineer:** Ratti Swenson Perbi, Seattle, Washington, Gary Swenson, *Principal*
**General Contractor:** Pleasant Beach Construction, Bainbridge Island, Washington, Don Heppenstall, *Principal*
**Geological Consultant:** General Testing Laboratories, Inc., Poulsbo, Washington, Allen L. Hart
**Total Area:** Garage/Shop/Guest House: 1496 Square Feet. House: 2308 Square Feet.
**Cost of Construction:** Withheld at owners' request.
**Watts/Square Foot per Year:** Not applicable because the house is heated with propane.
**Date of Completion:** 1994

---

### *Project Overview*

According to architect Jim Cutler, the design and construction of the Paulk site and house have one primary purpose, and that is to protect and nurture human awareness of the fragile nature of the earth's resources. "If we can't begin to change the way our culture views natural resources," says Cutler, "nothing else will matter. We have to love the earth, or it will die." Cutler's work is directed toward showing the essence and beauty of every material that he utilizes in his work, to honor its use to the fullest extent. In the tradition of Louis Kahn, with whom architect Jim Cutler studied, the fabrication of the building is intended to expose the nature of the materials and their assembly, as well as express regional traditions of wood construction. The form and the ornament flashings are a direct response to views, sun, wind, and rain.

Perched on a 200-foot bluff on the east side of the Hood Canal, the Paulk Residence property slopes both up to the bluff and down to the north. The land is wooded with a second growth cedar thicket in the center, tapering to young red alder with salal and evergreen huckleberry at the margins of the bluff. The Olympic Mountains dominate the views to the west and the northwest. To provide the residents with views, the building touches the ground at the garage on the south end and then proceeds north at the garage elevation, with the ground falling away beneath it. At the extreme north end the building is fifteen feet off the ground. The guest entrance is accessed by a ramp that rises from the east, passes through the building, and ends at a belvedere on the west edge of the bluff. The intent of the ramp is not only to access the house, but to have people intimately experience the forest.

#### Architect Profile

According to the *New York Times,* "Jim Cutler is one of a new breed of architects with little tolerance for fellow professionals who still spout old fashioned

***Site plan. The 2250-square-foot residence was carefully sited in a forest on part of an old logging road. Facing page, top: Exterior detail. In order to disturb the site as little as possible, the house was carefully situated between existing trees. Natural materials, lots of glass to integrate the outdoor with the interior, and meticulous detailing express a special reverence for the environment. Bottom: Floor plan. Photo: Art Grice. Drawings: James Cutler Architects.***

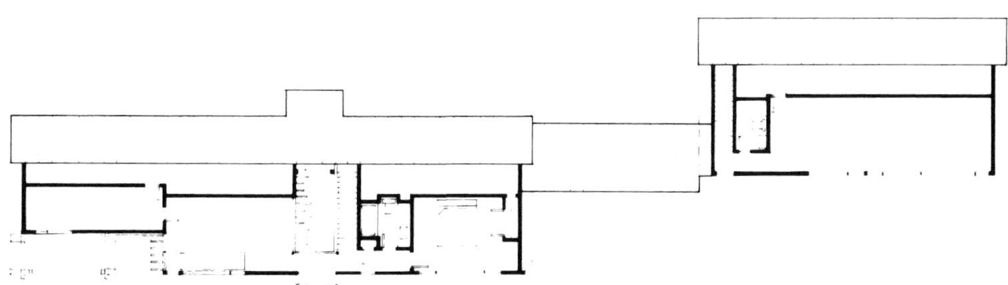

rhetoric about conquering the environment." The world, he believes, is too fragile for such master-of-the-universe myopia. "Today's architects," says Cutler, "must take the lead in building in ways that harmonize with nature and the industry will follow." Cutler begins his projects not by sketching on napkins, but by surveying the site himself, measuring his success inversely to the number of trees which are cut.

Since 1977, James Cutler Architects has been dedicated to design excellence and reverence for the environment. The firm is nationally recognized for its committment to creating architectural results that are particular to the site and the uniqueness of the owner's program, as in the Salem Witch Trials Tercentenary Memorial in Salem, Massachusetts, and the Virginia Merrill Bloedel Education Center located on Bainbridge Island in Washington State. James Cutler Architects has received over thirty regional and national awards, including three American Institute of Architects National Honor Awards. Currently involved in numerous projects throughout the country, Cutler is designing the Norfolk Armed Forces Memorial, the First Presbyterian Church of Wenatchee, and the Medina, Washington residence of Bill Gates III, chairman of Microsoft. He and his partner on the project, Peter Bohlin of Bohlin Cywinski Jackson, convinced Gates to fit his new 40,000-square-foot house on the land without unduly disturbing the local ecology. Prestigious clients and all, Cutler says that he will always build real houses for real people.

As an educator and critic for nineteen years, Cutler works to influence others in his profession to have a greater awareness of their physical and spiritual relationship to the land. He teaches at the University of Washington, and previously taught at Harvard and the University of Pennsylvania, where he completed his degree in architecture. Cutler frequently speaks to other professionals about his concern for architectural stewardship of the environment. He co-founded the Bainbridge Island Trust in 1988, a non-profit organization dedicated to increasing public awareness and understanding of land use issues. The membership includes 250 families who are working to preserve over 1000 acres of habitat and open space. "We are driven," says Cutler, "to generate site plans and buildings that fit into the landscape while revealing more fully its nature and beauty. To this end, we have developed methods of design and construction that allow us, our clients, and contractors to have a higher sensitivity to the uniqueness of a place." One way he achieves this is to personally survey the property with his project team and, if possible, the owners, instead of hiring a surveyor. "By physically apprenticing ourselves to the land we learn its secrets and nuances in a way that no technical drawing can reveal."

Cutler's zealous spirit attracted John and Elinor Paulk, a Chicago couple who dreamed of retiring to the Northwest. Cutler spoke to the Paulks about the importance of local building traditions, the beauty of weed trees, and the defenselessness of picturesque views if creating them meant clearing forests. "I'm sure you've heard his speech: save the trees, save the woods, save everything," remembers Elinor Paulk. "We were very impressed." At the same time, they wanted their dream house with a view, and not a mission statement. The Paulks wanted a home with two bedrooms, a workshop, detached garage, a kitchen that wasn't closed off from the living room, and places to display heirloom objects. Cutler was able to satisfy their requirements, as well as his own. "When we first heard that Jim was working on the Gates house, it impressed and scared us," says Mrs. Paulk. "We're just ordinary people, but Jim made a house that is just for us. It grabs you and makes you feel a part of nature." For John Paulk, the ramp is the point of indoctrination into nature. "Anyone who uses it is forced into an intimate experience with nature. Once they've had that, they'll become dedicated to preserving the forest, too."

### Design Solutions

The shape of the house is a simple shed design whose roof tilts up toward the view. Its details, however, are layered with imagination and soul. The entry ramp is 127 feet long, and is suspended over a gully which varies up to twelve feet off the ground. The entry sequence was directed through a cedar grove by this walkway which protects the floor of the forest and at once provides the visitor with a unique perspective of the forest and view. Once inside, a twenty-two-foot-high glass-gridded wall allows the view of the trees and the water to dominate the architecture.

To show respect for the nature of the building materials, all the building components were crafted and left exposed. Rafter tails were not trimmed; floor joists left uncovered; galvanized metal bracing revealed; and ceilings float with the rafters underneath showing. More than any other project, Cutler believes that this house is "most true," as it allows the materials to express themselves.

### Environmental Objectives

One of the goals of the Paulk Residence project was to disturb the site and the living things on it as little as possible. The owners wanted a house that complemented the land, not one that existed in spite of it. At the same time, they wanted the views of the mountains to be a part of the experience of the house. Respect for the materials from which the house was constructed was another primary concern. In this way, honor could be accorded to those resources that were sacrificed in order to build the house. Cutler also wanted to raise the consciousness of the house's owners and visitors with regard to the natural beauty of the land. It is his belief that if one intimately experiences the natural site, positive attitudes toward its preservation and care will be enhanced.

## *Working Methods*

### Project Team

The project team consisted of the architects, geological consultant Allen Hart, general contractor Don Heppenstall, and structural engineer Gary Swenson. Each of the members of the team understood the environmental goals of the project and worked with the owners to help to achieve them. One of the most important elements coordinated by the team was the earthwork that was done to preserve the integrity of the site's natural vegetation. The owner, for example, hand-dug footings for the entry ramp in order to minimize soil disturbance. Also in an effort to preserve the site, the construction team staged its work from the building's garage area. This significantly cut down on the circulation of heavy vehicles transporting materials around the work site.

### Construction Methodologies

Prior to construction, a meeting was held that included the owner, architects, contractor, and each of the sub-contractors. During that time, each person was alerted to the goals of the project, specifically the goal of preserving the native vegetation. Each worker was encouraged to participate in this team effort and as a result of the encouragement, craftspeople became even more protective of the site.

During construction, Cutler worked with the contractor to limit any incidental damage by organizing staging areas for equipment and materials within defined areas. Access was prohibited into any areas that would not necessarily be disturbed by the building, drives, or walks.

The team discovered that a ramp perpendicular to the residence could fit between the surrounding trees. The ramp begins at the guest parking and rises to meet the residence high above the forest floor. Because of the design of the residence, excavation for

***The entry walkway, 127 feet long and supported on piers up to 12 feet above the ground, directs the visitor through the cedar grove and provides a unique view of the forest. Photo: Art Grice.***

***Left:*** *Footings were dug by hand, and any vegetation that needed to be removed was immediately replaced.*

***Bottom:*** *The shape of the house is a simple shed design, with the roof tilting up toward the view. Materials are left exposed and detailed to express their natural properties. Photos: James Cutler Architects.*

the foundation took place from the inside out, limiting destruction of surrounding vegetation. Footings were hand dug, and vegetation was immediately replaced. As construction progressed and staging areas were vacated, the owners immediately replanted those areas to protect the soil and the natural landscape.

### Site Review

One of the most unique aspects of this project is the architect's approach to site design. In order to understand every nuance of the landscape, Jim Cutler, with the owners, surveyed it personally, tagging areas where vegetation would need to be removed and replanted. Mr. Paulk cleared the underbrush for the footings himself with a hand machete. "I felt like an old-time adventurer hacking through the forest," he recalls, "and we celebrated when I finally broke through." No extensively manicured garden area was planned around the house, rather it was left to its own devices with native plants and trees. Ringing the property was an old dirt logging road, compacted by years of use. There no longer, it was returned to the natural world by the Paulks, who planted it with alders and cedars.

Built in Seabeck, Washington, the site for the Paulk's house had no access to local utilities or drinking water, thus requiring that it be self-sufficient. In the design of the site, Cutler choreographed the experience of moving through the site and building so that the unique beauty of the land and the life on it is revealed. He describes the property as a paradise with wrinkles. "There was a strange perversity to its contours," he remembers. "The land sloped upward to the view of the water and the mountains, as well as sideways to the north. There was a depression at the center with a nearly imprenetrable thicket of young cedar. There wasn't much to latch onto." Additionally, zoning codes required a setback of eighty feet from the bluff's edge, making the spectacular view nearly inaccessible.

The solution to the difficult site was eloquent: the house itself is created as a platform in the forest. The architect anchored the house to the slope where a mass of twenty-foot-tall rhododendrons grew, then let it float out onto stilts at the brow of the bank, leaving one end raised nearly fifteen feet off the ground.

## *Environmental Economics*

### Life Cycle Costs

Though the Paulk Residence exceeded the 15% glazing to floor area by more than double, it not only met Washington state's stringent energy code, but actually surpassed it by five to ten percent. The architects achieved such high efficiency by spending more

***In order to build the house around the complex contours and vegetation of the site, it was created as a platform that is raised off of the forest floor. Photo: James Cutler Architects.***

money on Heat Mirror™ glazing, blown-in batt (BIB) and rigid insulation up front, thereby cutting energy costs and consumption in the long run.

## *Energy Conservation*

While the architects suggested a number of energy-saving measures such as high-efficiency insulation and glazing, the owners had some quite constructive ideas of their own. When it came time to design the septic system, John Paulk asked that a gravity syphon system be installed for pressurization rather than the usual pump powered by electricity. The gravity syphon is set up in a way that its positioning not only initiates the flow of effluent from the holding tank to the drainage field, but also controls the flow more evenly so that the effluent is uniformly distributed in the field.

### Building Envelope Insulation

The building envelope was designed to meet the code requirements of Washington State, which has some of the most stringent energy efficient requirements in the United States. The state requires an R value of 19 for walls and 30 for roofs, both of which were slightly surpassed by the Paulk Residence. Because the house contains so much glass, the architects decided to insulate as much as they could, wherever they could. The design team specified a blown-in batt (BIB) system, a type of fiberglass insulation tht fills the wall cavities and has an R value that beats the conventional rating

***A woodburning stove provides necessary heat during much of the region's mild winter climate. Photo: Art Grice.***

by twenty percent. In spaces where even higher efficiency was desired, such as behind headers and columns, rigid insulation was used.

GLAZING

The Paulk house incorporates lots of glass in order to bring its residents a continuous connection to their wooded surroundings and views of Hood Canal. So that heat loss would be minimized, Heat Mirror™ glazing was used in the windows throughout. Low-E Heat Mirror™ glazing with an R-value of 3.5–as compared to standard glass with an R value of approximately 1.8–protects the house from heat loss in the winter, and helps to reduce heat gain in summer. In addition, the windows are framed in wood, which provides better thermal performance than metal.

HEATING AND COOLING

Because of the house's remote location, an independent source of heat needed to be provided. Solar power was considered but ultimately ruled out for two reasons: first, it would have necessitated the clearing of a great deal of vegetation, a concession that was unacceptable to everyone involved; and second, the house's views and exposure are oriented northwest, severely limiting access to the sun. A woodburning stove provides necessary heat during much of the region's mild winter climate, and a propane hot air system generates heat during the harshest days of winter. While it is true that propane depletes the earth of valuable fossil fuels, it was more readily available than oil and also burns cleaner. The Paulk Residence's high-efficiency furnace generates so little exhaust that it doesn't even have a chimney. Water vapor and what little exhaust there is escape through a pipe.

## *Air Quality*

VENTILATION

"I don't think I've air-conditioned a house in this area yet," says project architect Bruce Anderson. Natural ventilation provides superior air changes per hour in the Paulk Residence, not only because of Washington's cool and breezy climate, but also because of the way the architects handled the building's fenestration. High and low windows are ordered in such a way to take advantage of prevailing winds, naturally enabling cross ventilation.

## *Resource Conservation*

RECYCLED OR SUSTAINABLE NATURAL CONTENT

"The woods that were incorporated were conventional," says Cutler. "However, the use of old growth lumber was avoided. The structure is built of second and third growth Douglas fir and Pine. We used standard 2 x 4s, which are second and third growth 99% Hem fir." Because old-growth forests are not renewable, the architects use only second and third growth woods and manufactured wood products such as TJIs and plywood, which are made from low-quality trees yet function like higher quality woods.

The house is built with natural materials, each of which is utilized to express its features. This approach to design minimizes waste of materials, while calling for a high level of craftsmanship. For example, floor decking, rafters, beams, columns, and metal strapping are left exposed to show the nature of the structure, and materials such as drywall ceilings and walls therefore become unnecessary.

COMPOSTING

The owners set up a composting area in the exterior breezeway, which also serves as a woodyard.

*Left: Window openings are organized to take advantage of prevailing winds and provide cross ventilation.*

*Below: Exposed materials reveal the nature of the structure, require a high level of craftmanship, and limit the need for unnecessary finish materials.*

*Bottom: The house was designed and built without gutters so that rainwater would disperse and permeate the soil naturally, as if the house didn't exist. Photos: Art Grice.*

***Top: The corridor at the second level is finished with natural woods and wool carpet.***

***Bottom: The kitchen is sparsely detailed with mixed-grain fir casework and stone countertops. Photos: Art Grice.***

### *Water Conservation*

Because of its remote location, the Paulk Residence needed a private well. A 120-foot casing well was drilled that reaches drinking water provided from the nearby Olympic mountains. After drilling, all of the spoil–a type of silt clay–was removed from the site so that vegetation could regenerate.

No gutters were used in the house so that rainwater could naturally be distributed along the length of the building. This prevents the water from passing through the land faster than it would were the structure not there, thereby limiting the building's effect on its natural surroundings. In other words, it allows the rainwater to be dispersed as if the house didn't even exist.

Low-flow toilets by American Standard and water-efficient faucets by Kohler were installed.

### *Materials and Products*

#### Criteria

The architects consider a number of elements when specifying materials for a project, namely their cost, durability, environmental impact, and aesthetic value. Perhaps the most important rule of thumb, however, is that the material should express itself: stone should look like stone, wood should look like wood. According to Bruce Anderson, you'll never catch anyone at James Cutler Architects using something that *looks* like something it's not. Wherever possible they try to use natural materials.

#### Toxicity

Toxic substances like plywood or products containing formaldehyde are always avoided, but when they simply can't be, Cutler tries to isolate them outside the building envelope or use materials that offgas as little as possible. With the exception of some vinyl tile in the bathroom, the Paulk Residence contains no synthetic materials. The kitchen counters are made of stone, the floors are covered with wool carpet and ceramic tile, and all of the floor finishes used were water-based.

#### Manufacturer's Environmental Impact

James Cutler Architects routinely requests MSDS sheets and other manufacturing information from its materials sources. Questions they are likely to ask a manufacturer about a material are How is it made? What are its characteristics? How far is the source from the site? This research is ongoing at the firm. In the case of the Paulk Residence, the architects were already familiar with all of their sources' environmental records.

***All materials were procured from local sources where possible. Fabrication and galvanizing for the building was done locally, and the hand rails were assembled by a nearby fishing net manufacturer. Photo: Art Grice.***

EMBODIED ENERGY

All materials used in the construction and design of the Paulk house were procured from local sources with the exception of two types of wood that were not available locally in commercial quantities. Fabrication and galvanizing for the building was done locally as well. The hand rails, for instance, were done by a nearby fishing net manufacturer, whose talented metal fabricators were more than happy to take the work during their off-season.

## *Post Occupancy Evaluation*

While the architects have not performed a formal evaluation of the Paulk Residence since its construction, they report that the Paulks are very pleased with their house and all its features.

## REEVES RESIDENCE

*Dewees Island, South Carolina*

**Architect and Environmental Consultant:** Design Harmony, Raleigh, North Carolina, Gail A. Lindsey, AIA, Cheryl Walker, AIA
**Structural Engineer:** Lysaght and Associates, PA, Raleigh, North Carolina, Chuck Lysaght, P.E.
**Electrical Contractor:** Frampton Electric, Charleston, South Carolina, Edmund Frampton, *President*
**General Contractor:** R. S. Structures, Inc., Isle of Palms, South Carolina, Tom Sanders, *President*, Rhonda Sanders, *Treasurer*
**Mechanical Contractor:** Sun Coast Heating and Air Conditioning Company, Inc., Charleston, South Carolina, Joe Bozzelli, *Vice President*
**Total Area:** Withheld at owner's request.
**Cost of Construction:** $127.00 per Square Foot
**Date of Completion:** July 1995

### *Project Overview*

The Reeves selected Dewees Island, a barrier island off the coast of South Carolina, as the location for their permanent residence because of its physical beauty, proximity to historic Charleston, and its island partnership's philosophy of preserving the island's natural environment. They chose Design Harmony and R.S. Structures after extensively interviewing other architects and builders recommended by the Island Preservation Partnership CEO, John Knott. The Reeves needed their new year round home to accommodate extended visits by five married children, grandchildren, and guests. In addition to meeting the environmental guidelines set forth by Dewees Island as well as the Reeves' concerns, the new home needed to meet additional criteria for the clients' allergy sensitivities.

#### Architect Profile

See The Body Shop U.S. Headquarters.

#### Design Solutions

The design of the Reeves residence and site is based on five major environmental elements: siting, energy efficiency, air and water quality, materials, resource efficiency, and waste management. The residence is located on Dewees Island, a community that was founded on sustainable principles. The architects for the Reeves Residence, Design Harmony, selected by the owners for their expertise and commitment to ecologically conscious design, created a place that joins comfort, spaciousness, and beauty with energy efficiency, ecological sensitivity, and health consciousness.

Orienting the house and locating windows to take advantage of coastal breezes for natural ventilation was a prime consideration in the design of the house. It was from this concern that the house's single-room deep, linear form footprint evolved. The two-story barrel vaulted living room frames a dramatic view of the ocean while increasing ambient light in all of the living spaces. More natural daylight is brought in by dormer windows located high in the barrel vault. The open configuration of the living spaces provides maximum air circulation and dispersion of natural daylight. "The barrel vault with dormer windows, a main feature of the house, merited the additional cost and difficulty required to build it," says Architect Cheryl Walker. "It not only expands the living area aesthetically, but increases the quality of ambient natural light and ventilation."

A series of outdoor porches serve a variety of important functions, taking advantage of unique site views and features. A long linear southern porch faces a wooded area, is screened to protect occupants from insects, and provides passive solar shading. The eastern porch provides a private ocean view with direct sun screening, and the northern porch provides guests with a private outdoor area view of the lagoon, and a cool shaded area in summer.

#### Environmental Objectives

Dewees Island is one of the barrier islands which lies twelve miles northeast of historic Charleston, South Carolina. The island, on which only four buildings stood as recently as 1992, is nearly 1200 acres of highland, lakes, salt marsh, and beaches. A state-approved Master Plan, developed in order to preserve Dewees Island's natural environment, governs the island's development. Designed and written by the Washington, D.C. architectural firm of Burt Hill Kosar Rittelman Associates, extensive design guidelines and island covenants regulate the building process. Focusing on environmentally sensitive design and construction strategies, these guidelines encourage, among other things, the construction of low, vernacular building forms. The Dewees Island Architectural Assistance Team also helps owners and architects work within the island's low-impact philosophy. Accessible by boat, Dewees limits residential development to 150 houses on 225 acres of land (1:8 ratio). Transportation on the island is limited to electric-powered golf carts and foot traffic. The northeastern section of Dewees Island is maintained as a pristine, 350-acre wildlife sanctuary.

In addition to the environmental goals and requirements of the community, Design Harmony established low-impact environmental and energy goals with the Reeves. These goals guided the design of the new residence:

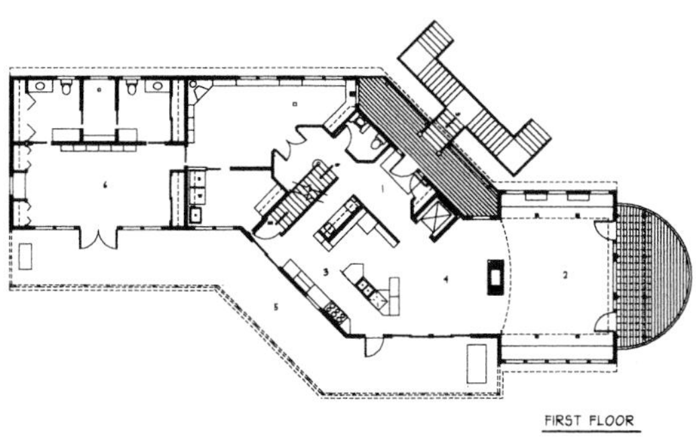
FIRST FLOOR

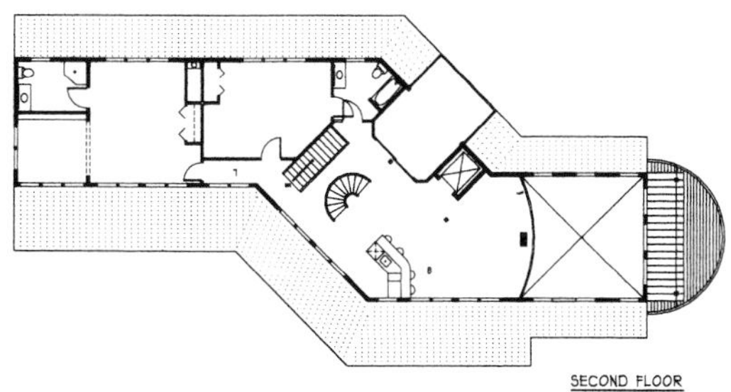
SECOND FLOOR

*Previous page: Orienting the house to take advantage of coastal breezes resulted in a footprint with a primarily single-room-deep linear form.*

*Above: Outdoor porches provide solar shading or access to direct sunlight, views and private outdoor rooms.*

*Right: Dewees Island is accessible by boat and transportation is limited to electric-powered golf carts and foot traffic. Photos: Michael W. Cox. Drawings: Design Harmony.*

***Aerial view of Dewees Island. Photo: Michael W. Cox.***

1. Develop the site with as little disturbance as possible.
2. Site and construct the house in a way that removes the fewest trees possible.
3. Establish and maintain good indoor air quality.
4. Be resource-efficient with respect to both available site resources and product/material/system selection and production.
5. Reduce transportation energy use by using regionally available products and materials.
6. Reduce construction waste.

## *Working Methods*

### Project Team

A traditional project team structure involving owner, architect, and contractor was used to create the Reeves Residence. Each member brought his or her own interests and experience regarding ecologically sensitive design to the table, including the builder, who was involved from the very beginning. The builder, Tom Sanders, had previously worked on several structures on the island, and so understood the logistics of barge transportation, alternative materials, and the realities of building ecologically on Dewees.

Aside from the guidance of Design Harmony, the Dewees Island Architectural Assistance Team played an important role in further evaluating environmental criteria.

### Computer Modeling

South Carolina Electric & Gas Company further analyzed energy efficiency criteria for the Reeves Residence and reviewed it by computer model. This step was taken to ensure that it complied with the utility's "Good Sense" rebate program.

The logistics and added expense of building on an island involve complex tranportation issues for the labor force, as well as difficult material choices for the architects. The Dewees Island boat could transport only six workers to the island per trip, with round trips requiring about thirty to forty minutes. Because building materials were transported to the site by barge, each trip increased the construction costs. Orders needed to be carefully calculated so that the materials would be on hand when needed. Since the builder had other projects under construction on Dewees, group deliveries and sharing of crews and equipment between several projects increased efficiency. Also, material waste–which had to be transported by barge off the island for recycling and disposal–was minimized. Island regulations limit the amount of land that can be disturbed during construction, and this further discouraged waste by confining staging areas and prohibiting traditional on-site disposal methods such as burning or burying.

### Site Review

Prior to site design, existing site features were analyzed and a site survey was prepared that indicated the location, type, and size of all vegetation. This allowed the designer to determine the best house location and optimum building footprint within the setbacks. Following the stated intent of the island's design guidelines, the house is sited in a linear fashion on a 100 x 975-foot-deep lot from southeast to northwest to maximize protection from winter winds and summer sun; to maximize ventilation from natural breezes; to benefit from passive solar heating in order to reduce fuel consumption; and to provide as many varied views of the island as possible. Directions for northeast storm winds and east and southeast summer breezes, as well as seasonal sunrises and sunsets, were taken into account in the design of the house.

When the Architectural Assistance Team expressed concern that a possible "wind shadow" might be created for the site to the north of the Reeves house, a local weather expert was consulted. After completing a careful analysis of the prevailing breezes, the size and height of the house, and the distance and topography of the adjacent site to determine possible effects, it was determined that no wind turbulence would be created and that the north neighbor would, in fact, benefit from an increased southern air current.

Island guidelines limit disturbed land during construction to 7500 square feet per lot, including one driveway. To maintain vegetation indigenous to the island, the Architectural Assistance Team required a survey of existing vegetation before work began; an approved landscape plan using only indigenous plants; and proposed tree removal plan. The Reeves' driveway of pine straw blends with the beach access drive.

## *Environmental Economics*

### Life Cycle Costs

The Reeves residence, at a cost of $127 per square foot, represents a slightly higher than market cost project than on nearby Isle of Palms or Sullivan's Island which have vehicular access. Barge transportation of materials to Dewees added roughly 25% to the total cost of the job. One side benefit of this was that it necessitated careful scrutiny of the quantity of materials ordered, so that little waste would result. "An additional 10% of the cost is attributable to the "green" materials, products, and systems incorporated into the

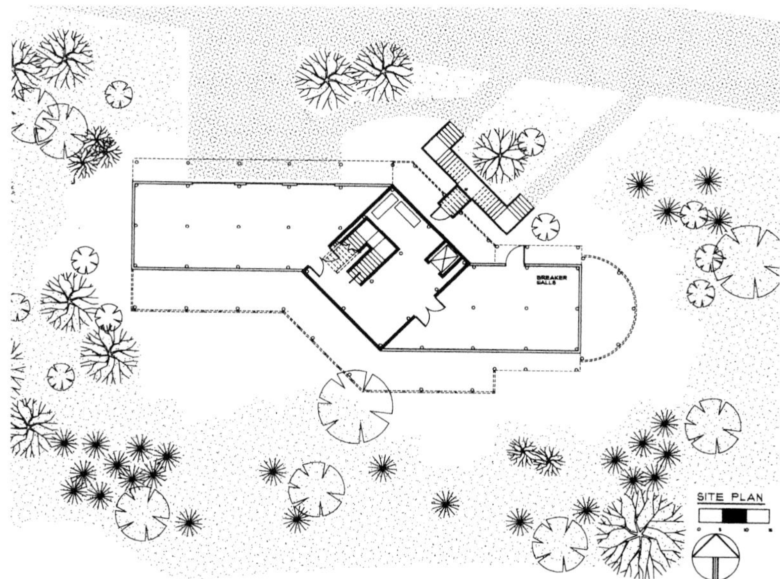


***In order to maintain and restore vegetation indigenous to the island, a survey of existing vegetation was required for approval of the proposed work. Drawing: Design Harmony.***

***After the devastation of the last hurricane, Dewees called for retaining existing vegetation, including damaged trees and scrub, leaving it in place to be restored to the original character and habitats of the island. Photo: Michael W. Cox.***

project," says architect Cheryl Walker, "but many of these items have paybacks of as little as two years, and reduce operational costs considerably. The total cost of the Reeves Residence was approximately 10% higher than average mainland costs, however the additional costs were more a result of barging materials to the island, than environmental features."

Environmental products or systems that added to the initial construction costs include:

•Closed loop geothermal HVAC system: It cost nearly twice the initial cost of a 17 SEER air-to-air system, but is only 60% as costly per year to operate.

•Asko Swedish appliances: These energy-efficient appliances were 50% more expensive than traditional appliances, but cost 50% less to operate per year.

•Quarter sawn oak flooring: While it cost 25% more than carpeting or other flooring, its water-based sealer provides a surface that does not absorb the dirt and dust that can aggravate an allergy sufferer.

•TREX decking: Costing 50% more than traditional "treated" wood, it is made of durable recycled plastic and "waste" wood chips. The advantage of TREX is less labor and maintenance since it does not need to be waterproofed, sealed, or painted.

•Cotton batt insulation: Its initial cost was 10% higher than fiberglass batts, but nonetheless made for a better choice because it is composed of a "waste" material (cotton mill scraps) that would otherwise be dumped into a local landfill.

### Grants and Rebates

The Reeves Residence profited from a $1650 rebate on electric bills because it met the South Carolina Electric & Gas Utility's "Good Sense" Energy Efficiency Program criteria for sealing, caulking, weatherproofing, and the utilization of a highly energy-efficient heating and cooling system.

To participate in the program and receive rebates, a new residential structure must be built to higher energy efficiency standards, including higher R-valued insulation, thorough caulking and sealing to prevent air infiltration, and higher efficiency heating and cooling systems than are required by building code. The utility company obtains plans, specifications, and window and door schedules for the new structure, and runs computer models to see that their standards are met or exceeded. They also determine the design loads that the HVAC system must meet. Per the Program requirements, the HVAC system cannot be oversized. The utility then inspects each project to ensure that the proper system components are installed correctly. Both the general contractor and the HVAC contractor for the Reeves Residence had worked and continue to work with South Carolina Electric and Gas Company to try to incorporate the "Good Sense" Program in all of their projects.

## *Energy Conservation*

### Building Envelope Insulation

The building envelope incorporates environmentally benign materials, including R-19 cotton fiber batt insulation in 2 x 6 stud walls (instead of the typical 2 x 4 construction), a radiant barrier in the roof construction, and low-emissivity argon-filled glazing.

One of the reasons the architects chose cotton fiber batt insulation is that they were concerned with the possible health risks faced by the workers who would be installing the more commonly specified fiberglass insulation. It is made of local waste materials, has a very good insulation value, and has an easy, non-messy installation procedure. As one of the Reeves suffers from allergies, the benign, natural content of the cotton insulation also made for a good choice. Air Krete, another possible insulation alternative, was rejected by the owners because it is a blown-in cementitious foam insulation that has less flexibility during future renovations. Later changes in a wall cavity, for instance, would destroy the integrity of the entire wall.

### Glazing

The architects selected Andersen glass doors and windows for many reasons. Their standard high-performance glazing system, its quality, availability, and cost competitiveness made Andersen windows a first choice. In addition, Andersen has initiated window recycling program. All of the glass installed at the Reeves Residence incorporates low-emissivity glazing filled with argon. This helps the windows to deflect heat from the sun while admitting light.

High-performance glazing was selected in order to reduce heating and cooling costs, increase summer comfort by reducing heat build up, and increase winter comfort by reducing heat loss. Andersen High Performance Sun II tinted glazing was used on southeast exposures for additional solar control. Features of this glazing include a microscopically thin metallic coating bonded to an inner surface of the sealed pane of glass, a low conductivity spacer made of stainless steel which is more resistant to heat conductivity than aluminum, and argon gas sealed between the two panes of glass. In winter, the Andersen II sun glazing is 35% more efficient than common double-pane windows; at 0°F outdoors and 70°F indoors, the temperature inside the glass is 57°F. In summer the glazing is 41% more efficient than the common double-pane windows, with an active heat gain under hot sun at 78 BTU per square foot per hour.

***R-19 cotton fiber batt insulation, made from recycled textile fibers, was specified. Photo: Michael W. Cox.***

### Heating and Cooling

To gain maximum energy efficiency from the building and its systems, passive solar features were incorporated. For instance, minimal glazing was used on the northwest face of the house in order to protect the indoors from cold prevailing winds. A trellis was installed on the southeast side deck to protect the east-facing interior from direct sun during summer months. Tinted windows were used on porches while roof overhangs on the southeast face were designed and constructed in order to minimize solar gain in summer and maximize solar gain in winter..

When it came time to specify an HVAC system, two systems were evaluated with respect to efficiency, longevity, initial cost, and operating costs. A closed loop geothermal heat pump system by Waterfurnace International had an initial cost of $27,000; an operational cost of $1500 per year; and a 15 EER (comparable to a 17 SEER or Super Energy Efficiency Rating). A conventional high efficiency air system by York had an initial cost of $15,000; an operational cost of $2500 per year; and a 12 SEER. Both systems met the high efficiency standards set by local utility company South Carolina Electric and Gas to qualify for the "Good Sense" Rebate Program, exceeding the South Carolina Building Code standard of SEER 10.

The Reeves team decided on a closed loop geothermal heat pump. The geothermal heat pump unit made by Waterfurnace International is an electrically powered device that uses the natural heat storage ability of the earth to heat and cool a building. In cool weather, the earth absorbs and stores energy, and this heat is extracted from the earth by water and pumped to heat exchangers to heat the house. In warmer weather, the process is reversed. Heat is extracted from the indoor air and transferred to the earth through the same liquid medium.

The owners selected the geothermal heat pump system over the high efficiency air to air heat pump

***A long expansive screened-in porch provides solar shading, passive cooling, and outdoor rooms.***

system for a number of reasons. Though the geothermal system cost significantly more than the air system, its operating costs are lower, the life span of the units is roughly twice that of conventional units in a salt air environment, no outside units were required, and the thermal comfort level it provides is superior to that of the other system.

Further cost savings are attributable to the rebate program and the downsizing of the overall HVAC system due to the reduced heating and cooling loads required. The reduction took place because of the efficient building envelope, insulation, glazing, and thorough caulking and sealing. In summmer, at 94°F outdoors and 75°F indoors, the HVAC's peak cooling load is 100,968 BTUs per hour. In winter, at 28°F outdoors and 70°F indoors, its peak heating load is 95,868 BTUs per hour.

### Lighting

Daylighting was maximized in the two levels of living spaces by introducing natural light through dormers in the two-story barrel vaulted ceiling and through the east-facing window wall, and by installing large windows in all habitable areas.

A variety of artificial lighting types was used, including compact fluorescent lights and high energy-efficient downlights.

To further increase energy efficiency, a programmable controls system made by Hybrid Technologies was installed. It governs lighting, hot water, and the HVAC system. No outdoor lighting is permitted on the island as it could interrupt the movements and cycles of the local wildlife.

***Natural daylight, light-colored surfaces, and a variety of energy efficient artificial lighting provide a high quality of interior light. Photos: Michael W. Cox.***

## *Air Quality*

### Ventilation

The house is essentially one room deep and has operable windows throughout to maximize the cooling benefits and cross ventilation from ocean breezes. All of the rooms plus the spaces which house the two gas fireplaces have good supply and return air grill locations, thereby providing consistently "clean" air. Transom windows and fans throughout the house help to admit and circulate fresh air at the ceiling where heat collects.

A central vacuum system was installed to maintain indoor air quality. Because of specific allergy sensitivities, the Reeves requested the installation of an AIR VAC central vacuum system during construction to provide better removal of dust and particulates from the indoor air environment. The central vacuum system is extremely powerful and tranports dust, dirt, and indoor air particulates through a sealed system to a holding bin for later removal. The system has the added convenience of attaching the vacuum tube to a number of wall receptacles. The owners think that while the central system is very effective in particulate removal, the tube is heavy and awkward to use.

Since the Reeves residence is sealed tight for energy efficiency, it requires substantial fresh air circulation, particularly in winter months.

### Materials Toxicity

In addition to general environmental concerns, indoor air quality was specifically important to the owners. To avoid indoor air quality problems associated with absorptive carpeting and padding, flooring was specified to be hardwood, marble, or ceramic tile. Non-VOC and low-VOC Glidden paints were specified and used throughout.

***Detail at circular stair. The use of hardwood flooring installed with water-based sealers helps eliminate indoor air quality problems associated with absorptive carpet and padding for the owner, who suffers from allergies. Photo: Michael W. Cox.***

***A screened porch, interior fans, and transom or operable windows help to circulate fresh air throughout the house. Photo: Michael W. Cox.***

## *Resource Conservation*

### Deconstructed Materials Reuse

The owner incorporated a number of salvaged items into the design of the house, including an antique beveled glass front entry door, refurbished stained glass panels as transoms, and a salvaged wood mantle. In addition, many of the furnishings are antiques, "early attic" consignment pieces, and found objects. For example, an old bureau was reconfigured as the base cabinet for the bathroom sink.

### Recycled or Sustainable Natural Content

Many of the building materials used in the Reeves Residence contain recycled material. The reconstituted wood and resin TREX™ decking was chosen because of its long-term durability, appearance, and recycled content. The cotton batt insulation is made of waste fibers from a South Carolina textile mill. Hardiplank cementitious siding contains recycled wood and plastic, and carries a fifty-year warranty.

### Composting

Composting of food and organic waste was addressed in the planning of the site. The kitchen has a center compost drop which allows food waste to drop directly from the sink into a food waste container. The container is twice weekly taken to the community composting area and emptied into the main system. The Reeves report that the community system, a three-stage system located at the Central Landings

Building, functions well, generates little odor, and attracts few insects.

### *Water Conservation and Quality*

Water conservation and quality is addressed in a number of ways. A state-of-the-art sewage treatment system that has received national recognition through coverage in Environmental Protection's "New Frontiers in Wastewater Treatment" has been installed on Dewees Island. The system is designed to accommodate all levels of occupancy on the island. According to Design Harmony, "even one homesite pump can pressurize the entire system. Liquid hydrogen sulfide is metered into the system for disinfection, and the pressurized system is connected to the absorption field for waste distribution." The low-technology design of the system reduces the need for human operations, helps to preserve and enhance the island's environment, and significantly reduces operations and maintenance costs. The Dewees Utility Corporation routinely samples water from the Dewees Inlet, the impoundment area and from six monitoring wells. Quarterly water inspections are performed, and the samples obtained by both sources during 1995 indicate that the sewer system is performing well.

Dewees Island has a 10,000-gallon capacity island community water system that provides a communal filtration system in lieu of many energy-intensive individual systems. The Reeves use the community's reverse osmosis water filtration system.

Low-flow commercial grade toilets (1.6 gal/flush) installed with a high riser and water-efficient shower heads were also specified throughout the Reeves Residence.

A cistern system was designed to collect rainwater from the roof for landscape irrigation and was built on site of standard components. Gutters direct the water from the roof through downspouts into a 500-gallon capacity storage tank. The storage capacity was estimated based on the amount of water necessary for landscape use in the immediate vicinity of the house only. Since the majority of plant materials are indigenous, little additional irrigation is needed on the site. Overflow water goes back into the ground water, and the raised tank has a spigot on the side to allow for a gravity feed connection to a garden hose. The owners also use the collected rainwater for watering houseplants. Once the final landscaping has been installed, collected water will provide irrigation for all vegetation on the property.

Concerning the use of pesticides on the site, the Reeves' mortgage company mandates the use of sprayed pesticides, a measure which can contaminate the water, in order to comply with building codes. The landscaping concepts proposed for the site, on the other hand, promote Integrated Pest Management (IPM) through the use of indigenous plants, insects, and organic soil treatments.

### *Materials and Products*

Energy efficient and low-water usage washer, dryer, and dishwashers by Swedish manufacturer Asko were installed. Even though their initial cost is 50% higher than other appliances, they reduce costs significantly by using both water and electricity at maximum efficiency. The dishwasher heats its own water, uses little detergent, and its stainless steel construction is more durable when exposed to island water. The washing machine uses less than 1/4 cup of detergent per load of clothes, and the spin cycle removes all water from the clothing, dramatically reducing drying time and energy use. The owners installed computers and faxes so that they could work from home, rather than commute to offices on the mainland.

#### Criteria

The following list illustrates the concerns that the Reeves Design/Construction Team considered when making decisions about materials and products:

1. Aesthetics
2. Cost-effectiveness
3. Energy efficiency
4. Good IAQ/low toxicity

***Water conservation and quality is addressed as a high priority in order to maintain the wildlife habitats and natural beauty of Dewees. Photo: Michael W. Cox.***

*Ceramic tiles, handmade by a local artist, were installed in the kitchen. Photo: Michael W. Cox.*

5. Easy maintenance/durability (especially due to harsh island weather conditions)
6. Availability
7. Regional sources

Toxicity

The owners were particularly concerned with their home's indoor air quality, as one of them suffers from allergies. Mold and mildew are common offenders contributing to poor indoor air quality, with humidity factoring in as a serious problem where the HVAC system is concerned. With this in mind, Design Harmony specified a closed loop geothermal HVAC system. Unlike air-to-air systems, whose units are located on the exterior, the geothermal system's units are underground and in the interior, thereby protected from the island's corrosive humidity.

Manufacturer's Environmental Impact

The Reeves Design Team weighed the environmental impact of manufacturing Corian for kitchen countertops against the material's durability and ease of maintenance, and decided in favor of the Corian. Hardiplank pressed concrete boards were chosen for the exterior siding over other options such as treated, sealed, or painted wood siding because of their low maintenance and good durability, important factors where the island's rugged weather is concerned. The finger-jointed, recycled wood trim was chosen not only because it was cost effective, but because it is composed of waste wood. The house's high-performance windows are manufactured by the Andersen Company, which has a recycling plan in place that appealed to the owners.

Embodied Energy

Not only is the R-19 cotton fiber batt insulation used in the Reeves Residence made from recycled fabric scraps, but it is available locally, thereby cutting down on the amount of fuel needed to transport it to the site.

Salvaged materials and antiques were selected by the owners because of their inherent beauty and craftsmanship. The Reeves incorporated an antique beveled front entry glass door, refurbished stained glass transoms, a salvaged wood mantle, and several antique pieces—all beautiful examples of "embodied energy."

## *Post Occupancy Evaluation*

Many of the features of the Reeves Residence have been very successful according to the architects and the owners. "The house is fantastic," say the Reeves. "It's the best house we've ever lived in. We think that it's the best designed house on the island." The natural daylight introduced into the barrel-vaulted two-story space greatly enhances the quality of the living areas, both on the main and upper levels of the house. When entering the main living space from the entrance, the whole living room opens up to the dramatic view of the ocean.

Within the very linear site constraints, the Reeves are pleased with the siting of the house. The slightly angled footprint allows outdoor privacy when using certain outdoor porches and decks by blocking views from more public areas, such as the nearby beach access. The angled design of the spaces inside the linear house footprint allows for privacy without having to close doors to individual rooms of the house. For

*Exterior materials include pressed concrete boards used for siding, recycled wood trim, and windows whose manufacturer implements a recycling plan. Photo: Michael W. Cox.*

instance, when entering from the main entrance, views into the private sitting room/ office and master bedroom are screened from public view due to the angled walls.

The house utilizes natural ventilation and summer breezes in a very pleasant and effective way. Many of the windows include operable transoms. The single-room depth and careful placement of windows and fans takes advantage of prevailing breezes that supplement summer cooling. If anything, the Reeves would add more transom windows above the double-hung windows to increase breezes into the main living room.

The owners are also pleased with the performance of the HVAC system; it provides excellent cooling in the summer and good heating in the winter. If harsher than average temperatures are anticipated, a slight modification can be made to increase the indoor air temperature. Based on two unusually cold winter storms during 1995–when outside temperatures went below 20°F–the average indoor temperature was about 55°F.

After the first year of occupancy, the owners are refining some of the original design decisions. The second floor guest bedroom/ sitting area on the west elevation receives too much sunlight. All other orientations of the house have good solar control because of the overhangs, porches, and sun screening devices. To remedy the overabundance of sunlight into the guest room, the owners are adding Bahamian shutters to the sitting room windows. This will provide storm control in addition to the desired solar control.

The Reeves also feel that the Hybrid energy controls system is too elaborate for their needs. The low-voltage system is sensitive to electrical noise disturbance and maintenance is a problem because there is no local system support. Electricians must be specially trained to work on the system, making repairs and modifications difficult.

As a last item, the Reeves noted the need for more large walk-in storage to store infrequently used items, bulk food, and supplies for year-round living on the island. Although an elevator was installed to service the main and second floors, the Reeves have encountered problems bringing large or heavy items to the third floor for storage in the attic. Plans to extend the elevator's reach are in the works.

## REEVES RESIDENCE MATERIALS RESOURCES

**Interior paint.** Spred 2000, No-and low-VOC, solvent-free and low odor; The Glidden Company, 925 Euclid Ave., Cleveland, OH 44115

**Siding.** HardiPlank siding; fiber- reinforced cement siding, asbestos-, formaldehyde-, and fiberglass-free, 50-year warranty; James Hardie Building Products, 10901 Elm Ave., Fontana, CA (909) 356-6300

***The barrel vaulted ceiling, a main feature of the house, adds drama to the living space and increases the quality of light and ventilation, thereby meriting the additional cost and difficulty required in building it. Photo: Michael W. Cox.***

**Sealers.** Ultra-Cure; water-borne urethane sealer for wood flooring; Bona-Kemi USA, Inc., Aurora, CA (303) 371-1411

**Batt Insulation.** Greenwood Cotton Insulation; Recycled cotton and polyester batt insulation from recycled textile scraps; Greenwood Cotton Insulation Products, Inc., P.O. Box 1017, Greenwood, SC 29648 (800) 546-1332

**Windows/Glazing.** Sun II High Performance low-emissivity, argon-filled glazing; R-value of 3.2 with shading coefficient of 0.35 was used on SE exposures, shading coefficient on other exposures was .51, manufacturer has initiated a window recycling program; Andersen Windows, Ft. of N. Fifth Ave., Bayport, MN (612)439-5150

**Window Treatment.** Optix™ heat-reflective window blinds; Reduce heat gain and glare, eliminate UV rays 100%; Nanik Division of Springs, Winslow Window Fashions, 7200 Stewart Avenue, Wausau, WI 54401 (800) 422-4544

**Deck Materials.** TREX™ decking; wood-polymer composite from reclaimed plastic and wood waste; Mobile Chemical Company, Composite Products Division, 800 Connecticut Ave., Norwalk, CT 06856 (800) BUY-TREX

**Heat System.** Electric, closed loop, geothermal heat pump system 3 (#SXH024) units w/ 15.5 EER rating 1 (#SXH030) unit w/ 14.3 EER rating (roughly equivalent to a 17 SEER rating); Waterfurnace International, 9000 Conservation Way, Fort Wayne, IN (800) 934-5667

**Appliances.** Energy/water conserving washer/dryer and dishwashers, Asko, 903 N. Browser, Richardson, TX 75081 (214) 644-8595

## WOMEN'S HUMANE SOCIETY ANIMAL SHELTER

*Bensalem, Pennsylvania*

**Architect:** Susan Maxman Architects, Philadelphia, Pennsylvania, Susan A. Maxman, FAIA, *Principal*, Jeffrey C. Hayes, AIA, *Project Architect*, Robert J. Hotes, AIA, *Project Team Member*, Missy Maxwell, AIA, *Project Team Member*, Linda Braley, *Project Team Member*, Robert Rudloff, *Project Team Member*, Kathryn Cleveland, AIA, *Project Team Member*
**Civil Engineer:** MGL, Inc. Bensalem, Pennsylvania, Ed McGill, P.E.
**Electrical Engineer.** Donald F. Nardy & Associates, Philadelphia, Pennsylvania, Donald F. Nardy, P.E.
**Mechanical Engineer.** Bruce E. Brooks & Associates, Philadelphia, Pennsylvania, Bruce E. Brooks, P.E.
**General Contractor:** Irwin & Leighton, Inc. King of Prussia, Pennsylvania, Edward Babcock, *Vice President*
**Landscape Architect:** Lager-Raabe Landscape Architects, Philadelphia, Pennsylvania, Anita Lager, ASLA
**Energy Analysis:** Ensar Group, Inc. Boulder, Colorado, Gregory Franta, AIA
**Lighting Design:** Clanton Engineering, Inc., Boulder, Colorado, Nancy Clanton, P.E.
**Total Area:** 24,500 Square Feet on 11 Acres
**Cost of Construction:** $3,119,208.00; $127 per Square Foot (With Parking, Landscaping and Off-site utility work, $3,915,000.00; $159 Per Square Foot)
**BTU/ Square Foot Per Year:** Administration Area (Zone 1): 83 kBtu/SF; Kennel Area (Zone 2): 416 kBtu/SF; Clinic Area (Zone 3): 297 kBtu/SF; Total Average: 265 kBtu/SF
**Watts/ Square Foot per Year:** 0.7-1
**Date of Completion:** 1994

### *Project Overview*

#### ARCHITECT PROFILE

Architect Susan Maxman reveals, "A good part of our practice involves recycling existing buildings and houses. Our design strategy always respects the site surroundings, and the client is always an integral part of the design process." During the time that the team began the design of the Women's Humane Society, Maxman recalls, "I heard Amory Lovins speak about how one could unscrew one light bulb and screw in another and save all sorts of coal in the power plant down the road, and I began to understand the role that I could play in minimizing energy consumption, halting further ecological degradation and designing in a way that promotes stewardship of our environment. I determined that our next challenge would be one in which we would attempt to design an environmentally sensitive building."

At the same time that this revelation came to Maxman, she was embarking on a term of office as President-elect of the AIA. "I felt compelled to speak about this issue wherever and whenever I could, to inform architects of the possibilities for our profession to assume a leadership role in this field. All architects today know the term 'sustainable design' and are far more aware of the issues involved in the stewardship of our planet and their role in it than they were when I first began talking about these issues in 1991." Maxman's commitment to environmental stewardship became a top priority for the AIA as well.

Ecological and energy concerns have become her firm's specialty. The firm received an Honor Award from the AIA for its design work at Camp Tweedale, a complex for the Freedom Valley Girl Scout Council. Through its sensitivity to and expertise in projects both rural and rustic in nature, Maxman Architects has attracted the National Park Service, several Girl Scout Councils, and the USDA Forest Service as clients.

The scope of Susan Maxman Architects' work with the USDA Forest Service in Seneca Rocks, West Virginia includes the design of a new 9000-square-foot visitor center complete with exhibit spaces, classroom, auditorium, and staff offices. The interpretive storyline incorporated into the visitors tour focuses on the ecosystem, as well as the recreational opportunities available to visitors in the nearby surroundings. Sustainable design practice governs the design of the building and energy efficiency is being maximized through the utilization of new energy analysis software developed by the National Renewable Energy Laboratory. This hour-by-hour simulation program was developed specifically for smaller commercial buildings of about 10,000 square feet.

Three new structures for the Girl Scout Council of Greater St. Louis' Camp Cedarledge are under construction. Its equestrian center includes a covered riding arena and stables for forty horses. The prominent hilltop site catches prevailing summer winds and provides dramatic views. Senior Hill Lodge, a troop house, has a narrow profile. Clerestory light/ventilation monitors and deep porches maximize passive cooling and daylighting of the building. The design also features environmentally responsible building materials such as wall board with a high content of recycled paper, more durable than conventional drywall.

#### DESIGN SOLUTIONS

Completed in the spring of 1994, the Women's Humane Society Animal Shelter rests on an eleven-acre site in Bensalem, Pennsylvania, just outside Philadelphia. The 25,000-square-foot facility combines an administrative area, management, education, humane and cruelty investigation staff offices, confer-

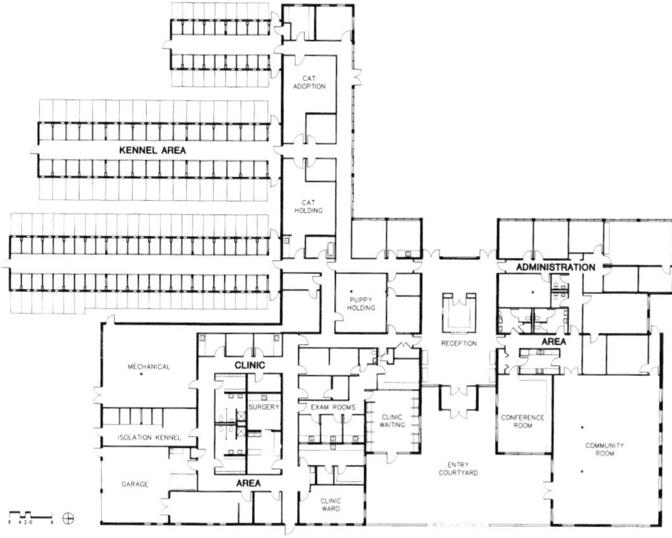


***Above: The entry area features exposed materials and is flooded with natural light. Photo: Catherine Bogert.***

***Left: The 25,000-square-foot facility includes an administrative area, conference area, animal holding, and clinic areas. Drawing: Susan Maxman Architects.***

***Low-maintenance corrugated metal siding and steel structural components manufactured in the region provide an aesthetic reference to industrial materials and reduce embodied energy consumption. Photos: Catherine Bogert.***

ence room, and multi-purpose community room. Three examination rooms, a surgery and surgery preparation room, an x-ray facility, and an isolation and hospital ward are incorporated with a shelter facility that houses 100 dog kennels, 88 feline cages, and an adoption staff and services area. The new facility was built according to environmental principles, starting with the design of the site itself. Also, recycled, managed growth, and non-toxic materials were utilized as much as possible together with increased ventilation to provide a high level of indoor air quality. Energy efficiency and CFC-free building systems specified for the shelter are expected to contribute an estimated $40,000 per year in energy savings.

A large tower owned by Philadelphia Electric Company dominates the site. To incorporate the tower with the aesthetics of the building, Susan Maxman Architects chose references to industrial materials–steel siding was used for cladding and a steel trussed arch marks the building's entry. A sign wall facing the turnpike forms the south wall of the service court.

Aspects of psychological and physical comfort for building users are taken into close account. For instance, a connection to the outside through a rear courtyard and planned nature trails afford employees the opportunity for a relationship with the outdoors. Operational windows encourage natural ventilation and provide an abundance of natural light, an advantage which has been clinically shown to benefit psychological well being. To prevent the light from becoming too harsh, a selection of light fixtures are equipped with glare reducing reflectors and windows are insulated with Heat Mirror™ glazing.

### Environmental Objectives

Early in the project, the architects established with their client an environmental objective of making the building as energy efficient as possible. They requested additional funding to do computer modeling of design strategies that would lead to energy efficiency. These studies also helped to identify the payback associated with each design strategy. "We committed to recommend only those strategies that had a payback of five years or less. Other design initiatives that were sustainable but did not require additional expense were simply incorporated into the project," says Maxman. "We added to the equation an awareness and sensitivity to the issues involved in sustainable design. We looked at the project as a whole and thought about where we could positively affect more benevolent solutions that would mitigate the effects of our development on the environment."

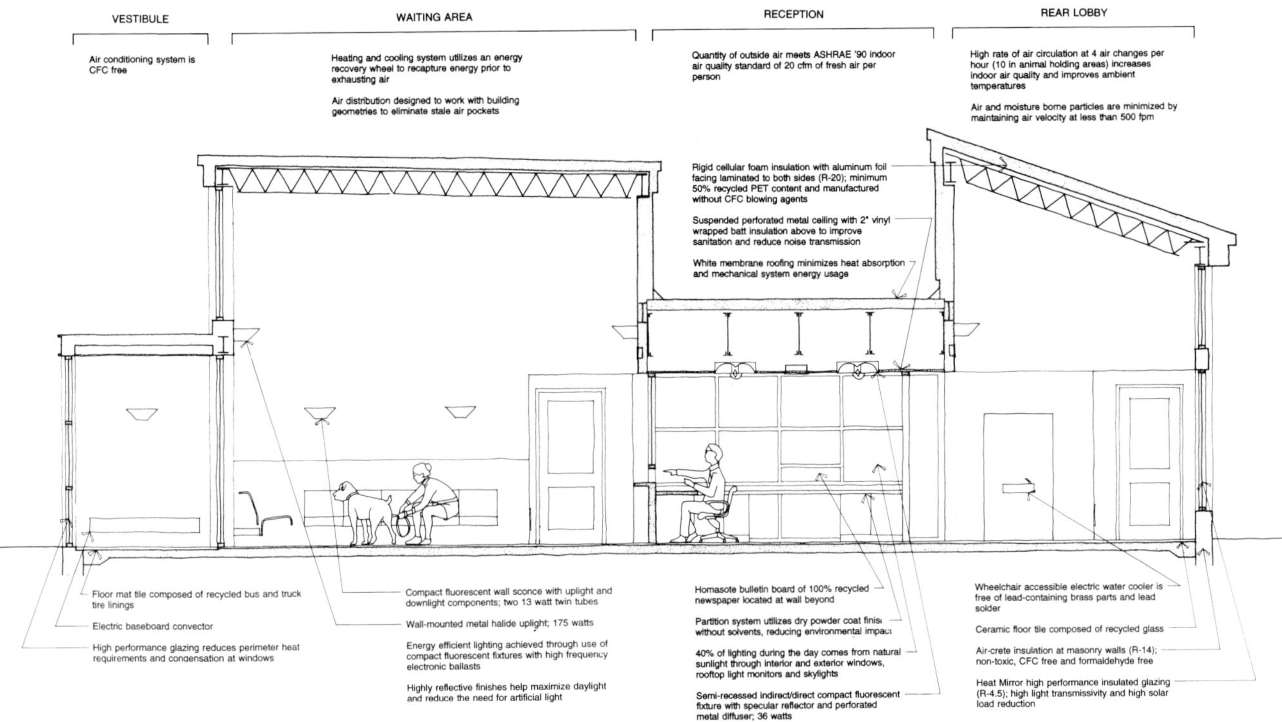


## *Working Methods*

### Project Team

Founded in 1864, the Women's Humane Society is the oldest Humane Society in the United States. After many years of planning this special project, the Humane Society went through a rigorous selection process to find an architect who would be sensitive to the Society's concerns. "During the interview," Maxman recalls, "our team suggested that the Society develop the five-acre wetland area as a wildlife refuge for animals displaced by the rapid development taking place in Bensalem Township, where the new building would be located." Maxman believes that it was this suggestion, plus their enthusiasm for the project, that won them the contract. "At the time of the selection of our team, the Society was not aware of our desire to make this a model of energy efficiency and environmental sensitivity, for it was not until the project began that I realized how one could achieve these goals. Once the Society was presented with the facts about energy conservation, CFCs, etc., they were quite willing to invest in a building that would tread lightly on the earth. In fact, when the inevitable budget cuts took place, our client was not at all willing to modify any design strategy that was a part of the sustainable design of the building," says Maxman.

Each member of the project team, selected for his or her commitment to sustainable design, was key in maintaining the environmental integrity of the project. Ensar Group was selected because of its experience in energy analysis and general knowledge of sustainable design. "We thought we needed their experience to supplement and enhance the design," explains Maxman. Ensar architect Greg Franta brought a certain design sensitivity to the analysis and design concepts. Nancy Clanton also had a proven working record with Ensar. Her expertise was helpful in the area of daylighting supported by artificial lighting, which Susan Maxman Architects wanted to feature in the design. Bruce Brooks, with whom Susan Maxman Architects had a long-term working relationship, "was open to non-traditional ideas about mechanical system design," according to Maxman.

Early in the design phase of the project, the energy consultant was brought in to charette with SMA and BEB to flesh out design concepts. This close dialogue between the team members continued as the design was refined, with input coming from all three. For example, the selection of window glazing affected energy analysis and decreased cooling loads, allowing for the downsizing of mechanical equipment. SMA did extensive research into materials selection, reviewing available data from manufacturer's literature, environmental guides, and periodicals.

### Computer Modeling

The SOLPATH Commercial Building Energy Analysis Program, a proprietary computer program of the Ensar Group, was used to study annual energy consumption. The program not only takes into account typical items such as glazing factors and thermal resistance values of walls and roof, but also the thermal storage capacity of building materials, the effect of changing solar position, the occupancy use profile, and other factors that affect annual operating cost. After establishing a base case building, a series of energy design strategies were tested for their effectiveness. The base case assumes the same building envelope and form as described in the plans and uses typical insulation values, glazing types, and other variables affecting energy use. Mechanical systems information is incorporated and, in this case, operating costs included 1991/92 Bensalem utility costs. Philadelphia, Pennsylvania weather and insulation data were also used in the analysis.

The first step of the analysis was to input the overall description and operating conditions of the base case building into the SOLPATH simulation program. The overall description and operating conditions include a description of building geometry and details such as wall characteristics, orientation, and roof; makeup of walls, roof, and floors; layers of various building materials and corresponding characteristics such as wall color and glass type; the occupancy, lighting, and equipment schedules; HVAC system specifications; operating parameters; and thermostat settings for cooling, heating, and natural air infiltration rates.

Once this is done, the building with its description and operating conditions is simulated for hourly cooling and heating loads; hourly cooling electric power consumption; hourly heating fuel consumption; annual total electric energy consumption; and annual total fuel consumption. Single-effect conservation measures such as insulation values for walls and roof, glazing type, lighting loads, efficiency of mechanical systems, use of heat exchanger, daylighting contribution, and reduction in building volume were identified and analyzed for energy use and cost savings in each of the three zones. The single-effects were then combined as multiple-effect conservation measures for another level of analysis. In doing this, the effect of one measure on another was analyzed. The design team was then able to evaluate what combination of effects best reduced energy costs..

### Construction Methodologies

The project was bid to a select bidders list. In general, typical construction techniques were employed during the construction of the Humane Society. Certain choices specified by the design team meant that the contractor had to work with unfamiliar materials, like the cementitious foam cavity wall insulation which required a specially approved installer. "Instead of the mason or carpenters on the job, a separate installer had to be called in. The process required more coordination than normal, but did not appear to impede the work," remarks Jeffrey Hayes, the project architect. "There were also many requests for substitutes, most of which were denied because the product did not meet environmental criteria."

### Site Review

The eleven-acre site presented a number of challenging environmental parameters. Much of the soil was not buildable, an existing stream bisected the prop-

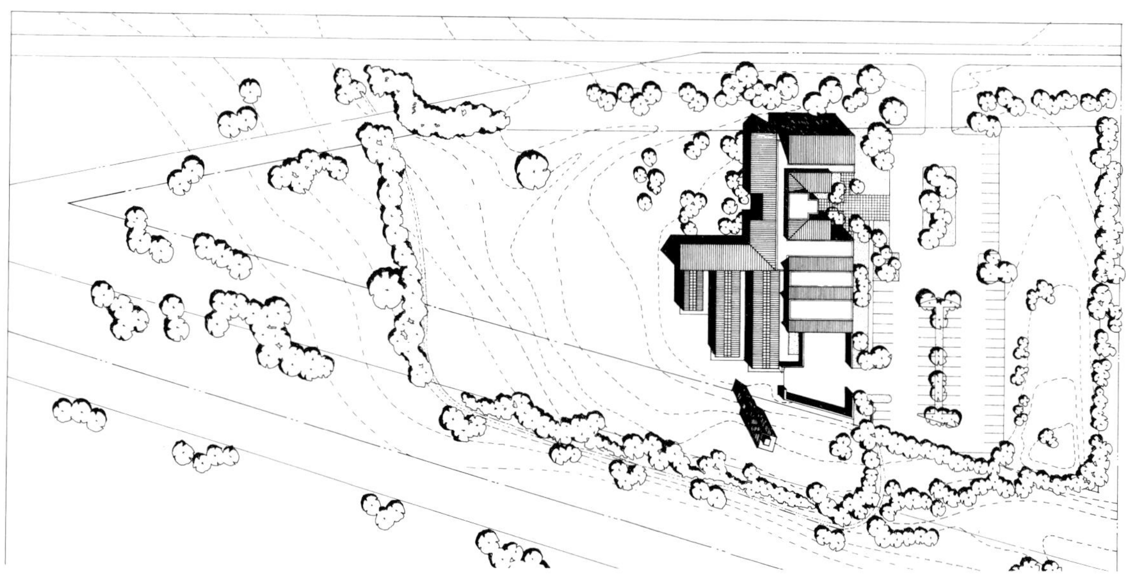

***Much of the soil on the eleven-acre site was not buildable, and many other features limited the planning possibilities. The wetlands were preserved to become a wildlife refuge. Drawing: Susan Maxman Architects.***

erty, the local utility easement limited the site planning possibilities, and a remaining third consisted of wetlands where construction can interfere with water quality and wildlife habitats. These features constricted the buildable areas of the site into a limited area. The architects responded by clustering the building and parking on the buildable sections of the site, freeing the wetlands to become a wildlife refuge and nature trails, a concept which supports the Society's education outreach program.

Near the building in an open area, a wildflower meadow encourages natural wildflower growth and requires little maintenance. Deciduous trees placed on the east and west facing elevations provide shade and reduce summer heat gain, while the building's orientation optimizes solar heat gain.

## *Environmental Economics*

### Life Cycle Costs

The life cycle cost analysis was performed by the architects with the energy analysis consultant and mechanical engineers using current energy rates for the Philadelphia area. Energy conserving features were evaluated and a payback period determined by comparing the initial additional cost over conventional construction with annual energy savings. Additionally, equipment cost savings were factored into the analysis. For example, the heat exchanger was

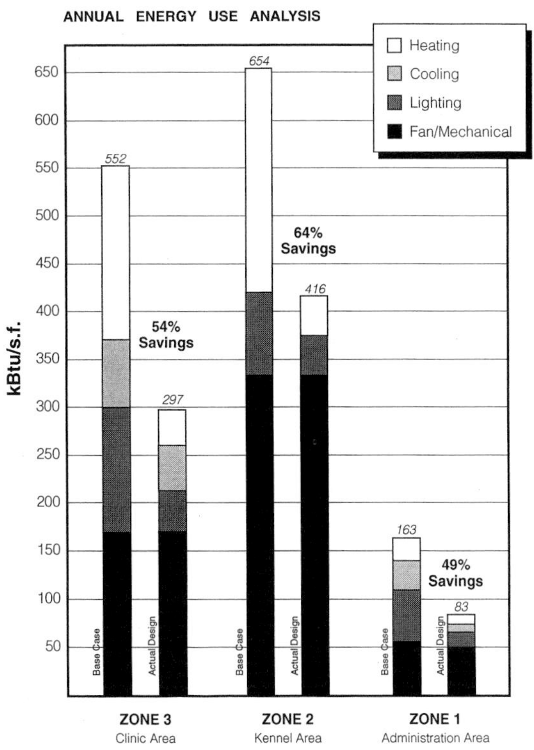


***Top:** The meadow encourages natural wildflower growth and requires little maintenance.*

***Bottom:** This chart compares actual annual energy use against conventional construction. Photo: Catherine Bogert. Drawing: Susan Maxman Architects.*

projected to save about $4300 per year. No significant rebate programs were in effect during the development of the Women's Humane Society project. An annual operating savings figure of $40,000 was identified by computer modeling in the architect's office. Even though the degree days were less than average, energy bills through the first nine months of occupancy indicate a savings greater than projected. Since the winter was milder than average, the project team believes that evaluation after two years of occupancy will yield more critical information.

**Estimated energy costs using typical construction–Base Case**

$113,880 per year    1370 kBTUs/SF/YR

**Estimated energy costs as designed with energy saving features**

$70,000 per year    796 kBTUs/SF/YR    39% Savings

**Actual energy cost for period June 10, 1994 to June 10, 1995**

$56,973 per year    kBTUs not available    19% savings over estimated 50% savings over base case

**Note:** Previous energy bills for Women's Humane Society were about $50,000 annually for a building less than half the size of the new facility.

The roof and walls, with R values well in excess of Pennsylvania code requirements, were constructed to contribute maximum energy efficiency. Photo: Catherine Bogert.

## *Energy Conservation*

### Building Envelope Insulation

According to Maxman, "The energy analysis indicated that due to the high volume of air changes at ten per hour, increasing the R values of the building had a small effect on the overall energy savings. Therefore, R values of R-19 for walls and R-24 for roofs were maintained, well in excess of that dictated by Pennsylvania code Act 222."

### ROOF AND WALL COMPOSITIONS

**Masonry Wall**

Two- to four-inch wythes of CMU with a 2" cavity, except at kennels where a single-width 8" CMU was used. Cavity and cores were filled with Air Krete™ cementitious foam insulation that is made up of magnesium oxide.

**Interior Wall**

Metal framing with 6" stud space filled with kraft-faced fiberglass batt insulation.

**Roof**

*Rigid Insulation:* 3.2" rigid polyisocyanurate/ R 22.2
*Batt Insulation:* 8" kraft-faced fiberglass batt insulation/ R 24

| | *Code Requirement* | *Provided* |
|---|---|---|
| Roof | R = 12 | R = 24 |
| Walls | R = 4 | R = 19 |
| Slab | R = 5 | R = 10 |

### Glazing

Heat Mirror™ insulating glass was specified for all exterior windows. Manufactured by Southwall Technologies, it features a thin coated film suspended between panes of glass. During the summer it helps cool the interior by letting in natural daylight while reflecting heat to the exterior. Conversely, it reflects heat to the interior during the winter. The Heat Mirror™ coating was designed to correspond with the building's orientation. North, south, and east facing glazing permit higher daylight levels than west facing glazing, which is designed for solar shading. In addition, all windows and storefront systems feature thermally broken frames. HM 77 was utilized on west-facing glass and HM 88 on north-, south-, and east-facing windows. The window units were provided by EFCO, which incorporates the film from Southwall Technologies.

### Heating and Cooling

The engineers produced a report detailing system options for the Women's Humane Society building. It described seven different systems, their estimated construction cost, and estimated annual energy usage.

From this analysis the owner and design team evaluated the pros and cons. The gas-fired absorption chiller/boiler option reflected low operating costs and used no CFCs or HCFCs of any kind for refrigeration. Gas-fired absorption cooling with hot water heating, a variation of the four-pipe fan coil system, is a water-based system that includes separate heating and cooling systems. The heating system consists of a natural gas-fired boiler, hot water circulation pumps, hot water coils at each air handling unit, and piping systems to transport the hot water through the building. The cooling system consists of a gas-fired absorption chiller, chilled water circulation pumps, chilled water coils at each air handling unit, and piping systems to transport the chilled water throughout the building. Absorption cooling is accomplished by using water as a refrigerant and lithium-bromide as an absorbent, both at low pressure. According to the engineer, because the system is centralized, it improves building aesthetics and isolates building noise. The system has only one outdoor component–a cooling tower–which is strategically located.

The challenge was to design a heating, ventilating, and air conditioning system to serve the facility's kennels, animal clinic areas, administrative offices, and public education spaces that would be both environmentally sensitive and cost effective to operate. Additional requirements included 100% outside air in the kennel (Zone 2) and clinic areas (Zone 3), and the need for a highly flexible operating schedule. The heart of the design is a carefully specified direct digital control system that allows the many spaces to be utilized on a random schedule while minimizing energy consumption. The HVAC system features variable volume controls in each room.

Because of the high level of necessary ventilation, a dessicant-coated energy recovery wheel was installed. This offsets the loss of energy involved in the high volume of air changes per hour required by reclaiming both sensible and latent energy from exhausted air and transferring it to the incoming outside air. The exhaust air is run through the reclaim device, transferring approximately 70% of its energy to incoming air. Constantly ventilated, the exhaust air from the kennel and clinic areas (Zones 2 and 3) is passed through a desiccant-coated energy recovery wheel whenever its enthalpy allows positive energy transfer to the makeup air stream. Exhaust and make-up air unit fans are modulated by variable frequency drive controls. The volume of make up air brought into the wheel is matched to the volume of exhaust air that has recoverable enthalpy. Latent energy and 80% of sensible energy are always returned to their original source. According to engineer Bruce Brooks, "The primary technical challenge in designing the building systems

***Each window features Heat Mirror™ film coating between panes of glass. The level of reflectivity varies, depending on the orientation of the window. Photo: Catherine Bogert.***

**ENERGY RECOVERY WHEEL (SUMMER)**

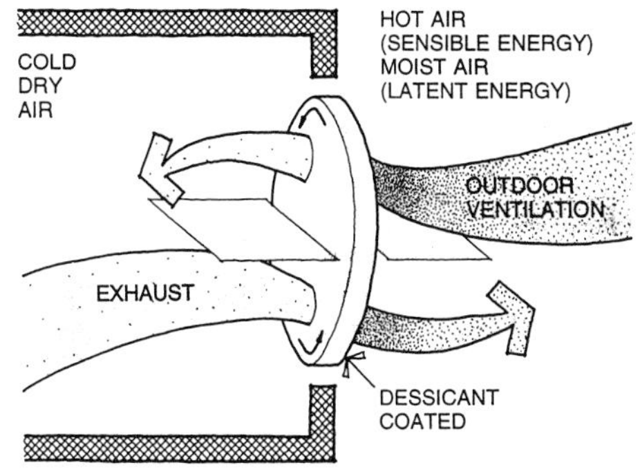


- Latent energy and 80% of sensible energy are always returned to where they came from
- Energy Recovery Wheel used only in kennel and clinic areas where there are 8-10 air changes per hour

***Drawing: Susan Maxman Architects.***

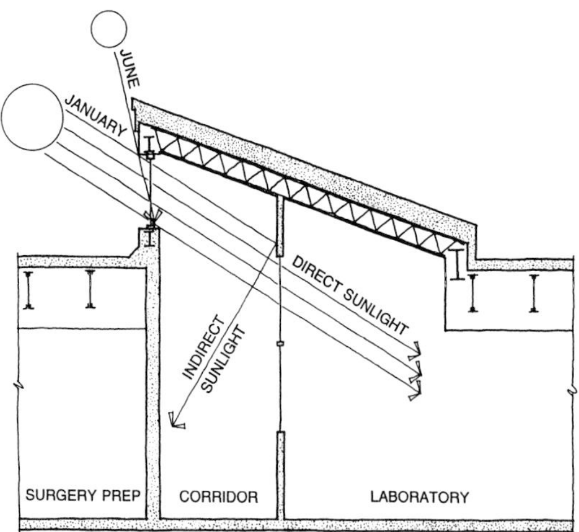

*Clockwise: High clerestory windows and a light paint color illuminate the interior corridor with natural light; Roof overhangs provide natural shading and passive cooling to the interior; Section diagram through clerestory windows illustrates patterns of natural daylighting. Photos: Catherine Bogert. Drawing: Susan Maxman Architects.*

was to handle diverse spaces without odor crossover while at the same time maximizing energy efficiency. Complicating this was the relatively small size of the facility which necessitated strict life cycle analysis for conservation measures. The measures were kept simple, but were carefully controlled. The heat exchange wheel with a cost of $30,000 actually produced a net saving as it allowed us to use smaller equipment."

## Lighting

The building is designed so that 40% to 90% (depending on the zone) of its lighting needs are supplied through natural daylight. Clerestory glazing, rooftop light monitors, and ridge skylights supplement exterior perimeter windows, thereby increasing natural light. Excessive heat generated by long summer days and late afternoon sun is mitigated with strategically placed overhangs and vegetation, coupled with high performance Heat Mirror™ glazing. In the administrative areas (Zone 1), extensive glazing provides for abundant natural lighting. At the kennel area (Zone 2), continuous ridge skylights provide even light distribution throughout. In the clinic (Zone 3) south facing roof monitors bring light to areas that have no exterior windows. Interior windows borrow light from the corridors.

Artifical lighting loads were reduced to under one watt per square foot in the administration, clinic, and shelter areas. Task lighting increases the level of illumination where required, and contributes to the overall efficiency of the lighting design.

Incandescent lamps were completely eliminated because they use up to 75% more energy than other types. In their place, compact and linear fluorescent and metal halide lamps were specified. These lamps also have a longer life than incandescent lamps (10,000 vs. 750 hours). Energy efficient lighting consisting of high frequency electronic ballasts was also specified. Multi-lamp ballasts, which reduce the number of ballasts needed, and T-8 lamps were employed to reduce energy usage and costs. High frequency ballasts with T8 lamps are used in linear fluorescent fix-

***In the kennel area, natural light, a high level of air changes, and exposed materials and systems contribute to energy efficiency, high indoor air quality, and easy maintenance. Photo: Catherine Bogert.***

tures. High-power factor ballasts are used with any compact fluorescent luminaires. Dimable photocell-controlled ballasts enable artificial light to be automatically adjusted in direct proportion to the daylight in a space, and ambient light fixtures help to control electrical energy costs. Occupancy sensor systems were eliminated from the design due to their ten- to twelve-year payback period.

## *Air Quality*

Among the many environmentally conscious features, "the concern for indoor air quality ranks among the most important," says architect Susan Maxman. Concerns for a high-performance ventilation system and minimal off-gassing were carefully considered.

### Ventilation

The rate of air circulation at four air changes per hour is maintained throughout the majority of the building, as prescribed by BOCA Mechanical Code of 1991, and is separated from the clinical and animal holding areas with a higher rate of ten air changes per hour. Ventilation requirements have been based on recommendations of the American Humane Association and the American Society of Heating, Ventilation, and Air Conditioning Engineers (ASHRAE) for veterinary facilities. Many of the spaces in the clinical area including cat holding, puppy holding, and isolation areas, as well as the hospital ward were provided with 100% exhaust for odor control.

### Materials Toxicity

Special care was taken to ensure the non-toxic content of materials in the project by reviewing the contents of products with ASTM reports from the manufacturers and consulting reviewed information by environmental publications like the AIA's *Environmental Resource Guide* and *Environmental Building News.* Air Krete™, a non-toxic wall insulation that is a non-CFC cementitious foam made of naturally ocurring magnesium oxide, was used instead of fiberglass batt insulation. Adhesive-backed carpet was specified in place of standard carpeting which would need to be installed with toxic glues. Instead of vinyl flooring, linoleum–a natural material–was installed with water based adhesives.

## *Resource Conservation*

RECYCLED OR SUSTAINABLE NATURAL CONTENT

The materials which were selected emphasize non-toxic and recycled products: floor tiles fabricated from glass-manufacturing by-products; adhesive-backed carpeting which does not require toxic glues for installation; CFC- and formaldehyde-free rigid insulation; rubber floor mats made of recycled tires; and benches and bathroom partitions composed of 65% recycled high-density polyethylene plastic.

## *Water Conservation and Quality*

The Women's Humane Society Animal Shelter was sited in a way that would preserve surrounding wetlands, allowing for the natural recharging of groundwater. In addition, one stormwater retention basin captures water and allows it to gradually return to the local water table. While the shelter gets most of its water from the municipal township, the kennel washdown facility relies on well water. This allows water from the site's existing location to be recycled into the water table, rather than importing it from a faraway source.

Low-flow water-conserving toilets with 3.0 gal/flush fixtures were specified, improving on the standard 5-6 gal/flush used in most buildings at the time. (Now, 1.5 gal/flush are commonly available.)

## *Materials and Products*

CRITERIA

Research was undertaken to identify building materials that were the least environmentally damaging yet feasible within the established budget. The materials specified were evaluated for their levels of toxicity, embodied energy, recycled content, and impact on the environment both during manufacturing and transport. Materials needed to be long-lasting and durable because of high use and frequent cleaning. For example, the plastic partitions used cost 50% more, but will last much longer than typical partitions.

MANUFACTURER'S ENVIRONMENTAL IMPACT

The AIA's *Environmental Resource Guide* and *Environmental Building News* provided critical data concerning the manufacturing processes of many materials and products used in the Women's Humane Society shelter. For example, in addition to providing non-toxic adhesives for their carpeting, Collins & Aikman initiated a recycling program for their products. GTE utilized waste light bulb scrap for their

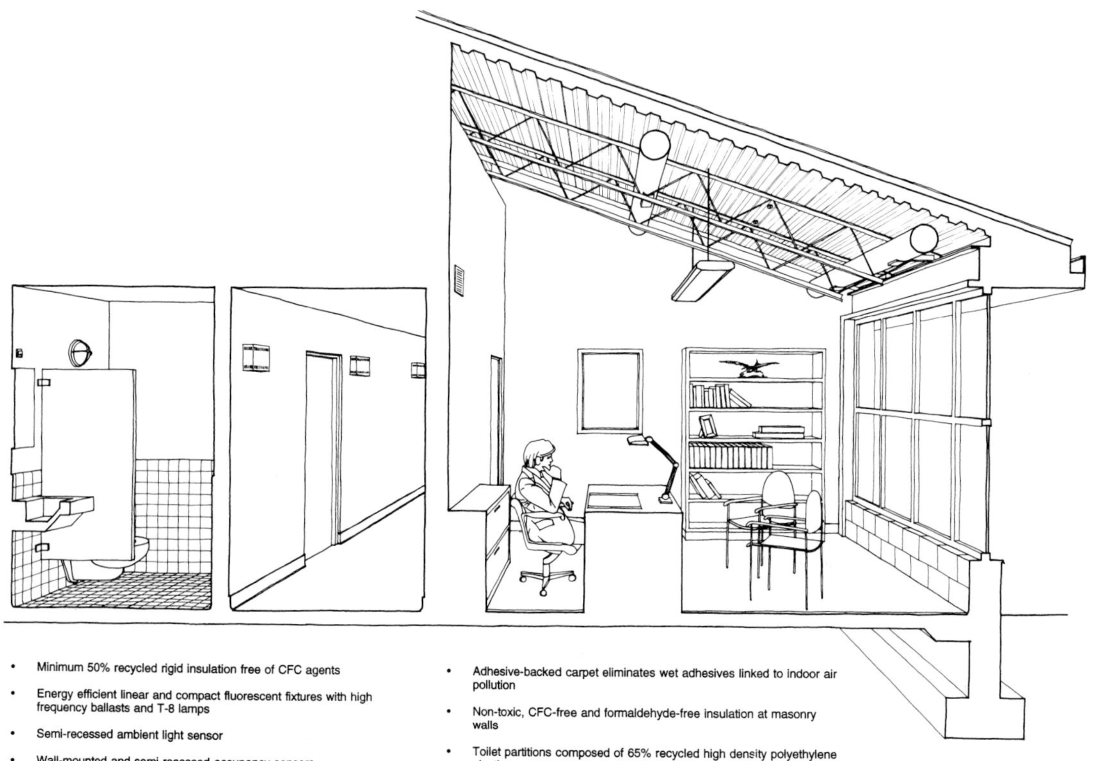

- Minimum 50% recycled rigid insulation free of CFC agents
- Energy efficient linear and compact fluorescent fixtures with high frequency ballasts and T-8 lamps
- Semi-recessed ambient light sensor
- Wall-mounted and semi-recessed occupancy sensors
- High performance Heat Mirror glazing with Low "E" coating
- Adhesive-backed carpet eliminates wet adhesives linked to indoor air pollution
- Non-toxic, CFC-free and formaldehyde-free insulation at masonry walls
- Toilet partitions composed of 65% recycled high density polyethylene plastic
- Low flow, water conserving toilet

ceramic tiles. Belting Associates uses recycled tire to produce their rubber floor mats, and Santana Products uses recycled plastic to produce their bench seating. Each of the manufacturers illustrated a commitment to environmental conciousness through its use of recycled materials and concerned manufacturing processes.

EMBODIED ENERGY

SMA also consulted the AIA's *Environmental Resource Guide* and *Environmental Building News* for data on embodied energy, which helped them to choose steel roofing and siding over aluminum, which uses ten times more embodied energy than steel. "We looked at how close to the site the manufacturer was located, and at local or regional products to consider transportation costs and energy use," says Hayes. "Steel siding and roofing, masonry, concrete pavers, and toilet partitions are some examples of the products we used that were manufactured in Pennsylvania." These choices reflect a concern for the amount of energy used to create and transport a product, as well as for providing economic support within the region.

## *Post-Occupancy Evaluation*

"People are comfortable in the building, and it seems to work well for the animal services," says Maxman. "The adoption rate is three to four times the national average, and we would like to think that this is to some extent due to the nature of the built environment." In particular, the quality of natural light and the operable windows throughout the building are receiving highly favorable comments. The payback in reduced utility costs is better than expected after a mild winter season. The architects have not yet performed a formal post-occupancy evaluation, but have proposed the idea to review the building after the first year of occupancy.

In retrospect, SMA would have liked to involve the contractor more in understanding the design goals for the project. As a result, they have developed a program for construction and demolition waste management. After working closely with the civil engineer, Maxman remarks, "I would have liked to develop site-related features such as waste and stormwater management to incorporate features like gray water disposal, constructed wetlands, and pervious paving materials."

***Photo: Catherine Bogert.***

### WOMEN'S HUMANE SOCIETY MATERIALS RESOURCES

**Steel Roofing.** SRS standing seam roof; Recycled content, lower embodied energy than aluminum; Smith Steelite, 1005 Beaver Grade Rd., Moon Township, PA 15108-2444 (800) 759-7474, (412) 299-8000

**White Membrane Roofing.** Mechanically fastened EPDM membrane; Reflects heat and enhances daylighting; Carlisle Syntec Systems, Division of Carlisle Corp., 1285 Ritner Highway, Carlisle, PA 17013-0925 (800) 4-SYNTEC, (717) 245-7000

**Steel Siding.** 3/4" Econolap corrugated panel siding; Recycled content, lower embodied energy than aluminum; Smith Steelite, 1005 Beaver Grade Rd., Moon Township, PA 15108-2444 (800) 759-7474, (412) 299-8000

**Wall Masonry Cavity Insulation.** Air Krete™; CFC- and formaldehyde-free, high R-value; Air Krete, Inc., P.O. Box 380, Weedsport, NY 13166 (315) 834-6609

**Foundation Wall Insulation.** Amofoam RX; 50% recycled content, CFC-free; Amoco Foam Products, 375 Northridge Rd. Suite 600, Atlanta, GA 30350 (800) 241-4402, (404) 901-5252

**Roof Insulation.** NRG2; High R-value CFC-free; NRG Barriers, Inc., 15 Lund Road, Saco, Maine 04072-1859 (800) 343-1285

**Windows.** Series 510 and 520; Thermally broken aluminum; Efco Corporation, P.O. Box 609, Country Road and Bridle Lane, Monnett, Missouri 65708-0609 (800) 221-4169

**Glazing Film.** Heat Mirror 88, Heat Mirror 77; High R-value, reduces heat gain; Southwall Technologies, 1029 Corporation Way, Palo Alto, CA 94303 (800) 365-8794, (415) 962-9111

**Carpeting.** Infinity; Adhesive-backed non-toxic glue, company program recycles carpets; Collins & Aikman, P.O. Box 1477, Dalton, GA 30720 (800) 214-4085, (404) 259-9711

**Floor Tiles.** Prominence; Ceramic from waste light bulb glass; GTE Engineered Ceramics, One Jackson Street, Wellsboro, PA 16901 (717) 724-8322

**Linoleum.** Solid Linoleum; Non-petroleum from sustainable natural material; DLW, Ltd. Gerbert Limited, P.O. Box 4944, Lancaster, PA 17604 (717) 724-8322

**Floor Mats.** Tirex; Recycled truck tire linings; Belting Associates Inc., 148 Lauman Lane, Hicksville, NY 11801 (800) 223-6287

**Heating/Air Conditioning.** Yazaki Model CH-L60; Gas-fired CFC-/HCFC-free lithium bromide absorption chiller; Energy Products Company, 868 Sussex Boulevard, P.O. Box 488, Broomall, PA 19008 (215) 544-3400

**Heat Recovery System.** Dessicant-coated, recovers latent and sensible heat from exhaust air; Semco, 1800 East Pointe Drive, Columbia, MO 65201-3508 (314) 443-1481

Chapter 6

# *Environmental Legislation*

## *Opportunities and Responsibilities*

In 1920, research scientist Thomas Midgley discovered a cheap chemical while working for General Motors that could be added to low-grade petrol to improve its octane rating and prevent knocking. Improving the efficiency of the gasoline engine, this breakthrough was leaded petroleum. In 1930, that same scientist produced an alternative for the unsafe ammonia that was then in use as a refrigerant. In two days he developed a group of cheap, stable chemicals that would do the job. Called chlorofluorocarbons, these chemicals are more commonly known as CFCs[1]. Since 1896, when Swedish scientist Svante Arrhenius established that the use of fossil fuels could cause a rise in average global temperature, legislative protection for global warming has remained in its infancy. One hundred years later, renewable resource technologies are only beginning to compete with fossil fuel technologies. Creating responsive environmental legislation has indeed been a slow process.

A spin-off of industrialization, a chemical revolution is at its height and continues to evolve despite complex and inconclusive scientific findings. A look at the history of environmental legislation illustrates that until significant damage occurs, little is done to rectify the problems. "Designing and building a structure merely to meet code requirements means designing the worst possible building allowable by law," Randolph Croxton remarks while discussing the work of his firm, whose environmental standards typically exceed those dictated by law. Building codes bind owners and building professionals to meet minimum acceptable standards. While these codes are intended to protect people from negligence that is health- or life-threatening, they have historically been created after the fact. For example, laws regarding mechanical equipment and maintenance were revised following deaths caused by Legionnaire's Disease. The lack of adequate codes related to environmental concerns is less about negligence and more about scientific ignorance and increased financial cost to owners. Many toxins, for instance, are listed as hazardous, but are not prohibited by law because of industry pressure. Even asbestos products, which were prohibited only after significant loss of life was established, are still the subject of massive court battles. Another element that complicates the regulation of environmental concerns is that codes vary from state to state. The states of California and Washington have some of the most sophisticated energy codes in the country, while other states resist them because of the immediate economic pressure that they create, primarily on business owners.

Building professionals who may not yet be knowledgeable or concerned about changing current methodologies that are damaging to our natural resources will soon be required to comply with some new ecologically responsible mandates. Creative legislative policies are providing numerous financial incentives for energy and resource conservation. For example, the Energy Plan Act, enacted in 1992, provided for numerous "sustainable" programs, setting aside millions of dollars in funding for this purpose. Professionals who work with government projects must meet resource conservation guidelines, and those who know how to incorporate this aspect into their practice are reaping vast benefits. Environmental requirements will undoubtedly increase. Property and building owners who are familiar with environmental policy know that they will benefit from the services of an architect who can address ecologically responsible concerns in building design and construction.

While a look at the past twenty-five years of legislation reveals a number of problem-response laws, it also shows an increasing number of creative initiatives toward the conservation of natural resources. According to the Natural Resources Defense Council (NRDC),

> Federal environmental laws since 1970 have, to cite just a few examples, stopped the flood of sewage and toxic chemicals into our rivers, greatly reduced lead in the air

and in children's blood, cleaned much of the unhealthy smog in our cities, brought the bald eagle and the grey whale back from the brink of extinction, preserved many of our most important and most breathtaking resources, stemmed mining practices that left the lands scarred and the rivers orange with coal waste, dramatically reduced toxic air pollution, revolutionized hazardous waste disposal, and put in place a workable program that, together with the efforts of other nations, is protecting our planet's fragile stratospheric ozone layer.

Thousands of pages of complex U.S. code outline federal legislation that relates directly or indirectly to building and site design and construction. This chapter can provide a fundamental understanding of environmental legislation, offering insight into the potential impact of ecological considerations in site and building design decisions. Professionals can increase the quality of the built and natural environment by recognizing the limitations of legislation and seeking to go beyond them. An awareness of the following laws provides a deeper understanding of the responsibility design professionals have in influencing the ecology and human health.

## THE DEVELOPMENT OF ENVIRONMENTAL LEGISLATION

The National Environmental Policy Act (NEPA) passed in 1969 directs the government to "use all practicable means to create and maintain conditions in which man and nature can exist in productive harmony." Sometimes referred to as our basic national charter for the protection of the environment, NEPA was the first legislation to require the government to consider environmental protection in its general decision-making process. NEPA regulations were designed to help public officials understand the environmental consequences of their actions, and to take steps to protect, restore, and enhance the environment. For instance, NEPA requires that an Environmental Impact Statement (EIS) be filed for any major construction project involving federal funds. This act also led to the creation of the Council on Environmental Quality (CEQ), an independent agency that advises and assists the president on environmental policy, regulation, and on the preparation of an annual report on environmental quality.

The last twenty-five years have shown a growing concern among the international community in the protection of the environment. A number of significant international and national conferences resulted in landmark treaties which provided the seeds for further important national environmental legislation. The hard-won successes of environmental legislation--plagued by scientific uncertainty, incomplete methods of enforcement, and huge financial cost–originate from these very conferences. Following are brief descriptions of some of the most notable.

The 1972 United Nations Conference on the Environment in Stockholm generated interest in such environmental matters as pollution and resource depletion. Some scientists attending the conference had suggested that CFCs could damage the Earth's ozone layer. Following years of argument in the scientific community as to whether these findings were conclusive, a report issued in 1976 said that this hypothesis warranted serious attention, and concluded that attempts should be made to seek alternatives.

That same year, a landmark treaty concerning the preservation of historical and architectural monuments was signed and ratified by most of the 178 countries in attendance at the 1972 United Nations Educational Scientific and Cultural Organization (UNESCO) Convention. Such sites as the Grand Canyon, Constitution Hall, and the Eiffel Tower were given special cultural significance and protection from destruction and indiscriminate alteration.

In 1987, The Montreal Protocol on Substances that Deplete the Ozone Layer, an international agreement to phase out substances destructive to the Earth's ozone layer, was signed. Three years later, ninety-three nations, including some not party to the original agreement such as China and India, accepted an amended protocol in London. The amended protocol called for phasing out five key chlorofluorocarbons (CFCs 11, 12, 113, 114, and 115), carbon tetrachloride, and nonessential uses of the fire-extinguishing halon gases (Halons 1211, 1301, and 2402) by the year 2000, and methyl chloroform (MC) by 2005. Hydrochlorofluorocarbons (HCFCs) were proposed as interim substitutes where no feasible alternatives exist, to be phased out by 2020 if feasible, and by 2040 at the latest. The 1990 agreement also established the Montreal Protocol Multilateral Fund to help developing countries finance the transition from ozone depleting chemicals.

*The Blueprint for the Environment: A Plan for Federal Action* was published in 1989 by the United States' environmental community to help the president address environmental problems. The landmark cooperative effort included the work of Defenders of Wildlife, Environmental Action, Friends of the Earth (and its affiliates, the Environmental Policy Institute and the Oceanic Society), Global Tomorrow Coalition, Izaak Walton League of America, National Audubon Society, National Parks and Conservation Association, National Wildlife Federation, Natural Resources Defense Council of America, Renew America, Sierra Club, Trout Unlimited, Union of

Concerned Scientists, Wilderness Society, and Zero Population Growth. Though the plan notes that not every organization agrees on all the advice contained in the book, over 750 detailed recommendations are included, organized by the appropriate cabinet department or agency that can coordinate federal efforts to ameliorate environmental problems.

Widely regarded as the largest gathering of heads of state in history, the United Nations Conference on Environment and Development (UNCED)–known as the Earth Summit–was held in Rio De Janeiro in June of 1992. It was attended by delegates from 178 countries and over 100 heads of state. The conference took on greater importance with the ending of the Cold War, which put widespread pressure on industrialized nations to redirect money from military expenditures to the protection of the environment and the development of poorer nations. The Earth Summit was the first international forum to address the full range of environmental concerns and sustainable development, most notably biological diversity, loss of forests, and global warming and climate change. "Two significant treaties were signed by most representative countries," says NRDC's Director of Earth Summit Watch, Jared Blumenfeld. "The Convention on Biodiversity was signed by 167 countries and ratified by 114, but has not been ratified by the United States at this writing. The Framework Convention on Climate Change has been signed and ratified by 162 countries including the U.S., providing for an agreement to return to the 1990 level of greenhouse gas emissions by 2000."

Another significant result of the Summit was Agenda 21, known as the "Blueprint for Sustainable Development." All nations agreed to Agenda 21, an 800-page document addressing in forty detailed chapters everything from human health, population, labor rights, and trade, to forestry, oceans, hazardous waste, and energy. The subsequent UN Commission on Sustainable Development (UNCSD) has fifty-three members and meets annually to review national progress in the implementation of Agenda 21.

Each of these international conferences has influenced U.S. legislation, which in turn has direct impact on the practice of architecture and the building professions. By international agreement and subsequent federal legislation to protect the ozone layer, chlorofluorocarbons are to be phased out of refrigeration manufacturing by the year 2000 "where reasonable alternatives exist." This affects all mechanical air conditioning systems and refrigerator and freezer products. To promote energy efficiency, minimum requirements have been established in new products such as windows, mechanical systems, lighting products, and appliances. By law, energy performance information must be available to consumers, who are often represented by design professionals. The legislation discussed in the paragraphs that follow represents the changes in U.S. environmental law in the wake of international treaties and scientific knowledge.

## PROTECTION OF NATURAL RESOURCES

### *Water*

Currently undergoing close scrutiny is the Clean Water Act, a keystone of environmental law, credited with significantly cutting the amount of municipal and industrial pollution fed into the nation's waterways. With the goal of making the nation's water fishable and swimmable, the Clean Water Act provides for the coordination of water pollution-control programs to eliminate the discharge of untreated municipal and industrial waste water into waterways. (Drinking water is primarily covered by the Safe Drinking Water Act of 1974). Known formally as the Federal Water Pollution Control Act Amendment of 1972, it stems from a much-amended 1948 law aiding commmunities in building sewage treatment plants. The Clean Water Act provided billions of dollars to states and municipalities for financing construction of sewage treatment facilities.

Protecting the nation's wetlands is another important goal of the Clean Water Act. "More than half of the wetlands in the lower forty-eight states are now shopping malls, industrial tracts, or parking lots," write Jon and Alex Naar in *This Land Is Your Land.* "Ninety percent of California and Connecticut wetland is gone, as is 95% of Iowa's. At the current rate, half of the remaining wetlands in the U.S. will disappear in less than 100 years." [2] Wetlands serve important functions, namely in protecting and providing stability for the natural and built environment. Referred to as the "cradle of life," they are nurseries and permanent habitats for many waterfowl, mammals, and freshwater and marine fish, as well as for one-third of the species currently on the endangered list. As millions of waterfowl breed in North American wetlands and rely on them for food during their seasonal migrations, the condition of our national wetlands affects regions beyond our borders. An asset in the protection of water supplies, wetlands keep the water table high, thereby blocking the intrusion of salt water, and additionally act as natural water purifiers by removing silt and filtering out or absorbing many pollutants. By holding water and replenishing soil moisture and groundwater supplies, wetlands prevent the subsidence that can occur when groundwater supplies are depleted. Excess water from floods can be contained in wetlands as well, preventing or lessening downstream destruction. And by slowing water currents, reducing the height of waves, and absorbing storm energy, wetlands prevent shoreline erosion and possible property damage. At this writing, Congress is seeking to pass legislation which will diminish the power of the Clean Water Act to protect water quality in the U.S.

Because the financial costs to property owners of following environmental regulations are substantial, the House of Representatives voted in favor of the Job Creation and Wage Enhancement Act (H.R.9) in 1995, legislation that would greatly reduce federal protection for wetlands under the Clean Water Act. In 1993, Congress had asked the National Academy of Sciences, the nation's most eminent scientific organization, to settle the debate on wetlands–namely, that they are important habitats for wildlife and significant to water quality. H.R.9 was approved before the review was complete, even while its opponents tried unsuccessfully to delay it. The bill was repudiated in the report issued by the Academy in May of 1995: "There is wide consensus about what constitutes a wetland, but the criteria it cites bear no resemblance to the definition in the bill." Strongly opposed by the Clinton Administration, the House bill would exempt many kinds of wetlands from federal regulation altogether, and would require the government to compensate property owners (commonly referred to as "takings") when it prevents them from developing their wetlands. The bill not only exposes drinking water supplies to new sources of pollution, but the quality of water in our rivers would be hurt as well because the bill weakens rules requiring industries to use the latest technologies to treat toxic waste. For coastal areas, significant damage to water quality would occur because of a weakening in the requirements of coastal towns to improve sewage treatment. In a statement to Congress, the AIA urged that they "resist efforts to include the concept of 'takings' in the legislation," cautioning that "the safety of the public, value of adjacent properties, and the stewardship of natural resources are of greater importance than the 'rights' of property owners without regard for public safety." The NRDC's report states:

> The Job Creation and Wage Enhancement Act threatens federal protection for wetlands in several devastating ways; by redefining wetlands, many properties currently under protection would no longer be safeguarded. "Takings" provisions would have the taxpayer paying for loss of property value to the owner, even in the case of criminal violation.

H.R.9's impact on the practice of architecture is significant. Owners, developers, architects, engineers, and construction professionals must currently meet stringent code requirements when working with wetland sites. By limiting wetland code requirements, H.R. 9 encourages owners to ignore responsive solutions and prevent the professionals whom they commission from appropriately addressing wetlands. Wetland protection not only costs clients money, but is also subject to local board approvals, which are in turn subject to political pressure. An architect or engineer who has an understanding of wetland ecosystems can provide creative solutions while educating his or her client about potential opportunities. The owner or developer who works with the ecology of a site will increase its quality and, therefore, the long-term value of the property.

Where drinking water is concerned, the Safe Drinking Water Act (SDWA) authorizes the EPA to set minimum national standards for quality based on the best "feasible" technology. The 1986 amendments to the Safe Drinking Water Act require the EPA to regulate eighty-three named contaminants. Designed to protect public health and welfare, the act covers every public water supply in the country serving at least fifteen service connections or twenty-five or more people. Primary Drinking Water Standards set under the original act established maximum contaminant levels (MCLs), or the largest permitted concentration in drinking water for various hazardous substances and other contaminants. MCLs are described as a "health goal equal to the maximum level of a contaminant which is not expected to cause any adverse effects over a lifetime of exposure," and are nonenforceable. They are scheduled to be replaced by the National Primary Drinking Water Regulation (NPDWR) before the year 2000, requiring a specific treatment method to control the contaminant.

The 1986 amendments also ban all future use of lead pipe and solder in public drinking water systems, requiring public authorities to tell their users of the potential sources of lead contamination, its health effects, and the steps that can be taken to mitigate it. The amendments extend federal protection to groundwater by establishing programs to protect critical groundwater sources of drinking water and areas around wells that supply public drinking water systems, and to regulate the underground injection of wastes above and below drinking water sources. Lead pipe and solder exist in the infrastructure of every municipality built prior to 1980, even though other materials such as PVC are likely to be found as well. This affects the water supply to every building. Lead pipes are also likely to exist in buildings that were built prior to the latter part of this century, which means that historic buildings across the United States are subject to higher levels of contamination.

Despite these efforts, many pollutants go unregu-

## PRIMARY DRINKING WATER STANDARDS

*Note: MCL is the Maximum Contaminant Level, expressed in milligrams per liter, unless otherwise noted.*

| *Contaminants* | *Health Effects* | *MCL** | *Sources* |
|---|---|---|---|
| Microbiological animal fecal matter Total Coliforms (Coliform bacteria, fecal coliform, streptococcal, and other bacteria) | Not necessarily disease-producing themselves, but can be indicators of organisms that cause assorted gastroenteric infections, dysentery, hepatitis, typhoid fever, cholera, and others; also interfere with disinfection process. | | 1 per 100 millileters** |
| Turbidity | Interferes with disinfection | 1 to 5 NTU** | Erosion, runoff, and discharges |
| INORGANIC CHEMICALS | | | |
| Arsenic | Dermal and nervous system toxicity effects | .05 | Geological, pesticide residues, industrial waste and smelter operations |
| Barium | Circulatory system effects | 1 | |
| Cadmium | Kidney effects | .01 | Geological, mining, and smelting |
| Chromium | Liver/kidney effects | .05 | |
| Lead | Central and peripheral nervous system damage; kidney effects; highly toxic to infants and pregnant women | .05** | Leaches from lead pipes and lead-based solder pipe joints |
| Mercury paper | Central nervous system disorders; kidney effects | .002 | Used in manufacture of paint, vinyl chloride, used in fungicides, and geological |
| Nitrate | Methemoglobinemia ("blue baby syndrome") | 10 | Fertilizer, sewage, feedlots, geological |
| Selenium | Gastrointestinal effects | .01 | Geological, mining |
| Silver | Skin discoloration (Argyria) | .05 | Geological, mining |
| Fluoride | Skeletal damage | 4 | Geological, additive to drinking water, toothpaste, foods processed with fluorinated water |
| ORGANIC CHEMICALS | | | |
| Endrin | Nervous system/kidney effects | .0002 | Insecticide used on cotton, small grains, orchards (cancelled) |
| Lindane | Nervous system/kidney effects | .004 | Insecticide used on seed and soil treatments, foliage application, wood protection |
| Methoxychlor | Nervous system/kidney | .1 | Insecticide used on fruit trees, vegetables |
| 2,4-D | Liver/kidney effects | .1 | Herbicide used to control broad-leaf weeds in agriculture, used on forests, range, pastures, and aquatic environments |
| 2,4,5-TP Silvex | Liver/kidney effects | .01 | Herbicide (cancelled in 1984) |
| Toxaphene | Cancer risk | .005 | Insecticide used on cotton, corn, gin |
| Benzene | Cancer | .005 | Fuel (leaking tanks), solvent commonly used in manufacture of industrial chemicals, pharmaceuticals, pesticides, paints, and plastics |

## PRIMARY DRINKING WATER STANDARDS *(continued)*

| *Contaminants* | *Health Effects* | *MCL** | *Sources* |
|---|---|---|---|
| Carbon tetrachloride | Possible cancer | .005 | Common in cleaning agents, industrial wastes from manufacture of coolants |
| p-Dichlorobenzene | Possible cancer | .075 | Used in insecticides, moth balls, air deodorizers |
| 1,2-Dichloroethane | Possible cancer | .005 | Used in manufacture of insecticides, gasoline |
| 1,1-Dichloroethane | Possible cancer | .007 | Used in manufacture of plastics, dyes, perfumes, paints, SOCs (synthetic organic compounds) |
| 1,1,1-Trichloroethane | Nervous system problems | .2 | Used in manufacture of food wrappings, synthetic fibers |
| Trichloroethylene (TCE) | Possible cancer | .005 | Waste from disposal of drycleaning materials and manufacture of pesticides,paints, waxes, varnishes, paint strippers, metal degreasers |
| Vinyl chloride | Cancer risk | .002 | Polyvinylchloride pipes and solvents used to join them, waste from manufacturing plastics and synthetic rubber |
| Total trihalomethanes (TTHM) (chloroform, bromoform, bromodichloromethane, dibrochloromethane) | Cancer risk | .1 | Primarily formed when surface water containing organic matter is treated with chlorine |
| RADIONUCLIDES | | | |
| Gross alpha particle activity | Cancer | 15 pCi/L | Radioactive waste, uranium deposits |
| Gross beta particle activity | Cancer | 4 mrem/yr | Radioactive waste, uranium deposits |
| Radium 226 & 228 (total) | Bone cancer | 5 pCi/L | Radioactive waste, geological |
| OTHER SUBSTANCES | | | |
| Sodium | Possible increase in blood pressure in susceptible individuals | None*** (20mg/1 reporting level) | Geological, road salting |

*Effective December 1990, the present total coliforms MCL will be superseded by these National Drinking Water Requirements (NPDWRs): 95% of samples taken shall be free of any coliforms; small systems can have one contaminated sample in 39. The present turbidity MCLs will be superseded by NPDWRs, which will be phased in between December 1990 and June 1993. These NPDWRs regulate *Giardia lamblia* (99.9% reduction), viruses (99.99% reduction), *Legionellae*, hetertrophic bacteria, and turbidity. The revised turbidity limits are 5 NTU (turbidity units) in the source water to avoid filtration; 0.5 NTU 95% of the time and 5 NTU at all times for conventional or direct filtration; 1 NTU 95% of the time and 5 NTU at all times for slow sand or diatomaceous earth filters.

**Agency considering substantially lower number.

***Monitoring is required and data is reported to health officials to protect individuals on highly restricted sodium diets.

***Source:** *Is Your Drinking Water Safe?* **Environmental Protection Agency, 1989.***

lated. In the EPA's own survey of drinking water, 127 pesticides and nitrates were measured. The EPA has been sharply criticized for failing to properly enforce the SDWA. In many cases, not enough information is available concerning potential hazards.

In 1988, California enacted the Safe Drinking Water and Toxics Enforcement Act, which sets an example of a state initiative resulting from public demand. Known as Proposition 65, this law was passed overwhelmingly despite a multimillion dollar campaign against it by industry and the governor. Under Proposition 65, no business may expose people to chemicals that cause cancer or reproductive problems such as birth defects, sterility, or miscarriage without giving "clear and reasonable warning." Failure to give warning can bring fines of up to $2500 a day for each exposure.

H.R.9 includes several provisions that would directly undercut public health protection under SDWA and make it impossible for the EPA to adopt new standards to protect the public from newly emerging contamination threats such as cryptosporidium, the parasite that devastated Milwaukee in 1993, sickening 400,000 people and killing over 100. H.R.9 would create huge barriers toward the adoption of standards for cryptosporidium that were agreed to in 1994 by state and local governments, the water industry, and public health and environmental groups, and would also block enforcement and public notification requirements for lead or dangerous bacteria in tap water.

Because of the ambiguities involved in controlling the quality of drinking water, one is well advised to consider filtering or purifying drinking water sources in a building. In older cities such as New York and Boston, where the infrastructure of the drinking water systems and many buildings is likely to contain lead, potential hazards are increased. Although not required by law, many building owners are seeking to improve drinking water quality by testing and filtering their drinking water.

### *Air*

The Clean Air Act (CAA), first passed in 1963 to reduce air pollution and protect air quality, has been amended many times since. The original authorized the U.S. Public Health Service to study air pollution and provided grants and training to state and local agencies for its control. Amendments in 1970 centered air quality control activities on the Environmental Protection Agency (EPA), charging it with conducting research and development programs, setting national standards and regulations, providing technical and financial assistance to states, and, where necessary, supplementing state implementation programs. The 1990 Clean Air Amendments brought wide-ranging reforms, dealing with all kinds of pollution on both large and small scales, from mobile or stationary sources, including routine and toxic emissions ranging from power plants to consumer products. Particular attention was paid to the depletion of the ozone layer, acid rain, urban smog, automobile emissions, and toxic pollutants. With acid rain, for example, the amendment targeted 50% reductions of sulfur dioxide and nitrogen oxides, with specific targets to be met as cuts phased through the 1990s. Concerning urban smog, Clean Air amendments established five categories–marginal, moderate, serious, severe, or extreme–for cities that did not meet limits on ozone, a key ingredient in smog. At the signing of the bill, only Los Angeles was included in the last category. Specific phased-in targets for ozone reductions are set for each category. The number of regulated toxic air pollutants was expanded from 7 to 189, compiled in a list entitled "Toxic Chemicals and Hazardous Substances."

CAA required the EPA to establish some 250 categories of hazardous pollutants; set new safety standards for residents living near plants where the largest amounts of toxic chemicals are concentrated; require polluters to install the best available pollution control equipment in order to reduce toxic emissions by 90% by 2003; prepare formal safety reviews to be made available to the public; and establish an independent Chemical Safety Board to investigate chemical accidents. This aspect of the act significantly affects the paint and furniture manufacturing industries, primarily regarding the finishing of manufactured goods. The EPA is currently reviewing technology for VOC emissions. H.R.9 could delay or indefinitely postpone future standards until more than a decade after their statutory deadlines, including standards for sodium cyanide production, lead smelting, lead acid battery manufacturing, and uranium hexafluoride production.

Clean Air legislation primarily affects architectural practice in the area of CFC production, as CFCs are commonly used in refrigeration systems and therefore affect typical mechanical cooling systems and refrigeration appliances. Manufacturers of products that incorporate these systems are required to substitute other less damaging products "where feasible" by the year 2000. In 1995, for example, the American automotive industry began using HCFCs instead of CFCs in its air conditioning systems. Major appliance manufacturers have begun, as required by law, to substitute HCFCs in refrigerators and freezers as well. The amendments called for phasing out ozone depleting chemicals (chlorofluorocarbons, hydrofluorocarbons, methyl chloroform, and carbon tetrachloride) and establishing new rules for the recycling and disposal of such chemicals. Under the Montreal Protocol, CFC production is to be completely phased out by 2000,

with production of all but essential uses phased out by 1996. Refrigeration and air conditioning represent the greatest total use of CFCs worldwide. "In the U.S., an estimated $135 billion in capital equipment relies on CFCs," states *Environmental Liability Insights*, a publication of EEA, Inc. "Retrofitting a large chiller for substitute refrigerants often involves the replacement of housings, impellers, gears, and motors, at a cost of up to $150,000. There are about 80,000 commercial chillers in the United States, most of them used in office building air conditioning units. However, many existing chillers can be used for years after CFC production phase-out by recycling existing refrigerant and repairing any leaks in air conditioning equipment." With the phasing out of CFCs in sight, alternative cost effective cooling systems exist. Architects can specify non-CFC equipment for new installations before the phase-out requirements are in place, thereby substantially upgrading a building system far in advance, saving billions of dollars in future retrofit requirements.

### *Land*

In reponse to Forest Service mismanagement and overcutting, Congress adopted the National Forest Management Act (NFMA) in 1976, ordering the Service to limit the timber cut to "an amount that each forest could sustain in perpetuity." It also directed the agency to "provide for diversity of plant and animal communities." In 1989, the Wilderness Society revealed that the Forest Service was selling timber at prices well below cost and subsidizing the lumber industry and timber-dependent communities in amounts of over $400 million a year. The Society also claims that in 1995, the Forest Service went so far as to clearcut a forest that protected Yellowstone National Park's western border and was home to the endangered peregrine falcon and bald eagle and the threatened grizzly bear. That same year the Society claimed that the Forest Service sold trees to timber companies for little more than $1. "The primary focus of the Service is logging," stated the Wilderness Society, "operated at a loss, costing taxpayers millions of dollars."

According to an NRDC study, damaging logging practices would increase under H.R.9, whose greatest impact on the implemenation of NFMA would come from its cap on regulatory costs. According to the Society,

> The least expensive approaches to logging are often the most destructive to forest resources, resulting in higher costs for private companies to cut public trees. NFMA standards require the Forest Service to pay for reforestation and rehabilitation of logged areas. The cap on regulatory costs would threaten those standards and require that cost-benefit analyses dictate their limits.[3]

Twenty-five percent of all the timber produced by the U.S. timber industry is utilized for construction. Architects can specify woods from sustainably managed sources, a task that is becoming less difficult due to numerous organizations and programs that have developed in recent years, such as the Rainforest Alliance's Smart Wood Programs, or Scientific Certification Systems.

## MANAGEMENT OF TOXIC SUBSTANCES

### *Hazardous Waste*

The primary goals of the Resource Conservation and Recovery Act (RCRA) are to protect human health and the environment from the potential hazards of waste disposal; to conserve energy and natural resources; to reduce the amount of all types of waste generated; and to ensure that waste is managed in an environmentally sound manner. Congress passed the Solid Waste Disposal Act in 1965, the first federal law to require safeguards and encourage environmentally sound methods for the disposal of household, municipal, commercial, and industrial refuse. Amended in 1970 by passing the Resource Recovery Act, and again in 1976 by passing the Resource Conservation Recovery Act, this federal law provides for the safe treatment and disposal of hazardous waste. It is the primary federal law regulating municipal waste disposal. Its predecessor, the Resource Recovery Act of 1970, provided funds for recycling materials and mandated a full investigation of the country's hazardous waste management practices. RCRA, passed in 1976, continued those provisions and was expanded to cover the disposal of used oil and waste, also closing most open dumps. Congress revised the law in 1980, and again in 1984. The 1984 amendments–referred to as the Hazardous and Solid Waste Amendments (HSWA)–were created largely in response to strongly voiced citizen concerns that existing methods of hazardous waste disposal were not safe.

RCRA requires the Environmental Protection Agency to identify hazardous wastes and to regulate their generation, transportation, treatment, storage, and disposal by requiring manufacturers to provide a cradle-to-grave tracking system for every waste shipment. The act focuses on the day-to-day management practices of the hazardous waste industry, covering hazardous waste and waste streams in general. By contrast, disposal of particular hazardous chemicals, such as Polychlorinated Biphenyls (PCBs), comes under the Toxic Substances Control Act. Problems associated with past mismanagement of hazardous wastes are covered by RCRA's companion law, CERCLA, or Superfund, which addresses the clean-up of

## AGENTS POSING CARCINOGENIC RISKS TO HUMANS

**Carcinogenic**

Aflatoxins
Aluminum production
4-Aminobiphenyl
Analgesic mixtures containing phenacetin
Arsenic and arsenic compounds*
Asbestos
Auramine, manufacture of
Azathioprine
Benzene
Benzidine
Betel quid with tobacco
*N,N*-Bis(2-chloroethyl)-2-naphthylamine (chlornaphazine)
Bis(chloromethyl)ether and chloromethyl methyl ether (technical grade)
Boot and shoe manufacture and repair
1,4-Butanediol dimethanesulfonate (Myleran)
Chlorambucil
1-(2-Chloroethyl)-3(4-methylcyclohexyl)-1-nitrosourea (methyl-CCNU)
Chromium compounds, hexavalent*
Coal gasification
Coal-tar pitches
Coal tars
Coke production
Cyclophosphamide
Diethylstilbestrol
Erionite
Estrogen replacement therapy
Estrogens, nonsteroidal*
Estrogens, steroidal*
Furniture and cabinet making
Hematite mining, underground, with exposure to radon
Iron and steel founding
Isopropyl alcohol manufacture, strong-acid process
Magenta, manufacture of
Melphalan
8-Methoxypsoralen (methoxsalen) plus ultraviolet radiation
Mineral oils, untreated and mildly treated
MOPP (combined therapy with nitrogen mustard, vincristine, procarbazine, and prednisone) and other combined chemotherapy, including alkylating agents
Mustard gas (sulfur mustard)
2-Naphthylamine
Nickel and nickel compounds*
Oral contraceptives, combined**
Oral contraceptives, sequential
The rubber industry
Shale oils
Soots
Talc containing asbestiform fibers
Tobacco products, smokeless
Tobacco smoke
Treosulfan
Vinyl chloride

**Probably Carcinogenic**

Acrylonitrile
Adriamycin
Androgenic (anabolic) steroids
Benz{a}anthracene
Benzidine-based dyes
Benzzo[*a*]pyrene
Beryllium and beryllium compounds
Bischloroethyl nitrosourea (BCNU)
Cadmium and cadmium compounds
1-(2-Chloroethyl)-3-cyclohexyl-1-nitrosourea (CCNU)
Cisplatin
Creosotes
Dibenz[*a, h*]anthracene
Diethyl sulphate
Dimethylcarbamoyl chloride
Dimethyl sulfate
Epichlorohydrin
Ethylene dibromide
Ethylene oxide
*N*-Ethyl-*N*-nitrosourea
Formaldehyde
5-Methoxypsoralen
4,4'-Methylene bis(2-chloroaniline) (MOCA)
*N*-Methyl-*N'*-nitro-*N*-nitrosoguanidine (MNNG)
*N*-Methyl-*N*-nitrosourea
Nitrogen mustard
*N*-Nitrosodiethylamine
*N*-Nitrosodimethylamine
Phenacetin
Polychlorinated biphenyls (PCBs)
Procarbazine hydrochloride
Propylene oxide
Styrene oxide
Tris(1-aziridinyl)phosphine sulfide (Thio-TEPA)
Tris(2,3-dibromopropyl) phosphate
Vinyl bromide

**Possibly Carcinogenic**

A-*a*-C (2-Amino-9H-pyrido[2,3-*b*]indole)
Acetaldehyde
Acetamide
Acrylamide
AF-2 [2-(2-Furyl)-3(5-nitro-2-furyl)-1,3,4-thiadiazole
*para*-Aminoazobenzene
*ortho*-Aminoazotoluene
2-Amino-5-(5-nitro-2-furyl)-1,3,4-thiadiazole
Amitrole
*ortho*-Anisidine
Aramite®
Auramine, technical grade
Azaserine
Benzo[*b*]fluoranthene
Benzo[*j*]fluoranthene
Benzo[*k*]fluoranthene
Benzyl violet 4B
Bitumens, extracts of steam refined and air refined
Bleomycins
Bracken fern
1,3-Butadiene
Butylated hydroxyanisole (BHA)
B-Butyrolactone
Carbon-black extracts
Carbon tetrachloride
Carpentry and joinery
Carrageenan, degraded
Chloramphenicol
Chlordecone (Kepone)
*a*-Chlorinated toluenes
Chloroform
Chlorophenols
Chlorophenoxy herbicides
4-Chloro-*ortho*-phenylenediamine
*para*-Chloro-*ortho*-toluidine

## AGENTS POSING CARCINOGENIC RISKS TO HUMANS *(continued)*

Citrus Red No. 2
*para*-Cresidine
Cycasin
Dacarbazine
Daunomycin
DDT
*N,N'*-Diacetylbenzidine
2,4-Diaminoanisole
4,4'-Diaminodiphenyl ether
2,4-Diaminotoluene
Dibenz[*a,h*]acridine
Dibenz[*a,j*]acridine
7*H*-Dibenzo[*c,g*]carbazole
Dibenzo[*a,e*]pyrene
Dibenzo[*a,h*]pyrene
Dibenzo[*a,i*]pyrene
Dibenzo[*a,l*]pyrene
1,2-Dibromo-3-chloropropane
*para*-Dichlorobenzene
3,3'-Dichlorobenzidine
3,3'-Dichloro-4,4'-diaminodiphenyl ether
1,2-Dichloroethane
Dichloromethane
1,3-Dichloropropene (technical grade)
Diepoxybutane
Di(2-ethylhexyl)phthalate
1,2-Diethylhydrazine
Diglycidyl resorcinol ether
Dihydrosafrole
3,3'-Dimethoxybenzidine (*ortho*-dianisidine)
*para*-Dimethylaminoazobenzene
*trans*-2-[(Dimethylamino)methylimino]-5-[2-(5-nitro-2-furyl)vinyl]1,3,4- oxadiazole
3,3'-Dimethylbenzidine (*ortho*-tolidine)
1,1-Dimethylhydrazine
1,2-Dimethylhydrazine
1,4-Dioxane
Ethyl acrylate
Ethylene thiourea
Ethyl methanesulfonate 2-(2-Formylhydrazino)-4-(5-nitro-2-furyl)thiazole
Glu-P-1 (2-Amino-6-methyldipyrido[1,2-*a*:3',2"-*d*]imidazole)
Glu-P-2 (2-Aminodipyrido[1,2-*a*:3'2'-*d*]imidazole)
Glycidaldehyde
Griseofulvin
Hexachlorobenzene
Hexachlorocyclohexanes
Hexamethylphosphoramide
Hydrazine
Indeno[1,2,3-*cd*]pyrene
IQ (2-Amino-3-methylimidazo[4,5-*f*]quinoline)
Iron-dextran complex
Lasiocarpine
Lead and lead compounds, inorganic
MeA-*a*-C (2-Amino-3-methyl-9*H*-pyrido[2,3-*b*]indole)
Medroxyprogesterone acetate
Merphalan
2-Methylaziridine
Methylazoxymethanol and its acetate
5-Methylchrysene
4,4'-Methylene bis(2-methylaniline)
4,4'-Methylenedianiline
Methyl methanesulfonate
2-Methyl-1-nitroanthraquinone (uncertain purity)
*N*-Methyl-*N*-nitrosouretha
Methylthiouracil
Metronidazole
Mirex
Mitomycin C
Monocrotaline
5-(Morpholinomethyl)-3-[(5-nitrofurfurylidene)amino]-2-oxazolidinone
Nafenopin
Niridazole
5-Nitroacenaphthene
Nitrofen (technical grade)
1-[(5-Nitrofurfurylidene)amino]-2imidazolidinone
*N*-[4-(5-Nitro-2-furyl)-2thiazolyl]acetamide
Nitrogen mustard *N*-oxide
2-Nitroropane
*N*-Nitrosodi-*n*-butylamine
*N*-Nitrosodiethanolamine *N*-Nitrosodi-*n*-propylamine
3-(*N*-Nitrosomethylamino)propionitrile
4-(*N*-Nitrosomethylamino)-1-(3-pyridyl-1-butanone(NNK)
*N*-Nitrosomethylethylamine
*N*-Nitrosomethylvinylamine
*N*-Nitrosomorpholine
*N'*-Nitrosonornicotine>*N*-Nitrosopiperidine
*N*-Nitrosopyrrolidine
*N*-Nitrososarcosine
Oil Orange SS
Panfuran S (containing dihydroxymethylfuratrizine)
Phenazopyridine hydrochloride
Phenobarbital
Phenoxybenzamine hydrochloride
Phenytoin
Polybrominated biphenyls
Ponceau MX
Ponceau 3R
Potassium bromate
Progestins
1,3-Propane sultone
B-Propiolactone
Propylthiouracil
Saccharin
Safrole
Sodium *ortho*-phenylphenate
Sterigmatocystin
Streptozotocin
Styrene
Sulfallate
2,3,7,8-Tetrachlorodibenzo-*para*-dioxin (TCDD)
Tetrachloroethylene
Thioacetamide
4,4'-Thiodianiline
Thiourea
Toluene diisocyanates
*ortho*-Toluidine
Toxaphene (polychlorinated camphenes)
Trp-P-1 (3-Amino-1,4-dimethyl-5*H*-pyrido[4,3-*b*] indole)
Trp-P-2 (3-Amino-1-methyl-5*H*-pyrido[4,3-*b*]indole)
Trypan blue
Uracil mustard
Urethane

* Applies to group of chemicals, not necessarily to individuals within the group.

** Conclusive evidence exists that these agents can protect against cancers of the ovary and endometrium.

inactive and abandoned hazardous waste sites.

Regarding the construction practice, RCRA governs proper disposal of any hazardous waste. General maintenance by owners of facilities involved in such practices as chemical manufacturing, vehicle maintenance, printing, leather products manufacturing, construction products manufacturing, cleaning products manufacturing, furniture, wood manufacturing and refinishing, and metal manufacturing requires direct compliance with RCRA. These manufacturers are required to identify, label, and dispose of listed hazardous wastes in accordance with RCRA's guidelines. Failure to do this can result in stiff financial penalties.

Indirectly related concerns include the contamination of groundwater by leachate, a mixture of rainwater or other liquid with pollutant. Groundwater, used for irrigating crops and drinking, naturally flows through and is stored in solid bodies beneath the land, such as rock. Almost half of the U.S. population relies on groundwater for some or all of its drinking water. Groundwater monitoring near hazardous waste storage facilities is required under RCRA. According to the EPA,

> In the South Bay area of San Francisco, California, leaks of toxic solvents from underground tanks severely contaminated the groundwater. In Truro on Cape Cod, Massachusetts, drinking water wells were contaminated with gasoline that had leaked from a nearby underground storage unit. Thousands of other communities are facing similar problems with leaking underground storage, hazardous waste, and contaminated groundwater and soils.

The careful review of any potential site should include water and soil testing for contamination.

The Environmental Protection Agency issued in 1994 the Comprehensive Procurement Guideline which designates items that are or can be made with recovered materials. Once the EPA designates an item, RCRA requires any procuring agency using appropriated funds to purchase that item with the highest percentage of recovered materials practicable. The proposed rule incorporates the previously issued guidelines which included construction materials such as building insulation, cement, and concrete, and adds to it many building-related products such as structural fiberboard and laminated paperboard, plastic pipe and fittings, geotextiles, carpet, floor tiles, and patio blocks. Architects and other contractors working with federal institutions will be required to comply with these requirements.

The Comprehensive Environmental Response Compensation and Liability Act (CERCLA), or Superfund, as it is more commonly known, was first passed in 1980 to deal with the release of hazardous substances in spills and from inactive and abandoned disposal sites. Its name comes from the fact that the Superfund law established large funds to pay for the cleanup of dump sites, such as Love Canal. CERCLA requires the EPA to identify hazardous substances, such as pesticides and other toxic chemicals that can present substantial danger. Superfund makes polluters financially accountable for the long-term maintenance, containment, and cleanup of sites contaminated with such substances, and allows the EPA to recover cleanup costs from the responsible party. Day-to-day management practices are governed by the Resource Conservation and Recovery Act (RCRA).

During the past fifteen years, Superfund has assessed over 36,000 sites and taken immediate action at more than 2,500. One in four Americans (73 million people) lives within four miles of at least one high-priority site. The fund also imposes a tax on

### EXAMPLES OF HAZARDOUS WASTE GENERATED BY BUSINESSES AND INDUSTRIES

| *Waste Generators* | *Waste Type* |
|---|---|
| Chemical manufacturers | Strong acids and bases<br>Spent solvents<br>Reactive wastes |
| Vehicle maintenance shops | Heavy metal paint wastes<br>Ignitable wastes<br>Used lead acid batteries<br>Spent solvents |
| Printing industry | Heavy metal solutions<br>Waste inks<br>Spent solvents<br>Spent electroplating wastes<br>Ink sludges containing heavy metals |
| Leather products manufacturing | Waste toluene and benzene |
| Paper industry | Paint wastes containing heavy metals<br>Ignitable solvents<br>Strong acids and bases |
| Construction industry | Ignitable paint wastes<br>Spent solvents<br>Strong acids and bases |
| Cleaning agents and cosmetics manufacturing | Heavy metal dusts<br>Ignitable wastes<br>Flammable solvents<br>Strong acids and bases |
| Furniture and wood manufacturing and refinishing | Spent solvents<br>Ignitable wastes |
| Metal manufacturing | Paint wastes containing heavy metals<br>Strong acids and bases<br>Cyanide wastes<br>Sludges containing heavy metals |

chemicals and petroleum to fund the immediate clean-up of urgent problems. Despite EPA's broad powers to order clean-ups, Superfund is plagued with long delays and innumerable law suits before long-term cleanup begins.

Superfund was later expanded under the Superfund Amendments and Reauthorization Act of 1986 (SARA, or Title III), as part of the Emergency Planning and Community Right to Know Act (EPCRA). This increased the amount of the fund from $1.6 to $8.5 billion over five years. To minimize lengthy litigation, it also introduced revised procedures designed to encourage voluntary settlements from Potentially Responsible Parties (PRP), adding an "innocent landowner" defense for people who had no reason to suspect that their property contained hazardous substances.

Superfund is currently undergoing review for reauthorization. Under H.R.9, if the EPA ordered a company to clean up a waste site, the company could bill the EPA for the costs. The most effective part of the Superfund program–immediate clean-up actions, such as providing clean water supplies or removing leaking drums–would be tied up in litigation over procedural issues. A full cost-benefit analysis would confuse the risks of hazardous waste sites, burden clean-up decisions with new paperwork and litigation, and inhibit improvements in the effectiveness of the fund to reduce hazardous waste.

Property owners and building professionals should be aware of hazardous waste sites in their communities, taking particular care to check the soil and water quality of a potential site. For current and specific information particular to your area, contact the Environmental Protection Agency.

### *Commercial Chemicals*

The Toxic Substances Control Act (TSCA or TOSCA), passed in 1976, authorizes the EPA to monitor and control the risks posed by commercial chemical substances that are not otherwise regulated by federal laws as drugs, food additives, cosmetics, tobacco, nuclear material, firearms, ammunition, or pesticides. The EPA maintains a chemical inventory of all commercial chemical substances that have been manufactured or imported into the United States since 1975, a list to which all new chemicals are added. The Agency is then charged with controlling the risks from over 65,000 existing chemicals–including those on the market before the law passed.

Critics point out that the EPA should have the authority to require testing of a chemical without first having to declare it to be an "unreasonable risk," as is the case with TOSCA. Where regulation authority is unclear, the EPA defers to other agencies, such as Occupational Safety and Health Administration (OSHA). *The Blueprint for the Environment* recommends that the EPA reassert its authority over any substance found to pose an unreasonable risk.

Regarding hazardous waste and toxic substances, building professionals should be alert to the business and manufacturing practices of the companies producing the materials they specify. While it does require extra research to be aware of specific environmental concerns, every specification implies a recommendation, and so should be carefully reviewed. Environmental publications from the Natural Resources Defense Council and the Sierra Club Legal Defense Fund make concerted efforts to provide objective information which can help inform concerned professionals. Ask your manufacturer's representative to provide documented information about their manufacturing practices regarding toxics. You can request MSDS sheets (Material Safety Data Sheet) on any product, and then review the information with the list of toxic substances. This is a time-consuming process that may require the assistance of a knowledgeable environmental consultant. Publications such as the *Environmental Building News* and the *Environmental Resource Guide* seek to provide this type of information on a continuing basis.

### *Asbestos*

Asbestos, a class of naturally occurring minerals composed of fibrous silicates, has long been known for its insulating properties. Asbestos was widely used in building materials during this century and earlier. Each of its three forms–white (crysotile), blue (crocidolite), and brown (amosite)–was found to be extremely hazardous to human health, causing lung disorders and various forms of cancer. Now listed as a toxic substance under TOSCA and controlled by state codes, asbestos had been installed in most schools, homes, offices, and commercial buildings by the 1960s. Used commonly as insulation for plumbing or electrical pipes, ceiling or floor material, asbestos products have been banned since the 1970s.

Practicing professionals are familiar with code requirements that address asbestos concerns in existing buildings, but building owners are often ill-prepared to face the issues involved when asbestos is present. The discovery of asbestos in existing buildings and its subsequent containment and/or removal can be fraught with huge costs–in health, time, and liability, as well as dollars. The problem remains of what to do with the asbestos that is in place, especially in schools where children are at high risk. Due to laws such as the Asbestos School Hazard Act and the Asbestos Hazard Emergency Response Act, the EPA provided funds of $88 million in 1988 alone to help

## General Guidelines for Handling Products Containing Asbestos

If you think that a material contains asbestos, and the material must be banged, rubbed, handled, or taken apart, you should hire a trained asbestos contractor, or obtain proper training yourself, before taking any action. Even if you are properly trained, you should not attempt anything more than minor repairs (approximately the size of your hand).

Special precautions should be taken during removal of exposed or damaged asbestos-containing material. Removal of the material is usually the last alternative.

In order to determine the experience and skill of a prospective asbestos-removal contractor, ask the contractor these questions:

- Are you certified? (Ask to see the certificate.)
- Have you and your workers been trained?
- Do you have experience removing asbestos from homes?
- Will you provide a list of references of people for whom you have worked with asbestos?
- Will you provide a list of places where you have worked with asbestos?
- Will you use the "wet method" (water and detergent)?
- Will you use polyethylene plastic barriers to contain dust?
- Will you use a HEPA (high efficiency particulate air) filter vacuum cleaner?
- Will your workers wear approved respirators?
- Will you properly dispose of the asbestos and leave the site free of asbestos dust and debris?
- Will the contractor provide a written contract specifying these procedures?

Make sure the trained asbestos contractor follows these procedures:

1. The contractor should seal off the work area from the rest of the residence and close off the heating/air conditioning system. Plastic sheeting and duct tape may be used. For some repairs (such as pipe insulation removal) plastic glove bags may be used which can be carefully sealed with tape when work is complete. The contractor should take great care not to track asbestos dust into other areas of the residence.
2. The work site should be clearly marked as a hazard area. Only workers wearing disposable protective clothing should have access. Household members and their pets should not enter the area until work is completed and inspected.
3. During the removal of asbestos-containing material, workers should wear approved respirators appropriate for the specific asbestos activity. Workers should also wear gloves, hats, and other protective clothing. The contractor should properly dispose of all of this equipment (along with the asbestos material) immediately after using it.
4. The contractor should wet the asbestos-containing material with a hand sprayer. The sprayer should provide a fine mist, and the material should be thoroughly dampened, but not dripping wet. Wet fibers do not float in the air as readily as dry fibers and will be easier to clean up. The contractor should add a small amount of a low-sudsing dish or laundry detergent to improve the penetration of the water into the material and reduce the amount of water needed.
5. The contractor should assure that if asbestos-containing material must be drilled or cut, the drilling or cutting is done outside or in a special containment room, with the material wetted first.
6. The contractor should assure that, if the material must be removed, it is not broken into small pieces. While it is easier to remove and handle small pieces, asbestos fibers are more likely to be released if the contractor breaks the material into small pieces. Pipe insulation is usually installed in preformed blocks and should be removed in complete pieces.
7. The contractor should place any material that is removed and any debris from the work in sealed, leak-proof, properly-labeled, plastic bags (6 ml thick) and should dispose of them in a proper landfill. The contractor should comply with health department instructions about how to dispose of asbestos-containing material.
8. The contractor should assure that after removal of the asbestos-containing material, the area is thoroughly cleaned with wet mops, wet rags, or sponges. The cleaning procedure should be repeated a second time. Wetting will help reduce the chance that the fibers get spread around. No asbestos material should be tracked into other areas. The contractor should dispose of the mop heads, rags, and sponges in the sealed plastic bags with the removed materials.

Source: *Asbestos in the Home*. U.S. Consumer Product Safety Commission and U.S. Environmental Protection Agency, 1989.

Caution: Do not dust, sweep, or vacuum particles suspected of containing asbestos. This will disturb tiny asbestos fibers and may make them airborne. The fibers are so small that they cannot be seen and can pass through normal vacuum cleaner filters and get back into the air. The dust should be removed by a wet-mopping procedure or by specially-designed "HEPA" vacuum cleaners used by trained asbestos contractors.

primary schools abate asbestos contamination. Management of asbestos remains an ongoing problem, incurring billions of dollars in costs to owners and threatening the health and lives of people who occupy buildings plagued with the toxic fiber. In New York City, for example, asbestos can still be found in buildings built before the 1970s which are regularly being renovated. In accordance with local codes, the problem is handled at a significant cost to owners.

### *Lead*

Lead has been utilized as a building material for thousands of years, especially in plumbing systems. In this century it has been widely used in paint, alloys, and gasoline, and is a common contaminant from many industrial processes such as mining and smelting. Known to have devastating effects on the kidneys, brain, nervous system, heart, and circulatory system, lead contamination is particularly damaging to children, whose brain development and intellectual functioning could become impaired, and to pregnant women, in whom fetal development is jeopardized. In the 1960s, government regulations regarded 60 micrograms of lead per deciliter (mg/dl) of blood as acceptable. By 1987, 15 mg/dl was considered acceptable.

Products containing lead, such as paint or gasoline, have been phased out since the 1970s, but lead still exists at dangerous levels in air, water, and soil. Lead is controlled as a toxic substance under TOSCA in water, food, paint, exterior sources such as air and soil, and occupational exposures. According to the EPA, the Lead-Based Paint Poisoning Prevention Act of 1971 was intended to attack the toxic threat of lead by requiring the removal of lead paint from all federally subsidized housing. However, it was not enforced because insufficient money was allocated to do the job, which costs several thousand dollars per dwelling.

Experts disagree about how to handle lead paint. As with asbestos, some believe that it may be safer to seal and cover lead paint than to remove it, while others believe that this postpones finding a solution to the problem. Sanding lead-filled paint produces lead-filled dust, creating an exposure risk to workers and occupants; the burning of lead-paint products is just as risky as it generates toxic fumes. The Toxic Substances Control Act outlines in Subchapter IV–Lead Exposure Reduction the qualifications and procedures for the abatement and measurement of lead. The Residual Lead-Based Paint Hazard Reduction Act of 1992, known as Title X, regulates lead paint, lead-contaminated dust, and lead-contaminated soil. It, too, goes unenforced because of a disparity of findings.

Building professionals who are ecologically conscious can be aware of potential sources of existing lead and suggest soil, water source, and existing paint tests to building owners.

### *Radon*

Radon was first recognized as a cause of lung cancer in underground miners in the 1930s. In 1955, the International Commission on Radiological Protection established the first occupational health standard for radon exposure in mines. In 1970, homes in the United States were found to have elevated levels of radon when uranium mill tailings were used as fill dirt or when built on reclaimed phosphate mining land. By 1984, it had become increasingly evident that homes could have elevated indoor radon levels caused by naturally occurring radium in the underlying soil and rock. In the past five years, homes with elevated radon levels have been found throughout the United States. Surveys indicate that up to six million homes may have radon levels above the EPA's action level guideline of 4 pCi/L. Based on studies by the National Academy of Sciences and other scientific organizations, it is believed that 7,000 to 30,000 lung cancer deaths per year can be attributed to elevated levels of indoor radon. There are also data that point to a synergistic effect between radon exposure and smoking, thereby placing smokers at a higher risk. The 1993 Federal Register provides information regarding radon occurence and its health risks.[4]

Title III of TOSCA, enacted in October of 1988, requires the EPA to develop model construction standards and techniques for controlling radon levels in new buildings. "To the maximum extent possible, these standards and techniques should be developed with the assistance of organizations involved in establishing national building construction standards and techniques and be made available in draft for public review and comment," advises the EPA. In 1993, the AIA joined with representatives of the building community to provide suggestions to the EPA of ways they could encourage builders to voluntarily use new radon-resistant construction techniques as a regular part of their building practice. The new construction standards are outlined in the EPA document "Model Standards and Techniques for Control of Radon in New Buildings." Most jurisdictions are several years away from developing codes for radon-resistant construction, and the representatives agreed that voluntary adoption of radon-resistant construction techniques is the most effective way of immediately reducing health risks.

### *Pesticides*

A U.S. federal law enacted in 1947 to govern pesticides, the Federal Insecticide, Fungicide, and Rodenticide Act (FIFRA) has been administered since 1970 by the EPA, and was amended in 1972 to focus more on monitoring the health and environmental consequences of pesticides. The EPA requires registration of all pesticides manufactured in or imported to the U.S. The manufacturer must "demonstrate evidence that when used in accordance with widespread and commonly recognized practice, the pesticide will not generally cause unreasonable adverse effects on the environment" and provide possible risk of cancer, birth defects, and other adverse effects to humans and wildlife. The EPA can remove from the marketplace pesticides deemed too dangerous for any use, such as DDT and several other chlorinated hydrocarbons. FIFRA directs the EPA to work with the Department of Agriculture "to develop and improve the safe use and effectiveness of chemical, biological, and alternative methods of pest control that reduce the quality and economical production and distribution of agricultural products."

Critics charge that the agency has not sufficiently emphasized such alternatives as biological control or integrated pest management (IPM). Environmentalists are also concerned that the process of registering pesticides is too slow, and that the setting of tolerance levels does not take into account increased susceptibility in pregnant women, children, and the elderly.

Although pest control does not come under typical architectural services, natural methods of pest control have been incorporated in the design and planning of many ecologically conscious buildings. Innovative solutions include encouraging the habitation of insect-eating species like bats and birds, and strategically locating plant species that naturally repel insects.

## BUILDING ENERGY EFFICIENCY STANDARDS

Until the 1990s, a building professional required great creativity in mechanical engineering to integrate energy efficiency into a project. With the exception of the work of innovative architects, engineers, contractors, and owners (including those in this book), U.S. buildings are only just beginning to benefit from innovative solutions to energy concerns. The following legislation has had a powerful impact on building products and systems, which in turn are helping to make energy efficiency a technologically available, feasible, and even profitable alternative.

### *Energy Legislation*

Commonly referred to as EPACT, the National Energy Policy Act was signed into law by President George Bush in October of 1992. EPACT directs the reduction of energy consumption through competitive electricity generation and conservation initiatives, providing millions of dollars in funding for this purpose. This policy affects every aspect of energy policy in the United States: resources, consumption, conservation, utility initiatives, income tax exclusions for rebates, renewable energy fuels, vehicle fuels, and product efficiency standards as applied to motors, distribution transformers, and lamps.

EPACT set substantial groundwork for energy efficient technology that directly affects building owners, architects, and designers. Some provisions of interest to building professionals include:

**State Building Energy Codes.** Each state was required by 1994 to certify to the Secretary of Energy that the energy efficiency standards of its residential building code met or exceeded the energy efficiency provisions for residential space of the 1992 CABO Model Energy Guide. If the standards had not met/exceeded the requirements outlined in the guide, they needed to be revised.

**Commercial Building Energy Codes.** Each state was to certify by 1994 to the Secretary of Energy that it had reviewed and updated the provisions of its commercial building code regarding energy efficiency. States needed to prove that their code provisions met or exceeded the requirements of ASHRAE Standard 90.1-1989.

**Federal Building Energy Standards.** By October of 1994, the Secretary of Energy, after consulting with appropriate federal agencies, the AIA, and other professional organizations, was required to issue federal building energy efficiency standards requiring technologically feasible and economically justified energy efficiency measures in new buildings.

**Government-Assisted Housing Energy Codes.** By October of 1993, the Secretary of Housing and Urban Development (HUD) established energy efficiency standards for new construction of public and assisted housing and single- and multifamily residential housing subject to mortgages insured under the National Housing Act. The Secretary of Agriculture established energy efficiency standards for new construction of single-family housing with mortgages insured, guaranteed, or made under Title V of the Housing Act of 1949.

The impact that EPACT has had on energy related products for the building professions will continue to be felt for a number of years. Other legislation that has already encouraged the building professions includes the Public Utilities Regulatory Policies Act (PURPA), which facilitates the development of renewable energy and small-scale power production by requiring electric utilities to buy power at "just" rates from smaller power producers using renewable sources. Under PURPA, utilities must purchase power offered at "appropriate rates, whether they want to or not." This is administered by the Federal Energy Regulatory Commission, which is also charged with establishing conditions under which independent power producers may easily connect their electricity into the public-utility grid.

Appliance efficiency standards are addressed in three laws: the National Appliance Energy Conservation Act of 1987 (NAECA); the National Appliance Energy Conservation Amendments of 1988; and the Energy Policy Act of 1992 (EPACT). NAECA contains initial minimum efficiency standards for various appliances, and requires the Department of Energy to set future standards for consumer products based on criteria that include cost-effectiveness and economic impacts. This act sets minimum efficiency standards for new home heating and cooling systems, refrigerators, freezers, small gas furnaces, and other appliances. EPACT oversees other regulated products such as lamps, motors, and commercial heating and cooling equipment.

Standards on refrigerators, freezers, dishwashers,

clothes washers and dryers were issued in 1989 and 1991. "Standards already adopted are expected to save consumers $125 billion," according to the NRDC report. New standards on refrigerators and freezers that took effect in 1993 should save $9 million. Currently proposed standards would increase this savings by over $60 billion. H.R.9 would delay implementation of the proposed standards and cost the U.S. economy billions of dollars. Appliance standards that have a small cost but large benefits would count as net costs in the budget, discounting their long-term cost effectiveness.

Architects can increase energy efficiency in a building by becoming familiar with these standards, and by seeking to specify appliances that meet or exceed them. Owners will benefit by considering long-term energy cost savings while evaluating the costs of appliances.

### *Pending Legislation*

Passed in the Senate in October of 1993, the Indoor Air Quality Act (IAQ) requires indoor air quality research and risk management activities such as federal and private research, management practices, guidance and training, assessment of and recommendations for ventilation standards, federal and other building demonstration programs, and an IAQ clearinghouse. The required research activities include a technology demonstration program, contaminant health advisories, a national response strategy, assessment of corrective actions, and state grants.

Indoor air pollution ranks as one of the top five environmental risks to health in the United States. The EPA estimates that one in six commercial buildings produces Sick Building Syndrome, costing tens of billions of dollars annually in medical expenses and reduced productivity. The U.S. Department of Labor's Occupational Safety and Health Administration (OSHA), the standard-setting agency that regulates indoor air quality as a workplace condition, has proposed groundbreaking indoor air quality legislation.[5] The OSHA rule is the most comprehensive effort to control indoor air quality in the history of environmental regulation, requiring all employers, including tenants and building managers in non-industrial workplaces, to prepare and implement an IAQ compliance program. Some minimum proposed actions include:

- HVAC system must operate to specifications during facility occupancy with regular inspection and maintenance required.
- Carbon dioxide levels are to be monitored and should not exceed 800 parts per million (1,000 ppm is the threshold recommended by ASHRAE). Outdoor ambient carbon dioxide concentrations typically range from 250 to 350 ppm.
- Natural ventilation is required in buildings without mechanical ventilation. Relative humidity must be maintained below 60% in buildings with mechanical cooling.
- Outdoor air contaminants must be restricted at air intakes.
- General or local exhaust ventilation is to be used in areas where maintenance activities or use of equipment or products could cause emissions of hazardous chemicals or particulates.
- Smoking must be limited to designated areas that are fully enclosed and directly exhausted to the outside.
- Microbial contamination of HVAC systems must be controlled.
- Friable asbestos-containing materials in non-ducted air plenums of chases must be encapsulated or removed so that these materials do not enter the HVAC system.
- Employees are to be given training and information, and complaints must be filed with a designated program implementation person.

The AIA endorses the proposed rule, believing that "it will save lives, money, and protect the right of people to use public spaces without suffering a health hazard from airborne substances." Due to the controversial and complex issues, final rule making is not expected until 1996.

The Indoor Air Act of 1993 requires the EPA to establish guidelines for identifying and preventing indoor air hazards in new and existing buildings; train and certify IAQ contractors; establish a national education campaign including health advisories with action levels; publish technology bulletins; create an IAQ clearinghouse and federal buildings program; provide state grants; and conduct IAQ research.

These concerns and pending laws regarding indoor air quality are changing how building professionals and owners address legal and moral responsibilities in the creation of healthy buildings. Pending legislation such as the Indoor Air Quality Act, the Global Climate Change Prevention Act, and the Tropical Forest Protection Act will inevitably change the way all building professionals and property owners create the built environment by requiring the implementation of environmentally conscious community and building design.

### *EPA Voluntary Non-Regulatory Programs*

In January of 1991, the Environmental Protection Agency began its most substantial voluntary non-regulatory program, the Green Lights Program. The Green Lights Program uses the initiative of organizations nationwide to reduce pollution and conserve energy by upgrading inefficient light fixtures and replacing them with newer, more efficient models. Electrical utility companies have strongly supported this program by offering substantial rebates and, in some cases, completely subsidizing to participants.The reason for this is because it is less expensive for utilities to manage their customer's demand for electricity than it is to invest in new sources of electrical supply. According to the EPA, "Since the program began, over 500 private companies and institutions like American Express, Mobil, and Westin Hotels and Resorts have upgraded their facilities, saving $11.9 million annually." The EPA estimates that by the year 2000, a full implementation of Green Lights would save 39.8 million kilowatts of electricity, freeing 59.7 billion that would otherwise be needed for power plant construction. Program participants include large corporations, state and local governments, environmental organizations, electric companies, and major members of the lighting industry. By treating lighting as an investment opportunity, participants realize returns of over 25% on average.These organizations are reducing their lighting bills by 50% or more while maintaining or improving lighting quality.

Each program participant agrees to survey all of his/her domestic facilities, upgrade lighting where profitable, and complete the lighting upgrades within five years.The participants assign an employee to be responsible for ensuring the timely implementation of the lighting upgrades.Additionally, they work with the EPA to publicize the benefits of energy-efficient lighting.

Another of the EPA's programs is the Energy Star Buildings Program, which provides incentives to upgrade HVAC equipment with variable speed drives. Similarly, the Energy Star Computers program seeks to increase market penetration of new energy-efficient personal computers.

After reading this chapter on environmental legislation, one thing is glaringly clear: the current climate of environmental protection is changing.Americans voted in 1994 for less government bureaucracy, not weaker environmental protection.The 104th Congress reflects voters' concerns about crime, taxes, and government bureaucracy and their frustration with an ineffective former Democratic Congress. In 1994, an election night poll conducted by the LCV further indicated that 83% of voters "want stronger environmental protection and are willing to pay more for it." Instead, "This Congress looks as though it will be the most unsympathetic to environmental issues since the 1970s," says the NRDC's *Amicus Journal*. "It threatens to undo thirty years of environmental policy." The Contract with America, "the campaign gambit of Newt Gingrich that was adopted by the House of Representatives as the legislative agenda, is the most radical set of special interest wish lists composed in the last twenty-five years," says Daniel Weiss, political director for the Sierra Club.

On March 3, 1995, the House of Representatives passed legislation adopted under the Contract known as H.R.9, or the Job Creation and Wage Enhancement Act. H.R.9 is currently the subject of debate before the Senate.Without directly addressing the environment, it threatens environmental protection across the board by requiring extensive cost-benefit analyses of federal standards and regulations, granting businesses easier access to regulators, stopping "unfunded mandates" to state and local governments, and compensating property owners for regulatory takings. H.R.9, designed according to its supporters to complete the Reagan agenda, goes further than the Reagan administration ever proposed in imposing curbs on federal safety and health agencies, while allowing regulated industries to influence the process at each step, even before the public has an opportunity to comment. Regarding takings, it proposes compensation when property loses 10% of its value, a level that even supporters agree will cost taxpayers billions of dollars. Property owners could easily request compensation to the concerned agency, which would be required to pay the amount within six months.

Launching its "most important environmental campaign ever," NRDC warns in *Breach of Faith,* a detailed case study report that reviews the impact of H.R.9 on the environment, that "Congress is on the brink of dismantling the legal underpinnings that made gains in environmental protection possible, and is doing so in such a fashion that there will be no opportunity for a national debate on what will be lost." The legacy of H.R.9, as well as other significant anti-environmental legislation recently passed in Congress, currently comprises an unfinished chapter in U.S. history.

As a result of the last twenty years of environmental legislation in the United States, building owners and building professionals are required to answer to an increasingly stringent set of requirements set in place to protect the environment, actions which have reversed the devastation caused by ignorance and damaging industrial processes. Environmentally conscious building professionals are increasingly aware of their role in protecting the environment and restoring natural resources and human health, while building owners look to their design professionals for this guidance. In 1995, with the goal of balancing the United States budget, Congress passed legislation that reflects the tenets of The Contract with America and the "Wise Use Movement," both of which would relax many environmental laws and allow business and industry to regulate themselves regarding environmental protection. While surveys indicate that Americans are concerned with environmental protection, citizens must be made aware of the environmental positions of those they elect. An acute awareness of environmental legislation, scientific information, available technology, and community needs is critical to the successful practice of environmentally conscious building design. Professionals who create the built environment must increasingly understand the impact of their choices, not only as professionals, but as community leaders, citizens, and human beings. Designers of the built environment, through daily actions and through representative organizations such as the AIA or ADPSR, can influence education, the protection of natural resources, and the future of environmental policy in the United States.

# A Call to Action

*The Ecology of Architecture* was written to inspire building professionals, provide tested information through examples of groundbreaking projects, and highlight the ecologically sound building materials and techniques available to practitioners today. This is a field that is constantly changing, benefitting on an almost daily basis from our rapid advances in science and technology. Even during the course of the writing of this book, a number of new alternatives have become readily available.

The work of building professionals has the greatest long-term impact on our world's resources. Up to 54% of all energy used in the United States is consumed by the construction and operation of buildings, and we have long known that we use far greater amounts of energy per capita than any other country in the world. The decisions of building professionals, particularly in the design and planning phases, affect the local, regional, and global environments of the future. After a decade of building environmentally conscious projects in the U.S., it is clear that the groundwork is set, but much more needs to be done. A design professional's job has become increasingly complex and litigious these days, requiring practitioners to exercise greater caution, work more with consultants, and meet difficult cost challenges. In light of these demands, it is important that they update business practices to support ecologically conscious practices.

In an effort to promote the practice of environmentally conscious building, the American Institute of Architects is working to implement "sustainable" elements into standard contracts used by professionals throughout the United States. Research programs established at federal, regional, and local levels by both the public and private sectors are working to fund and highlight ecologically conscious work, thereby educating others in this discipline. Thus far, laws have been implemented that will continue to change products, systems, and materials to the year 2020. The increased use of life cycle costing–beyond the scope of typical design practice–exhibits the common sense and dollar value in using energy efficient systems. Technology for renewable resources, then, is entering the mainstream of reasonable use. An increased level of communication between the professionals in architecture, engineering, building construction, and real estate about long-term social and environmental impact will serve to create ecologically conscious communities and buildings.

The most important point here is that building professionals and owners must think of themselves as human beings first, and that their professional work is done in service to the community. The community, in turn, should attempt to not only conserve resources, but restore them. Beyond our professional practices, as human beings and citizens, there is much more that we can do.

When I started writing this book, federal environmental legislation was being celebrated by national environmental organizations across the country. The Natural Resources Defense Council, the Sierra Club, and many others applauded the results of twenty-five years of groundbreaking federal environmental legislation. Over the last two years, this optimism has dwindled and the political climate changed, creating true cause for concern. The 104th Congress, adopting "wise use" legislation, began to pass anti-environmental legislation, and new legislation such as responsive indoor air regulations were set aside, awaiting passage by a more sympathetic Congress.

It is more critical than ever that we be aware of the environmental positions of our representatives. This can be done by contacting environmental organizations, such as the League of Conservation Voters, who follow candidates' voting track records and create environmental scorecards on elected officials. Write, fax, and e-mail your elected officials; they make decisions according to what they hear from their constituents. There are also many organizations that represent building professionals and owners. The American Institute of Architects (AIA) or Architects/ Designers/ and Planners for Social Responsibility (ADPSR), for example, represent thousands of professionals in the United States, work to promote environmentally conscious programs, and lobby for environmental legislation.

How we conduct our personal lives can also have a significant effect on the environment. As head of a household, learning what resources were used for the manufacture of consumer products and practicing a self-sustaining lifestyle create the greatest platform for experimentation available. When you are concerned with the details of creating and running your home and office as resourcefully and consciously as possible, a ripple effect reaches local, regional, and global resource markets. Thoughtful choices will serve to educate and inspire others.

# *Appendix*

## TOXIC CHEMICALS AND HAZARDOUS SUBSTANCES

| *Chemical Name* | *HS* | *TC* | *HAP* | *CAS #* |
|---|---|---|---|---|
| Acenaphthene | X | | | 83329 |
| Acenaphthylene | X | | | 208968 |
| Acetaldehyde | | X | X | 75070 |
| Acetamide; aka: | | | | |
| Ethanamide | | X | X | 60355 |
| Acetone | | X | X | 67641 |
| Acetonitrile | | X | X | 75058 |
| Acetophenone | | | X | 98862 |
| 2-Acetylaminofluorene | | X | X | 53963 |
| Acrolein | X | X | X | 107028 |
| Acrylamide; | | | | |
| aka: 2-Propenamide | | X | X | 79061 |
| Acrylic acid | | X | X | 79107 |
| Acrylonitrile | X | X | X | 107131 |
| Aldrin | X | X | | 309002 |
| Allyl chloride | | X | X | 107051 |
| Aluminum (fume or dust) | | X | | 7429905 |
| Aluminum oxide | | X | | 1344281 |
| 1-Amino-2-methyl- | | | | |
| anthraquinone | | | X | 82280 |
| 2-Aminoanthraquinone | | X | | 117793 |
| 4-Aminoazobenzene | | X | | 60093 |
| 4-Aminobiphenyl | | X | X | 92671 |
| Ammonia | X | X | | 7664417 |
| Ammonium nitrate | | | | |
| (solution) | | X | | 6484522 |
| Ammonium sulfate | | | | |
| (solution) | | X | | 7783202 |
| Aniline; aka: | | | | |
| Benzenamine | X | X | X | 62533 |
| 0-Anisidine | | X | X | 90040 |
| p-Anisidine | | X | | 104949 |
| o-Anisidine | | | | |
| hydrochloride | | X | | 134292 |
| Anthracene | X | X | | 120127 |
| Antimony | X | X | | 7440360 |
| Antimony | | | | |
| compounds | | X | X | – |
| Antimony tris | | X | | 27288444 |
| (iso-octyl mercapto- | | | | |
| acetate) aka: | | | | |
| ATOM | | | | |
| Aramite | | X | | 140578 |
| Arsenic | X | X | | 7440382 |
| Arsenic compounds | | X | X | – |
| Asbestos | X | | X | 1332214 |
| Asbestos (asbesti- | | X | | – |
| form varieties of | | | | |
| chrysotile (serpentine); | | | | |
| crocidolite (rieeckite); | | | | |
| amosite (cummin | | | | |
| gtonitegrunerite); | | | | |
| anthophyllite; | | | | |
| tremolite; and | | | | |
| actinolite) | | | | |
| Atrazine | X | | | 1912249 |
| Auramine | | X | | 492808 |
| Barium | X | X | | 7440393 |
| Barium compounds | X | X | | – |
| Benzal chloride; | | | | |
| aka: Benzene, | | | | |
| dichloromethyl- | | X | | 98873 |
| Benzamide | | X | | 55210 |

| *Chemical Name* | *HS* | *TC* | *HAP* | *CAS #* |
|---|---|---|---|---|
| Benzenamine, | | | | 88744 |
| 2-nitro-; aka: | | | | |
| 2-Nitroaniline, or | | | | |
| o-Nitroaniline | X | | | |
| Benzenamine, | | | | |
| 3-nitro-; aka: | | | | |
| m-Nitroaniline | X | | | 99092 |
| Benzenamine, | | | | |
| 4-chloro; aka: | | | | |
| 4-Chloroaniline | X | | | 106478 |
| Benzene (HAP | X | X | X | 71432 |
| includes benzene | | | | |
| from gasoline) | | | | |
| Benzene, bromo- | | X | | 108861 |
| Benzene, | | | | |
| chloromethyl- | | X | | 100447 |
| Benzene, 1,2-dinitro-; | | X | | 528290 |
| aka: o-Dinitrobenzene | | | | |
| Benzene, 1,3-dinitro-; | | X | | 99650 |
| aka: m-Dinitrobenzene | | | | |
| Benzene, 1,4-dinitro-; | | X | | 100254 |
| aka: p-Dinitrobenzene | | | | |
| Benzene, methyldinitro-; | | X | | 25321146 |
| aka: Dinitrotoluene | | | | |
| (mixed isomers) | | | | |
| Benzene, | | X | | |
| 608935 | | | | |
| pentachloro- | | | | |
| Benzene, 1,2,3- | X | X | | 108907 |
| trichloro-; aka: 1,2,3- | | | | |
| Trichlorobenzene | | | | |
| 1,2-Benzenedi- | X | | | 84617 |
| carboxylic acid, | | | | |
| dicyclohexyl ester | | | | |
| 1,4-Benzenediol; | | X | | 122319 |
| aka: Hydroquinone | | | | |
| Benzidine; aka: | X | X | X | 92875 |
| [1,1'Biphenyl]- | | | | |
| 4-4'-diamine | | | | |
| 1,3-Benzodioxole, | | X | | 120581 |
| 5-(1-propenyl)-; | | | | |
| aka: Isosafrole | | | | |
| Benzo[a]anthracene | X | | | 56553 |
| Benzo[b] | X | | | 205992 |
| fluoranthene | | | | |
| Benzo(k) | X | | | 207089 |
| fluoranthene | | | | |
| Benzo[g,h,i] | X | | | 193395 |
| perylene | | | | |
| Benzo[a]pyrene | X | | | 50328 |
| Benzoic acid | X | | | 65850 |
| p-Benzoquinone; | | X | X | 106514 |
| aka: or 2,5-Cyclo- | | | | |
| hexadiene-1,4-dione, | | | | |
| or Quinone | | | | |
| Benzotrichloride; | | X | X | 98077 |
| aka: Benzene, | | | | |
| trichloromethyl- | | | | |
| Benzoyl chloride | | X | | 98884 |
| Benzoyl peroxide | | X | | 94360 |
| Benzyl alcohol | | X | | 100516 |
| Benzyl chloride | | | X | 100447 |
| Beryllium | X | X | | 7440428 |

| *Chemical Name* | *HS* | *TC* | *HAP* | *CAS #* |
|---|---|---|---|---|
| Beryllium compounds | | X | X | - |
| Biphenyl; aka: | | | | |
| 1,1-Biphenyl | | X | X | 92524 |
| Bis(2-ethylhexyl) adipate | | X | | 103231 |
| Boron | X | | | 7440428 |
| Boron compounds | X | | | - |
| Bromochlorodifluoromethane; | | | | |
| aka: Halon 1211 | | X | | 421012 |
| Bromoform; aka: | | | | |
| Methane, tribromo- | X | X | X | 75252 |
| 1-Bromo-4- | | | | |
| phenoxybenzene | X | | | 101553 |
| Bromotrifluoromethane; | | | | |
| aka: Halon 1301 | | X | | 75638 |
| 1,3-Butadiene | X | X | | 106990 |
| 1,3-Butadiene, | | | | |
| 2-chloro-; aka: | | | | |
| Chloroprene | X | | | 126998 |
| Butyl acrylate; aka: | | | | |
| 2-Propenoic acid, | | | | |
| butyl ester | X | | | 141322 |
| n-Butyl alcohol; aka: | | | | |
| Butanol | | X | | 71363 |
| sec-Butyl alcohol | | X | | 78922 |
| tert-Butyl alcohol | | X | | 75650 |
| Butyl benzyl phthalate; | | | | |
| aka: 1, | | | | |
| 2-Benzenedicarbo- | X | X | | 85687 |
| xylic acid, | | | | |
| butyl phenylmethyl | | | | |
| ester; Benzyl butyl | | | | |
| phthalate; or BBP | | | | |
| 1,2 Butylene | | | | |
| oxide; aka: | | | | |
| 1,2-Epoxybutane | | | X | 106887 |
| Butyraldehyde; aka: | | | | |
| Butanal | | X | | 123728 |
| Cadmium | X | X | | 7440439 |
| Cadium compounds | | X | X | - |
| Calcium cyanamide | | X | X | 156627 |
| Caprolactam | | | X | 105602 |
| Captan | | X | X | 133062 |
| Carbaryl; aka: Sevin | X | X | X | 63252 |
| Carbon disulfide | X | X | X | 75150 |
| Carbon tetrachloride | X | X | X | 56235 |
| Carbonyl sulfide | | X | X | 463581 |
| Catechol | | X | X | 120809 |
| Chloramben | | X | X | 133904 |
| Chordane | | X | X | 57749 |
| Chlorine | | X | X | 7782505 |
| Chlorine dioxide | | X | | 10049044 |
| Chloroacetic acid | | X | X | 79118 |
| 2-Chloroacetophenone | | X | X | 532274 |
| Chlorobenzene | | | X | 108907 |
| Chlorobenzilate | | X | X | 510156 |
| Chlorodiben- | | | | |
| zodioxins | X | | | - |
| Chlorodibenzofurans | X | | | - |
| Chlorodifluoro- | | | | |
| methane | X | | | 75456 |
| Chloroform; aka: | | | | |
| Methane, trichloro | X | X | | 67663 |
| p-Chloro-m-cresol | X | | | 59507 |
| Chloromethyl | | | | |
| methyl ether; aka: | | | | |

| *Chemical Name* | *HS* | *TC* | *HAP* | *CAS #* |
|---|---|---|---|---|
| Methane, | | X | X | 107302 |
| chloromethoxy- | | | | |
| Chlorophenols | | X | | - |
| 2-Chlorophenol | X | | | 95578 |
| 4-Chlorophenyl | | | | |
| phenyl | X | | | 7005723 |
| Chloroprene | | | X | 126998 |
| Chlorothalonil | | X | | 1897456 |
| Chromium | X | X | | 7440473 |
| Chromium compounds | | X | X | - |
| Chrysene | X | | | 218019 |
| C.I.Acid Blue 9, | | | | |
| diammonium salt | | X | | 2650182 |
| C.I.Acid Blue 9, | | | | |
| disodium salt | | X | | 3844459 |
| C.I.Acid Green 3 | | X | | 4680788 |
| C.I. Basic Green 4 | | X | | 569642 |
| C.I. Basic Red 1 | | X | | 989388 |
| C.I. Direct Black 38; | | | | |
| aka: 2,7-Naphthalenedisul- | | X | | 1937377 |
| fonic acid, 4-amino-3[ | | | | |
| [4'-[ (2,4-diaminophenyl)azo] | | | | |
| [1,1'-biphenyl]-4-yl] | | | | |
| azo]-5-hydroxy-6-(phenylazo)-, | | | | |
| disodium salt | | | | |
| C.I. Direct Blue 6; aka: | | | | |
| 2,7-Naphthalenedisulfonic | | X | | 2602462 |
| acid, 3,3'- [[1,1'-biphenyl]- | | | | |
| 4,4'-diylbis(azo) ]bis[5- | | | | |
| amino-4-hydroxy-, | | | | |
| tetrasodium salt | | | | |
| C.I. Disperse Yellow 3 | | X | | 2832408 |
| C.I. Food Red 5 | | X | | 3761533 |
| C.I. Food Red 15 | | X | | 81889 |
| C.I. Pigment Green 7 | | X | | 1328536 |
| C.I. Solvent Orange 7 | | X | | 3118976 |
| C.I. Solvent Yellow 3 | | X | | 97563 |
| C.I. Solvent Yellow 14 | | X | | 842079 |
| C.O.Vat Yellow 4 | | X | | 128665 |
| Cobalt | X | X | | 7440484 |
| Cobalt compounds | X | X | X | - |
| Coke oven emissions | | | X | - |
| Copper | X | X | | 7440508 |
| Copper compounds | | | X | - |
| Copper, [1,3,8,16,18, | | | | |
| 24-hexabromo- | | | | |
| 2,4,9,10,11,15,17,22, | | | | |
| 23,25-decachloro-29H, | | | | |
| 31HH-phthalocyaninato | | | | |
| (2-)-N (29), N (30), | | | | |
| N (31), N (32)]-, (SP-4-1)-; | | | | |
| aka: C.I. Pigment | | | | |
| Blue 15 | | X | | 147148 |
| Creosote | X | X | | 8001589 |
| p-Cresidine | | X | | 120718 |
| Cresoles Creslylic | | | | |
| acid (isomers and | | | | |
| mixture); | X | X | X | 1319773 |
| aka: Phenol, methyl- | | | | |
| m-Cresol; aka: | | | | |
| Phenol, 3-methyl- | | X | X | 108394 |
| o-Cresol; aka: Phenol, | | | | |
| 2-methyl- | X | X | X | 95487 |
| p-Cresol; aka: | | | | |
| Phenol, 4-methyl- | X | X | X | 106445 |

| *Chemical Name* | *HS* | *TC* | *HAP* | *CAS #* |
|---|---|---|---|---|
| Cumene | | | X | 98828 |
| Cumene hydroperoxide; aka: Hydroperoxide, 1-methyl-1-phenylethyl- | | X | | 80159 |
| Cupferron | | X | | 135206 |
| Cuprate(2-), [5-[ [4'-[2,6-dihydroxy-3-[ (2-hydroxy-5 sulfophenyl)azo] phenyl] azo] [1,1'-biphenyl]-4-yl]lazo]-2-hydroxy benzoato (4-) ]-, disodium | | X | | 16071866 |
| Cyanide | X | X | | 57125 |
| Cyanide compounds | | X | X | - |
| Cyclohexane | | X | | 110827 |
| Cyclohexane, 1,2,3,4,5,6-hexachloro-, (1alpha, 2alpha, 3beta, 4alpha, 5beta, 6beta)- | X | | | 319846 |
| Cyclohexanone | X | | | 108941 |
| Cyclonite; aka: RDX | X | | | 121824 |
| DDE | | | X | 3547044 |
| 4,4'-DDE, DDT, DDD | X | | | 72559 |
| Decabromodiphenyl oxide; aka: Decabromodiphenyl ether | | X | | 1163195 |
| Diallate | X | | | 2303164 |
| 2,4-Diaminoanisole sulfate; aka: 1,3-Benzenediamine, 4-methoxy-; or m-Phenylenediamine, 4-methoxy- | | X | | 615054 |
| 2,4-Diaminoanisole sulfate; aka: 1,3-Benzenediamine, 4-methoxy-, sulfate (1:1) | | X | | 39156417 |
| 4,4'-Diaminodiphenyl ether | | X | | 101804 |
| 2,4-Diaminotoluene; aka: 2,4-Toluene diamine, or 1,3-Benzenediamine, 4-methyl-, of 1,3-Diamino-4-methylbenzene | | X | X | 95807 |
| Diazomethane | | X | X | 334883 |
| Dibenzo[a,h] anthracene | X | | | 53703 |
| Dibenzofurans | X | X | X | 132649 |
| Dibromotetrafluoro ethane; aka: Halon 2402 | | X | | 124732 |
| 1,2-Dibromo-3-chloropropane | | | X | 961281 |
| Dibutyl phthalate; aka: 1,2-Benzene dicarboxylic acid, dibutyl ester; or Di-n-butyl phthalate | X | X | X | 84742 |
| Dichlorobenzene; aka: Benzene, dichloro (mixed isomers) | | X | | 25321226 |
| m-Dichlorobenzene; aka: Benzene, 1, 3-dichloro- | X | X | | 541731 |
| o-Dichlorobenzene; aka: Benzene, 1, 2-dichloro | X | X | | 95501 |
| p-Dichlorobenzene; aka: Benzene, 1, 4-dichloro- | X | X | | 106467 |
| 1,4-Dichlorobenzene(p) | | | X | 106467 |
| 3,3'-Dichloro-benzidine | X | X | X | 91941 |
| Dichlorobromomethane; aka: Methane, bromodichloro- | X | X | | 75274 |
| Dichlorodifluoro-methane; aka: CFC-12 | X | X | | 75718 |
| 1,2-Dichloro-ethylene | X | X | | 540590 |
| cis-1,2-Dichloro-ethylene | X | | | 156592 |
| Dichloroethyl ether; aka: Bis(2-chloroethyl) | X | X | X | 111444 |
| Dichloroisopropyl ether; aka: Propane, 2,2'-oxybis[1-chloro-; aka: Bis(2-chloro-1-methylethyl)ether, or Bis(2-chloroisopropyl) ether | | X | | 108601 |
| Dichloro-methylether; aka: Bis(chloromethyl) ether | X | X | X | 542881 |
| 2,4-Dichloro-phenol | X | X | | 120832 |
| 2,4-D; aka: 2,4-Dichlorophenoxy-acetic acid (HS includes salts and esters) | X | X | X | 94757 |
| 1,3-Dichloro-propene | | | X | 542756 |
| cis-1,3-Dichloro-propene | X | | | 10061015 |
| trans-1,3-Dichloro-propene | X | | | 10061026 |
| Dichlorotetrafluoro-ethane; aka: CFC114X | | | | 76142 |
| Dichlorvos | | X | X | 62737 |
| Dicofol | | X | | 115322 |
| Dieldrin/aldrin | X | | | 60571 |
| 1:2,3:4-Diepoxy-butane; aka: 2,2'-Boxirane | | X | | 1464535 |
| Diethanolamine | | | | 111422 |
| Diethyl sulfate | | | X | 64675 |
| Di(ethylhexyl) phthlate; aka: 1,2-Bis(2-ethyl-hexyl) phthalate; or Benzenedicarboxylic | X | X | X | 117817 |

| *Chemical Name* | *HS* | *TC* | *HAP* | *CAS #* |
|---|---|---|---|---|
| acid, bis(2-ethylhexyl) ester, or DEHP | | | | |
| Diethyl phthalate; aka: 1,2-Benzene-dicarboxylic acid, diethyl ester | X | X | | 846627 |
| 3,3'-Dimethoxy benzidine | | X | X | 119904 |
| Dimethyl amino-azobenzene; aka: 4-Dimethyl-aminoazobenzene | | X | X | 60117 |
| N,N-Dimethylaniline; aka: N,N-Dimethyl aniline | | X | X | 121697 |
| 3,3'-Dimethyl-benzidine; aka: o-Tolidine | | X | X | 119937 |
| Dimethyl-carbamyl chloride | | X | X | 79447 |
| Dimethyl formamide; aka: DMF, or Formamide, N,N-dimethyl- | X | | X | 68122 |
| 1,1-Dimethyl-hydrazine | | X | X | 57147 |
| 2,4-Dimethyl-phenol | X | X | | 105679 |
| 1,2-Dimethyl phthalate; aka: Benzene-dicarboxylic acid, dimethyl ester; or Dimethyl-phthalate | X | X | X | 131113 |
| Dimethyl sulfate | | | X | 77781 |
| 4,6-Dinitro-o-cresol; aka: 4,6-Dinitro-2-methyl-phenol (HAP includes salts) | X | X | X | 534521 |
| 2,4-Dinitro-phenol | X | X | X | 51285 |
| 2,4-Dinitro-toluene | X | X | X | 121142 |
| 2,6-Dinitro-toluene | X | X | | 606202 |
| Di-n-octyl phthalate; aka: carboxylic acid, dioctyl ester | X | X | | 117840 |
| Di-n-propylnitro-samine; aka: 1-Propanamine, N-nitroso-N-propyl; or Nitrosodipro-pylamine | X | X | | 621647 |
| 1,4-Dioxane; aka: 1,4-Diethyl-eneoxide; or Dioxane | X | X | X | 123911 |
| 1,2-Diphenylhy-drazine; aka: Hydrazine, 1,2-diphenyl-; or Hydrazobenzene | X | X | X | 122667 |
| Disulfoton | X | | | 298044 |
| Endosulfan; aka: Alpha, beta, sulfate | X | | | 115297 |
| Endrin aldehyde/ endrin | X | | | 7221934 |
| Epichlorohydrin; aka: Oxirane, chloromethyl-, or 1-Chloro-2, 3-epoxypropane) | | X | X | 106898 |
| Ethanamine, N-ethyl-; aka: diethylamine | | X | | 109897 |
| Ethane, 1, 1-dichloro-; aka: Ethylidene dichloride | X | | X | 75343 |
| Ethane, 1,1'-[methylenebis (oxy) ]bis[2-chloro-; aka: Bis(2-chloro-ethoxy)methane | X | | | 111911 |
| Ethanol, 2,2'-iminobis-; aka: Diethanolamine | | X | | 111422 |
| Ethene, (2-chloroethoxy); aka: 2-Chloroethyl vinyl ether | X | | | 110758 |
| Ethene, 1,2-dichloro-, (E)-; aka: 1,2-trans-Dichloroethene | X | | | 156606 |
| Ethyl acrylate; aka: 2-Propenoic acid, ethyl ester | | X | X | 140885 |
| Ethyl benzene; aka: Benzene, ethyl- | X | X | X | 100414 |
| Ethyl carbamate; aka: Urethane | | X | | 51796 |
| Ethyl chloride; aka: Ethane, chloro | X | X | X | 75003 |
| Ethyl chloroformate | | X | | 541413 |
| Ethylene | | X | | 74851 |
| Ethylene dibromide; aka: 1,2-Dibromo-ethane, or EDB | X | X | X | 106934 |
| Ethylene dichloride; aka: Ethane, 1,2-dichloro- | X | X | X | 107062 |
| Ethylene glycol | X | X | X | 107211 |
| Ethylene glycol monoethyl ether; aka: 2-Ethoxyethanol | | X | | 110805 |
| Ethyleneimine; aka: Aziridine, or Ethylene imine | | X | X | 151564 |
| Ethylene oxide; aka: Oxirane | X | X | X | 75218 |

| *Chemical Name* | *HS* | *TC* | *HAP* | *CAS #* |
|---|---|---|---|---|
| Ethylene thiourea | | X | X | 96457 |
| Fluometuron | | X | | 2164172 |
| Fluoranthene | | X | | 206440 |
| Fluorene | X | | | 86737 |
| Fluorides/fluorine/ hydrogen fluoride | X | | | 16984488 |
| Fluorotrichloromethane; aka: Trichlorofluoromethane, or CFC-11 | X | X | | 75694 |
| Formaldehyde | X | X | X | 50000 |
| Freon 113; aka: Ethane, 1,1,2-trichloro-1,2,2,-trifluoro-, or Chlorinated fluorocarbon | X | X | | 76131 |
| Glycol ethers | | X | X | - |
| Heptachlor (heptachlor/ Heptachlor epoxide under HS) | X | X | X | 76448 |
| Heptachlor epoxide | X | | | 1024573 |
| Heptane | X | | | 142825 |
| Hexachlorobenzene | X | X | X | 118741 |
| Hexachlorobutadiene; aka: 1,3-Butadiene, 1,1,2,3,4,4-hexachloro- | X | X | X | 87683 |
| Hexachloro cyclopentadiene; aka: 1,3-Cyclopentadiene, 1,2,3,4,5,5-hexachloro- | X | X | X | 77474 |
| Hexachloroethane; aka: Ethane, hexachloro- | X | X | X | 67721 |
| Hexachloronaphthalene; aka: Naphthalene, hexachloro- | | X | | 1335871 |
| Hexamethylphosphoramide | | X | X | 680319 |
| Hexane | X | | X | 110758 |
| Hydrazine | X | X | X | 302012 |
| Hydrazine sulfate | | X | | 10034932 |
| Hydrochloric acid | | X | X | 7647010 |
| Hydrogen cyanide; aka: Hydrocyanic acid | | X | | 749008 |
| Hydrogen fluoride; aka: Hydrofluoric acid | | X | X | 7664393 |
| Hydrogen sulfide | X | | X | 7783064 |
| Hydroquinone | | | X | 123319 |
| Indeno[1,2,3-cd]pyrene | X | | | 193395 |
| Isobutyraldehyde | | X | | 78842 |
| Isophorone; aka: 2-Cyclohexen-1-one, 3,5,5- | X | | X | 78591 |
| trimethyl- | | | | |
| Isopropyl alcohol; aka: Isopropanol or 2-Propanol | | X | | 67630 |
| 4,4'-Isopropylidenediphenol; aka: Phenol, 4,4'-(1- methylethylidene)bis-; aka: Bisphenol A | | X | | 80057 |
| Lead | X | X | | 7439921 |
| Lead compounds | | X | X | - |
| Lindane (HAP includes all isomers) | | X | X | 58899 |
| Malathion | X | | | 121755 |
| Maleic anhydride; aka: 2,5-Furandione | | X | X | 108316 |
| Maneb | | X | | 12427382 |
| Manganese | X | X | | 7439965 |
| Manganese compounds | | X | X | - |
| MBI; aka: 4,4'-Methylenebis (N,N-dimethylbenzenamine) | | X | | 101688 |
| Melamine | | X | | 108781 |
| Mercury | X | X | | 7439976 |
| Mercury compounds | | X | X | - |
| Methane, bromochloro- | X | | | 74975 |
| Methane, dibromochloro-; aka: Chlorodibro momethane | X | | | 124481 |
| 4,4'-Methylenebis (N,N-dimethyl-benzenamine) | | X | | 101611 |
| Methylene bromide; aka: Methane, dibromo- | | X | | 74953 |
| Methylene chloride; aka: Methane, dichloro-, or Dichloromethane | X | X | X | 75092 |
| 4,4-Methylenedianiline; aka: Benzenamine, 4,4'-methylenebis-, or MDA | | X | X | 101779 |
| Methanol | X | X | X | 67561 |
| Methoxychlor | X | X | X | 72435 |
| 2-Methoxyethanol | | X | | 109864 |
| Methyl acrylate; aka: 2-Propenoic acid, methyl ester | | X | | 96333 |
| Methyl bromide; aka: Bromomethane, or Methane, bromo- | X | X | X | 74839 |
| Methyl n-butyl ketone; aka: 2-Hexanone | X | | | 591786 |
| Methyl chloride; aka: Methane, chloro- | X | X | X | 74873 |
| 1-Methylethylbenzene; aka: Cumene, or Benzene, (1-methylethyl)- | | X | | 98828 |
| Methyl ethyl ketone; aka: 2-Butanone or MEK | X | X | X | 78933 |
| Methyl hydrazine; | | | | |

| *Chemical Name* | *HS* | *TC* | *HAP* | *CAS #* |
|---|---|---|---|---|
| aka: Methylhydrazine | | X | X | 60344 |
| Methyl iodide; aka: | | | | |
| Iodomethane | | X | X | 74884 |
| Methyl isobutyl | | | | |
| ketone; aka: 2- | | | | |
| Pentanone, | X | X | X | 108101 |
| 4-methyl-, or Hexone | | | | |
| Methyl isocyanate | | X | X | 624839 |
| 4-4'-Methylenebis(2- | | | | |
| chlorobenz- | | | | |
| enamine); | X | X | X | 101144 |
| aka: 4,4'-Methy- | | | | |
| lenebis (2-chloro- | | | | |
| aniline), or MBOCA | | | | |
| Methylene diphenyl | | | | |
| diisocynate; aka: | | | | |
| Benzene, | | X | X | 101688 |
| 1,1'-methylene- | | | | |
| bis[4-isocyanato-, | | | | |
| Methylenebis | | | | |
| (phenylisocynate), | | | | |
| or MDI Methyl | | | | |
| methacrylate; aka: | | | | |
| 2-Propenoic acid, | X | X | X | 80626 |
| 2-methyl-, methyl ester | | | | |
| 2-Methylnaph- | | | | |
| thalene | X | | | 91576 |
| Methyl tert-butyl | | | | |
| ether; aka: Propane, | | X | X | 1634044 |
| 2-methoxy-2-methyl- | | | | |
| Michler's ketone | | X | | 90948 |
| Mineral fibers | | | | |
| (includes mineral fiber | | X | | - |
| emissions from | | | | |
| places manufacturing | | | | |
| or processing glass, | | | | |
| rock, slag, or other | | | | |
| mineral-derived | | | | |
| fibers, avg. under 1 | | | | |
| micrometer) | | | | |
| Mirex | X | | | 2385855 |
| Molybdenum | X | | | 7439987 |
| Molybdenum | | | | |
| trioxide; aka: | | | | |
| Molybdenum | | X | | 1313275 |
| oxide | | | | |
| (Mono)chloropent- | | | | |
| afluoroethane; | | X | | 76153 |
| aka: CFC115 | | | | |
| Mustard gas; aka: | | | | |
| Ethane, 1,1'- | | | | |
| thiobis[2-chloro- | X | X | X | 505602 |
| Naphthalene | X | X | X | 91203 |
| alpha-Naphthylamine; | | | | |
| aka: 1-Naphthylamine | | X | | 134327 |
| beta-Naphthylamine | | X | | 91598 |
| Nickel | X | X | | 7440020 |
| Nickel compounds | | X | X | - |
| Nitrates/nitrites | X | | | 14797558 |
| Nitric acid | | X | | 7697372 |
| Nitrilotriacetic acid | | X | | 139139 |
| Nitrobenzene; aka: | | | | |
| Benzene, nitro- | X | X | X | 98953 |
| 4-Nitrobiphenyl | | X | X | 92933 |
| Nitrofen | | X | | 1836755 |

| *Chemical Name* | *HS* | *TC* | *HAP* | *CAS #* |
|---|---|---|---|---|
| Nitrogen mustard; aka: | | | | |
| Mechlorethamine | X | X | | 51752 |
| Nitroglycerin | | X | | 55630 |
| 5-Nitro-o-anisidine | | X | | 99592 |
| Nitrophenol | X | | | 25154556 |
| 2-Nitrophenol | X | X | | 88755 |
| 4-Nitrophenol; aka: | | | | |
| p-Nitrophenol | X | X | X | 100027 |
| 2-Nitropropane | | X | X | 79469 |
| N-Nitrosodiethylamine | | X | | 55185 |
| N-Nitrosodimeth- | | | | |
| ylamine | X | X | X | 62759 |
| N-Nitrosodiphen- | | | | |
| ylamine | X | X | | 86306 |
| p-Nitrosodiphen- | | | | |
| ylamine | | X | | 156105 |
| N-Nitrosodi-n- | | | | |
| butylamine; aka: | | | | |
| 1-Butanamine, | | X | | 924163 |
| N-butyl-N-nitroso-; | | | | |
| or Nitrosodibutylamine | | | | |
| N-Nitroso-N-ethylurea | | X | | 759739 |
| N-Nitroso-N-methylurea | | X | | 684935 |
| N-Nitrosomethylvinylamine | | X | | 4549400 |
| N-Nitrosomorpholine | | X | X | 59892 |
| N-Nitrosonornicotine | | X | | 16543558 |
| N-Nitrosopiperidin | | X | | 100754 |
| Octane | X | | | 111659 |
| Octachloronaphthalene; | | | | |
| aka: Naphthalene, | | X | | 2234131 |
| octachloro- | | | | |
| Osmium tetroxide | | X | | 20816120 |
| Oxirane, ethyl- | | X | | 106887 |
| Parathion; aka: | | | | |
| DNTP | X | X | X | 56382 |
| PCBs-Aroclor 1016 | X | | | 12674112 |
| PCBs-Aroclor 1221 | X | | | 11104282 |
| PCBs-Aroclor 1232 | X | | | 11141165 |
| PCBs-Aroclor 1242 | X | | | 53469219 |
| PCBs-Aroclor 1248 | X | | | 12672296 |
| PCBs-Aroclor 1254 | X | | | 11097691 |
| PCBs-Aroclor 1260 | X | | | 11096825 |
| Pentachloronitro- | | | | |
| benzene; aka: | | | | |
| Quintozene | | X | X | 82688 |
| or PCNB | | | | |
| Pentachlorophenol; | | | | |
| aka PCP | X | X | X | 87865 |
| n-Pentane | X | | | 109660 |
| Peracetic acid | | X | | 79210 |
| Phenathrene | X | | | 85018 |
| Phenol | X | X | X | 108952 |
| p-Phenylenediamine; | | | | |
| aka: 1,4-Benzenediamine, | | X | X | 106503 |
| p-Diaminobenzene, or p-PDA | | | | |
| 2-Phenylphenol | | X | | 90437 |
| Phosgene | X | X | X | 75445 |
| Phosphine | | | X | 7803512 |
| Phosphoric acid | | X | X | 7664382 |
| Phosporous | | | | |
| (yellow or white) | | X | | 7723140 |
| Phthalic anhydride | | X | X | 85449 |
| Picric acid | | X | | 88891 |
| Plutonium-239 | X | | | 15117483 |
| Polybrominated | | | | |

| *Chemical Name* | *HS* | *TC* | *HAP* | *CAS #* |
|---|---|---|---|---|
| biphenyls; aka: | | | | |
| PBBs | X | X | | - |
| (brominated biphenyl | | | | |
| molecules having the | | | | |
| molecular formula | | | | |
| CC(12)H (x)Br (y), | | | | |
| where x +y = 10 and | | | | |
| y ranges from 1 to 10) | | | | |
| Polychlorinated | | | | |
| biphenyls; aka: PCBs | | | | |
| (any | | X | X | 1336363 |
| chemical substance | | | | |
| that is limited to the | | | | |
| biphenyl molecule that | | | | |
| has been chlorinated | | | | |
| to varying degrees, or | | | | |
| any combination of | | | | |
| substances which | | | | |
| contains such | | | | |
| substances), or | | | | |
| Archlors Polycyclic | | | | |
| organic matter | | | | |
| (organic matter with | | X | | - |
| more than one benzene | | | | |
| ring, with a boiling point | | | | |
| at or above 100°C) | | | | |
| Propane, 1,2-dibromo- | | | | |
| 3-chloro- | X | X | | 96128 |
| 1,3-Propane sultone; | | | | |
| aka: Propane | | | | |
| sultone, or 1,2- | | | | |
| Oxathiolane, 2,2- | | | | |
| dioxide | | X | X | 1120714 |
| Propane, 1,2,3- | | | | |
| trichloro | X | | | 96184 |
| 2-Propen-1-ol; aka: | | | | |
| Allyl alcohol | | X | | 107186 |
| 1-Propene, 1,3-dichloro-; | | | | |
| aka: 1,3-Dichloro- | | X | | 542756 |
| propylene | | | | |
| 1-Propene, 2,3-dichloro- | | X | | 78886 |
| beta-Propiolactone | | X | X | 57578 |
| Propionaldehyde | | X | X | 123386 |
| Propoxur; aka: Baygon | | X | X | 114261 |
| Propylene; aka: Propene | | X | | 115071 |
| Propylene dichloride; | | | | |
| aka: Propane, 1,2- | | | | |
| dichloro- | X | X | X | 78875 |
| Propyleneimine; aka: | | | | |
| 1,2-Propylenimine, or | | X | X | 75558 |
| 2-Methyl aziridine | | | | |
| Propylene oxide; aka: | | | | |
| Oxirane, methy- | | X | X | 75569 |
| Pyrene; aka: Benzo | | | | |
| [def]phenanthrene | X | | | 129000 |
| Pyridine | | X | | 110861 |
| Quinoline | | X | X | 91225 |
| Radionuclides | | | | |
| (including radon) | | | X | - |
| Radium | X | | | 7440144 |
| Radium | | | | |
| compounds | X | | | - |
| Radon and its | | | | |
| compounds | | | | |
| (HAP under | X | | X | 10043922 |

| *Chemical Name* | *HS* | *TC* | *HAP* | *CAS #* |
|---|---|---|---|---|
| Radionuclides, above) | | | | |
| Saccharin (manufacturing) | | X | | 81072 |
| Safrole | | X | | 94597 |
| Selenium | X | X | | 7782492 |
| Selenium compounds | | X | X | - |
| Silver | X | X | | 7440224 |
| Silver compounds | | X | | - |
| Sodium sulfate | | | | |
| (solution) | | X | | 7757826 |
| Strontium | X | | | 7440246 |
| Styrene; aka: | | | | |
| Benzene, ethenyl- | X | X | X | 100425 |
| (Styrene monomer) | | | | |
| Styrene oxide; aka: | | | | |
| Oxirane, phenyl- | | X | X | 96093 |
| Sulfur dioxide | X | | | 7446095 |
| Sulfuric acid | X | X | | 7664939 |
| Sulfuric acid, | | | | |
| diethyl ester; aka: | | | | |
| diethyl sulfate | | X | | 64675 |
| Sulfuric acid, | | | | |
| dimenthyl ester | | X | | 77781 |
| Terephthalic acid | | X | | 100210 |
| 2,3,7,8-Tetrachloro- | | | | |
| dibenzo-p- | | | | |
| dioxin; aka: | X | | X | 1746016 |
| tetrachlorodibenzo- | | | | |
| p-dioxin | | | | |
| 1,1,2,2-Tetrachloro- | | | | |
| ethane; aka: | | | | |
| Ethane, | X | X | X | 79345 |
| 1,1,2,2,-tetrachloro- | | | | |
| Tetrachloroethylene; | | | | |
| aka: Perchloroethylene, | | X | X | 127184 |
| or Ethene, terachloro- | | | | |
| Tetrachlorvinphos | | X | | 961115 |
| Tetrahydrofuran | X | | | 109999 |
| Thallium | X | | | 7440280 |
| Thallium compounds | | X | | - |
| Thioacetamide | | X | | 62555 |
| 4,4'-Thiodianiline | | X | | 139651 |
| Thiourea | | X | | 62566 |
| Thorium | X | | | 7440291 |
| Thorium | | | | |
| compounds | X | | | - |
| Thorium dioxide | | X | | 1314201 |
| Tin | X | | | 7440315 |
| Titanium dioxide | | X | | 13463677 |
| Titanium tetrachloride | | X | X | 7550450 |
| Toluene; aka: | | | | |
| Benzene, methyl- | X | X | X | 108883 |
| Toluenediamine; aka: | | | | |
| Benzenediamine, | | X | | 25376458 |
| ar-methyl-; or | | | | |
| Diaminotoluene | | | | |
| Toluene diisocynate | | | | |
| (mixed isomers); | | | | |
| aka: | X | X | | 26471625 |
| Benzene, 1,3- | | | | |
| diisocyanatomethyl- | | | | |
| Toluene-2,4- | | | | |
| diisocyanate | | X | X | 584849 |
| Toluene-2,6- | | | | |
| diisocyanate; aka: | | | | |
| Benzene, | | X | | 91087 |

| *Chemical Name* | *HS* | *TC* | *HAP* | *CAS #* |
|---|---|---|---|---|
| 1,3-diisocyanato-2-methyl-o-Toluidine; aka: Benzenamine, 2-methyl- | X | | X | 95534 |
| o-Toluidine hydrochloride | | X | | 636215 |
| Toxaphene; aka: Chlorinated camphene | X | X | X | 8001352 |
| 2,4,5-T | X | | | 93765 |
| 2,4,5-TP acid; aka: Silvex | X | | | 93721 |
| Triaziquone | | X | | 68768 |
| Trichlorfon | | X | | 52686 |
| 1,2,4-Trichlorobenzene; aka: Benzene, 1,2,4-trichloro- | X | X | X | 120821 |
| 1,1,1-Trichloroethane; aka: Methyl chloroform; or Ethane, 1,1,1-trichloro- | X | X | X | 71556 |
| 1,1,2-Trichloroethane; aka: Ethane, 1,1,2-trichloro- | X | X | X | 79005 |
| Trichloroethylene; aka: Trichloroethene | X | X | X | 79016 |
| 2,4,5,-Trichlorophenol | X | X | X | 95954 |
| 2,4,6-Trichlorophenol | X | X | X | 88062 |
| Triethylamine | | | X | 121448 |
| Trifluralin | | X | X | 1582098 |
| 1,2,4-Trimethylbenzene; aka: Benzene, 1,2,4-trimethyl- | | X | | 95636 |
| 2,2,4-Trimethylpentane; aka: Pentane, 2,2,4-trimethyl- | | X | X | 540841 |
| 1,3,5-Trinitro benzene | X | | | 99345 |
| Trinitrophenylmethylnitramine | X | | | 479458 |
| 2,4,6-Trinitrotoluene | X | | | 118967 |
| Tris (2,3-dibromopropyl) phosphate | | X | | 136727 |
| Tritium | X | | | 10028178 |
| Uranium | X | | | 7440611 |
| Uranium compounds | X | | | - |
| Vanadium (fume or dust) | X | X | | 7440622 |
| Vinyl acetate; aka: Acetic acid, ethenyl ester | X | X | X | 108054 |
| Vinyl bromide; aka: Ethene, bromo- | | X | | 593602 |
| Vinyl chloride (monomer) | X | X | X | 75014 |
| Vinylidene chloride; aka: 1,1-Dichloroethylene, or 1,1-Dichloroethene | X | X | X | 75354 |
| Xylenes; aka: Benzene, dimethyl- (Total xylenes–HS; isomers and mixtures-HAP) | X | X | X | 1330207 |
| m-Xylene; aka: Benzene, 1,3-dimethyl- | | X | X | 108383 |
| o-Xylene; aka: Benzene, 1,2-dimethyl- | | X | X | 95476 |
| p-Xylene; aka: Benzene, 1,4-dimethyl- | | X | X | 106423 |
| 2,6-Xylidine | | X | | 87627 |
| Zinc (fume or dust) | X | X | | 7440666 |
| Zinc borate hydrate; aka: ZB-2335 | | X | | 12513278 |
| Zinc compounds | | X | | - |
| Zineb | | X | | 12122677 |

Key
HS = Hazardous substances
TC = Toxic chemicals
HAP = Hazardous air pollutants
aka = also known as; used when material has alternate name(s)

***Sources: Chemicals on Reporting Rules (CORR) Database, 6/30/90, compiled by the Office of Toxic Substances (OTS), Existing Chemical Assessment Division, Chemical Screening Branch. Also Clean Air Act of 1990; available in U.S. Environmental Laws (Bureau of National Affairs, 1991).***

## ECOLOGICAL BUILDING PUBLICATIONS


Alexander, Christopher. A Pattern Language. New York: Oxford University Press, 1977.

Alexander, Christopher. *The Timeless Way of Building.* New York: Oxford University Press, 1979.

Architects for Social Responsibility. *The Source Book for Sustainable Design: A Guide to Environmentally Responsible Building Materials and Processes.* 248 Franklin Street, Cambridge, MA 02139.

Bower, John. *Healthy House Building.* New York: John Stuart Lyle, 1989.

Center for Resourceful Building Technology. *Guide to Resource Efficient Building Elements.* PO Box 3866, Missoula, MT 59806.

Dadd-Redalia, Debra. *Sustaining the Earth: Choosing Consumer Products That Are Safe for You, Your Family, and the Earth.* New York: Hearst Books, 1994.

Day, Christopher. *Places for the Soul: Architecture as a Healing Art.* Glasgow: Collins, 1990.

Devall, Bill, ed. *Clearcut: The Tragedy of Industrial Forestry.* San Francisco: Sierra Club Books/ Earth Island Press, 1994.

Durning, Alan. *How Much Is Enough?* New York: Norton, 1992.

Eisenberg, David. *Straw Bale Building and the Building Codes.* Out on Bale, 1037 E. Linden Street, Tuscon, AZ 85719.

Fromm, Dorit. *Collaborative Communities: Co-Housing, Central Living and other New Forms of Housing with Shared Facilities.* New York: Van Nostrand Reinhold, 1991.

Giradet, Herbert. *The Gaia Atlas of Cities: New Directions for Sustainable Urban Living.* London: Gaia Books, 1992.

Girdlestone, Rodney and Cowan, David. *Safe As Houses? Ill-Health and Electro-Stress in the Home.* New York: Gateway Books, 1994.

Good, Clint and Dadd, Deborah Lynn. *Healthful Houses: How to Design and Build Your Own.* Guaranty Press, 1988.

Greater Toronto Homebuilders' Association. *Making A Molehill Out Of A Mountain.* 20 Upjohn Road, North York, Ontario, Canada M38 2V9.

Harland, Edward. *Eco-Renovation.* Real Goods Independent Living Books, 966 Mazzoni St., Ukiah, CA 95482.

Heschong, Lisa. *Thermal Delight in Architecture.* Cambridge, MA: MIT Press, 1980.

Hurst Thomas, David. *Exploring Ancient Native America.* New York: Macmillan.

Lanning, Bob. *Straw Bale Portfolio.* Out on Bale, 1037 E. Linden Street Tucson, AZ 85719.

Lawler, Anthony. *The Temple in the House.* New York: Tarcher Putnam, 1994.

Loomis, Ruth and Wilkinson, Merv. *Wildwood: A Forest for the Future.* Reflections Publisher, PO Box 178, Gabriola, BC, Canada VOR IXO.

MacDonald, Stephen and Oren. *A Straw-Bale Primer.* PO Box 58, Gila, NM 88038.

MacDonald, Stephen O. and Myrman, Matts. *Build it with Bales.* 1037 E. Linden St., Tuscon, AZ 85719.

Marinelli, Janet and Bierman-Lytle, Paul. *Your Natural Home.* New York: Little, Brown, and Company, 1995.

McCamant, Katherine and Durrett, Charles. *CoHousing: A Contemporary Approach to Housing Ourselves.* Habitat Press/ Ten Speed Press, 1988.

Mollison, Bill. *Permaculture: A Designer's Manual.* Permaculture Resources, 56 Farmersville Rd., Califon, NJ 07830.

Mollison, Bill. *Permaculture: A Practical Guide for a Sustainable Future.* Permaculture Drylands, PO Box 27371, Tucson, AZ 85726-7371

National Association of Home Builders. *Builders Guide to Residential Construction Waste Management and Resource Conservation Research House Guide* and video. 400 Prince George's Boulevard, Upper Marlboro, MD 20772.

Nobokov, Peter and Easton, Robert. *Native American Architecture.* New York: Oxford University Press, 1989.

Norwood, Ken and Smith, Kathleen. *Rebuilding Community in America: Housing for Ecological Living, Personal Empowerment, and the New Extended Family.* Berkeley: Shared Living Resource Center.

Papanek, Victor. *Design for the Real World: Human Ecology and Social Change.* London: Thames and Hudson, 1984.

Pearson, David. *Earth to Spirit: In Search of Natural Architecture.* San Francisco: Chronicle Books, 1995.

Pearson, David. *The Natural House Book.* New York: Simon and Schuster (Fireside), 1989.

Perlin, John. *Forest Journey: The Role of Wood in the Development of Civilization.* Cambridge, MA: Harvard University Press, 1991.

Rainforest Action Network. *The Wood User's Guide.* 450 Sansome St., San Francisco, CA 94111.

Robinson, Gordon. *The Forest and the Trees: A Guide To Excellent Forestry.* Corvelo, CA: Island Press, 1988.

Roodman, David Malin and Lenssen, Nicholas. *A Building Revolution: How Ecology and Health Concerns are*

*Transforming Construction: A Worldwatch Paper.* 1776 Massachusetts Avenue NW, Washington, DC 20036.

Roy, Rob. *Super Insulated Houses and Underground Houses.* New York: Sterling Publishing, 1994.

Roy, Rob. *Underground Houses.* Earthwood Building School, 366 Murtagh Hill Rd., West Chazy, NY 12992.

Schurcliff, William Schurcliff. *Air to Air Heat Exchangers.* Andover, MA: Brick House Publishing, 1980.

Schurcliff, William. *Thermal Shutters and Shades.* Andover, MA: Brick House Publishing, 1980.

Steen, Steen, and Bainbridge. *Straw Bale House.* Back Home Books, PO Box 70, Hendersonville, NC 28792.
Teitel, Martin. *Rainforest In Your Kitchen.* Washington, DC: Island Press, 1992.

The Clean Washington Center, Department of Trade and Economic Development. *Directory of Recycled Building and Construction Products.* 2001 6th Ave., Suite 2700, Seattle, WA 98121.

Tibbets, Jo. *Earth Building Encyclopedia.* Southwest Solaradobe, PO Box 153, Bosque, NM.

Venolia, Carol. *Healing Environments.* California: Celestial Arts, 1992.

Walters, Derek. *Feng Shui: The Chinese Art of Designing a Harmonious Environment.* New York: Simon and Schuster (Fireside).

Wells, Malcolm. *Gentle Architecture.* New York: McGraw-Hill, 1982.

## MATERIALS RESOURCE GUIDES

American Institute of Architects Environmental Resource Guide
1735 New York Ave., NW, Washington, DC
(800) 365-2724

Austin Environmental Directory
PO Box 1374, Austin, TX 78767
(512) 447-8712

Bay Area Green Pages
Green Media Group, PO Box 11314, Berkeley, CA 94701
(510) 534-3470

Environmental Building News
RR1 Box 161, Brattleboro, VT 05301
(802) 257-7300

Environmental by Design/Vol 1: Interiors
Kim Leclair and David Rousseau, Hartley and Marks, Inc.
79 Tyee Dr., Point Roberts, WA 98281
(360) 945-2017

Environmental Outfitters
44 Crosby St., New York, NY 10012
(212) 334-9659

Greater LA Green Pages
Green Media Group, PO Box 11314, Berkeley, CA 94701
(510) 534-3470

The Green Guide/ Washington DC
523 Constitution Ave., NE, Washington, DC 20002
(202) 543-1214

The Green Pages: The Contract Interior Designer's Guide to Environmentally Responsible Products and Materials
Kim Nadel, C.I.D. & Andrew Fuston, Co-Authors
399 4th St., Brooklyn, NY 11215
(718) 369-2578

The Harris Directory
B.J. Harris
508 Jose St., Suite 913, Santa Fe, NM 87501-1855
(505) 995-0337

Houston Very Green Pages
PO Box 27630, Houston, TX 77227
(713) 524-6077

Interior Concerns Resource Guide
Victoria Schomer
131 W. Blithedale, Mill Valley, CA 94941
(415) 389-8049

Minnesota Green Pages
Minnesota Chapter of the International Alliance for Sustainable Agriculture
1701 University Ave. SE, Minneapolis, MN 55414
(612) 331-1099

Natick Green Pages
75 West St., Natick, MA 01760
(508) 651-7310

National Park Service, Denver Service Center
Sally Small
(303) 969-2466

Sourcebook for Sustainable Design
Boston Society of Architects
52 Broad St., Boston, MA 02109

Vermont Green Pages
RD 1 Box 85A, Groton, VT 05046
(802) 592-3447

Willamette Green Pages
PO Box 12156, Eugene, OR 97440
(503) 485-0177

# Notes

## Chapter 1
## A History of Ecology in Architecture

1. Bernard Rudofsky, *Architecture Without Architects: A Short Introduction to Non-Pedigreed Architecture* (Garden City, New York: Doubleday & Co., Inc., 1964).

2. Clive Ponting, *A Green History of the World: The Environment and the Collapse of Great Civilizations* (New York: Penguin Books, 1991).

3. Ibid.

4. James Lovelock, *Gaia: A New Look at Life on Earth* (New York: Oxford University Press, 1987).

## Chapter 2
## Defining Environmentally Conscious Architecture: Pioneering American Practitioners

1. Croxton Collaborative and National Audubon Society, *Audubon House: Building the Environmentally Responsible Energy-Efficient Office* (New York: John Wiley & Sons, 1994).

2. Crosbie, Michael J., *Green Architecture: A Guide to Sustainable Design* (Washington, DC: AIA Press, 1994).

3. Calmenson, Dianne Wintroub, "Industrial Revolution II: William McDonough's New Way of Thinking," *Interior Sources* (May 1995).

4. McDonough, William, The Hannover Principles, 1992

5. Wagner, Michael, "William McDonough: Why Green Means Go," *Interiors Magazine* (March 1993).

6. DesignTex, *Environmental Textiles: William McDonough Collection* (1995).

7. McDonough, William, and Hawken, Paul, "A Centennial Sermon: Cathedral of St. John the Divine," *Design, Ecology, and the Making of Things* (1993).

8. Wintroub Calmenson, Diane, "Healing the Environment with Bricks and Bytes: John Picard's Vision of the Future of Design and Architecture," *Interiors & Sources* (New York: BPA International, October 1995).

9. Gunts, Edward, "Green Architecture: Nature's Revenge," *Architecture Magazine* (May 1991).

10. "Aquatorium, Chattanooga, Tennessee," *Architecture Magazine* (June 1993).

11. U.S. Department of the Interior, National Park Service, Denver Service Center, *Guiding Principles of Sustainable Design* (September 1993).

12. The White House, Office of the Press Secretary, *Council on Sustainable Development* (June 14, 1993).

13. Pearson, David, *The Natural House Book* (New York: Simon and Schuster (Fireside), 1989).

## Chapter 3
## Renewable Resource Technologies

1. One Btu is the amount of energy required to warm 1 pound of water 1 degree Fahrenheit. The kilowatt-hour can be regarded as the amount of energy consumed in lighting ten 100-watt light bulbs for a period of one hour. A kilowatt, however, is the rate at which energy must be used to light ten 100-watt bulbs. 'Megawatt' (1 million watts) and 'gigawatt' (1 billion watts) are terms commonly used to describe the generating capacity of power plants. A large nuclear of coal-powered plant, for example, might have a capacity of 1,000 megawatts or 1 gigawatt and would produce 8.76 billion kilowatt-hours of energy in one year if it operated continuously at full power. "The quad, short for 1 quadrillion Btu, is often used to refer to massive amounts of energy. For example, in 1990 the total amount of energy worldwide was about 321 quads, and the world's largest energy consumer, the United States, used about 79 quads," according to *The Almanac of Renewable Energy.*

2. Golub, Richard and Eric Brus, *The Almanac of Renewable Energy: The Complete Guide to Emerging*

*Energy Technologies* (New York: Henry Holt and Company, 1993).

3. Ibid.

4. See "China's Inevitable Dilemma: Coal Equals Growth," *The New York Times* (November 29, 1995).

## Chapter 4
## The Process: Creating Ecologically Conscious Architecture

1. Rocky Mountain Institute with Lopez Barnett, Dianna and Browning, William, *A Primer On Sustainable Building* (Aspen: Rocky Mountain Institute, 1995).

2. Fanney, AH, Whitter, KM, et al., *NIST Special Publication 863, US Green Building Conference* (Washington, DC: US Department of Commerce Technology Administration, 1994).

3. Audin, Lindsay, "Poisonous Power and Light," *Architectural Record Lighting Technology* (November 1994).

4. "Trouble in the Air," *Interiors & Sources Magazine* (New York: BPA Publishing, April 1995), reprinted with permission from Steelcase Inc.'s magazine, *Workwell.*

## Chapter 6
## Environmental Legislation: Opportunities and Responsibilities

1. Vale, Brenda and Robert, *Green Architecture: Design for an Energy Conscious Future* (London: Thames and Hudson Ltd., 1991).

2. Naar, Jon and Alex, *This Land Is Your Land: A Field Guide to North America's Native Ecosystems* (New York: HarperCollins, 1993).

3. Natural Resources Defense Council, "Breach of Faith: How the Contract's Fine Print Undermines America's Environmental Success" (February 1995).

4. AIA Documents Sources, "Radon Mitigation Standards," *The Energy Policy Act of 1992*.

5. Federal Register 15.968 (April 15, 1994).

# Bibliography


Albrecht, Donald. "Urban Oasis," *Architecture.* June 1993.

Bryant Logan, William. "The Recyclable Nest," *House and Garden.* October 1991.

Crosbie, Michael. *Green Architecture: A Guide to Sustainable Design.* Washington, DC: AIA Press, 1994.

Croxton, Randolph and Childs, Kirsten. "Office Design and the Environment," *Skylines.* June 1991.

Dodge, Sue E. "Green by Design," *National Parks Magazine.* September/ October 1994.

Dunkel, Tom. "Environment: Going Green at Harmony Resort on St. John," *Travel & Leisure.* March 1994.

Dunlap, David W. "Audubon Society Creating Power Saving Offices," *The New York Times.* December 30, 1990.

Iovine, Julie. "A House With a View as Well as a Conscience," *New York Times.* January 26, 1995.

Kalosh, Anne. "The Travel Industry's Green Guru: An Interview with Stanley Selengut," *Hemispheres.* April 1994.

Karon, Paul. "Exercise In Utility," *Los Angeles Times.* July 27, 1994.

Langreth, Robert. "Eco Resort," *Popular Science.* March 1994.

Nasatir, Judith. "National Audubon Society," *Interior Design.* August 1991.

National Audubon Society, Croxton Collaborative Architects. *Audubon House: Building the Environmentally Responsible Energy-Efficient Office.* New York: John Wiley & Sons, 1994.

Nemanic, Jerry. "Stan Selengut," *Caribbean Travel and Life.* January/ February 1991.

Nesmith, Lynn. "Technology: Ready or Not Recycling is on the Way," *Architectural Record.* December 1993.

Novitski, B.J. "Energy Conservation Software," *Architecture.* May 1991.

Oldam, Jeff. "Powering the Harmony Resort," *Solar Today.* September/October 1994.

Oliver, Suzanne. "Eco-Profitable," *Forbes.* June 20, 1994.

Rosenbaum, David. "Pioneers Plead for Green Design," *Engineering News Record.* May 13, 1991.

Rosenbaum, David. "Sustainable Design," *Engineering News Record.* October 3, 1994.

Seldon, Jr., W. Lynn. "Plastics in Paradise," *EcoTraveler.* Premiere Issue.

Selengut, Stanley. "Sustainable Development in Paradise," *Solar Today.* September/October 1994.

Slatin, Peter D. "Blueprint for Off-the-Shelf Energy Efficiency," *Architectural Record.* June 1991.

Stites, Janet. "Caribbean Green: Sun, Sand, Surf and Conservation," *Omni Magazine.* July 1994.

Wagner, "90's Alert: Virgin Green," *Interiors.* March 1994.

Wagner, Michael. "90's Alert: Energy Wise," *Interiors.* June 1991.

# Index

Art Center College of Design
Library
1700 Lida Street
Pasadena, Calif. 91103

3/26/99 Daedalus 9.98 74560
(55)